Penguin

Freud and Psychology

Edited by S. G. M. Lee
and Martin Herbert

Penguin Modern Psychology Readings

General Editor
B. M. Foss

Freud and Psychology

Selected Readings

Edited by S. G. M. Lee and Martin Herbert

Penguin Books

Penguin Books Ltd, Harmondsworth,
Middlesex, England
Penguin Books Inc., 7110 Ambassador Road,
Baltimore, Md 21207, U.S.A.
Penguin Books Australia Ltd, Ringwood,
Victoria, Australia

First published 1970
This selection copyright © S. G. M. Lee and Martin Herbert, 1970
Introduction and notes copyright © S. G. M. Lee and
Martin Herbert, 1970

Made and printed in Great Britain by
Richard Clay (The Chaucer Press) Ltd,
Bungay, Suffolk
Set in Monotype Times

Contents

Introduction

Three thinkers, probably more than any others, have contributed to the dethronement of Man's confidence in himself as being of unique importance in the Universe. In physical and cosmological terms, Copernicus displaced him from the central place in that Universe; Charles Darwin showed clearly that he had much in common with 'lower' animals and that he did not owe his existence as a species to an act of *special* creation by an omniscient deity, but that the pressures of selective evolution had been brought to bear, through millenniums, on him as on others. Freud, against a background of the surge of 'progress' and technical development in the nineteenth century, sowed grave doubts about the rationality of man and about his ability to solve his problems – particularly individual ones – by conscious ratiocination alone.

All these men have had enduring effects upon their world. In the social and cultural climate of our times Freud's thinking has been more pervasive than that of any other researcher into the more complex elements of man's behaviour – his 'mind'. If one were asked to name claimants to the title 'genius' in the field of psychology, one would find it difficult not to concede the palm to Freud. No other original thinker in psychology has had as wide an effect on psychological debate and research. The least that can be said of Freud is that he has been an enormous and significant stimulus to fresh inquiry in a wide variety of fields, from anthropology and aesthetics to laboratory studies of memory. In everyday terms, the child-rearing practices of much of the Western world have been influenced, for some three generations, by his dicta. To many laymen the statements above would seem to guarantee for Freud adherence from the majority of psychologists, academic, experimental and empirical. But Freud's theories have always been the subject of great dispute, often very emotional in tone. This volume attempts to bring together some of the more pertinent contributions to the enormous task of 'checking up on Freud'.

Freud was essentially a proponent of *verstehende* or 'understanding' psychology; he wished to answer the 'whys' of human conduct. Despite his training in medicine and research work in physiology he was not content with the mere observation of surface behaviour or with the investigation of neurophysiology; he was determined to explain the *mental* mechanisms underlying complex sequences of behaviour. He set up models of such underlying entities and mechanisms – the former exemplified by his division of the personality into id, ego and super-ego, the latter by such abstractions as repression, projection, reaction-formation, etc. He wished to account for the whole of human mentation at the *psychological* level of explanation. While he did not deny the possibility, indeed probability, of physiological accompaniments for all mental phenomena, he did not concern himself with these in any detail. He was concerned with the *experience* of the neurotic patient, with the *meaning* of his symptoms (in a semantic sense), and not with the functioning of the patient's cells or nerves.

Most of Freud's thinking was inductive in character. He was not an experimentalist and did not use, formally, the hypothetico-deductive method in his work. Steadily, through a long life, he added further findings and theoretical formulations to the huge body of psychoanalytic statements. This accounts partly for the contradictions and changes of mind in the writing of Freud. While it is a tribute to his flexibility of mind that he was able to modify his ideas over so long a time, this makes the task of the academic psychologist even harder in that he has to spend time trying to pin down a Freudian dictum to its definitive form before he can even begin to try to verify its truth. In addition, the experimentalist is in difficulty in that Freud did not specifically set out his formulations in the form of specific, experimentally testable hypotheses (see Farrell, Reading 1, p. 19).

As we have said, Freud was talking about *mental* entities; the experimental psychologist, observing and predicting *behavioural* variables, is at a great disadvantage in testing propositions derived from Freud's theories.

Again, the empirical psychologist is usually attempting to check on the validity of Freudian *theory*. Freud's own aims were primarily therapeutic and there has been a tendency in the past (particularly on the part of convinced Freudians) to assume that if the patient appears better, then this is proof positive of Freud's concepts that have been applied by the analyst in the treatment of the particular individual. This is, logically, a *non sequitur*. For example, it might be conceivable that any improvement was due merely to the talking to a sympathetic listener by the patient, rather than to the uncovering of unconscious conflicts, etc. Or the effectiveness of the therapy might be merely the result of hetero-suggestion by the therapist. In this book we are not concerned with the efficacy of psychoanalysis as a therapy, but with its validity as an explanation of some facets of the mental life of the human individual.

Another almost insuperable difficulty lies in the fact that psychoanalysis is, to a very large extent, a closed system of thought. What academic psychologist, or, indeed, any other scientist, has not been frustrated and infuriated by the apparently smug statement: 'No one can assess the truths of psychoanalysis who has not himself undergone psychoanalysis and seen the truth of it in the therapeutic situation.' On a similar note, the experimentalist is likely to be deterred in his inquiries by: 'The only proofs occur in the psychoanalytic session itself. Clinical proof is the only kind possible.'

By its devotees, Freudian theory is regarded as applicable in the explanation of all problems of human behaviour. Thus it has often been adopted as a conceptual framework for investigations within social anthropology, aesthetics, linguistics, literary studies, and so on. To many people, this is a great attraction – it has, potentially at least, 'all the answers'. But any event can be conveniently fitted in by the uncritical Freudian to bolster the main body of theory: for example, a person may act generously either from a genuine impulse of kindliness or through 'reaction-formation', against an underlying meanness. This is very much a 'heads I win, tails you lose' approach, diametrically opposed to K. Popper's central criterion for the scientific value of a theory – 'A theory which is not refutable by any conceivable event is non-scientific. Irrefutability is not a virtue of a theory (as people often think) but a vice' (see Popper, in Mace, 1957, p. 159).

Psychoanalysis is concerned with vast molar segments of human behaviour, with thousands of the variables of one human life elicited over a considerable period of time. The records of a year's psychoanalytic sessions with one patient would fill many volumes of print. The experimental psychologist, on the other hand, is concerned with a deliberately curtailed and simplified series of events in the life of his subjects. One result of the interaction between the two approaches has been the partly justified claim by Freudians that laboratory situations are far too limited and artificial – too far removed from the great complexity of the individual personality – to represent adequate tests of Freud's ideas.

Here, too, we have a further clash of method in that all the natural sciences do their utmost to reduce the 'personal equation' of the experimenter. His idiosyncratic acts should have no appreciable effect on the result of the experiment. In the psychoanalytic session, on the other hand, the patient (or 'subject') is perforce in close and unique interaction with the therapist (or 'experimenter') – the analyst's 'personal equation' is, in many aspects, maximized. From the standpoint of science, it is obvious that the validity of psychoanalysis cannot be, simultaneously, both 'clinically' and 'scientifically' put to the test – and this gives grounds for further accusations of unreality in the experimental situation in the laboratory.

Problems such as these, and many others, have led to intense debates about the scientific status of psychoanalysis (Parts One and Two of this book). There is wide disagreement among distinguished thinkers as to whether it is science, myth or a premature synthesis. Professor T. R. Miles (1966) has argued that unless the word 'science' is understood in a very rigid and narrow sense, it is perfectly possible for psychoanalytic investigations to be scientific. Professor H. J. Eysenck (1963), on the other hand, is of the opinion that unless the scientific canons are to be so flexible as to become valueless, psychoanalysis cannot be termed a science. But even a critic as severe as Eysenck adds that,

like most psychologists, I appreciate that breath of fresh air which Freud introduced into the musty, dry-as-dust atmosphere of nineteenth-century academic psychology. The brilliance of his mind has opened doors which no one now would wish to close again, and his keen insight has given us a store-house of theories and hypotheses which will keep researchers busy for many years to come.... It is only by bringing to bear the traditional methods of scientific inference and experimentation that we can hope to reap all the benefit of its founder's genius.

From Parts Three to Six of the book, there is a selection of studies which have attempted to do just this. The reader can form his own opinion as to the benefits and success of such an approach. Part Three deals with Freud's genetic propositions which describe how any condition under observation has grown *out* of the individual's past and extended through his total life span. A variety of methods – observational, experimental, cross-cultural and comparative – have been used to elucidate these psychoanalytic propositions. In Part Four, which concerns the psychosexual development of the child and the character formations that are said to result from experiences during these formative (some say 'critical') years, research on this aspect is reviewed.

The dynamic propositions in psychoanalysis, such as the 'defence mechanisms', are probably the most susceptible of experimental analysis. A selection of investigations designed to confirm or disconfirm the validity of concepts such as repression, projection, fixation, regression, displacement and identification is to be found in Part Five. Part Six marshals some of the evidence for unconscious motivation and Freud's theory of dreaming, as well as the possible links between contemporary research into sleeping and dreaming and psychoanalytic concepts.

To complicate an already confusing issue, several writers such as Dr Charles Rycroft (1966) are of the opinion that the controversy between psychoanalysts and critics like Eysenck is not a meaningful one. Both sides are said to be arguing from different and from wrong premises. Rycroft believes that analysts are claiming that psychoanalysis is what it is not, while Eysenck is critical of the system for failing to be what it has no need to claim to be. Rycroft maintains that what Freud was engaged in was not to explain the patient's symptoms causally but to understand them and give them meaning. This was not the scientific procedure of elucidating causes, but the semantic one of making sense of them. Rycroft says it can be argued that much of Freud's work was really semantic, namely, that neurotic symptoms are meaningful disguised communications, but that owing to his

13

scientific training and allegiance, he formulated his findings in the conceptual framework of the physical sciences.

Whatever the merits of these arguments, psychology itself is considered as a *science* of behaviour, and psychoanalysis is commonly viewed as a specialized (and isolated) branch of psychology. In the words of Ernest Hilgard (Reading 2):

Psychoanalysis is, first of all, a medical psychology, concerned with the treatment of human suffering, and as such represents the procedures used by those trained in it as they treat the patients who come to them for help. It is also a general psychology, with its interpretations of human development, memory, thought processes, creativity, social behaviour – fitting all of the subject matter of psychology into its categories.

Freud's passion was psychology. His biographer Ernest Jones (1966) makes it clear that Freud had constantly in mind the ambition of incorporating his discoveries into the body of psychopathology, and then of working through this into a normal psychology which by that means would be transformed into a new science, to be called 'metapsychology'. Freud himself wrote (see Jones, 1966):

A man like myself cannot live without a hobby-horse, without a dominating passion: in fact, without a tyrant, to use Schiller's expression, and that is what it has become. For in its service I know no moderation. It is psychology which has been the goal beckoning me from afar, and now that I have come into contact with the neuroses the goal has drawn much nearer. Two aims plague me: to see how the theory of mental functions would shape itself if one introduced quantitative considerations, a sort of economics of nervous energy; and, secondly, to extract what psychopathology has to yield for normal psychology.

Considerations such as these: the definition of psychoanalysis as a branch of psychology – the latter a discipline struggling to find a respectable place alongside the older and highly respected empirical disciplines – and Freud's own attitude to psychology, have determined the title of this book, *Freud and Psychology*. The choice of Readings, in turn, reflects the attempts to find empirical answers to the questions about the status of particular psychoanalytic propositions.

References

EYSENCK, H. J. (1963), *Uses and Abuses of Psychology*, Penguin Books.

JONES, E. (1966), *The Life and Work of Sigmund Freud*, Penguin Books.

MACE, C. A. (ed.) (1957), *British Philosophy in the Mid-Century*, Allen & Unwin.

MILES, T. R. (1966), *Eliminating the Unconscious*, Pergamon.

RYCROFT, C. (ed.) (1966), *Psychoanalysis Observed*, Constable.

STRACHEY, J. (ed.) (1966), *The Standard Edition of the Complete Psychological Works of Sigmund Freud*, Hogarth Press.

Part One
Psychoanalysis as Science:
General Theoretical Considerations

Freud's aim was to establish a 'scientific psychology' and his wish was to achieve this by applying to psychology the same principles of causality as were at that time considered valid in physics and chemistry. Part One consists of papers by Farrell and Hilgard; they deal with general theoretical considerations – the logical and metaphysical properties of psychoanalytic propositions. The requirements of a scientific theory are discussed. It is argued that psychoanalysis is really a complex of propositions of different types and differing explanatory value. The question of whether psychoanalysis is science, myth or a premature synthesis is considered.

1 B. A. Farrell

Psychoanalytic Theory

B. A. Farrell, 'Psychoanalytic theory', *New Society*, no. 38, 20 June 1963, pp. 11–13.

'How much truth is there in psychoanalytic doctrine? How sound is it?'

It is not easy to give a brief answer to this large question from the layman. To begin with, there is no one psychoanalytic doctrine. A number of psychoanalytic doctrines or theories have been developed in the course of the last fifty years – Freudian, neo-Freudian, Jungian, etc. It will be appropriate to concentrate on classical Freudian theory and the neo-Freudian doctrine of Melanie Klein as examples of psychoanalytic doctrine.

The classical Freudian theory is primarily a doctrine about mental energy. This takes two fundamental forms which, in the early and better known version of the theory, are the sexual and the self-preservative; and this energy goes to determine the character of the stages (oral, anal, etc.) through which the mind develops. In the course of this development the mind becomes differentiated into the structures of id, ego and super-ego, cut across by the critically important barrier separating the unconscious from the pre-conscious elements of the mind. The total balance and distribution of energy is controlled by the mechanisms of defence, such as repression, regression, displacement, and so on. Where this control had not been satisfactorily achieved in the past, the repression barrier keeping the unconscious interests of the system at bay is apt to break down under frustration; and the unconscious comes to the surface in the compromise form of symptoms. The Kleinian theory has a different emphasis. This is primarily a doctrine about the 'object relations' the infant forms (especially with the objects of mother and her breast), and about the internal world of the infant's unconscious phantasies. From the outset the infant experiences

19

the anxieties of living and is faced, in particular, with the breast that both satisfies and frustrates it. It deals with these difficulties by means, especially, of the defences of introjection, projection and splitting. Thus, to begin with, it introjects the breast (i.e. incorporates it in phantasy), and splits the good breast from the bad. Aggressive impulses are as important as sexual ones, and the infant experiences early anxiety as persecution. So the first stage it goes through is the 'paranoid-schizoid position'. At about five months or so, it comes to synthesize the good and bad breast, and passes into the 'depressive position'. The ego is at work from birth, but in a weak, unintegrated form; and a primitive super-ego is already at work in the fifth and sixth months. The Oedipus complex is also operating during the first year in a pre-genital form. The character of the infant's object relations – their good or bad quality – and the extent to which it gets through these early stages satisfactorily are all of crucial importance to it. For the liability of the grown-up Jane to break down and the character of her collapse when it comes are critically dependent on what happened *inside* baby Jane during her first year of life.

How much truth is there in Freudian or Kleinian theory? There is no generally accepted answer to this question. The reason is that there is no consensus in our culture about the position of psychoanalytic theory on our map of knowledge and belief. Is it a scientific theory, as Freud himself apparently believed? Or is it just a pre-scientific myth, as Popper has argued? Or is it the doctrine of the faith to which one is converted in the course of one's own psychoanalysis, as Sargant has suggested?

Is It a Scientific Theory?

Let us, then, take a look at some of the logical properties of psychoanalytic theory which are among the chief sources of the trouble. Suppose we fall into temptation and say that 'the theory embodies as much truth, no doubt, about human nature as a new and developing scientific theory can be expected to do'. We then run slap up against a formidable and, by now, familiar objection. On a widely accepted use of the word 'scientific', the theory of analysis is not a scientific one at all, and whatever knowledge is embodied in it is not scientific in character. For the following reasons:

1. The theory does not exhibit the degree of logical determinateness required of a theory in science. Consider, for example, that part of the doctrine concerned with the mechanisms of defence (i.e. repression, projection, displacement, etc.). It is unclear what precise set of mechanisms is covered by this part of the theory. It is unclear what generalizations are included in it, or what their precise formulation is to be. Because the theory does not (typically) state that, under certain conditions $C_1 \ldots C_n$, a person will defend by projecting (say), the generalizations offered about the mechanisms of defence are (typically) statements of non-numerical likelihoods, of what 'may happen', etc. And of course, such generalizations are so vague as to be very dubious candidates for membership of a scientific theory.

2. Psychoanalytic theory does not exhibit the degree of empirical determinateness required of a theory in science. Thus, a key concept such as 'repression' is not tied to empirical fact by what are generally called 'operational definitions' or 'correspondence rules'. It is linked to fact via the analyst's clinical judgement. The latter will judge that patient Smith has repressed his memory of certain events in the light of the total picture or impression Smith presents in the analytic sessions – an impression in which Smith's silences, affect and 'resistance' behaviour generally will play a prominent part. Such a judgement may be skilful, illuminating and therapeutically necessary. But it is not a scientific procedure. Without correspondence rules, it is not possible to test objectively whether Smith has repressed his memory of certain events. No usable correspondence rules seem to have been constructed so far for any of the large number of concepts of psychoanalytic theory. It would seem, therefore, that the generalizations of psychoanalytic theory embodying these concepts cannot be tested scientifically. So the theory is not a scientific one.

The situation is not much better if we give up the strict demand for 'operational definitions' or 'correspondence rules', and merely put the layman's question. 'What does a term such as *repression* mean?' We will find that the key concept of repression can only be elucidated by means, in part, of the concept of psychic energy. But in the present state of analytic theory this is an explanation *per obscurius*. What is worse, if we seek for the elucidation of the key Kleinian notion of 'the phantasied incorporation by the infant to the breast', it is difficult to avoid an abrupt plunge into psychological absurdity. If we try to rescue the whole Freudian, or Kleinian, story by saying that it provides 'a model' of the mind, we are confronted with the problem of tying some, at least, of the important theoretical concepts of the theory to fact with sufficient precision for it to function as a scientific model, and not just as a string of metaphors. It is very doubtful whether this problem has been solved at the present time.

Is It the Doctrine of a Faith?

Now consider quite a different way of looking at the theory. If we have been struck by the cult-like orthodoxy of analysts and noted the character of the training they go through, we may be tempted to look upon the theory as the ideology of a faith. We may say: 'When one examines the actual character of psychoanalytic method, it is clear that an analysis, especially a training analysis, closely resembles a technique of religious conversion and indoctrination. The person, or trainee, who is subjected to the process comes out of it with a faith, into the truth of which he is no longer interested, or even able, to inquire. So the theory is the doctrine of a faith, and not an empirical theory about human nature.'

This point of view will not do either. It may be true that psychoanalytic method closely resembles the techniques of religious conversion and indoctrination. It may also be true that analysts are usually so maimed psychologically by their training as to be incapable of, and/or uninterested in, investigating the truth of their theory. But plainly it does not follow from this that the theory is one into whose empirical truth or falsity it is not possible or profitable to inquire. The fact that analysts sometimes use the theory like a theology in defence of a faith does not mean that they always use it like this, and that it has no empirical character at all. Even if it be a fact that analysts come to accept the theory as true via something like a conversion experience, this fact does not mean that no rational and empirical grounds can be found to support and even establish it. In this respect, psychoanalytic theory differs markedly from the theology of the faith of Moral Rearmament, for which, presumably, no empirical grounds can logically be found. It would seem to differ less markedly from the doctrine of Yoga – for though parts of this doctrine are occult in character and hence logically untouchable by empirical evidence, other parts do seem to be open to empirical support and refutation.

Is It a Pre-Scientific Myth?

So psychoanalytic theory is not a scientific story, on one important use of the word 'scientific'. Yet it appears to possess some sort of empirical character. This suggests that the theory may be a pre-scientific myth – a story that may contain, in Popper's words, 'most interesting psychological suggestions, but not in a testable form'; and yet which 'may be developed, and become testable'. But this view of the matter also runs into difficulties. If psychoanalytic theory were a myth, it would presumably be a closed story. But this is just what it is not. Though it may be closed to the sort of testing characteristic of science, it is open to the influence and control of fact – experimental, clinical and sociological. This becomes plain when one looks at the history of the theory. Thus, it was empirical fact in one form or another that led to Freud's view of narcissism, to the second instinct theory and to the emphasis on character development; to the Kleinian stress on early development and the importance of early personal relations; to the acceptance of a non-genital view of the Oedipal situation, and so on. The picture of the theory as a myth does not square very easily with the history of its development. The theory is used daily to generate clinical expectations about patients, and to help in their diagnosis, care and treatment. It seems doubtful whether pre-scientific myths have, and could have, functioned in this sort of way. Just what the precise relations are between psychoanalytic theory and fact is a complex matter still enveloped in considerable obscurity. But it seems clear that, whatever these relations turn out to be, they will be found to bring the theory into much closer and more intimate relations with fact than those enjoyed by any pre-scientific myth.

Is It a Premature Synthesis?

But let us reformulate the suggestion we have just considered. Suppose we say that psychoanalytic theory represents an empirical and speculative synthesis, which is premature in that it runs far ahead of the evidence that can upset or support it with reasonable certainty. This suggestion may very well be true, but it does not say much because it is so vague. What we need is an analysis of the way in which psychoanalytic theory is an empirical synthesis; and of the detailed manner in which it is related to empirical fact. As we have just hinted above, it is doubtful whether any such analysis of the theory has ever yet been made. In its absence the suggestion we are now considering necessarily tells us little. Moreover, there is a further difficulty about it. Even though this suggestion may be true — that the theory is a premature empirical synthesis – it may or may not be worth while offering this suggestion, and describing the theory in this way. For the theory may be premature in one of two ways: in the way that characterizes pre-Daltonian atomic theory or Prout's theory of matter; or in the way that characterizes Aristotle's physics and cosmology or Phlogiston theory. That is to say, the synthesis embodied in psychoanalytic theory may be shown by future scientific work and discovery to be on the right lines; or it may be shown to be substantially mistaken. So the theory may represent, in large measure, a correct anticipation of future advance, or it may point up a blind alley. Now it is only worth while asserting that the theory is a premature empirical synthesis if it does correctly anticipate the future. But to assert that it is premature in this way is to say something that, though possibly true, is very difficult to establish. This assertion contains a gamble that the future will go the way psychoanalytic theory has indicated; and there is no need to stress the hazards of betting on the future of science.

Is It a Rational Theory?

There are some workers in the psychological field who may still be moved to reject this view of the theory as false. 'No psychoanalytic theory can be an empirical synthesis which the future may favour, because they are all unscientific and irrational stories, and it is difficult to conceive how an irrational story can ever point the way to the truth.' Now we have seen that it may very well be true that psychoanalytic theories are not scientific. But it does not follow from this that they are irrational. We need only think of theories in fields such as history, economics, jurisprudence, social anthropology and sociology. These are (typically) not scientific narratives; but they are (typically) quite rational ones. The domain of the rational is wider than that of the scientific. Hence, to suppose or imply that an unscientific theory is necessarily an irrational one is to perpetrate a howler. (It is tempting to argue that this howler is embedded in some of Eysenck's criticism of psychoanalysis.)

However, it may nevertheless be the case that any psychoanalytic theory, in addition to being unscientific, is indeed also an irrational story. We all know that there has been much criticism of psychoanalysis. Part of the point of this vast body of criticism has been to show that the theory as a whole is a confused and incoherent business without rational support. But it is open to doubt whether the critics have established this thesis. For, in general, they seem to have judged the theory in the light of the logic (usually implicit) of some *other* type of theory or discourse, which serves for them as the model of rationality. Then, when they have shown that psychoanalytic theory fails to satisfy the standards of the particular discourse they have taken as a model, they have rejected it as irrational. But all such criticism commits a crucial sin. It disregards a fundamental rule of intellectual virtue which states that to each type of discourse its own logic. Before we can reject psychoanalytic theories as irrational, we must first elucidate their logic without preconceptions. If we then find that they contain inconsistencies, absurdities, are without rational support, and so on, we are safe to reject them as irrational stories. It is doubtful whether any such elucidation of any psychoanalytic theory has ever been carried out. The upshot, therefore, is that an analytic theory may or may not be a pointer to the truth – it may or may not be a harbinger of part of the future in the psychological field. But we will find it difficult to argue that it fails to point to the truth because it is an irrational doctrine. The irrationality of psychoanalytic theory has not been established.

Are There Grounds to Support It?

But if we are to look on, say, Freudian theory as a premature empirical synthesis that is a harbinger of future scientific discovery, there must be some rational grounds to support the theory. Consider three important ones.

1. The use of psychoanalytic method has produced an enormous amount of factual material. This material demands ordering, description and explanation. Freudian theory grew up to satisfy this demand. Now it is in fact the case that the theory has succeeded to some degree in ordering, describing and explaining this clinical material or data. It is also the case that this material suggests, more or less strongly, that we should use the theory to talk about it, and that the theory represents the correct way of doing so. This complex relationship between the theory and the clinical material of analysis constitutes a rational ground in support of the theory; and, it is tempting to argue, a *good* ground at that.

2. In recent years psychologists have conducted many studies of concepts and generalizations that are psychoanalytic or near analytic in character. Some of these studies have thrown doubt on Freudian doctrine, others have tended to support it; and the precise relevance and outcome of this work is still uncertain. Thus, these studies have generally supported the Freudian view of erotogenesis, or sensual development, though it has not yet been shown that the infant's sexual behaviour is an innate matter, as the Freudian doctrine of sexual energy requires. Nor has it yet been shown that the concept of 'infantile sexuality' is required at all; and in so far as studies in this field have thrown any light on the Oedipal hypothesis (in its sexual or non-sexual forms), the present picture seems a very confused one. Experimental studies on animals do suggest that the formation of an

attachment to mother or litter mates during a critical early period is of great importance – which is consistent with the whole Freudian and Kleinian emphasis. But studies with hospital children suggest that the critical period is between six and eighteen months, and therefore later than the period Kleinians stress. Just what are the effects of maternal deprivation is still unsettled. As we have implied above, the psychoanalytic model of mental functioning is too poor to permit of straightforward testing. An aspect of it that has been investigated is the unconscious. This has been approached in particular via analogues of the concept of repression, and the results have been suggestive. What little work has been done on projection Kleinians would probably not regard as very relevant. However, the body of studies that has been made into the mechanisms of defence, or their analogues, has produced results that, generally speaking, support or are consistent with the Freudian story. On the other hand, though, there is some work at present that supports the idea of the oral character; there is very little, as yet, to support the related idea of the anal character.

But whatever the precise relevance and outcome of these scientific studies, it is plausible to argue that in places Freudian theory is 'on to something'. The theory may not have the whole truth on these topics; it may be very wrongheaded about them; and in any case it does not (typically) state its insights in ways that are scientifically acceptable. But, it can be argued, the work of the psychologists has brought out that the Freudian version of psychoanalytic theory is pointing, in part, to something authentic.

3. Suppose we are considering a theory in science. Suppose we find that it can also be used to explain sets of phenomena that it was not originally designed to explain, and that are apparently remote in character from the original ones. We should then regard this as a good, additional ground for supposing that the theory is true, or an approximation to the truth. Now something analogous applies to Freudian theory. Originally designed to order and explain the data of the analytic session, the theory has been used 'to explain' all sorts of other phenomena – religion, the creative artist, the character of Hamlet, jokes, the incest taboo, human character development, and so forth. No doubt the sense in which the theory does explain these phenomena is unclear, and

the success of these explanations is uncertain. But the concepts and generalizations of the theory are sufficiently powerful to illuminate these very different phenomena by exhibiting them as manifestations of certain fundamental, psychological processes. The fact that the theory is able to do this constitutes a good ground for saying that it is, at the least, an approximation to the truth.

But are these grounds good enough to establish that the Freudian or any other psychoanalytic theory is true or an approximation to the truth? It will be generally agreed that the second and third grounds, separately or jointly, are not good enough for this purpose. It will also be generally agreed that the chief support for an analytic theory comes from the first ground – from the clinical material thrown up by psychoanalytic method. But before we can decide how good this support is, we have to ask whether the clinical material can be relied upon. In other words, is psychoanalysis a valid method of discovery? This doubt is connected with the stock question: What is the therapeutic effectiveness of the method?[1]

1. See Reading 3 [Eds.].

2 Ernest R. Hilgard

The Scientific Status of Psychoanalysis

Ernest R. Hilgard, 'The scientific status of psychoanalysis', in E. Nagel,
P. Suppes and A. Tarski (eds.), *Logic, Methodology and Philosophy of
Science: Proceedings of the 1960 International Congress*, Stanford
University Press, 1962, pp. 375–90.

Psychoanalysis is, first of all, a medical psychology, concerned
with the treatment of human suffering, and as such represents the
procedures used by those trained in it as they treat the patients
who come to them for help. It is also a general psychology, with
its interpretations of human development, memory, thought
processes, creativity, social behavior – fitting all of the subject
matter of psychology into its categories. Finally, it presents a
general view of man's place in nature, of how man may live with
his heritage of unconscious processes if he is to be at peace with
himself, and if he is to be as rational as he can be in planning for
the future of human society. The influence of psychoanalysis
upon literature and drama rests upon this implied *Weltanschau-
ung*.

Every young science goes through a number of stages in its
development from naturalistic observation, through the detection
of areas of lawfulness and construction of more limited theories,
to more comprehensive, parsimonious and elegant theories.
While these states can be assigned some sort of historical order,
observations are guided by theories, theories are modified by
observations and some theories of very wide scope may be proposed early to be supplemented later by less ambitious models.
Hence any particular body of scientific material can be assessed
only according to its history, its achievements along the way, the
course of revision and its promise for the future.

Psychoanalysis has a special history because it was dominated
so long by Sigmund Freud, a man of great genius, who made
most of the observations upon which psychoanalysis is built,
who began theory construction at the very start of his career and
fought the social battles for recognition against a hostile clientele.

He thus defined the field of inquiry, invented the techniques of investigation, proposed the theories and set the stage for the fervent social interactions that have characterized psychoanalysis as a profession. He continued to think, to change his mind, to propose new ways of looking at things, throughout a long life. Despite the changes in detail, there is a remarkable unity to his thinking, if one looks for the guiding ideas rather than for the changing metaphors that expressed them. One guiding idea is the *continuity of development* from earliest infancy; new ways of behaving are built on earlier ways through subtle transformations and shifts, in which the old and outgrown ways are somehow carried along, also, on occasion becoming manifest. This idea has had a profound influence upon general psychology. The notion that these residues from earlier experience affect behavior *unconsciously* is a second guiding idea. The nature of the active unconscious, the number of fundamental drives, the nature of repression, may be matters of some dispute, but some equivalent of unconscious motivation, of the regulation of what man does by thought-like processes that are out of awareness, is now part of general psychological thinking. A third guiding idea, that present behavior is often a result of *conflict* and exhibits ways of meeting, resolving or compromising issues, brings the results of the past into the present. This feature of Freud's teaching has also become a commonplace of academic psychology. There are many other guiding ideas, such as the distinction between impulse-driven thinking, called primary process thinking, and more rational or conceptual thinking, called secondary process thinking. This distinction has not yet been fully domesticated in academic psychology, but it is influential in current research. The special processes assigned to the dreamwork (condensation, displacement, symbolization) are significant original formulations. Thus far I have not discussed the contributions of the psychoanalytic method. Again, to Freud we owe free association, the role of interpretation, and the very important problems of transference and countertransference.

Most of these ideas were spelled out in the seventh chapter of *The Interpretation of Dreams* (Freud, 1900), Freud's major announcement of his theory, but they had already been worked out in 1895 in his 'Project for a scientific psychology' that came to light only recently with the Fliess papers (see Freud, 1887–1902). It is significant that Freud was searching for a theoretical framework for his ideas before the turn of the century, and had four more decades in which to develop them before his death in 1939.

For philosophers of science, the history of psychoanalysis provides a unique opportunity to study the evolution of a science. It of course had many roots and was influenced by the *Zeitgeist*, but it would not have been the same without Freud. We know now the kinds of germinal ideas he had as early as 1895. Many of these were imaginative, novel, inventive, but they were not weird or fantastic, and they foreshadowed developments in neurophysiology as well as in psychoanalysis. Freud built upon the available methods and scientific ideas that were current, molding them honestly and courageously on the basis of his careful observations of himself and of his patients. Frenkel-Brunswik (1954) assessed his inferred variables from the point of view of the logic of science and she found that, *in principle*, he was doing what any conceptualizer of science does. He was aware of the problems of scientific logic; while he often used metaphor when events were too difficult to systematize more precisely, he would have preferred to abandon metaphor for better anchored concepts. The interaction between creative imagination, on the one hand, and careful observations, on the other, as exemplified in Freud, bears dispassionate study. His speculations doubtless outran his data at some points, but this is perhaps essential if a young science is to grow.

We are now considering where psychoanalysis stands today, twenty years after Freud's death. As students of the history of science, we need to recognize the personal and social problems that faced psychoanalytic practitioners and theorists following his death. There had been defections from the ranks during his lifetime by such early favorites as Adler, Jung and Rank, so that the central core of psychoanalysis was both defined and dominated by Freud. During his lifetime a unity within a developing theory could be maintained by accepting his leadership; after his death those who wished to remain within the tradition had to retain a kind of unity that would be social as well as intellectual. That is, those who now remained within the mainstream of

31

psychoanalysis had to be free to modify their views (as Freud would have done were he still alive), but they felt some obligation to show that they followed Freud's main teachings both as to method and theory, enough at least to preserve unity among themselves. This has inevitably resulted in a certain amount of in-group rigidity and out-group antagonism, understandable in view of the social history of psychoanalysis during Freud's lifetime. Seldom has a man with a new scientific message been greeted with as much antagonism and hostility as Freud met, from both medical and non-medical groups. This is part of the social history that we have to understand if we are to study the evolution of psychoanalysis as a science. Post-Freudian psycho-analysis has its own social history, too, with in-group and out-group relations internal to psychoanalysis. The nature of these relationships, in the light of their history, will some day contribute an interesting chapter to the sociology of knowledge. There is no point at present in passing judgement on these matters, except to note that there is flux. For example, in several large cities psycho-analytic institutes have fissioned into separate groups differing on some matters of doctrine, yet leaders at the national level have managed to keep these factions united within the American Psychoanalytic Association, with graduates of the separate insti-tutes validated as psychoanalysts. Thus the groundwork exists for the eventual reduction of the barriers between the groups that now find themselves somewhat in conflict.

In order to proceed with an assessment of the status of psycho-analysis as a science today, some choices have to be made. I have chosen to discuss what the analysts call their *metapsychology* rather than their theory and technique of psychoanalytic treat-ment of patients. There fortunately exist two papers providing information about contemporary psychoanalytic thinking within the social tradition of classical psychoanalysis. One is a long chapter by David Rapaport. 'The structure of psychoanalytic theory: a systematizing attempt' (see Koch, 1959, pp. 55–183). Prepared after this chapter, but appearing in print at about the same time, is a paper also by Rapaport, in collaboration with Merton Gill, entitled 'The points of view and assumptions of metapsychology' (Rapaport and Gill, 1959). These papers are serious efforts to state the structure of psychoanalysis 'from the inside' and can be taken as a fair specimen of the best of current thinking among those who feel themselves at home within the classical Freudian tradition, while yet ready for new developments ahead. My initial task becomes a review and commentary upon these statements. I shall lean primarily upon the paper by Rapaport and Gill.

Psychoanalytic Metapsychology

In undertaking their formal statement of the propositions of metapsychology, Rapaport and Gill begin by distinguishing four kinds of propositions within psychoanalysis: empirical propositions, specific psychoanalytic propositions, propositions of the general psychoanalytic theory and propositions stating the metapsychological assumptions. Their own examples follow.

Empirical propositions

'Around the fourth year of life boys regard their fathers as rivals.'

This is empirical in the sense that it could be investigated directly by available methods, and is thus either demonstrably true or false on the basis of directly relevant evidence.

Specific psychoanalytic propositions

'The solution of the Oedipal situation is a decisive determinant of character formation and pathology.'

This is a step removed from direct empirical study because it implies some substantiated theory regarding the Oedipus complex, character formation and pathology. It is specific in that its reference is to a set of events taking place at one time in the life cycle. Even though the proposition were confirmed, its explanatory value would be limited to this set of events.

General psychoanalytic proposition

'Structure formation by means of identifications and anticathexes explains theoretically the consequence of the "decline of the Oedipus complex".'

Note that this proposition says something more about the

33

preceding one, placing it in the larger context of identification and cathexes, that will be used to explain other events as well. Hence this proposition is of more general scope.

Metapsychological proposition

'The propositions of the general psychoanalytic theory which explain the Oedipal situation and the decline of the Oedipus complex involve dynamic, economic, structural, genetic and adaptive assumptions.'

This is, of course, the most general statement of all.

In their paper Rapaport and Gill attempt to limit themselves to the metapsychological propositions in relation to general psychoanalytic propositions, avoiding the two levels of specific psychoanalytic propositions and the empirical propositions. The metapsychological theory that they present, already hinted at in the illustration, can be restated as follows: *The psychoanalytic explanation of any psychological phenomenon must include propositions reflecting the dynamic, economic, structural, genetic and adaptive points of view.*

Those familiar with psychoanalytic theory will recall that Freud formulated three metapsychological points of view, which he called dynamic, topographic and economic. Rapaport and Gill, in order to make explicit what was implicit in Freud, and to include current developments within psychoanalytic ego psychology, accepted the three points of view of Freud (modifying topographic to structural, in view of changes during Freud's lifetime), and added two points of view (genetic and adaptive). These five points of view are in some respects five separate models. Let us see how each of them is characterized.

The dynamic point of view

This is perhaps the most widely understood aspect of psychoanalysis and gives psychoanalysis its designation as a dynamic psychology. The general psychoanalytic propositions of the dynamic point of view employ the concepts of *unconscious forces and conflicts*, and the concept of *drive or instinct*. Contemporary psychoanalysts commonly refer only to the two specific innate drives of sex and aggression; other drives (if any) are thought to be derivatives of these.

The metapsychological assumptions within this point of view are thus summarized by Rapaport and Gill:

The *dynamic* point of view demands that the psychoanalytic explanation of any psychological phenomenon includes propositions concerning the psychological forces involved in the phenomenon.

The major assumptions are: (a) there are psychological forces; (b) the effect of simultaneously acting psychological forces may be the simple resultant of the work of each of these forces; and (c) the effect of simultaneously acting psychological forces may not be the simple resultant of the work of each of these forces.

It is evident that these assumptions are a mere scaffolding upon which a more precise theory has to be built. For example, the third assumption as stated negates the second, so that the two can be combined into this statement: 'The effect of simultaneously acting psychological forces may *or may not* be the simple resultant of the work of each of these forces.' In this form the statement is a mere truism, but of course there is more intended. The third assumption actually implies something like this: under some circumstances the effect of simultaneously acting forces is modified by drive fusion and overdetermination; under these circumstances the effect is not a simple resultant of the work of each of these forces. This statement draws in, however, some notions from general psychoanalytic theory (e.g. drive fusion and overdetermination), and hence belongs with a next elaboration of the theory rather than with the metapsychological assumptions at the level of generality that Rapaport and Gill seek to hold.

The economic point of view

This is the point of view that all behavior is regulated by psychological energy, and concerns the principles by which psychological energy is disposed of. The term 'economic' means 'economical', that is, that psychological energies operate along paths of least effort, leading toward tension reduction and homeostasis.

Psychoanalytic theory when approached from this point of view has to do with the processes by which tension is reduced by energy discharge either directly or through devious means, or by suspending energy discharge until conditions are more favorable. The basic concepts here are primary and secondary process, wish fulfilment, cathexis and countercathexis. There are additional related concepts of binding and neutralization of psychological energy. The level of concepts represented by primary and secondary processes and cathexes belongs, however, to the general psychoanalytic theory, rather than to the metapsychological assumptions.

The metapsychological assumptions are that there are psychological energies, that they follow laws of conservation and entropy, and that these energies are subject to transformations that increase or decrease their entropic tendency.

The use of physical analogies in the assumptions of both the dynamic and economic points of view requires discussion, to which we shall return.

The structural point of view

The structural point of view replaced the earlier topographic one when Freud introduced the tripartite division of id, ego and super-ego to displace (or supplement) the emphasis upon unconscious, preconscious and conscious topography. More recently there has developed within classical psychoanalysis an emphasis known as ego psychology in which various kinds of structure are proposed, e.g. defense-, control- and means-structures. The control- and means-structures are considered to be relatively autonomous structures within the ego, and thus part of the conflict-free sphere (Hartmann, 1939).

I shall not repeat the formal language of the assumptions with respect to structure. The main points are that structures are configurations with a slow rate of change, that these structures have a hierarchical order, and that mental processes take place within, between and by means of these structures.

The genetic point of view

The course of individual development is very important within psychoanalytic theory, and emphasis upon early childhood is one of the most influential contributions of psychoanalysis to general psychology. The developmental point of view was so taken for

36

granted within psychoanalysis that it has not traditionally been separately formulated as parallel to the dynamic, economic and structural viewpoints. The general theory of psychosexual development is well known, in which the child passes through the anal, oral, phallic, latency and genital stages on the way to maturity. This aspect of the theory is the source of some controversy between those who insist that the crises related to these stages are primarily rooted in the nature of the organism (the more classical position), and those who attribute a major influence to the impact of the culture in which the child is reared (the more dissident position). The terminology is somewhat unforfunate, because 'genetic' means ontogenetic or epigenetic, and not gene-controlled as in the more familiar current use of the term. However, we may continue here to use the term as synonymous with developmental.

The metapsychological assumptions of the genetic point of view are that all psychological phenomena have an origin and development, originating in innate givens that mature according to an epigenetic ground plan. The earlier forms of a psychological phenomenon, though superseded by later forms, remain potentially active; at any point in psychological history the totality of potentially active forms codetermines all psychological phenomena.

It may be noted, in passing, that the level of generality of these assumptions is such that the content of general psychoanalytic theory could be greatly changed without violating them. For example, psychosexual development could be replaced by some other content without violating any of these assumptions.

The adaptive point of view

This relative newcomer to psychoanalytic theory permits statements that cover most of the ground familiar to functional psychology and frees the psychoanalyst from the need to find a libidinal explanation for all behavior. Among the conceptions are the organism's preparedness (through evolution) for an average expectable environment, 'apparatuses' that are essentially abilities by which to cope with the environment, dependence upon external stimulation, achieved relative autonomy from the environment.

The adaptive assumptions include statements concerning adaptation to internal states, to the physical and social environment and the mutual adaptations between man and environment.

This completes the listing of the five points of view and their assumptions, according to Rapaport and Gill. This summarization cannot do justice to their treatment, which at many points includes reservations, nor to the sources they have used in arriving at the assumptions. They illustrate each of the assumptions by reference to the psychoanalytic theory of affects; for the sake of brevity, these references have been ignored in my summary. Only a reading of their original paper can fill in these gaps.

Rapaport and Gill concluded their paper by a statement of confidence that the five points of view are likely to prove necessary and sufficient 'to a degree which recommends that they should be accepted – for the time being – as the framework of psychoanalytic metapsychology'. They felt less sure about their assumptions: 'It is not yet possible to assess whether all these assumptions are necessary, and whether this set of assumptions is sufficient – when coupled with observational data – to yield the existing body of psychoanalytic propositions.'

Five Models or One?

What is implied in the assertion that a psychoanalytic explanation requires a minimum of one proposition from each of the five points of view? It could mean that this is a five-dimensional system with the coordinates of any event being the five yielded by the dimensions. The dimensions are not of this kind, however, and this interpretation can be rejected. A second possibility is that there are five independent models. An event can be explained according to *any one* of the models, but the explanation has not become exhaustive until it has been explained according to *every* model. That this is possibly the intent of Rapaport and Gill appears to be demonstrated in the empirical use of the five-model scheme in the interpretation of hypnotic phenomena by Gill and Brenman (1959). Each point of view in turn serves for the characterization of what happens within hypnosis; the story is completed when the last of the five points of view has been discussed. The models of course overlap, and references to other points of view are not excluded when a given view provides the background for discussion. The manner of the interaction is not specified, however, and this is one of the weaknesses of the Rapaport and Gill presentation. It is not clear, for example, whether non-interchangeable kinds of information emerge from each model or whether, by appropriate transformations, the yield of one of the models could be made more powerful by using information from the others.[1]

We have Rapaport (see Koch, 1959, p. 152) saying of the points of view:

The 'points of view' seem to be the equivalents of 'principles' in psychoanalytic theory. Yet their form shows that the time to examine them one by one, for their long-range significance, has not yet arrived. Instead of formal principles we will present here a few general conceptions, which compound the various points of view, and which seem likely to survive whatever the fate of the more specific ingredients of the psychoanalytic theory should prove to be.

His discussion then proceeds at a level quite different from that of the Rapaport–Gill paper.

The vacillation between the points of view as models, as principles, as components to be compounded, is understandable in view of the complexity and looseness of contemporary psychoanalytic formulations.

It is in accordance with good scientific practice to seek for principles of unification, and I have therefore examined the five viewpoints to see if some subgrouping might be plausible. One principle that appears to be a possible guide for combining the five models into a smaller number is the *time-span* of the processes to which the models refer. The reference of the dynamic and economic models is to events which have primarily a *short* time-span: the resolution of forces and the transformation of energy into work. The reference of the other models is to events with a *long* time-span: genetic, structural and adaptive models refer to processes developing over the life-span, changing slowly and

1. A statement that '*all* psychoanalytic propositions involve *all* meta-psychological points of view' does not clarify the status of the separate points of view.

leading in the end to the contemporary situation which the dynamic-economic model is called upon to explain. A first step in simplification would be to unite the dynamic-economic models into one and the genetic-structural-adaptive models into a second one.[2]

If there are just two models, one historical covering a long time-span, one historical covering a short time-span in the present, then both the independence and the interrelationship of the models are easier to comprehend. Let me give an analogy from problem solving. The *historical* understanding of problem solving requires that we know what the problem solver brings to the situation from his past learning, what relevant information he has, what techniques he knows, what attitudes he has toward himself as a problem solver. We can make certain assertions or predictions on the basis of this knowledge. The *ahistorical* understanding of problem solving requires that we know the manner in which our problem solver makes use of his past experience in relation to the present, how he analyses the problem, selects the relevant information and techniques, how the present display of the problem influences what he is able to do. There are many relationships here that cannot be discussed in purely historical terms. One way of putting this is that sufficient past experience to solve a problem does not guarantee that the subject will solve the problem, unless the present demands upon him are made in an appropriate manner and unless he has his past experiences available in a form suitable for use.

Translating this example into the language of the clinic, we might say that an individual's relations to his parents in childhood were such as to produce an abiding structure of anxiety-dependency. Now he takes a job in which the boss reminds him (unconsciously) of his father, the anxiety (based on the dynamics of transference) overwhelms him and he develops neurotic symptoms. The abiding structure is a historical fact, to be explained by the genetic-structural-adaptive model; the breakdown with the present boss is to be explained by the dynamic-economic model. Obviously the two interact in that we understand the

2. Hartmann and Kris (1945) have also recognized that the explanatory propositions of psychoanalysis classify chiefly into two groups: genetic and dynamic.

individual's present behavior in relation both to his life history and to the provocative circumstances of the present.

The separation of the two models is a practical convenience because data come both from the life-history and from the present, though as a scientific enterprise the two models should be combined. If a single equation is written to describe what is happening in the present, it can have terms in it that represent the residues from the past, as well as terms that represent the present. Thus Hull's equations for reaction potential (1952) include the simultaneous interactions of habits (including generalized habits) built up in the past, along with the drive state, stimulus dynamisms, and so on, in the present. There is no formal obstacle to including historical and ahistorical data in the same equation.

For convenience, we may discuss the five Rapaport–Gill models as though they were two, turning aside from the problem of their eventual integration into one.

The Dynamic-Economic Model

Some contemporary model of this kind is needed to deal with the problem of conflict and its resolution, and the energetics of behavior including facilitation, inhibition, distortion, symbolization.

The physical metaphors as used at present are unsatisfactory, but perhaps they can be built upon to do what the models are intended to do. The physics is not literal: there is no mass for force to accelerate, there is no distance by which to determine how much work a force has done, there is no dissipation of energy into unavailable heat by which to make precise the meaning of entropy; when energy is transformed it is not changed from potential to kinetic (Skinner, 1956). Non-psychoanalytic psychologists have also used physical metaphors, such as threshold and drive, not out of the vocabulary of systematic physical science, or force, distance, direction, as by Kurt Lewin, with more of the flavor of systematic physics. When the vocabulary remains too close to that of strictly physical science, the metaphors are strained and the result has usually been unsatisfactory (Leeper, 1943; London, 1944).

Uneasiness with the quantitative concepts of the dynamic-economic model has been expressed by psychoanalysts. Thus Kubie (1947) states:

Assumptions as to changes in quantities of energy are admissible only if alterations in the pattern of intrapsychic forces are ruled out. A failure to recognize this has made all so-called economic formulations a species of *ad hoc* speculative allegory in quantitative terms.

Note that this statement of Kubie's not only is critical of the economic theory, but indicates clearly that the dynamic-economic models must be thought of at one and the same time.

Colby (1955) has given thoughtful consideration to these problems. He finds the hydraulic analogy used to describe psychological energy (i.e. a reservoir with pipes to regulate the flow) entirely unsatisfactory, and builds his own cyclic-circular model. He recognizes that his energy concept is actually far removed from the physicist's concept: 'Our psychic energy provides a synoptic way of talking about activity and change' (1955, p. 27). While energy within his system has some descriptive characteristics (pulsation, period, synchrony, etc.), it is transported through the system essentially as a modifiable message and its 'energetic' aspects are minimal. He is struggling with genuine problems within the psychoanalytic description of events and processes and finds some sort of 'feedback' model essential. Without going into his solution of the problems, we can here merely indicate that this is a serious effort to find an alternative to the classical model. It supports the position that the status of the dynamic-economic metapsychology of contemporary psychoanalysis is very provisional.

The Structural-Genetic-Adaptive Model

Freud's tripartite structure – id, ego, super-ego – is a heuristic convenience in the discussion of typical intrapsychic conflicts. The impulsivity of the id, the intellectual realism of the ego and the moral flavor of the super-ego epitomize ways of talking about stress within the person that are familiar in the Hebraic-Christian tradition. Thus the spirit may be willing while the flesh is weak, one may start out on a course of action but be troubled by a nagging conscience. Anyone raised in Western culture can easily understand the id/ego/super-ego conflicts, at least in their broad outlines.

This simplicity, while an initial advantage, rises up as an obstacle when the parts of the personality become reified as almost three persons, the id telling the ego what to do, the ego actively fighting the id, the super-ego being a party, too, to the internal battles. Actually, as Colby (1955, p. 77) says, 'its simplicity (i.e. that of the tripartite scheme) makes it insufficient to conceptualize specifically enough the manifold functions of psychic activity.'

The id, ego, super-ego structural divisions have been supplemented more recently chiefly by differentiations within the ego. The ego psychology of Hartmann has multiplied the structures within the ego, calling them 'ego apparatuses'. Some of these apparatuses are said to rest on constitutional givens (e.g. perception, motility, intelligence). Other secondary apparatuses develop through interaction with the environment; both kinds may be relatively autonomous, that is, free of control through the instinctual drives. These ego apparatuses and structures are very numerous, and I have not found a systematic list of them if, indeed, such a list is possible. Apparently some primary-process defense mechanisms such as displacement, condensation, substitution, symbolization, repression, isolation, reaction-formation and projection, can be included among ego apparatuses or structures (Rapaport, in Koch, 1959, p. 154). Other structures include control- and means-structures, which are not defenses.

The acceptance of conflict-free ego structures has been viewed as a great advance within classical psychoanalysis, permitting not only the greater differentiation of the structural viewpoint, but the addition of the adaptive viewpoint. The psychoanalyst no longer faces the burden of explaining everything in terms of one or two primordial drives; he can now accept the drive theory as he has always done, but can supplement it with the structures of the conflict-free ego sphere, and thus comprehend the problems of perception, problem solving, esthetics, play, that were forced into a somewhat artificial perspective when everything had to be derived from drive. The concept of sublimation no longer has to be stretched to cover everything that appears on the surface to be non-sexual. While the multiplication of apparatuses and structures within the ego gives this new freedom, some of the unifying value of the older structural theory has been sacrificed. This is probably inevitable when a theory is in transition, and seeks to encompass new facts under new assumptions.

Because the structural conceptions relate to enduring aspects of the personality, aspects with slow rates of change, these conceptions are intimately bound to the developmental ones represented by the genetic and adaptive viewpoints. Erikson (1959) has combined the psychosexual states of classical psychoanalysis with adaptive crises associated with each of these stages, thus integrating the genetic and the adaptive viewpoints as these are characterized by Rapaport and Gill.

While Erikson takes off from Freud, accepting the psychosexual stages associated with the prominence of certain body orifices as the individual matures, he attempts to go beyond Freud and to meet the problem of interaction with the environment, showing how the resolution of each developmental crisis affects the manner in which later crises are met. He introduces some stages beyond the Freudian genital stage, or perhaps as differentiations within it, with the three successive polarities in adolescence and adult life of ego identity versus role diffusion, generativity versus self-absorption, and integrity versus despair and disgust.

Erikson's proposals are insightful, sensitive to the human situation, and provide important supplements to the encapsulated and intrapsychic flavor of the more traditional psychosexual theory of psychogenesis. Yet from the point of view of a logical or systematic plan of human development, intended to hold across cultures, it lacks criteria by which its stages are distinguished and according to which the major problems associated with each stage have been identified.

In general, examination of the structural-genetic-adaptive model indicates that, like the dynamic-economic model, it is a very provisional one, although useful in giving direction to the kind of tighter theory eventually to be achieved.

Ernest R. Hilgard

The Validation of Psychoanalytic Propositions

There have been many attempts to submit theoretical propositions from psychoanalysis to experimental tests, either of a quasi-clinical sort (as in projective tests and hypnosis) or in non-clinical tests (as in studies of memory, animal behavior, child development in other cultures, etc.). While indeed many of these have come out rather favorably to psychoanalytic conceptions, the general attitude of the classical psychoanalyst has often been one of skepticism, if not of hostility, to these attempts. Why should this be?

1. The first reason for a negative attitude by the psychoanalyst toward these attempts is his confidence that the psychoanalytic method is the only appropriate method for revealing some of the relationships. A depth psychology, it is said, requires a depth method for its study. The only person qualified to interpret evidence is the one who has himself been through a psychoanalysis and is thus familiar at first-hand with the phenomena. Thus psychoanalysis is needed to produce the phenomena and a psychoanalyst is needed to interpret them.

We may accept this objection to studies by non-psychoanalysts, but with two qualifications. First, it applies to *some* aspects of the psychoanalytic theory only. We need to become clearer about which aspects require the analyst and the analytic method, and which do not. Second, when a psychoanalyst obtains the data and assists in its interpretation, then third persons (including non-psychoanalysts as well as other psychoanalysts) may be helpful in arranging for critical hypothesis testing.

2. The second reason for a negative attitude by some psychoanalysts toward empirical attempts at testing psychoanalytic propositions is the complexity of psychoanalytic theory, and hence the fear that tests of separate propositions will be either trivial or irrelevant. According to Rapaport, most of those who try to test the theory either do not understand it, or they ignore what they know. 'The overwhelming majority of experiments designed to test psychoanalytic propositions display a blatant lack of interest in the meaning, within the theory of psychoanalysis, of the propositions tested' (Rapaport, in Koch, 1959, p. 142).

This second argument has some force, but it can be overstated. To be sure there have been those who interpreted the Freudian theory of forgetting to mean that unpleasant things are forgotten and pleasant things remembered; then they went about constructing lists of words including quinine (unpleasant) and sugar (pleasant) to test the Freudian theory. This sort of thing has not happened much in the last few years, as the knowledge of psychoanalytic theory has become more sophisticated.

The reason that the argument may be overstated is that psychoanalytic propositions at all levels lack the tightness of conceptual integration that makes the very general test possible. Hence more low-level propositional testing is in order before the larger system can be tightened up for a testing within this larger network of theory.

The empirical propositions to be tested are not necessarily trivial, and they usually imply some of the special or general psychoanalytic propositions as these are outlined by Rapaport and Gill. For example, it is not easy to get good evidence as to the age ranges within which boys are especially rivalrous with their fathers. This information (and other of the same general sort) is important to test some of the inferences from the more general theory.

We are led into a paradox when we insist that the superstructure of psychoanalytic theory (including metapsychology) ought to be accepted before we attempt to test theory. Sophistication demands that we do test theory. The idea that a single hypothesis can be disconfirmed by evidence, but not confirmed, is logically sound, but scientifically trivial. A single hypothesis, embedded in a theory, can be neither confirmed nor disconfirmed in any important sense without knowing more about the theory. One needs to know the interactions: for example, under one circumstance praise will improve learned performance, under another it will handicap performance. The proposition 'praise improves performance' is thus not established by a score-card, in which it more often improves than handicaps, but rather by additional propositions which specify when it does the one and when it does the other. Thus we test what Cronbach and Meehl (1955) call the *nomothetic network;* we do not test one proposition at a time, or if we do, we do not draw our conclusions from these tests in isolation from each other. The paradox arises because the psychoanalytic theory is not quite good enough for systematic testing. Hence the best we can do is some theory construction, integrating a few of the propositions that appear consonant with the general theory. Then it is *these* propositions that we test. These smaller models, or miniature systems, as Hull called them, will not reconcile the devotee to the whole system, but is the best that can be done at this stage.

Who is to do the testing? For some purposes the psycho-analytic interview is the best source. It may yield inferences that can be checked in other ways, however, and if experimental and clinical evidence agrees, so much the better all around. For example, the adult consequences of loss of a parent in childhood (Hilgard, Newman and Fisk, 1960) can be studied through inter-views with the adult, but these will raise conjectures about what went on at the time of parent loss. These conjectures can be studied by doing some investigations of children who have recently lost a parent. Thus the nature of the hypotheses being tested will often rule on the best method of studying them. There need be no *a priori* decision that the best method will be the psychoanalytic interview, or observational studies of children, or experimental studies. The nature of the hypotheses, and availa-bility of methods and of facilities, will guide investigations within psychoanalysis as they do in any other field of science.

There are some inhibiting factors within professional psycho-analysis that tend to reduce the research productivity of the analysts themselves. One is the long course of training, so that training is typically completed at about age forty, when families are established, obligations are great and research initiative is on the decline. Another is the nature of a practice involving long and expensive commitments to aid the suffering, so that the analyst must have faith in what he is doing. This leads to a conservative tendency with respect to change of doctrine or method which, while not to be condemned, is less favorable to research than a situation lacking such commitments. The training institutes have tended to neglect research in their training pro-grams; in the recent report on training in psychoanalysis (Lewin and Ross, 1960) covering 460 pages, but four pages were devoted to research. Only three of the fourteen institutes bring research at all prominently into the training pattern. The job of consolidating psychoanalysis as a science will continue to call for the collaboration of others if it is to move ahead with any rapidity.

The reconstruction of psychoanalytic theory can be expected to take time. It would be undesirable to throw present formulations aside and to start all over again, for too much would be lost even though some communication today is by way of rather loose metaphor. The gradual reconstruction may in time produce drastic revisions, but that possibility does not mean that these revisions have to be made all at once. The theory has enough body that investigators can choose segments of the theory within which to work out smaller models to be coordinated with others as the work advances. There are a number of avenues available to them besides those that open up only within the psychoanalytic interview. Among these are the study of child development and child rearing (including studies by anthropologists), studies of perception, learning and memory (especially where there is ambiguity and perhaps conflict), projective tests, hypnosis and the study of sleep and dreams. A great many pertinent investigations are now under way in these fields and we have every reason to expect a reconstruction of psychoanalysis to emerge from them. It will be a reconstruction rather than a validation, for the very act of validation requires reconstruction. In the process a better science will emerge, with firmer data encompassed within a more elegant system.

References

COLBY, K. M. (1955), *Energy and Structure in Psychoanalysis*, Ronald Press.

CRONBACH, L. J., and MEEHL, P. E. (1955), 'Construct validity in psychological tests', *Psychol. Bull.*, vol. 52, pp. 281–302.

ERIKSON, E. H. (1959), 'Identity and the life cycle', *Psychol. Iss.*, vol. 1, no. 1.

FRENKEL-BRUNSWIK, E. (1954), 'Psychoanalysis and the unity of science', *Proc. Amer. Acad. Arts Scien.*, vol. 80, pp. 271–350.

FREUD, S. (1887–1902), *The Origins of Psychoanalysis: Letters to Wilhelm Fliess, Drafts and Notes*, Basic Books, 1954.

FREUD, S. (1900), *The Interpretation of Dreams*, Basic Books, 1955.

GILL, M. M., and BRENMAN, M. (1959), *Hypnosis and Related States: Psychoanalytic Studies in Regression*, International Universities Press.

HARTMANN, H. (1939), *Ego Psychology and the Problem of Adaptation*, International Universities Press, 1958.

HARTMANN, H., and KRIS, E. (1945), 'The genetic approach in psychoanalysis', in R. S. Eissler *et al.* (eds.), *The Psychoanalytic Study of the Child*, vol. 1, International Universities Press, pp. 11–29.

HILGARD, E. R., NEWMAN, M. F. , and FISK, F. (1960), 'Strength of adult ego following childhood bereavement', *Amer. J. Orthopsychiat.*, vol. 30, pp. 788–98.

HULL, C. L. (1952), *A Behavior System*, Yale University Press.

KOCH, S. (1959) ,*Psychology: A Study of a Science. Vol. 3. Formulations of the Person and the Social Context*, McGraw-Hill.

KUBIE, L. S. (1947), 'The fallacious use of quantitive concepts in dynamic psychology', *Psychoanal. Quart.*, vol. 16, pp. 507–18.

LEEPER, R. (1943), *Lewin's Topological and Vector Psychology: A Digest and a Critique*, University of Oregon Press.

LEWIN, B. D., and ROSS, H. (1960), *Psychoanalytic Education in the United States*, Norton.

LONDON, I. D. (1944), 'Psychologists' misuse of the auxiliary concepts of physics and mathematics', *Psychol. Rev.*, vol. 51, pp. 266–91.

RAPAPORT, D., and GILL, M. M. (1959), 'The points of view and assumptions of metapsychology', *Intern. J. Psychoanal.*, vol. 40, pp. 153–62.

SKINNER, B. F. (1956) ,'Critique of psychoanalytic concepts and theories', in H. Feigl and M. Scriven (eds.), *The Foundations of Science and the Concepts of Psychology and Psychoanalysis*, University of Minnesota Press, pp. 77–87.

Part Two
Psychoanalysis as Science: Methodological Considerations

In Reading 3 Farrell concerns himself with the questions:
1. Is psychoanalysis a valid method of discovery?
2. When is an interpretation correct?
3. Is the method artefact-free?
4. Why has the method given rise to different psychoanalytic theories?
5. Can analysis be justified therapeutically?

He provides a useful short discussion of some of the problems in this field.

3 B. A. Farrell

Psychoanalysis: The Method

B. A. Farrell, 'Psychoanalysis – II. The method', *New Society*,
no. 39, 27 June 1963, pp. 12–14.

Is psychoanalysis a valid method of discovery? An analyst, no
matter what his persuasion, usually just assumes that, if the
analysis can be satisfactorily prosecuted for long enough, he will
arrive at part, at least, of the truth about the patient. Hence the
point of the analyst's claim that by means of the analysis the
patient comes 'to understand himself', 'to develop insight', 'to
know himself as he really is, free from self deception and distortion', and so forth. The assumption that psychoanalytic
method is a technique of valid discovery is so deeply seated in
the work and thinking of analysts of all schools that they are apt
to find it difficult to realize that they are making any assumption
here at all. If and when they do realize it they are apt to find
themselves quite incapable of taking the problem seriously – 'It
may be an assumption that in analysis we discover the truth about
a patient. But this assumption is so obviously true that it does
not need defending.'

This view of psychoanalytic method is a complete mistake. The
assumption that the method does really uncover the facts about
a patient runs into a range of objections of quite Himalayan
proportions.

When is an interpretation correct? An essential and important
feature of the method consists in the appropriate offer of interpretations to the patient. (A reference to Freud's case histories
will show something of the extent and importance of this feature
of the method.) Consider, now, the work of an analyst who
happens to be an orthodox Freudian, and who claims to have
discovered in the course of analysis that a particular patient has
certain Oedipal difficulties. If the claim is challenged, he will
then (typically) defend it by saying it is supported by certain

material in the analysis. This material centres round the Oedipal interpretations he offered the patient, and it shows that these Oedipal interpretations are correct. Hence the patient does indeed have the particular Oedipal difficulties he claims tó have discovered in him. In defending his claim in this way, the analyst is pointing to a corner stone of the support for his alleged discovery, and is just adopting a standard type of defence that is well nigh universal among analysts.

Now there is a critical snag about this defence. It supposes that the material of analytic sessions is such that we can use it to distinguish interpretations that are correct from those that are not. In other words, it supposes that it is possible to arrive at criteria which enable us in practice to distinguish interpretations that are true from those that are not. But it is very doubtful indeed whether this supposition is correct. Analysts have made various attempts to arrive at such acceptance, or truth, criteria of psychoanalytic interpretations, but without much success. For example, among the criteria suggested have been the following: acceptance by the patient, helping to make the material as a whole coherent, testing the interpretation by reference to the patient's consequential response to it. It is easy to construct a strong case against each and all of these suggestions.

The acceptance criterion is sometimes very difficult to apply at all; and even when it is easy, it is not sufficient (for reasons connected with the psychological character of the analytic session). Coherence does not work because, even if we waive the vagueness and obscurity surrounding this criterion, the support it gives to, say, a particular Oedipal view about the patient is weak support if there is a plausible alternative story available. The criterion of consequential responses is poor, if only because it is very doubtful whether the scientific model of 'prediction-cum-testing of consequences' can be applied at all to the material of analytic sessions.[1]

What is the relevance of this failure to arrive at satisfactory truth or acceptance criteria of a psychoanalytic interpretation?

1. It is evident that an adequate examination of these criteria is a very technical matter. It is also a very lengthy one, as it requires the detailed examination of analytic material. The problem is discussed – with reference to a (tape recorded) transcript of an analytic session – by Farrell, Wisdom and Turquet (1962).

It means that the analyst cannot tell us what properties his analytic material must possess for it to show that, say, his Oedipal interpretations are correct. Hence he cannot claim that it does show that his Oedipal interpretations are correct in any given instance. But the claim that his interpretations are correct in *this* given instance that we are considering is a standard way of defending his (alleged) discovery that his patient has certain Oedipal difficulties. Hence, he cannot do much, in this way, to support his assumption that psychoanalytic method has really discovered the truth here about his patient, and that it is, in general, a valid procedure.

Is the method artefact free? If psychoanalytic method is a valid procedure, it must reveal or uncover the facts about a patient without distortion. The material thrown up in analysis must be veridical. A strong case, however, can be made out for the view that, whatever the method may or may not really discover about the patient, it also helps to manufacture the material it produces. This case is based upon the psychological character of the analytic session. It can be incompletely summarized and expressed commonsensically as follows.

1. To the extent that the method does its therapeutic job, it does so, in part, by disorganizing the patient's habits, attitudes, etc., thereby making him labile and suggestible.

2. The analyst presents the patient with a stream of interpretations; and the patient is under great pressure in the analytic situation to accept the themes involved in these interpretations as being a correct account of himself. If the analysis has successfully rendered the patient confused and suggestible in respect of any such theme, the pressures on him in the analytic situation will be even more effective. If the analysis continues in a manner that the analyst judges to be satisfactory, the patient will in fact come to accept, with sincerity and conviction, the account of himself which is contained in the interpretations that the analyst has presented to him.

3. These interpretations will serve, either before or after acceptance, to direct the patient's attention, recall, daydream life, etc., along lines indicated by, and consonant with, these interpretations. Hence the patient will subsequently and continually produce material in the analysis along the lines previously

indicated by the analyst. This material will probably be rather different from what he *would* have produced if he had gone to a different analyst of some other theoretical persuasion, who would naturally have presented him with interpretations along quite different lines. So the patient of a Freudian is apt to produce Freudian material, the patient of a Horneyian, Horneyian material, and so on.

This psychological account of the analytic situation suggests that psychoanalytic method is not so much a tool of observation and discovery as a technique of human transformation, with obvious resemblance to the techniques of religious conversion and brain washing. Whatever the ultimate truth about the method may be, this psychological account is strong enough to suggest that the method does help to manufacture the material it produces. Hence it is strong enough to throw serious doubt upon the assumption that psychoanalytic method is a valid procedure for uncovering the facts of human nature.[2]

Why has the method given rise to different psychoanalytic theories? Different theories are suggested by different sorts of analytic material. But if the method is a valid procedure, how is it that it uncovers different sorts of material? How is it that it reveals Oedipal material when used by a classical Freudian, and fails to reveal it when used by a Horneyian?

Suppose we answer the question by saying that they do *not* use the same psychoanalytic method, but different ones, in that they handle the patients by means of different analytic theories. We might then account for the different material thrown up by saying that this is the outcome of the fact that different psychoanalytic theories are injected into the analytic situation via, in particular, the interpretations presented.

But this answer will hardly do. For it then follows from it that the material one gets out of the analytic situation will support whatever theory one puts into it; and this greatly reduces the value of the evidential support the material is alleged to lend to any one psychoanalytic theory. However, we could answer the question in another way. We could agree that differences in the theory injected do not constitute differences of method. We could

2. For a discussion of the analytic and therapeutic situations see Frank (1961). Cf. also Lifton (1961), ch. 23.

say, instead, that the differences in the material produced arise from differences among the patients, and in the actual techniques used – for example, in the amount of use made of transference, in the stress placed on reconstructing the past in contrast with emphasizing the patient's difficulties in the here and now, and so forth.

Now there seems good reason to believe that these variations in method will result in differences in the material produced. But are they sufficient to account for *all* these differences? This is very doubtful. However, assuming these variations in method *are* sufficient, it then seems to follow that no *one* psychoanalytic theory can be true. For we are now faced by the fact that one and the same method produces material that suggests different and partly incompatible psychoanalytic theories. This is all very awkward.

The trouble seems to hinge round the fact that analysts do not make clear when we have to accept the use of the method on any occasion as correct, and modify the analytic theory employed; or when we have to reject the use of the method as incorrect or illegitimate, and retain the theory employed.

The difficulties we have raised about psychoanalytic method are sufficient to throw grave doubts on its validity. These doubts do much to weaken the support that the clinical material of analysis lends to any psychoanalytic theory; and they strongly suggest that this material is not sufficient to establish the truth of any of the well-known theories of analysis. The logical ties between material and theory are much more complex and much weaker than analysts are apt to assume.[3] What is more, when we consider the clinical material in conjunction with the other supporting grounds for Freudian theory we mentioned in the first article, it is at best very doubtful whether the *joint* support they all provide for any psychoanalytic theory is sufficient to establish its truth.

3. On some of these ties, see again Farrell (1963). It is important to remember, of course, that Kleinian theory was suggested originally by the material of psychoanalytic play technique, or therapy, on children – not by the ordinary analysis of adults. See Klein (1932) and Klein *et al.* (1955), ch. 1. But whatever the difficulties of adult analysis, those of Klein's play technique are just as bad, if not much worse.

Can Analysis be Justified Therapeutically?

Suppose we now challenge an analyst: 'Why do you practise analysis? Why do you use it on a patient?' He *could* say: 'I do so in part for research purposes – to uncover the truth about the patient and so add something to the corpus of clinical experience.' If he produces this answer, he is susceptible to the objection we have just considered, namely that he is using a method of research of doubtful validity. In actual fact he is much more likely to meet the challenge in a different way in the first instance. 'I use analysis on a patient because I believe that it will be of help to him.' Well, will it be? What is the therapeutic effectiveness of analysis?

There are some old, and well known, clinical reports from analysts on this question. H. J. Eysenck has examined their figures, and found that, if one classes together the cases reported by analysts as 'cured', 'much improved' and 'improved', such cases constitute 44 per cent out of the total of 760. Peter Knight examined what appear to be the same figures, and arrived at a more favourable result. The outcome was successful in 78·1 per cent of organic neuroses and related conditions, 63·2 per cent of the psychoneuroses, 56·6 per cent of character disorders, 48·5 per cent of sexual disorders and 25 per cent of psychoses.

Professor Eysenck has also brought together a large collection of cases which were treated by various forms of psychotherapy, and found that the figure for those 'cured', 'much improved' or 'improved' is 64 per cent out of nearly 7400 cases. But these figures do not have much significance unless one can compare them with a base line figure of cases of, say, neurotics who have received little or no psychotherapy, but who have recovered or improved to a considerable extent. Such a figure was worked out some years ago by C. Landis. He found that the percentage of neurotics who were discharged annually as recovered or improved from custodial hospitals in the United States, in the years 1926 to 1933, was 68 per cent.

This figure clearly suggests that neurotics who receive analysis are likely to do worse or about as well as those who merely receive custodial care; and that neurotics who receive some form of non-analytic psychotherapy are likely to do about as well as those who get custodial care alone.

But, of course, it is perfectly obvious (and surely everyone will agree?) that these figures are not worth much. They are subject to all the manifold and serious uncertainties of clinical assessments. (For instance, the low figure of 44 per cent that Eysenck found for psychoanalytic method may be due, in part, to the strict criterion of cure and improvement the analysts adopted.) Still, these figures are the best of this type that we have in this field. We cannot deal with these figures by just ignoring them.

However, they are unsatisfactory in another sort of way that needs emphasizing: they are obtained from clinical assessments, and these are made without the benefit of information from comparable control groups. Clearly, what is wanted are studies on comparable groups, one of which is treated by psychoanalysis and the other not; and where the character and progress of the groups is also objectively, and not only clinically, evaluated. Studies which satisfy these requirements even approximately are rare gems of great value. A good example is the Cambridge–Somerville Youth Study. In this we find that the therapists, ranging in character from 'big brother' to psychiatric social workers, considered that about two thirds of the treated group had substantially improved; and when the treated group was compared objectively with the untreated control group, the former showed no greater improvement than the latter.

This control study is typical of the few that have been made, in that it is difficult to extract from them good evidence that psychoanalysis, or psychotherapy generally, benefits the persons treated. This negative result is important; and workers such as Eysenck have been quite right to stress it.

But how serious or lethal is this negative result for analysis? Let us, first of all, see the whole matter in proportion. When we turn to look at the standard methods of treatment used in psychiatry, a somewhat similar, negative and inconclusive picture emerges. Consider the much favoured electroconvulsive therapy (ECT). A consensus seems to have developed in the psychiatric world that ECT is valuable in the treatment of psychotic depression and involutional melancholia. High recovery rates of 70, and even 90 per cent have been reported. But these are clinical assessments of improvement; and so far psychologists have discovered no base line of a 'natural' remission rate against which we can judge the significance of these figures. Furthermore, these high recovery rates are apt to drop somewhat drastically when one compares the figures of treated and untreated groups (e.g. a drop to 48 per cent for ECT groups and 30·5 for non-shock groups). Moreover, ECT is a complex treatment, involving at least three factors – application of an electric current, rapid loss of consciousness and motor convulsion. In an experimental study of these factors, Brill and others found that patients who were just made unconscious, under the belief that they were being shocked, improved just as well as those who were shocked, either with convulsions or without.

So the rationale of ECT seems completely uncertain. When one turns to other forms of psychiatric treatment such as drugs or psychosurgery, the position is even worse. When one looks at what is called behaviour therapy, one finds that no controlled studies have apparently yet been made into its therapeutic effectiveness. The stricture that Eysenck has applied to psycho-therapy seems equally applicable to behaviour therapy – it is 'not proven'.

But does the fact that other methods of treatment are in much the same negative and uncertain boat as psychoanalysis help the analyst to justify his belief that analysis will help a patient? No, obviously not. It seems clear that the analyst cannot give us reasonable grounds to believe that analysis *will* help a patient. But just as a psychiatrist can give us reasonable grounds to believe that some form of treatment, such as ECT, *may* help a patient, so a psychoanalyst can do the same for analysis. No doubt the evidence he will have at his disposal to show that analysis may help in a given instance will be pretty poor in quality. If, however, it is sufficient to give us ground to believe that analysis is the most suitable weapon in the psychiatric armoury for this patient; and that it is better to try out some form of treatment on him rather than none at all, then the analyst will be justified in recommending analysis for the patient. This will be true even though further knowledge about the patient shows that this assessment was mistaken, and his recom-mendation of analysis an error.

Can Analysis be Justified Non-Therapeutically?

But this is not the whole story. Consider a prospective patient about whom the evidence gives us ground to believe both the points just mentioned above. There is now an additional case for recommending the use of psychoanalytic method with this patient – a case which is independent of any possible therapeutic benefit to him. It can be argued that it is very necessary for us to keep the technique of psychoanalysis alive; and this can virtually only be done by using it on suitable patients, such as the one we are now considering. It is necessary to keep it alive for more than one reason. Though we cannot demonstrate its therapeutic value at the present time, we may be able to do so in 50 or 100 years' time, with the more refined techniques of investigation we may then possess. In any case contemporary psychiatry is in a state of messy flux; and in the present uncertainties it is obviously advisable to retain analysis as part of the psychiatric armoury. Moreover, analysis is one of the important methods of psychotherapy, and the whole argument about the value of psychotherapy in general is still quite unsettled.

But just as important as all this is the place of psychoanalytic method in Western culture. It is the chief source of the material that has led to psychoanalytic theory. Whether rightly or wrongly, this theory has revolutionized our view of human nature in the West, it has affected many aspects of our culture, and has permeated our thinking and practice about mental health. But in spite of its importance in Western life, its intellectual standing is quite uncertain. Until, therefore, the status of psychoanalytic theory and its contribution are resolved, it is very necessary to keep alive the technique that was responsible for this whole influential body of doctrine. So it is very necessary for a Western society such as ours to put aside some social and economic resources to maintain the psychoanalytic profession, and the expertise that goes with it. When the National Health Service, or the Hospital Boards, or other bodies are asked to support analysis, they should realize that they are being asked, in part, to make a small contribution to our cultural resources. They must not regard their support of analysis as just a business investment – to be judged solely in the light of its immediate therapeutic returns.

And the obligations of the medical world do not end at this point. It is a scandal of our time that psychoanalytic doctrine, in spite of its extraordinary impact upon us, should still exhibit such an uncertain standing. Careful scientific research on a massive scale into personality development, adjustment and maladjustment is obviously required to resolve the uncertainty about analysis, and end the scandal. It is plain that the medical world is also under an obligation, along with other bodies, to contribute to this end.

However, it is quite understandable that the present relationship between the psychoanalytic profession and the society that supports it is an uneasy one, and is likely to remain so for some time to come. For the doctrine of the profession is at best a premature empirical synthesis; and it will be many years before psychologists and other scientific workers will be able to extract from it what is of permanent value, and so absorb it into the corpus of scientific knowledge. In the long interim our society will just have to tolerate the logical ambiguity of the doctrine. The analysts themselves inhabit at present some dubious no man's land among the professions. The uncertainty about their standing stems in part from their own methods of professional training.

It will be difficult to bring analysts satisfactorily within the world of medicine, or the universities, or research institutes and the like, as long as strong suspicions remain that their methods of training resemble techniques of indoctrination rather than those of education. Again, it will probably be many years before this problem is resolved. In the long interim our society will just have to tolerate in its midst a small group of queer and insecure fish, whom the society cannot comfortably house, and who do not themselves know where they belong.

References

FARRELL, B. A. (1963), 'Introduction', in S. Freud, *Leonardo* (trans. A. Tyson), Penguin Books, pp. 11–91.

FARRELL, B. A., WISDOM, J. O., and TURQUET, P. M. (1962), 'Criteria for a psychoanalytic interpretation', *Aristot. Soc. Suppl.*, no. 36.

FRANK, J. D. (1961), *Persuasion and Healing*, Oxford University Press.

KLEIN, M., (1932), *The Psycho-Analysis of Children*, Hogarth Press.

KLEIN, M., *et al.* (1955), *New Directions in Psychoanalysis*, Tavistock.

LIFTON, R. J. (1961), *Thought Reform and the Psychology of Totalism*, Gollancz.

Part Three
Freud's Genetic Theories:
Infant Experience and Adult Behaviour

Reading 4 by Albino and Long reports on a replication and modification of the well-known experiments by J. McV. Hunt, using rats, where he claimed that infantile weaning experience affected hoarding behaviour in adult life – a demonstration, using animals, of the effects of 'oral frustration' in infancy on later acquisitive habits, which parallels the Freudian theory of 'oral character' development.

4 R. C. Albino and M. Long

The Effect of Infant Food-Deprivation upon Adult Hoarding in the White Rat

Ronald C. Albino and M. Long, 'The effect of infant food-deprivation upon adult hoarding in the white rat', *British Journal of Psychology*, vol. 42, 1951, pp. 146–54.

Introduction

This paper describes a repetition of the experiments designed by Hunt (1943; Hunt *et al.*, 1947) to determine the effect of infant feeding-frustration upon hoarding behaviour in the adult white rat. Our results confirm the original findings (Hunt, 1943), and provide additional data on the phenomenon and its nature.

Hunt (1943) set out to devise a controlled experimental situation to verify directly the hypothesis, originally propounded by the psychoanalysts and cultural anthropologists, that infant experience can endure and affect adult behaviour. Using rats as subjects, on account of their short life span, he found that animals submitted to a period of feeding-frustration after weaning hoarded significantly more pellets of food in adult life than their fully fed litter-mate controls.

There were two parts to the original experiment. In the first part two litters comprising fourteen animals were weaned at twenty-one days and split into experimental and control groups of seven animals each. At twenty-four days the experimental group was submitted to feeding frustration consisting of group feedings of wet mash at irregular intervals varying from nine to thirty-six hours over a period of fifteen days. The control group had unlimited access to wet mash during this period. Thereafter the two groups were treated alike. Five months after the infant feeding-frustration both groups had equal mean weights, and only hoarded very few pellets of food when satiated. Both groups were then submitted to adult feeding-frustration consisting of a two-day period on a subsistence diet and then thirty-minute feedings of wet mash at twenty-four-hour intervals for three successive days: twenty-three and a half hours after the last feeding they were tested in the hoarding alleys. Three more tests were made on successive days, the animals being allowed to retain the pellets they had hoarded. It was shown that neither sex nor litter contributed to the variance of the number of pellets hoarded but that the experiment did so, a *t*-test showing that the difference between the mean number of pellets hoarded by the controls (14) and the mean number hoarded by the experimentals (37·7) would have been obtained by chance in only one out of fifty trials.

In the second part of the experiment two litters weaned on the twenty-eighth day were again split into two groups of seven each. The experimental group was submitted to the same infant feeding-frustration procedure as was used in the first experiment, beginning, however, on the thirty-second day. From this point on, the experiment was identical with part one. The mean difference in the number of pellets hoarded by the two groups after a period of adult frustration was statistically insignificant.

Hunt (1943) concluded that infant experience does affect adult behaviour, but that the intensity of the effect depends upon the age at which the infant experience occurs.

This original experiment has been repeated three times (Hunt *et al.*, 1947), each repetition giving results of a lower degree of statistical significance than those obtained in the original. The procedure adopted in the repetitions differed from that of the original in several respects. Larger groups were used, weaning occurred at twenty days and infant feeding-frustration began on this day. The infant frustration differed in that the experimental animals were allowed several hours continuous access to wet mash on the first day, the time being decreased daily until by the eleventh day the length of the feeding period was reduced to five minutes. The experimental group was without food for two periods of thirty-six hours and for six periods of twenty-four hours. Adult feeding-frustration prior to the hoarding tests consisted of three days on thirty-minute feedings of wet mash. The hoarding trials were executed at various ages and consequently the weight differences between the two groups had not been eliminated in two of the repetitions, the experimental groups being lighter than the control. The findings resembled those in the first part of the original experiment, but the differences between the two groups were of a lower degree of statistical significance.

Hunt *et al.* (1947) estimated the probability of the collective results of the original experiment and its repetition being due to chance to be 0·00108, and took this as evidence of the correctness of his original conclusions (1943).

There was slight evidence in the repetitions that animals from different litters reacted differently to the infant feeding-frustration, and also, that the experimental animals ate more than the controls after adult feeding frustration.

In the above description of the three repetitions of the experiment we have quoted the results based on raw hoarding scores. Hunt *et al.* (1947) also used logarithmic hoarding scores in his calculations but, as these do not materially affect the conclusions and as the results of this experiment are expressed in raw scores, we have not quoted the logarithmic data.

The uncertain nature of the findings of Hunt (1943; Hunt *et al.*, 1947) led us to repeat the experiment. We also wished to determine whether there were any behavioural differences between the experimental and control groups besides the more specific hoarding difference, and, if such differences were observed, whether they were permanent.

The Experiment

The sample

The animals used were white rats of an inbred strain supplied to us by the University of the Witwatersrand. There were, at the beginning of the experiment, twenty-nine rats belonging to four litters born on the same day. The litters were split at random into experimental and control groups. One animal was lost from the experimental group during infant food-deprivation and one of the controls died in the course of the experiment. Finally there were fourteen animals in the control group divided into an equal number of males and females, and thirteen in the experimental group of which six were males and seven females.

Procedure

On weaning at twenty-one days the animals of both groups were individually caged and were freely fed wet mash. Infant food-deprivation began at twenty-four days, as in the original experiment of Hunt (1943), and consisted of irregular feedings of wet mash for twelve days. We did not attempt to keep each animal on an identical feeding schedule as we believed that the frustration value of a given degree of deprivation would vary from animal to animal. Instead we attempted to keep the weight curves of all animals in the experimental group parallel during the period of deprivation, a procedure which ensured that the animals were subjected to more or less identical and measurable treatments. We avoided the technique used by Hunt (1943) of giving irregular group feedings as this involves so many unisolable variables, such as individual differences in eating rate, varying food preferences and inability to eat due to inanition. Prior to ending the period of deprivation the experimental group was fasted for thirty-six hours. If any experimental animal showed signs of marked inanition during deprivation it was fed warm milk and cod-liver oil until it recovered. The control group had free access to wet mash during the time the experimental group was being deprived.

Table 1

The Percentage Weight Loss of the Experimental Group as Compared with the Controls for all Repetitions of the Experiment

This experiment	Original experiment (Hunt, 1943)	First repetition (Hunt et al., 1947)	Second repetition (Hunt et al., 1947)	Third repetition (Hunt et al., 1947)
29%	29%	49%	49%	61%

The percentage loss of weight[1] of the experimental group was the same as that obtained by Hunt in his original experiment but considerably less than was found in the repetitions (Table 1). In this respect, as well as in the age at which frustration began, our experiment resembles the original experiment more nearly than the repetitions.

1. Calculated by the formula of Hunt et al. (1947).
Percentage weight loss

$$= \frac{100 \text{ (mean weight of controls} - \text{mean weight of experimentals)}}{\text{mean weight of controls}}.$$

At the end of infant deprivation the two groups were mixed and caged in colony cages according to sex where they remained until 108 days, and from this time until the end of the experiment they were reared in isolation. The food pellets (mean weight five grammes) which were later to be used for hoarding were fed to both groups from the end of the period of deprivation.

The hoarding trials were undertaken by both groups after a period of absolute deprivation lasting six days. This procedure, which does not attempt to differentiate between frustration and deprivation, is somewhat more severe than the one adopted by Hunt *et al.* (1947). One half hour before the first trial of each run every animal was given a half-pellet of food. We did this because Hunt (1943) had observed that some hoarding time in the early part of the hoarding trials was wasted in eating. We assumed that the preliminary feeding would eliminate this uncontrolled variable, and would provide the optimal conditions of deprivation followed by partial satiation stated by Marx (1950) to be essential for maximum hoarding motivation.

In all, the animals were given three hoarding runs commencing on the 119th day, the 174th day and the 196th day. Each run consisted of one twenty-minute trial in the hoarding apparatus at successive twenty-four-hour intervals. The trials were given in a hoarding apparatus identical to that designed by Hunt (1943), but were carried out in the dark and at a constant environmental temperature ($67 \pm 3°$ F), the latter condition being observed in order to eliminate the known effect of temperature on hoarding (McCleary and Morgan, 1941). All trials took place between 11.00 and 15.00 hours. Prior to the period of frustration before the first and last runs the animals were given a trial in a condition of satiation. This was omitted in the second run as it was desired to give the animals as little practice in hoarding as possible outside that obtained in the post-deprivation trials. As the hoarding difference between the two groups had disappeared by the end of the second run a satiation trial was given prior to the third run to determine what had happened to satiation hoarding in the interval.

Table 2 summarizes the hoarding procedure.

At the time of the first run the percentage differences between the mean weights of the experimental and control groups was 2·8 per cent, the experimental group being the lighter. This difference remained until the conclusion of the experiment.

Table 2

Summary of Hoarding Procedure

Run	Satiation trials	Post-deprivation	
		No. of trials given	Day of first trial
a	1	3	119
b		6	174
c	1	4	196

Results of the Experiment

Qualitative

The two groups differed markedly after the period of infant deprivation. The experimental animals were all very timid, withdrawing from the experimenter's hand and starting at any loud noise. They were continually active and the shaking of a bunch of keys near their cage would stimulate them into violent running activity. They also appeared to fight a great deal. The control animals demonstrated none of these symptoms; they lay asleep most of the day, were only disturbed by very loud noises like hand clapping, and sought out the hand of the experimenter when he put it into their cage. These differences became daily less marked and had disappeared by the fifty-sixth day.

There were, however, permanent differences of behaviour which were evident during the adult deprivation. Again, the experimental animals were more active and more easily stimulated into activity by noise than the controls. It was not possible to determine whether they fought more as they were individually caged at this time, but they did show a more marked tendency than the controls to attack the experimenter's hand. These differences were present in all three periods of adult deprivation and thus persisted when differences in hoarding were lost.

On all the hoarding trials any loud noise caused the experimental animals to cease hoarding and to begin agitated exploration of the apparatus.[2]

Quantitative

Table 3 displays the results for all runs. It will be seen that on the first run the ratio of the mean number of pellets hoarded by the control and experimental groups is 1 : 2·2. An analysis of

Table 3

The Mean Number of Pellets Hoarded on each Hoarding Trial

	Satiation hoarding	Post-deprivation hoarding trials						Mean no. of pellets hoarded by each rat per trial
		1	2	3	4	5	6	
Run *a*:								
Experimental	0·6	10·1	5·3	1·4	—	—	—	5·6
Control	0·4	5·2	0·9	1·3	—	—	—	2·5
Run *b*:								
Experimental	—	23·3	17·5	7·3	4·3	1·1	5·4	9·81
Control	—	23·8	17·8	5·1	2·4	4·0	5·2	9·72
Run *c*:								
Experimental	2·2	21·6	42·8	19·1	3·2	—	—	21·67
Control	1·1	20·0	36·6	10·1	3·5	—	—	16·55

variance [3] (Table 4) carried out on the data from this first run shows that the variance due to the experimental treatment (infant deprivation) exceeds the contribution of the other factors included in the table and gives an F-value 6·69, a value which would be exceeded by chance in only one instance out of fifty. We are, therefore, justified in assuming that the effect is most probably due to the experimental treatment and not to accidents of random sampling.

2. All these behaviour changes in the experimental group gave the impression of being 'anxious'. We have refrained from mentioning this in the text in case it should be merely an artefact of our own bias.

3. A preliminary test showed that there was no sex difference. As the numbers in the litter subgroups were unequal it was necessary to weight our data in accordance with the method of Snedecor (1946).

Table 4

Analysis of Variance Carried out on the Data from the First Run

	Sum of squares	df	Variance	F	P
Experiment	7·239	1	7·239	6·69	0·02 (approx.)
Litter	3·404	3	1·135	1·05	0·05
$E \times L$	3·976	3	1·325	1·22	0·05
Error	20·556	19	1·082	—	—

This result, taken together with Hunt's findings (Hunt, 1943; Hunt et al., 1947), confirms the enduring effect of infant food deprivation, for if we combine the individual probabilities of all

Table 5

The Probability of the Collective Results of the Various Experiments being due to Random Sampling

Experiment	Probabilities combined by multiplication P	Probabilities combined by treating each as χ^2 value		
		χ^2	df	P
Hunt et al. (1947)	0·00108	18·36	8	0·02–0·01
Hunt et al. (1947) and this experiment	—	24·56	10	0·01

four experiments being due to chance we find that the collective results would be accounted for by accidents of random sampling in less than one instance in a hundred (Table 5).[4]

On the second and third runs a difference between the two

4. Hunt et al. (1947), noting that the experimental group hoarded more than the controls in all the experiments but that the probability of such a difference being due to random sampling was high in each of the replications, felt justified in combining the probabilities of the four experiments to obtain an estimate of the probability of the collective results being due to chance. They simply multiplied the independent probabilities to get this combined probability. The authors felt that the uncertain nature of the results demanded a more conservative estimate. They therefore used the method described by Lindquist (1940) in which the individual probabilities are treated as χ^2-values. It will be seen (Table 5) that this method gives a higher value of P, but one which makes it unlikely that the findings are due to random sampling.

groups is maintained, but in both instances it is statistically insignificant ($P < 0.05$). Both groups hoarded more on the pre-deprivation trial in the third run than they did on the corresponding trial in the first run and the experimentals again hoarded more than the controls, but this latter difference can be attributed to random sampling.

Not only does the difference in the mean amounts hoarded disappear in the course of the experiment, but other changes occur in hoarding behaviour from run to run. These are best seen when the results are expressed graphically (Figure 1). The maximum amount hoarded increases from run to run, and hoarding diminishes more rapidly from one trial to the next in the later runs.

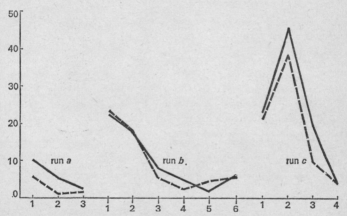

Figure 1 Mean hoarding scores for each rat in the experimental and control groups on all trials. (The abscissa represents the number of hoarding trials, and the ordinate the number of pellets hoarded. The experimental group is indicated by a continuous line and the control group by a broken line)

Hunt *et al.* (1947) believed they had found a litter effect in his experiments. The analysis of variance (Table 4) carried out on the data from the first run gives little evidence of such an effect as the *F*-values obtained for litter by experiment interaction might have been obtained by accidents of random sampling in as much as one instance out of twenty.

As the experimental group demonstrated symptoms of a kind which would imply a decreased tolerance to disturbing stimuli we decided to test all animals for frustration tolerance. Maier and Longhurst (1947) have shown that rats experiencing severe frustration are more susceptible to audiogenic convulsions than normal rats and, therefore, if the adult deprivation was more frustrating to the experimental group than to the controls we

Table 6

Day	Convulsive behaviour (mean rating)		Mean difference	P
	Experimental	Control		
(a) Difference in convulsive behaviour between groups rated on a five-point scale during bell ringing				
1	2·15	2·57	0·42	0·05–0·10
2	2·31	2·57	0·26	0·40
3	2·15	2·50	0·35	0·10–0·2
4	1·77	2·15	0·38	0·02–0·05
(b) Differences in convulsive behaviour between the experimental and control groups rated on a five-point scale after bell ringing				
1	1·85	3·00	1·15	0·1 –0·20
2	2·85	3·36	0·51	0·4 –0·50
3	1·31	2·68	1·37	0·01–0·02
4	2·38	2·29	0·09	0·2

would expect the former to show a greater incidence of convulsions than the latter. To test this hypothesis all animals were put through the same procedure beginning on the 288th day. They were placed in a wooden box (dimensions nine × twelve × seven inches), with a wire-netting lid and floor, in which was a loud electric bell. The bell was rung for two minutes, and the rats were rated on a five-point scale for convulsive behaviour during and after the bell ringing. The first trial was done on satiated animals, after which the animals were returned to their cages and fasted for three days. On each of these days the rats were subjected to the convulsive procedure. With only one exception (Table 6), the controls showed an unexpected greater susceptibility than the experimentals, but a t-test showed that all the differences except two could be attributed to differences of random sampling.

No valid conclusions can be drawn from these few data but there is presumptive evidence that there may be some difference between the two groups and that it is in the direction of an increased tolerance to frustration in the experimental animals.

Conclusions

There is no doubt that our experiment confirms the original findings of Hunt (1943) on his twenty-four-day group. It does, however, produce new findings which are difficult to explain. Hunt (1943) observed that infant feeding-frustration commenced as late as thirty-two days after birth had no effect upon adult hoarding behaviour, whereas our results clearly show that frustration in adult life will have as great an effect as early deprivation commencing on the twenty-fourth day. This result could be reconciled with the findings of Hunt on his thirty-two-day group if it were found that the differences appeared again after a period of rest from hoarding, for under these conditions we would be free to assume that the effect of adult experience, though equal in the sense that it temporarily reduces the difference between the two groups, is less enduring. We did not attempt to determine whether this was so, but the fact that the difference in hoarding is still present at the end of the third run indicates that the expected finding would be unlikely to occur.

There is an alternative explanation. We observed that the experimental animals started to hoard food during the period of infant deprivation, many taking small balls of wet mash into the back of their cages to feed there. The control animals showed no tendency to hoard during this period, always eating from the dish placed near to the cage door. It seems likely that the experimental animals learned to hoard in infancy whereas the controls did not, and, therefore, when placed in the hoarding alleys in adult life had an advantage over the control group. However, after the practice of the first run the control group equalled the experimental animals in hoarding speed and thereafter the difference disappeared. On this hypothesis the difference between the two groups (so far as the hoarding habit is concerned) is merely one of practice. If this is so, then support is given to the views of Hunt *et al.* (1947) and Marx (1950) that the observed differences in hoarding between infant-deprived and normal animals, as well as hoarding behaviour itself, are the result of learning.

This hypothesis does not exclude the existence of behavioural differences between the two groups which cannot be equalized by additional practice by the controls. Our qualitative findings make it appear as if the rat deprived in infancy responds with greater activity and sensitivity to a given adult deprivation than do fully fed animals subject to the same deprivation. Also, the continuous experience of frustration in adult life does not appear to produce the same effect in this respect as infant deprivation. These results can only mean that the infant-deprived animal suffers a more or less permanent intensification of drive in response to a given adult deprivation.

The experiment clarifies the clinically derived concept of fixation, demonstrating, as it does, that the permanent and essential difference between animals who, at first, show fixation of a response as a result of infant deprivation, lies not in the specific response (or instrumental act) but in an intensified drive manifestation, to which the fixated instrumental act is secondary. This conclusion confirms the psychoanalytical view (Fenichel, 1947) that intense frustration of a drive in infancy will have the effect of causing minor frustrations in adult life to lead to an impending traumatic state – a state which is nothing more than a heightened manifestation of drive. Our hesitant conclusion that the behaviour of the experimental animals in adult deprivation appeared 'anxious' gives further confirmation of the psychoanalytic view, for an impending traumatic state is believed by the psychoanalysts to be an anxious unpleasant state, as well as a heightened manifestation of drive. The instrumental act may be regarded, as the psychoanalysts would maintain it to be, as a secondary mechanism defending the animal against the unpleasant traumatic state. Our experiment thus directs attention away from the hoarding itself towards the more fundamental effect of infant deprivation on drive manifestation.

The increased rate of decrease in hoarding from run *a* to run *b* (Figure 1) may imply that both groups develop a frustration tolerance in the course of the experiment, and there is slight evidence from the convulsive experiment that the experimental group ultimately show a greater tolerance than the control. This latter finding is paradoxical in the light of clinical findings but gives some support to the popular view that the neurotic who breaks down will, if immediately confronted with the situation which caused him to break down, show less tendency to relapse.

Summary

1. A modified repetition of Hunt's experiment (Hunt *et al.*, 1947) designed to determine the effect of infant experience upon adult behaviour is described.

2. The original conclusions of Hunt concerning the effect of infant experience upon adult behaviour have been confirmed for the twenty-four-day group.

3. It was observed that the hoarding differences between the animals frustrated in infancy and those who were fully fed disappear if sufficient hoarding practice is given.

4. However, general behavioural differences of a kind involving 'drive' were observed between the two groups, and these differences were maintained until the end of the experiment. The experimental group appeared to show a more marked reaction to adult deprivation than the controls.

5. There was evidence that both groups developed a tolerance to food deprivation in the course of successive periods of absolute deprivation, and there was an indication that the experimental animals were superior in this respect.

6. The relation of the findings to the psychoanalytic concepts of the traumatic state and of fixation is discussed.

References
FENICHEL, O. (1947), *The Psycho-Analytic Theory of the Neuroses*, Routledge & Kegan Paul.
HUNT, J. McV. (1943), 'The effects of infant feeding frustration upon adult hoarding in the albino rat', *J. abnorm. soc. Psychol.*, vol. 36, pp. 338–60.
HUNT, J. McV., SCHLOSBERG, H., SOLOMON, R. L., and STELLAR, E. (1947), 'Studies of the effect of infantile experience on adult behavior in rats. I. Effects of infantile feeding frustration', *J. comp. Psychol.*, vol. 40, pp. 219–304.

LINDQUIST, E. F. (1940), *Statistical Analysis in Educational Research*, Houghton Mifflin.

MCCLEARY, R. A., and MORGAN, C. T. (1941), 'Food hoarding in rats as a function of environmental temperature', *J. comp. Psychol.*, vol. 32, pp. 531–41.

MAIER, N. R. F., and LONGHURST, J. V. (1947), 'Studies of abnormal behavior in the rat. XXI. Conflict and "andiogenic seizures"', *J. comp. Psychol.*, vol. 40, pp. 397–412.

MARX, M. H. (1950), 'A stimulus–response analysis of hoarding in the rat', *Psychol. Rev.*, vol. 57, pp. 80–93.

RIDER, P. R. (1939), *An Introduction to Modern Statistical Methods*, Wiley.

SNEDECOR, G. W. (1946), *Statistical Methods*, Iowa State College Press, 4th edn.

Part Four
Psychosexual Development and Character Formation

This Part includes detailed investigations of the psychosexual stages of development of the child: the oral phase of development and the anal phase. The character formations discussed are said to result from experiences during these 'sensitive' years in the development of the child. The Readings are chosen to illustrate different methods of testing psychoanalytic propositions. Observational techniques, experimental methods, cross-cultural and comparative studies have been used at one time or another in the various investigations of psychosexual concepts.

5 Arnold Bernstein

Some Relations between Techniques of Feeding and
Training during Infancy and Certain Behaviour in
Childhood

Arnold Bernstein, 'Some relations between techniques of feeding
and training during infancy and certain behavior in childhood',
Genetic Psychology Monographs, vol. 51, 1955, pp. 7–44.

Introduction

Although childhood has long been regarded as the important
formative period of life, the significance of early infancy has only
been fully appreciated during the past half century. The work of
Freud (1905, 1908) and Abraham (1916, 1924) was instrumental
in calling attention to the potential influence of infantile experience upon adult character. Continuing interest in the part played
by infant training in the development of later behavior is evidenced by the writings of Levy (1943), Ribble (1938) and Spitz
(1945), among others.

Up to the present time, the exact nature of the influence of the
infantile period upon later personality and behavior has not been
subjected to sufficient experimental investigation, and thus the
hypotheses have been largely deductive rather than inductive,
and supported by logical considerations rather than empirical
evidence. In particular, the classical psychoanalytic generalizations were based upon inferences drawn from the memories of
adult psychoneurotic patients, and from retrospective predictions
made from the larger body of self-consistent theory. Freud wrote:
'I need not emphasize the fact that the processes of development
here described – just as others found in psychoanalysis – have
been inferred from the regressions into which they had been
forced by neurotic processes' (1916, p. 165).

The psychoanalytic formulations, although a fertile source of
hypotheses, have lacked careful definition and experimental
verification. Several major psychoanalytic postulates, however,
seem capable of incorporation into the designs of experiments.
Especially susceptible to experimental study are the hypotheses

concerning the relationship between sucking activity and certain subsequent mouth-centered behaviors, and between coercive toilet training and certain later behavioral propensities. The hypotheses are described in the sections that follow. The study here reported tests several of these hypotheses.

Review of the literature

Early reinforcement of sucking and its relation to oral activity. One of Freud's earliest formulations in his theory of character formation is the following assertion (1905, p. 586) concerning the relation of infant sucking to later oral activities:

It is, moreover, clear that the action of the thumbsucking child is determined by the fact that he seeks a pleasure which he has already experienced and now remembers. . . . It is also easy to conjecture on what occasions the child first experienced this pleasure which he now strives to renew. The first and most important activity in the child's life, the sucking from the mother's breast (or its substitute), must have acquainted him with this pleasure. . . .

Not all children suck their thumbs. It may be assumed that it is found only in children in whom the erogenous significance of the lip-zone is constitutionally reinforced. If the latter is retained in some children, they develop into kissing epicures with a tendency to perverse kissing or, as men, they show a strong desire for drinking and smoking.

While it is clear from the foregoing quotation that Freud related thumbsucking and other oral activities to the child's experience at the mother's breast or substitute, it is not clear whether he proposed a learning-theory (reinforcement) explanation or hypothesized the existence of an inborn constitutional need for sucking. Both of these interpretations have found a measure of acceptance, with the result that two conflicting sets of hypotheses appear in the literature.

Glover (1924), another psychoanalytic theorist, added:

There seems to be little question that . . . with sucking gratification, there is an optimum period with individual variation, the shortening or prolongation of which constitutes either a traumatic experience, or a situation of fixation. I should be inclined to say that shortening of the period is almost invariably traumatic, whilst the effect of lengthening depends on the stage of ego development reached in the civilization concerned.

Glover's formulation suggested that the effect of sucking experience on the child was related to the period of gratification (reinforcement). He inclined to the view that a shorter period of reinforcement was traumatic and a longer period led to fixation.

The effect of sucking reinforcement upon certain food habits was suggested in the following observation recounted by Abraham in an early paper on oral erotism (1916, pp. 260–61):

It is well known that after being weaned children preserve a tendency to suck sweet things. We frequently find in neurotic men with strongly suppressed libido, an intense, impulsive desire for sweet things. They take a particular pleasure in sucking at sweets very slowly. In two very pronounced cases I could establish with certainty that it was the sucking-pleasure originating in infantile auto-erotism. . . . One of these patients used to suck sweets in bed in the evening, and then go off to sleep with the feeling of having been gratified. The similarity of this behavior with that of the child in the sucking period is very obvious.

Independently of the psychoanalytical school, Mursell (1925) concluded that candy and food can serve non-nutritional needs:

We may enumerate some of the food practices which obviously seem to depend upon vestigial remainders of infantile sucking. . . . Perhaps the most prominent of these is the use of candy. . . . Candy offers a respectable chance to munch and chew and suck without exciting derision . . . there is a decided preference for the more lasting forms of candy. If candy eating were merely a means of receiving a ration of sugar, then evidently the preference would be for some form . . . on which it would be easy to satiate oneself in a very short time. But there is a special pleasure derivable from the humble all-day sucker and the more aristocratic caramel which the more readily soluble confections will not yield. And when we turn to chewing gum we have a perfectly clear case of a commercial product whose sale depends absolutely on the ability of human beings to enjoy chewing and sucking for their own sake.

While a test of these hypotheses requires a means of estimating the strength of oral reinforcement as well as objective data on later oral activity, no such experimental controls were set up by the early analytic theorists.

Infant oral activity and its relation to other behavior. Another basic psychoanalytic hypothesis concerns the development of certain reaction patterns which the child is said to learn from his experience in using his mouth. It is held that oral responses generalize to and affect other areas of behavior. The hypothesis is similar to the theory of transfer of training involving similar elements. According to Abraham (1924, pp. 396–8):

What is of particular significance is that the pleasure in sucking undertakes a kind of migration. At about the time that the child is being weaned it is also being trained in habits of cleanliness. An important prerequisite for the success of this latter process lies in the gradually developing function of the anal and urethral sphincters. The action of these muscles is the same as that of the lips in sucking, and is obviously modelled on it.

. . . the child . . . attempts to resume the abandoned act of sucking in an altered form and in another locality. We have already spoken of the sucking activity of the sphincters at the excretory apertures of the body, and have recognized that the inordinate desire to possess, especially in the form of abnormal parsimony and avarice, stands in close relation to this process. Thus we see that those traits, which belong to the clinical phenomena of the anal character, are built up on the ruins of an oral erotism whose development has miscarried.

Abraham's hypothesis that the action of the anal sphincter is related to the action of the oral sphincters has not yet been subjected to any objective tests. Such a test is suggested, however, by the following passage in which Freud argues that constipation may be used as a symptom of anal retentiveness (1905, pp. 589–90):

Children utilizing the erogenous sensitiveness of the anal zone can be recognized by their holding back of fecal masses. . . . One of the surest premonitions of later eccentricity or nervousness is when the infant refuses to empty his bowel when placed upon the chamber. . . .

The retention of fecal masses . . . is at least one of the roots of constipation so frequent in neurotics.

Freud's opinion that constipation is related to anal erotism suggests a means by which the analytic contention that oral experience influences anal behavior may be tested. If anal retentiveness (anal sucking) is a function of the transfer of reinforced oral erotism to the anal sphincters, then anal retentiveness (retention of bodily contents) should increase with reinforcement of the oral sucking drive. Thus the hypothesis that the pleasure in

sucking migrates to the anus and takes the form of anal retentiveness can be tested objectively by comparing data on oral
reinforcement and constipation.

The psychoanalytic hypothesis is summarized in the following
quotation from Abraham (1924): 'Whereas to begin with,
pleasure was only associated with taking in something coming
from without or expelling bodily contents, now there is the added
pleasure in retaining bodily contents, which leads to pleasure in
all forms of property.'

Abraham's hypothesis can be tested if it is reformulated in
objective terms using operationally defined variables. The relation
of oral reinforcement to retention of bodily contents (constipation) and to pleasure in all forms of property (collecting
stamps, etc.) can be explored empirically.

Cleanliness training and its relation to other behavior. In addition
to the psychoanalytic theory concerning the role which the
mouth plays in the development of personality, is the psychoanalytic theory relating the function of the anus to the formation
of character. According to Freud (1916, p. 164):

The constant co-existence in any person of the three character-traits of
orderliness, parsimony and *obstinacy* indicated an intensification of the
anal-erotic components in . . . that person, and that these were modes
of reaction specially favored by his ego which had been established
during his development in the course of his absorption of his anal
erotism. . . .

. . . Each one of the three qualities, avarice, pedantry and stubborn-
ness, springs from anal-erotic sources – or, to express it more cautiously
and more completely – draws powerful contributions from these
sources.

Abraham indicated that the development of what Freud had
called anal character traits was related to the child's response to
cleanliness training:

The original unchecked voiding of bodily excretions was accompanied
by stimulation of the apertures of the body which undoubtedly was
pleasurable. If the child adapts itself to the demands of training and
learns to retain its excretions this new activity also gets to be accompanied by pleasure. The pleasurable sensations in the organ connected
with this process form the foundations upon which the mental pleasure

in retention of every kind of possession is gradually built up. (1924, p. 394.)

In that the child's training demands strict regularity in its excretions as well as cleanliness it exposes the child's narcissism to a first severe test. The majority of children adapt themselves sooner or later to these demands (1921, p. 373).

The severity of cleanliness training techniques can be evaluated by considering the age at which toilet training was initiated, and whether or not punishment was employed. Abraham (1921) enumerated specific behaviors which he stated were a function of the individual's attitude toward evacuation:

Self-will in regard to any demand or request made to them by some other person (p. 377).

Pleasure in painting, modelling, and similar activities (p. 371).

Often collect all sorts of broken objects . . . bits of paper, old envelopes, worn-out pens and similar things (p. 385).

The hypothesis that certain behavior is related to the way in which the child adapts itself to the demands of toilet training can be tested by comparing data on the severity of toilet training and data about behavior which has been characterized as having been derived from anal sources.

Purpose of the present research

The lack of experimental evidence supporting the psychoanalytic contentions regarding the influence of infancy was noted by Murphy, Murphy and Newcomb (1937, p. 575) after a comprehensive survey of the evidence:

Although we have now been exposed for some time to psychoanalytic and other psychiatric hypotheses regarding the effects of . . . weaning trauma, extreme emphasis on early control of urination and defecation . . . we have almost no objective records of the development of children going through these experiences, or of experiments controlling certain aspects of the problem.

Orlansky reviewed 149 publications bearing upon the relation of infant care to personality. His evaluation of the data led him to a negative and pessimistic conclusion (1949, p. 38):

Social scientists have failed to produce a definite answer to the question of the relation between infant disciplines and character development, because of . . . the difficulty of establishing the validity of the personality measurements employed, and the difficulty of isolating single factors for study. It is hard to see how the latter obstacle, in particular, can be overcome.

According to Orlansky (1949) one of the great findings of psychoanalysis was the importance of childhood experience on the formation of personality. He felt that social scientists do not dispute the general finding, but only wish for further elucidation and experimentation. He concluded (1949, p. 38): 'we are led to reject the thesis that specific nursing disciplines have a specific, invariant psychological impact upon the child.'

The primary purpose of the present research is to meet the need, so urgently felt by Murphy, Orlansky and others for more quantitative and objective data on infant experience and later childhood behavior.

In the interests of objectivity, the research is confined to a study of the effects of certain parent *behavior* upon the infant, rather than the effects of parental motives and attitudes. In a sense, the parents' behavior toward an infant is determined by the attitudes that they hold toward him. Whether parental motives eventually will be shown to be the critical intervening varible remains to be seen. Ultimately it would seem that parental attitudes can be transmitted to the infant only through what the parent does to the infant, that is, through parental behavior. How the parent behaves will, of course, be determined by his motives. If this is true, then the study of the effects of motives and the study of the effects of behavior on infant development will frequently lead to similar findings.

The choice between the use of parental behavior or the use of parental attitudes as an independent variable will necessarily depend upon the nature of the problem under consideration as well as the demands of experimental design.

Summary

The role that the parent plays in the control of the infant and its environment has been emphasized by Fries (1944), Levy (1943), Ribble (1943), Spitz (1945), Spock (1946) and others. General agreement exists that while the parent–child interaction is extremely complex and subtle, certain areas have more universality than others and seem to be more critical in determining developmental sequences.

The two areas considered to be of central importance are infant feeding and the acquisition of sphincter control. Freud (1905) was one of the first to emphasize the special significance of sucking and excretory functions when he hypothesized the existence of oral and anal character traits. He attributed these traits to the specific channeling of the infant's physiological urges by the parents' training procedures.

Unfortunately, the amount of quantitative and objective data that has been gathered concerning these two nodal areas has been slight and only a few attempts have been made to correlate data of this kind with later personality development (Childers and Hamil, 1932; Maslow and Zzilagy-Kessler, 1946; Peterson and Spano, 1941; Rogerson and Rogerson, 1939; Simsarian, 1947). This lacuna in data gathering may be attributed in part to the methodological difficulties involved and in part to the amount of time which the longitudinal character of the definitive research will require.

Within specified limits, the present research is designed to gather data about the feeding and training of infants, together with data about the behavior of the same children at a later age. The general hypothesis that experience during infancy produces demonstrable behavioral consequences in later life can then be tested empirically. Two subordinate hypotheses derived from the psychoanalytic theory of psychosexual development will be tested:

1. Oral reinforcement during infancy will affect behavior in later childhood.

2. Coerciveness of bowel training during infancy will affect behavior in later childhood.

Description of the Research

The well-baby clinic

The present research was carried out at a well-baby clinic in the City of New York, which offers free pediatric care and instruction to mothers in the neighborhood. The clients for the most part come from working-class families and many have foreign-born parents. The health station is wholly supported by municipal funds, and the service is free to all applicants, regardless of ability to pay. It serves almost half the newborn babies in the area. Many referrals to the station are made by word of mouth, one mother telling another. The hospitals in the district automatically refer all new mothers to the district health center.

Attendance at the health center is not compulsory, but the center maintains a visiting-nurse service, and mothers who are delinquent in attending are visited by the nurses. Babies are seen and examined frequently during the first year, averaging almost one visit per month. The frequency of visits diminishes as the child grows older, and the visits are terminated after he enters school or earlier if the mother so desires. The service endeavors to persuade the mother to continue until the child reaches school age.

At each visit, the child is examined by a pediatrician, and the mother is interviewed by a nurse. Instruction on child rearing, cleanliness training, hygiene, nutrition, etc., is given. When signs of illness are detected, the child is referred to a hospital or a private physician for treatment. The service is for normal, average babies and is designed to reach all neonates, not merely those who are sick or those from low income groups.

The impression gained by the experimenter during the months spent at the clinic was that the relations between the mothers and the clinic staff were warm and cordial. Considerable confidence in the staff was evidenced.

The station keeps a continuous medical record of each child in attendance. Information on diet, prescriptions, physical data, etc., are entered on these records.

A small room was assigned to the experimenter for research purposes. It was furnished with a small desk and chair for the experimenter, a chair for the interviews, a small kindergarten-size chair and table for the children, and a white medical screen with which the window in the door could be covered to insure privacy. Clearly visible upon entering the room were a set of rag dolls representing a mother, a father and a child; a box of finger paints; some paper towels and a basin of water. Although the room possessed the typical institutional atmosphere of a medical clinic, no medical equipment or instruments were present. The room opened from the clinic waiting room and was isolated from the examination rooms in which the babies were examined and inoculated.

Procedure

When the mothers arrived at the clinic for their regularly scheduled appointments, they often had to wait to see the examining pediatrician. Taking advantage of this delay, the nurse in charge asked the mother if she would 'consent to an interview with the psychologist who is doing research at the station.' In each instance the nurse accompanied the mother and child to the interview room and introduced them to the experimenter.

The experimenter began with the following statement: 'We are doing research on all of the five-year-old children who are coming to the clinic. I would like an opportunity to play alone here with your child and then to talk to you about him (her) afterwards.' The play session with the child was conducted before the pediatric examination in order to avoid the emotional repercussions which frequently follow inoculations, etc.

The child's reaction to separation from the mother was then rated (see p. 113). If the child refused to be separated, the mother was interviewed first, and then the experimenter again attempted to convince the child to stay alone and play. If the child still refused, the play period was conducted in the presence of the mother.

The children were asked to play a game with the dolls, to finger paint, to play with cold cream, to draw a person and to accept a piece of candy.

The mother was interviewed regarding the infancy and present behavior of her child.

Every effort was made to conduct the play session and the interview according to a standardized procedure. With few exceptions the mothers appeared eager to talk about their children and to ask questions.

Sample

The sample consisted of fifty children of American-born mothers who had been seen continuously at the health station from shortly after the birth of the child. Medical records covering a span of five years since birth were available on each case and were used whenever possible to verify the data obtained directly from the mothers.

The sample included twenty-three white male and twenty-seven white female children, 84 per cent of whom were in the fifth year of life (forty-eight to fifty-nine months). The remaining 16 per cent consisted of one child aged forty-seven months and seven children between sixty and sixty-eight months.

Sources of data

Data were gathered from three independent sources: a play interview with the child, an interview with the mother and the medical chart kept by the child-health station.

Play interview. Data obtained in the play interview consisted of ratings of the child's behavior and his responses to the candy choice and the draw-a-person tests, and his responses to the smearing test conducted with finger paints and cold cream.

Interview with the mother. The interview with the mother was discursive, but the interviewer made certain to cover a schedule of items including:

1. Number of months the child was breast fed.
2. Number of months the child was bottle fed.
3. Number of feedings per day before three months.
4. Number of minutes required for one feeding.
5. Age at which spoon-feeding was begun.
6. Age at which weaning was completed.
7. Willingness to accept the bottle in place of the breast.
8. Willingness to accept spoon-feeding in place of sucking.
9. Time required for the transfer to spoon-feeding.
10. Ease or difficulty in weaning from sucking.
11. Existence of a scheduled feeding time.
12. Description of feeding routine.
13. Age at which toilet training was begun.
14. Age at which child stopped wetting himself.
15. Age at which child stopped soiling himself.
16. Description of training method.
17. Age at which thumbsucking or fingersucking was begun.

18. Parental attitude toward fingersucking.
19. Method(s) of prevention (if any) of fingersucking.
20. Propensity of the child for collecting stamps, marbles, junk, etc.
21. Constipation.

Medical records. Valuable objective information was obtained from the medical chart that was kept for each child. On the face of each medical chart the following spaces were provided for the entry of development data:

1. Birth date of the child —
2. Sex of the child —
3. Mother's birthplace —
4. Feeding history:
    a. Breast only until — months old;
    b. Breast and bottle from — months until — months old;
    c. Age at which bottle was discontinued — .

Space was also provided on the back of the medical chart for the entry of progress notes by the physician and nurse. A short entry was made there each time the child was examined. The contents of these notes varied with each visit and, although the entry was always made on the same date as the visit, there was no systematic coverage of data. The notes were made from a clinical rather than a research point of view.

The systematic entries required on the face of the chart were sometimes omitted. When the entries on the front of the chart were not completed, the desired information was sought in the progress notes made by the clinical staff on the rear of the chart and was used when available. In some cases the formal quantitative data entries on the face of the chart were contradicted by remarks entered in the progress notes. Since the progress notes were always current and the formal entries were sometimes entered as afterthoughts, the current notes were always accepted when contradictions arose. In cases where the information could not be found on the medical record, the mother's report was used.

The Treatment of Historical Data

The data obtained and used in the experiment fell into two classes: current data about the child's present behavior and historical data concerning the child's earlier experiences. Some of the current data were obtained by direct observations of the child's behavior and some from reports on his behavior obtained from his mother. The historical data were obtained from both medical records and mothers' reports and raised the problem of reconciling the two sources of data with each other. Because the medical records were more reliable than the mothers' reports, the medical records were used whenever possible as a primary source of data and as a means by which the mothers' reports could be substantiated.

The general rule was to accept the medical records if they were precise and unambiguous and if there was no reason to question them. When the medical records contained data that were ambiguous, they were used as a basis for substantiating or rejecting the mothers' reports. In the event of the absence of information on the medical chart, the mothers' report was accepted.

Data on sucking reinforcement

The data obtained on the amount of sucking opportunity (reinforcement) that the subjects experienced during infancy consisted of (a) the number of months during which the infant had access to the breast or bottle as a main source of nutrition; (b) the number of months during which the infant had any access to the breast or bottle at any time, including time when it had an occasional bottle or a night bottle only; (c) the average number of meals a day that the mother estimated she gave the infant during the first three months of life; and (d) in round numbers the average number of minutes that the mother estimated that it took the infant to finish an average meal at the breast or bottle.

The information concerning the number of months of infantile sucking experience was obtained both from the medical records and the mothers' reports. The estimates regarding the number of meals a day and the average number of minutes it took the infant to finish an average meal were obtained from the mothers' reports only.

Indices of sucking. Three measures of sucking opportunity (reinforcement) were readily derived from the data: a minimum estimate, a maximum estimate and a composite estimate. Each of these three indices was computed for each of the fifty subjects used in the experiment.

Minimum estimate of sucking opportunity. The minimum estimate of sucking opportunity was the number of months during which the breast and bottle were a main source of nutrition. This estimate is hereinafter referred to as *Sucking Index I*.

In twenty-five of the fifty cases, there was evidence to show that the children experienced a period of sucking opportunity during which they were given an occasional bottle or a night bottle only. In eighteen of these cases, the medical record contained remarks such as, 'eighteen months, four days: . . . not weaned from night bottle,' and, 'fifteen months, ten days: . . . partially cup trained.' The minimum estimate was based on the date on which the record showed that the bottle had ceased to be used as a main source of feeding. In the remaining seven cases, the mothers reported the date on which the bottle had ceased to be used as a main source of nutrition.

In twenty-five cases, there was no evidence in the medical records or the mothers' reports to indicate that there had been a period of partial weaning, and in these cases, the date on which the bottle was reported to have been discontinued was used as the minimum estimate of sucking opportunity.

Maximum estimate of sucking opportunities. The maximum estimate of sucking opportunity was the number of months during which, at any time, the child was ever given the breast or bottle. This estimate is hereinafter referred to as *Sucking Index II*.

In thirty-six of the fifty cases, the medical records showed the month in which the bottle had been discontinued, and there was no reason to question the accuracy of the records. In these cases, the date on which the bottle was discontinued was accepted as the maximum estimate of sucking opportunity. In two cases, the records and the mothers' reports differed strikingly, and the mothers asserted that they had given false information to the nurse to escape criticism. In these two cases, the mothers' reports were accepted instead of the medical records. In one case only, there was no entry on the medical chart, and the mother's unsubstantiated report was accepted. In the remaining eleven cases, the information on the medical chart was somewhat ambiguous, but provided some basis for accepting or rejecting the mothers' reports.

In nine of these cases, the date on which the bottle was discontinued was not entered on the medical record, but the progress notes contained relevant remarks, such as, 'thirty months, four days: still taking the bottle,' and 'forty-three months, twenty days: ... bottle at night.' Thus, while the final date on which the bottle was discontinued was not available, there was some evidence that could be used for accepting or rejecting the mothers' reports. (a) In six of these cases, the dates reported by the mothers were later than those entered in the progress notes, and the mothers' reports were accepted. (b) In the remaining three cases, the progress notes showed that the child was still receiving the bottle after the date reported by the mother. In these cases, the date in the progress notes was considered the better estimate. In two cases, the progress notes indicated that the bottle had been discontinued since the previous visit. The dates reported by the mothers fell earlier than the dates reported in the progress notes. The weaning date was therefore arbitrarily considered to be midway between the two recorded visits.

The date on which the bottle was discontinued was a datum that could be used to estimate the reliability of the mothers' reports. In thirty-six cases the medical records showed the month in which the mother reported to the clinic that she had discontinued the bottle and completed weaning. The coefficient of correlation (r) between the date in the medical records and the date reported from memory by the mothers was equal to 0·50. This correlation was somewhat attenuated by the fact that the medical records were not absolutely reliable estimates of the true date on which the bottle was discontinued.

If the average number of months that the children had any access to the bottle or breast was computed solely on the basis of the mothers' reports, it was equal to 24·3 months. If it was computed solely on the basis of the medical records, it was equal to 24·9 months. The difference in the means was negligible. However, neither of these estimates was completely accurate. If the mean was computed on the basis of the best information available in both the mothers' reports and the medical records, it was equal to 26·14 months. This probably was a more accurate estimate than would have been possible if either the mothers' reports or the medical records had been used exclusively.

Composite estimate of sucking opportunity. The composite estimate of sucking was designed to give weight to factors such as the number of meals per day and the number of minutes per meal, in addition to the number of months of sucking. It is referred to as *Sucking Index III.*

A number of alternative methods for computing a composite index might have been used. At first glance, it would appear that a simple computation consisting of the number of months of sucking, multiplied by the number of meals per day, multiplied by the number of minutes per meal, would yield a figure representing the actual amount of sucking time that each of our subjects enjoyed. For the following reasons, this method of computation was not used.

In the first place, since the number of months of sucking (Sucking Index II) is the most reliable datum, it should be given greater weight than either of the other measures. Furthermore, the mother's estimate of sucking time in minutes is a very crude estimate, as is the rather arbitrary estimate of the average number of meals per day. On the basis of these two measures, little more can be done than to rank the subjects with regard to sucking time.

It might be assumed that a child whose mother reported an average of eight thirty-minute meals had more sucking reinforcement than a child whose mother reported an average of three ten-minute meals, but further generalization would probably be unwarranted. To weight the index of the first child by the figure of 240 (8 × 30), and the index of the second child by the figure 30 (3 × 10) would be misleading. Moreover, it would be erroneous to assume that these averages remain constant during the entire period of sucking. The schedule of infant feeding undergoes rapid changes during the first twelve months of life.

It was decided to base the composite index (Sucking Index III) upon the maximum number of months of sucking weighted by *adding* to it the number of meals per day *plus* one for every ten minutes of sucking time. In the examples cited above, the sucking index of the child who averaged eight thirty-minute meals would be weighted by adding 8 plus 3, and the sucking index of the child who averaged three ten-minute meals would be weighted by adding 3 plus 1. In this manner, the difference in sucking opportunity indicated by the mothers' estimates of frequency and duration of meals would be preserved but not overweighted, while at the same time, the index would be most heavily weighted by the most reliable measure, i.e. the number of months of sucking.

To the extent that these indices are estimates of the amount of sucking reinforcement during infancy, they may be used to test the hypothesis that behavior in later childhood is affected by the amount of sucking reinforcement during the period of early infantile feeding experience. The sucking indices are multi-determined estimates of sucking opportunity rather than direct measures of the amount of sucking reinforcement. A number of other factors would have to be considered to obtain a more clearly definable and more accurately measurable variable. The resistance of a response to extinction is determined by the number of reinforcements, the periodicity of reinforcements, as well as the number of cues to which the response has been attached. It will be seen that in the ordinary course of infant feeding, each feeding situation involves a complex of variables. Direct observations of considerable detail would have been necessary to obtain data on sucking reinforcement comparable to those obtainable in controlled laboratory experiments.

Data on constipation and fingersucking

Constipation. The data on constipation were obtained from the mothers' reports. In twenty-four cases, the mothers reported the occurrence of constipation in their children and, in twenty-six cases, the occurrence of constipation was denied.

Data on constipation were not wholly entered on the medical records. However, in seven cases, there were remarks in the progress notes reporting the occurrence of constipation. In all seven of these cases, the medical records substantiated the mothers' reports. In no case were the mothers' reports regarding the occurrence or non-occurrence of constipation contradicted by the medical records.

Fingersucking. The data on fingersucking were obtained from the mothers' reports. In seventeen cases, the mothers reported the occurrence of fingersucking in their children and, in thirty-three cases, the occurrence of fingersucking was denied.

Data on fingersucking were not ordinarily entered on the medical records. However, in four cases, fingersucking was reported in the progress notes. These four cases were among those reported by the mothers. In no case were the mothers' reports contradicted by the medical records.

Tests of Hypotheses

The method employed and the results obtained in the present research are described in the sections that follow. Care has been taken to use only variables that have been defined operationally and to test only hypotheses that have been formulated objectively. The use of psychoanalytic terms has been avoided in order to obviate the need to explain or postulate the validity of untested psychoanalytic assumptions.

Relation of sucking opportunity to oral drive in infancy

Wide variations exist among infants with regard to the times at which they finally relinquish sucking at the breast or bottle as a means of taking nourishment. The differences are partly based on external conditions, but in part they are the consequences of variations in the individual child.

In his discussion of thumb-sucking, Freud (1938, p. 586) presented the hypothesis that the lips and mouth become erotogenic, i.e. capable of giving pleasurable sensations when stimulated, as a result of the association of the act of sucking with the act of food taking. He recognized the difficulty, from a systematic standpoint, of explaining how the sensory apparatus of the lips and mucosa obtained their pleasure-giving power from this association. This difficulty disappears if the concept of eroto-genesis is disregarded, and if the relationship between sucking and nourishment is described in terms of instrumental acts and goal responses. Any instrumental act consistently leading to a goal response (consummatory act, gratification, reward) develops the properties of a goal response in its own right; i.e. it becomes a final act in a motivated behavior sequence. There can then be said to be a *secondary*, or learned, drive to make that response. Freud's hypothesis may be restated as follows: sucking is an almost universal instrumental act in infant feeding. It is closely followed on nearly every occasion by the goal response of eating. Sucking therefore becomes a secondary goal response, and children may be said to possess an oral drive that instigates sucking and other related oral manipulatory actions (Sears and Wise, 1950).

According to Sears and Wise (1950), if the oral drive is in part a product of reinforcement of the sucking act during food taking, its strength should vary with the number of opportunities for reinforcement. With reference to the actual feeding of children, the longer the child feeds by means of sucking, the stronger his oral drive will be. Partial support for this hypothesis was secured in an earlier study by Davis *et al.* (1948), who found that infants who were breast fed from birth had a stronger sucking response at the end of ten days than did infants fed by cup or bottle.

An indirect test of the hypothesis that sucking reinforcement during infancy increases the strength of the oral drive may also be undertaken. In the case of oral drive, weaning represents frustration. If the strength of the oral drive increases with reinforcement, then the more reinforcement, the stronger the drive and the greater should be the frustration experienced at weaning. The degree of frustration resulting from weaning may be supposed to manifest itself in the amount of disturbance that occurs in the child as a reaction to weaning, i.e. crying, refusal to eat, restlessness, etc.

Sears and Wise (1950) evaluated the strength of the frustration reaction to weaning on the basis of mother's reports and found that weaning disturbance was significantly greater the longer the child had been fed by sucking.

Experimental findings. On the basis of the mothers' replies to the question: 'Did your child give up the bottle readily?' the subjects in the present research were divided into two groups: those who acquiesced easily to weaning and those who resisted weaning. Table 1 shows that the average amount of sucking reinforcement experienced by the group of twenty children whose mothers reported that they had resisted weaning exceeded the average of the group of thirty children whose mothers reported that they had no weaning trouble. This mean difference is significant at the 0·01 level of probability for Sucking Index II and the 0·05 level for Sucking Index III. But the difference is not significant for Sucking Index I.

The evidence lends partial support to the hypothesis that strength of oral drive during infancy is related to the amount of reinforcement experienced by the infant. The findings are in agreement with those of Sears and Wise (1950). Although the

Table 1

Relation of Resistance to Weaning and Sucking Opportunity

| | Sucking opportunity | | |
	Index I	Index II	Index III
Mean of group that resisted	21·35 months	29·55 months	37·05 months
Mean of group that acquiesced	20·47 months	23·87 months	30·70 months
Difference between means	0·88 months	5·68 months	6·35 months
Fisher's t-ratio	0·65	3·12	2·16
Probability	greater than 0·10	less than 0·01	less than 0·05

findings have been phrased in terms having more currency among present-day psychologists, the findings also lend some support to the early psychoanalytic formulations of Karl Abraham, who pioneered in this area (1927, pp. 259–60):

There are, however, children who resist with great obstinacy the transition from breast to the bottle. This resistance becomes quite manifest when the child is expected finally to give up taking nourishment by sucking. . . .
Such behavior on the part of the child can be explained in no other way than as an obstinate adherence to the pleasure which sucking affords him through the agency of the lips as an erotogenic zone.

Although the finding that resistance to weaning is related to the amount of sucking opportunity was predicted from reinforcement theory, an alternative explanation of the relationship may be offered. The mothers of children who resisted weaning may have tended to prolong the period of sucking in response to the difficulty they encountered when they attempted to wean their children. If this were true, then the amount of sucking reinforcement would have been in part a consequence of resistance to weaning. If it is assumed that resistance to weaning is a cause of additional sucking reinforcement, then the question as to the variable responsible for resistance to weaning remains unanswered. The present study offers no satisfactory answer to the question.

Hypotheses relating early sucking opportunity to later oral behavior

Two opposed hypotheses. The hypotheses concerning the relation between early infantile sucking experiences and later oral activity have fallen into two classes. On the one hand, learning theory suggests a *reinforcement* hypothesis, i.e. the more sucking experience or practice an individual experiences, the greater will be the strength of his oral drive and the greater the expression of this oral drive at a later age. In contrast, the *need deprivation* hypothesis holds that frustration of the oral drive leads to increased oral activity later.

The critical question is whether the child who has had the *greatest* amount of sucking practice as an infant continues to use the sucking act as a preferred mode of behavior, or whether the child with the least amount of sucking practice continues to seek satisfaction through sucking. Is it reinforcement or frustration of the oral drive during infancy which plays the critical role in the determination of oral activity in later childhood?

Evidence supporting the frustration hypothesis. The frustration hypothesis is supported by the work of Levy (1928, 1934, 1937), whose classical experiment controlling the amount of sucking by six puppies led him to the conclusion that those who apparently suffered oral deprivation engaged in considerably more nonnutritional sucking than the others. It is unfortunate that Levy's experiment has not been duplicated with a larger sample.

Roberts (1944) seemed to verify Levy's findings with observations made upon a group of seven- and eight-month-old infants. Comparing the average daily time in minutes spent at the breast or bottle by fifteen fingersucking infants with the time spent by fifteen non-fingersucking infants, she found that the infants who sucked their fingers averaged less time at the breast or bottle than those who did not suck their fingers. Her findings apparently support the hypothesis that fingersucking is related to sucking deprivation rather than sucking reinforcement. Roberts' observations, however, covered only the first eight months of infancy. Moreover, in seven of the fifteen cases of fingersucking, the onset of fingersucking occurred during the first month of life. A follow-up would be necessary to determine whether such early manifestations of fingersucking persist and affect behavior in later childhood.

Levy (1937) has stated, 'the primary cause of fingersucking is insufficient sucking at the breast or bottle.' If this were true and Roberts' findings were valid, then fingersucking in infants might be used as evidence in support of the hypothesis that sucking activity is increased when the oral drive is frustrated.

Evidence supporting the reinforcement hypothesis. A number of research workers have made observations upon children's sucking activities that contradict the observations reported by Levy and Roberts. For example, Bakwin (1948) reports having 'frequently seen babies nursing at the breast and seemingly satisfied in every way who sucked their thumbs'.

Trainham, Pilafian and Kraft, (1945) found that one of a pair of twins brought up on a self-demand schedule, who voluntarily gave up sucking at the age of nine months, began to suck his thumb almost constantly at about four months of age, and at thirteen months still sucked his thumb in moments of stress.

Fredeen (1948), a pediatrician who prescribed cup feeding from birth, reported: 'The impression gained after having watched and cared for several hundred cup-fed infants . . . is that the incidence of thumb-sucking was no greater . . . than in those who were breast or bottle fed from birth.'

Sears and Wise (1950) separated their eighty subjects into three groups based upon age of weaning, i.e. early, middle and late weaning. They found no significant difference in the incidence of thumbsucking among the three groups. A comparison of the total distribution of scores combining the early and middle groups yielded a chi-square equal to 3·9, with a p equal to 0·15. Sears and Wise concluded that, in general, thumbsucking occurred more frequently among children who had the *greater* amount of sucking opportunity. Although the difference was not statistically significant, it was in the direction opposite to the one expected from Levy's hypothesis.

Experimental findings. (1) Fingersucking as a test of the reinforcement hypothesis. On the basis of the mothers' reports, it was possible to divide the subjects in the present research into two groups consisting of seventeen children who had sucked their fingers and thirty-three children who had never sucked their fingers (see Table 2). On the average, the fingersucking group had 2·83

Table 2

Relation of Fingersucking to Sucking Opportunity

| | Sucking opportunity | | |
	Index I	*Index II*	*Index III*
Mean of finger-sucking group	21·29 months	27·71 months	34·88 months
Mean of non-fingersuckers	20·58 months	25·33 months	32·45 months
Difference between means	0·71 months	2·38 months	2·43 months
Fisher's *t*-ratio	0·23	0·81	0·81
Probability	greater than 0·10	greater than 0·10	greater than 0·10

months *more* sucking reinforcement than the non-fingersucking group. While this difference is not statistically significant, the direction of the difference supports the findings of Sears and Wise (1950).

Insufficient sucking opportunity does not appear to be the determining factor in the etiology of fingersucking. On the contrary, the observed difference is in the direction predicted by the reinforcement hypothesis.

Langford (1939) and others, however, suggest that finger-sucking during the first year of life may be differently motivated than fingersucking among children between two and five years of age. He notes further that fingersucking is commonly a reaction to boredom, fatigue, illness, frustration and punishment. The occurrence of reflex fingersucking among infants lends support to Langford's hypothesis: 'Some infants are born sucking their thumbs or some of their fingers and, occasionally, swollen and macerated thumbs of the newborn give evidence of sucking before birth' (Ribble, 1943).

For these reasons, fingersucking is not a satisfactory criterion for determining whether sucking practice during infancy affects oral activity in later life. Although the evidence so far adduced suggests a reinforcement hypothesis, fingersucking appears to be a multi-determined criterion, which weakens the argument and complicates the analysis. This conclusion agrees with that of Orlansky (1949, p. 12), who states: 'It is clear, in any case, that no single-factor explanation of its (fingersucking's) etiology will suffice, and that it cannot, therefore, be used as an *unqualified* index of oral deprivation.' A more precise and less contaminated criterion for testing the reinforcement hypothesis would be desirable.

Experimental findings. (2) *Choice of candy as a test of reinforcement hypothesis.* In order to provide a simpler and more conclusive test of the reinforcement hypothesis, each of the fifty subjects was asked to choose between a lollipop and a piece of chocolate. The choice was suggested by the previously cited observations of Abraham (1916) and Mursell (1925). The function of a lollipop as a sucking device is clear.

Before each child was permitted to see the candy, he was asked to make a choice as follows. The experimenter said: 'Would you like to have a piece of candy? I have some chocolate bars and some lollipops. Which would you rather have?' After the child stated his choice, he was given the candy and observed to see what he did with it.

Of the twenty-two children who chose lollipops, nineteen sucked them, two chewed them and one took it home. Of the twenty-five children who chose chocolate, twenty-one chewed, one sucked and three took it home. The mean sucking time on the lollipops was between fourteen and fifteen minutes, while the mean time spent eating the chocolate was between one and two minutes.

Table 3 shows that the children who chose lollipops averaged 5·38 more months of sucking practice (Sucking Index II) than the group that selected the chocolate. The difference is almost significant at the 0·05 level of probability.

Further examination of Table 3 reveals that when an over-all measure of sucking reinforcement (Sucking Index III) is used to compare the groups, the mean difference in sucking reinforcement is significant at the 0·02 level. Sucking Index I shows a difference in the same direction, but the difference is not significant. The differences are clearly in a direction supporting the reinforcement hypothesis.

Table 3

Relation of Candy Choice to Sucking Opportunity

| | Sucking opportunity | | |
	Index I	Index II	Index III
Mean of Lollipop Group	22·50 months	28·86 months	37·04 months
Mean of Chocolate Group	18·84 months	23·48 months	29·80 months
Difference between means	3·66 months	5·38 months	7·24 months
Fisher's t-ratio	1·36	1·90	2·52
Probability	greater than 0·10	0·10 < 0·05	less than 0·02

The candy choice was a simple behavioral observation designed to test the reinforcement hypothesis. Although a measure of its reliability might seem desirable, it was not feasible to obtain one. Moreover, the question was not whether the child would *always* choose a lollipop or a chocolate bar, but simply whether he *did* choose one or the other. It would perhaps be possible to undertake a more extensive exploration of the problem by offering the children a variety of different food choices rather than just one. Further studies along such lines would undoubtedly yield considerable data.

Summary. The relationship between the amount of sucking reinforcement during infancy and the propensity of the individual to favor sucking activity in later childhood was investigated. The hypothesis that thumbsucking is related to sucking deprivation during infancy was not verified, but, on the contrary, the evidence tended to support a reinforcement explanation more strongly. Using a food choice under controlled conditions, it was demonstrated that selection of the sucking choice in childhood bore a significant relationship to the amount of sucking reinforcement experienced during infancy.

Hypotheses relating sucking opportunity to other behavior

Psychoanalytic investigations resulted in a number of hypotheses suggesting that certain character traits and modes of behaving were derived from the individual's oral erotic experiences.

In the present paper the somewhat ambiguous term, 'oral-erotism', has been avoided. The operationally defined variable, 'amount of sucking reinforcement', is a more satisfactory concept for experimental purposes.

Sucking opportunity and anal retentiveness. Abraham states that retention of bodily contents is related to oral experience. Children who retain fecal material for prolonged periods of time are described as constipated infants. Using 'amount of sucking reinforcement' as a criterion for the amount of training to suck that each child experienced and constipation as a criterion for anal retentiveness, a striking relationship between the two criteria is revealed (see Table 4).

Table 4

Relation of Constipation to Amount of Sucking Opportunity during Infancy

| | *Sucking opportunity* | | |
	Index I	*Index II*	*Index III*
Mean of constipated group	24·54 months	30·33 months	37·58 months
Mean of non-constipated group	17·38 months	22·27 months	29·31 months
Difference between means	7·16 months	8·06 months	8·27 months
Fisher's *t*-ratio	2·72	3·26	3·19
Probability	less than 0·01	less than 0·01	less than 0·01

Each of our mothers was asked if her child had ever been constipated. The average amount of sucking reinforcement experienced by the twenty-four children whose mothers reported them to have been constipated exceeded the average for the twenty-six infants who were reported 'never to have been constipated'. The difference is highly significant at the 0·01 level.

The finding will not prove surprising to the experienced pediatrician and nurse. Apparently the observation that prolonged sucking and constipation are associated is common knowledge in the well-baby clinic. The fact that the occurrence of constipation is associated with the amount of sucking reinforcement verifies the psychoanalytic hypothesis that retention of bodily contents is related to oral experience.

Relation of sucking opportunity to collecting. The relation that was suggested between collection of objects (parsimoniousness) and sucking was tested as follows. The children were divided into two groups on the basis of mothers' replies to the question, 'Does your child collect things such as marbles, stamps, junk, etc.?' A summary of the findings is contained in Table 5.

Table 5

Relation of Collecting to Sucking Opportunity during Infancy

	Sucking opportunity		
	Index I	*Index II*	*Index III*
Mean of non-collectors	27·50 months	31·21 months	38·86 months
Mean of collectors	18·22 months	24·16 months	31·11 months
Difference between means	9·28 months	7·04 months	7·75 months
Fisher's *t*-ratio	2·64	2·06	2·14
Probability	less than 0·02	less than 0·05	less than 0·05

The average amount of sucking reinforcement of the thirty-six children whose mothers reported that they collected things exceeded the average for the fourteen children whose mothers gave negative replies. The difference is significant at the 0·02 level for Sucking Index I and the 0·05 level for Sucking Index II and Sucking Index III. The difference, however, is in an unexpected direction. The tendency to collect appears to be inversely related to sucking reinforcement, which means that the children reported to be collectors at five years of age experienced considerably less sucking reinforcement during infancy than the non-collectors.

These data are somewhat analogous to those of Hunt (1941) who reported that rats who suffered food deprivation during infancy tended to hoard food pellets later. In our case children who collect (hoard) objects are those who by comparison to non-collectors have suffered a deprivation during infancy averaging 9·28 months of sucking. The finding would seem to support the theory that collecting is related to oral deprivation, not to anal retention.

Constipation and collecting. It logically follows from the foregoing that strong doubts must be entertained regarding the expected connexion between constipation and parsimony, which has been hypothesized by Abraham (1921, p. 387):

> We find a tendency to extravagance less frequent than parsimony in our patients. In an observation communicated to the Berlin Psychoanalytical Society, Simmel made the parallel between extravagance and neurotic diarrhoea just as evident as that between avarice and constipation, which has long been clear to us.

Table 6

Frequency with which Children Reported to have been Constipated were Reported to have been Collectors

	Constipated	*Non-constipated*
Collectors	62·5% (15)	81% (21)
Non-collectors	37·5% (9)	19% (5)

$\chi^2 = 2·2$
$P > 0·10$

The relation between constipation and parsimony (collection) is shown in Table 6. The relationship between constipation and collecting is in a direction opposite to that expected from the analytic hypothesis, although the difference is not statistically significant ($\chi^2 = 2 \cdot 2$). Collecting objects seems to be related to sucking deprivation rather than to anal retentiveness. The findings suggest that some clarification of the psychoanalytic theory of the anal character is required. Perhaps a distinction between *anal* retentiveness and *oral* retentiveness would be appropriate. Constipation might then be described as anal retentiveness and collecting as oral retentiveness.

Summary. The relations between sucking reinforcement, anal retentiveness and retention of objects was investigated. A direct relation was found to exist between sucking reinforcement and constipation. An inverse relationship was found between sucking reinforcement during infancy and retention of objects in later childhood. The relationship between retention of feces and retention of objects, while not statistically significant, was found to be in a direction opposite to that expected from the psychoanalytic hypotheses.

The psychoanalytic hypothesis that oral reinforcement affects other behavior was partly verified. The specific hypothesis that constipation leads to collecting all kinds of objects was rejected. The data lend support to an alternate hypothesis that oral deprivation in infancy may bear a relation to collecting and hoarding in later childhood.

Hypotheses relating coercive toilet training in infancy and behaviour in later childhood

On the basis of the date toilet training was begun and whether or not punishment was employed, it is possible to rate coerciveness of toilet training and compare the behavior of children who were coercively trained with that of those who were not. According to Huschka (1942):

Coercive toilet training is used to denote premature institution of a toilet training régime and overactive, destructive training methods . . . frequent and marked employment of shame [and] punishment for failure to comply . . . [it is] reasonable to consider training which was started before the age of eight months as forced or coercive as far as the time factor is concerned.

Each of the mothers in the present study was asked at what age she began toilet training her child, and the method she used.

Information was obtained on forty-seven children. In thirteen cases, training was reported begun at six months of age or earlier. In eighteen cases, training was begun later than six months, but the mothers reported that they had punished the children for failure to comply. Among the remaining sixteen cases, training was begun later than six months of age and the mothers denied using punishment. Thus about 66 per cent of our cases were rated as having been coercively toilet trained. This finding agrees with that of Huschka and McKnight (1943), who rated 68 per cent of their sample as having been coercively toilet trained.

Huschka and McKnight (1943) used nine months of age as the sole criterion for their ratings. The criterion of six months used in the present study for rating coerciveness is a more conservative estimate, but cases characterized by '... frequent and marked employment of shame and punishment for failure to comply ...' were included in the group rated as coercively trained.

Having divided the subjects into two groups using the coerciveness of bowel training as the criterion, these groups can be used to test the hypothesis that toilet training technique employed during infancy affects the behavior and character of the same infants in later childhood.

Relation of coercive training to collecting and constipation. Parsimony, as measured by the tendency of children to collect, seems to be inversely related to oral reinforcement, while the tendency to be constipated is positively related to oral reinforcement.

Tables 7 and 8 indicate that collecting (parsimony) and constipation are independent of coercive bowel training.

Table 7

Frequency with which Children Reported to have been Constipated were Reported to have been Coercively Toilet Trained

	Constipated	Non-constipated
Coercive training	73% (16)	60% (15)
Non-coercive training	27% (6)	40% (10)

$\chi^2 = 0.84$

$P > 0.30$

Table 8

Frequency with which Children Reported to have been Collectors were Reported to have been Coercively Toilet Trained

	Collector	Non-collector
Coercive training	65% (22)	69% (9)
Non-coercive training	35% (12)	31% (4)

$\chi^2 = 0.47$
$P = 0.50$

Coercive training and responses to smearing tests. The hypothesis that pleasure in painting, modeling and similar activities are related to the child's response to toilet training was tested by means of a smearing test.

Each child was asked to play with finger paints and to play with a jar of cold cream. The child was supplied with a sheet of paper for painting and a square of oil cloth for smearing the cold

Table 9a

Relation of Smearing to Coercive Bowel Training

	Smearing (Ratings 1–3)	Non-smearing (Ratings 4–5)
Finger painting		
Coercive training	68% (17)	56% (9)
Non-coercive training	34% (9)	44% (7)

$\chi^2 = 0.35$
$P > 0.50$

Cold-cream test		
Coercive training	69% (16)	53% (10)
Non-coercive training	31% (7)	47% (9)

$\chi^2 = 1.27$
$P > 0.20$

Table 9b

Frequency Distribution of Children's Responses to Smearing Tests

| | Ratings | | | | |
	1	2	3	4	5
Finger painting					
Coercive training	6	0	11	3	6
Non-coercive training	1	0	8	1	6
Cold-cream test					
Coercive training	9	3	4	2	8
Non-coercive training	4	2	1	1	8

cream. The child's response was rated in terms of the area he covered with the smearing material
1. The child refuses to touch material.
2. The child touches the material but refuses to smear it.
3. The child smears but not extensively (less than half the area).
4. The child smears but uses the material with control and form.
5. The child smears extensively with enjoyment.

Table 9 shows no significant relationship between the tendency to smear and the technique of toilet training. The hypothesis that pleasure in smearing is a response to toilet training is not supported by these findings.

Coercive training and negativism. Obstinacy or negativism was rated by the willingness of the child to perform the six tasks requested of him by the experimenter, i.e. separate from his mother, play with the dolls, choose a piece of candy, draw a

Table 10

Frequency with which Children who were Negativistic were Reported to have been Coercively Toilet Trained

	Negativistic	*Cooperative*
Coercive training	87% (13)	56% (18)
Non-coercive training	13% (2)	44% (14)

$\chi^2 = 5 \cdot 21$
$P < 0 \cdot 05$

person, play with finger paints, play with cold cream. Children who refused more than three requests were rated as negativistic.

Table 10 shows that negativistic behavior occurred more frequently among those children who were coercively toilet trained than among those who were not coerced. The difference is significant at the 0·05 level of probability ($\chi^2 = 5·21$). This finding supports the analytic hypothesis that obstinacy and refusal to comply with requests are related to the child's response to toilet training.

Coercive training and other behavior. The possibility that coercive bowel training might be related either directly or indirectly to a constellation of negativistic behavioral traits such as anxiousness, immaturity and uncommunicativeness, noted by the experimenter during the play session, was tested. Three behavioral criteria were used by the experimenter to rate each child with regard to these behavioral traits.

Table 11

Frequency with which Children who Exhibited Anxiety at Separation from their Mother were Reported to have been Coercively Toilet Trained

	Anxious (Ratings 3 and 4)	Non-anxious (Ratings 1 and 2)
Coercive training	84% (16)	54% (15)
Non-coercive training	16% (3)	46% (13)

$\chi^2 = 4·73$
$P < 0·05$

Separation anxiety. For convenience, the first of these criteria was called separation anxiety. Separation anxiety was rated by the amount of difficulty the experimenter experienced in convincing the child to separate from his mother and to remain alone in the playroom. A four-point rating scale was used to rate the child's anxiety about separation:
1. The child remained alone with the experimenter without hesitation or manifest anxiety.
2. The child was easily persuaded to separate from his mother.

3. The child was persuaded to separate from his mother but with difficulty.

4. The child refused to separate from his mother.

Table 11 shows that separation anxiety occurred more frequently among children who were coercively trained than among those who experienced non-coercive training. The difference is significant at the 0·05 level of probability ($\chi^2 = 4·73$).

Spontaneous verbalization. The second comparison variable was based on the amount of spontaneous verbalization that the child exhibited during the experimental play period. A four-point scale was used by the experimenter to rate the child's verbal performance:

1. Child did not talk.
2. Child talked a little.
3. Child talked freely.
4. Child was bossy or verbose.

Table 12 shows that uncommunicative performances occurred more frequently among the coercively trained children. The difference is significant at the 0·05 level of probability ($\chi^2 = 4·23$).

Table 12

Frequency with which Children who were Uncommunicative during the Experimental Play Period were Reported to have been Coercively Toilet Trained

	Uncommunicative (Ratings 1 and 2)	Verbal (Ratings 3 and 4)
Coercive training	81% (17)	52% (13)
Non-coercive training	19% (4)	48% (12)

$\chi^2 = 4·23$
$P < 0·05$

Draw-a-person test. The third comparison variable was called immaturity. Each child was asked to draw a person. A six-point rating scale was used by the experimenter to rate the drawings:
0. Child says, 'Won't.'
1. Child says, 'Can't.'
2. Child scribbles.
3. Child uses some form.

4. Child draws main body parts.

5. Child draws details as well as main body parts.

Table 13 shows the predominance of immature responses among the coercively trained children. However, some reservation about this conclusion is warranted by the large number of negativistic

Table 13a

Frequency with which Immature Responses to the Draw-a-Person Test Occurred among Children who were Reported to have been Coercively Toilet Trained

	Immature ratings (0,1,2)	Mature ratings (3,4,5)
Coercive training	80% (20)	48% (10)
Non-coercive training	20% (5)	52% (11)

$\chi^2 = 5.27$
$P < 0.05$

Table 13b

Frequency Distribution of Ratings of Children's Responses to the Draw-a-Person Test

	0	1	2	3	4	5
Coercive training	12	2	6	7	2	1
Non-coercive training	0	0	5	4	3	4

refusals with which this finding is weighted. Nevertheless, it may be noted that even without the fourteen refusals, the relationship still holds. Of the drawings made by the coercively trained children, 81 per cent were rated (2) and (3), while only 56 per cent of the drawings made by the non-coercively trained children were equally immature.

Discussion. The findings regarding the relation between coercive bowel training and anxious, uncommunicative and immature responses during the play session were not explicitly predicted. They must, therefore, be regarded as hypotheses in need of cross-validation. Coercive toilet training is a procedure that may be symptomatic of a general attitude of coerciveness on the part of the mother, and this general attitude may be the intervening variable responsible for the anxious attitude and immature responses observed in the children.

Summary. On the basis of mothers' reports of how and when toilet training was begun, children were rated with regard to coerciveness of toilet training. Using fourfold contingency tables, it was shown that contrary to predictions made from psychoanalytic theory, the relation between coercive toilet training and collecting, constipation and pleasure in smearing was not above chance.

A relation significant at the 0·05 level of probability, using the χ^2 test was shown to exist between coercive toilet training during infancy, on the one hand, and negativistic behavior, separation anxiety and uncommunicativeness on the other.

The relation shown between coercive training and immature responses on the draw-a-person test may be considered questionable, due to the large number of refusals with which this item is weighted.

The finding that negativistic behavior is related to coercive toilet training was predicted from psychoanalytic theory.

The findings regarding anxiety, immaturity and uncommunicativeness must be treated as hypotheses requiring cross-validation, since they were not specifically predicted.

The general analytic assumption that toilet training affects later behavior has in part been verified.

Summary and Conclusions

The purpose of the study was to examine certain relations between infant experiences and behavior in later childhood, particularly the effects of the methods of feeding and training employed during infancy.

Problem

An empirical test of the general hypothesis that experience during infancy produces demonstrable behavioral consequences in later life was undertaken. Two subordinate hypotheses derived from the psychoanalytic theory of psychosexual development were tested: oral reinforcement during infancy will affect behavior in later childhood and coerciveness of bowel training during infancy will affect behavior in later childhood.

Subjects

Fifty children between forty-seven and sixty-eight months of age were selected at random from the current files of a well-baby clinic. Each child had attended the clinic since shortly after birth.

Procedure

Data were gathered from three sources: (a) a play interview with the child, (b) an interview with the mother and (c) medical records of the well-baby clinic. Data obtained from the mothers were checked against the medical records whenever possible.

Data

With regard to each child, data were gathered on: (a) the amount of sucking reinforcement experienced during infancy; (b) the date and method of bowel training; (c) constipation; (d) response to weaning; (e) propensity to collect things; (f) fingersucking; (g) responses to requests by experimenter, i.e. to separate from the mother, to play with dolls, to draw a person, to play with finger paints, to play with cold cream and to accept a piece of candy.

Results

1. The hypothesis that reinforcement increases the strength of oral drive during infancy was supported by the findings.

2. The hypothesis that thumbsucking is due to sucking deprivation during infancy was not supported.

3. The possibility that thumbsucking may, in part, be due to reinforcement of oral drive during infancy was suggested by the findings.

4. Using a food choice under controlled conditions, it was demonstrated that the selection of the sucking choice during childhood bore a significant relationship to the amount of sucking reinforcement in infancy.

5. A relationship was found between the amount of sucking reinforcement during infancy and the tendency to be constipated.

6. An inverse relationship was found between the amount of sucking reinforcement during infancy and the tendency to collect objects in later childhood.

7. The psychoanalytic hypothesis that the propensity to collect objects is directly related to constipation was rejected.

8. Using fourfold contingency tables, it was found that relationships significant at the 0·05 level existed between coercive toilet training and separation anxiety, negativistic behavior, uncommunicativeness and immaturity in the experimental play interview.

9. No relationship was found between coercive toilet training and collecting, constipation or response to smearing tests.

Discussion

The conclusions are somewhat limited by the undermined reliabilities of many of the variables. However, as a general rule, lower reliabilities tend to obscure rather than magnify the true differences between groups. Therefore, somewhat more confidence may be placed in the positive findings of the present study than in the negative findings.

It must also be emphasized that the findings of the present study pertain to the general effect of certain variables upon group averages in the long run. The findings therefore cannot be used to predict behavior in individual cases. Not only was there considerable overlap between the different groups, but the level of statistical significance of the observed differences clearly indicated the existence of other important variables, which were not considered in the present study.

Conclusions

While many questions remain unanswered, the results indicate that psychoanalytic speculations regarding the importance of the oral and anal experiences of the infant are a rich source of hypotheses deserving careful study and consideration. The findings also offer evidence that *a priori* assumptions about the specific consequences of infantile experiences are to be received with considerable caution. In principle, the assertion that infantile experiences have demonstrable effects in later life has been verified.

References

ABRAHAM, K. (1916), 'The first pregenital stage of the libido', in *Selected Papers: International Psychoanalytic Library*, no. 13, Hogarth Press, 1927, pp. 248–79.

ABRAHAM, K. (1921), 'Contributions to the theory of the anal character', in *Selected Papers: International Psychoanalytic Library*, no. 13, Hogarth Press, 1927, pp. 370–92.

ABRAHAM, K. (1924), 'The influence of oral eroticism on character formation', in *Selected Papers: International Psychoanalytic Library*, no. 13, Hogarth Press, 1927, pp. 393–406.

BAKWIN, H. (1948), 'Thumb- and finger-sucking in children', *J. Pediat.*, vol. 32, pp. 99–101.

CHILDERS, A. T., and HAMIL, B. M. (1932), 'Emotional problems as related to the duration of breast feeding in infancy', *Amer. J. Orthopsychiat.*, vol. 2, pp. 134–42.

DAVIS, H. V., SEARS, R. R., MILLER, H. C., and BROBECK, A. J. (1948), 'Effects of cup, bottle, and breast feeding on oral activities of newborn babies', *Pediatrics*, vol. 2, pp. 549–58 .

FREDEEN, R. C. (1948), 'Cup feeding of newborn infants', *Pediatrics*, vol. 2, pp. 544–8.

FREUD, S. (1905), 'Three contributions to the theory of sex', in *Basic Writings*, Modern Library, 1938, pp. 553–632.

FREUD, S. (1908), 'Character and anal eroticism', in *Collected Papers*, vol. 2, Hogarth Press, 1924, pp. 45–50.

FREUD, S. (1916), 'On the transformation of instincts with special references to anal eroticism', in *Collected Papers*, vol. 2, Hogarth Press, 1924 , pp. 164–71.

FREUD, S. (1923), 'The infantile genital organization of the libido', in *Collected Papers*, vol. 2, Hogarth Press, 1924, pp. 244–9.

FRIES, M. E. (1944), 'Psychosomatic relationships between mother and infant', *Psychosom. Med.*, vol. 6, pp. 159–62.

GLOVER, E. (1924), 'The significance of the mouth in psychoanalysis', *Brit. J. med. Psychol.*, vol. 4, pp. 134–55.

HUSCHKA, M. (1942), 'The child's response to coercive bowel training', *Psychosom. Med.*, vol. 4, pp. 301–8.

HUSCHKA, M. (1943), 'A study of training in voluntary control of urination in a group of problem children', *Psychosom. Med.*, vol. 5, pp. 254–65.

HUSCHKA, M., and McKNIGHT, W. K. (1943), 'Psychiatric observations in a well-baby clinic', *Psychosom. Med.*, vol. 5, pp. 42–50.

HUNT, J. McV. (1941), 'The effects of infant-feeding frustration upon adult hoarding in the albino rat', *J. abnorm. soc. Psychol.*, vol. 36, pp. 338–60.

JONES, E. (1918), 'Anal-erotic character traits', *J. abnorm. Psychol.*, vol. 13, pp. 261–84.

LANGFORD, W. S. (1939), 'Thumb and finger sucking in childhood', *Amer. J. Dis. Child.*, vol. 58, pp. 1290–300.

LEVY, D. M. (1925), 'Resistant behavior of children', *Amer. J. Psychiat.*, vol. 4, pp. 502–7.

LEVY, D. M. (1928), 'Finger sucking and accessory movements in early infancy', *Amer. J. Psychiat.* vol. 7, pp. 881–918.

LEVY, D. M. (1934), 'Experiments on the sucking reflex and social behavior of dogs', *Amer. J. Orthopsychiat.*, vol. 4, pp. 203–24.

LEVY, D. M. (1937), 'Thumb or finger sucking from the psychiatric angle', *Child Devel.*, vol. 8, pp. 99–101.

LEVY, D. M. (1943), *Maternal Overprotection*, Columbia University Press.

LEVY, D. M. (1944), 'On the problem of movement restraint', *Amer. J. Psychiat.*, vol. 14, pp. 644–71.

MASLOW, A. H., and ZZILAGYI-KESSLER, I. (1946), 'Security and breast feeding', *J. abnorm. soc. Psychol.*, vol. 41, pp. 83–5.

MURPHY, G., MURPHY, L. B., and NEWCOMB, T. M. (1937), *Experimental Social Psychology*, Harper.

MURSELL, J. L. (1925), 'Contributions to the psychology of nutrition: III. Nutrition and the family', *Psychol. Rev.*, vol. 32, pp. 457–71.

ORLANSKY, H. (1949), 'Infant care and personality', *Psychol. Bull.*, vol. 46, pp. 1–48.

PETERSON, C. H., and SPANO, F. L. (1941), 'Breast feeding, maternal rejection and child personality', *Charact. Personal.*, vol. 10, pp. 62–4.

RIBBLE, M. A. (1938), 'Clinical studies of instinctive reactions in newborn babies', *Amer. J. Psychiat.*, vol. 95, pp. 145–60.

RIBBLE, M. A. (1939), 'The significance of infantile sucking for the psychic development of the individual', *J. nerv. ment. Dis.*, vol. 90, p. 455.

RIBBLE, M. A. (1941), 'Disorganizing factors of infant personality', *Amer. J. Psychiat.*, vol. 90, pp. 459–63.

RIBBLE, M. A. (1943), *The Rights of Infants*, Columbia University Press.

ROBERTS, E. (1944), 'Thumb and finger sucking in relation to feeding in early infancy', *Amer. J. Dis. Child.*, vol. 68, pp. 7–8.

ROGERSON, B. C. F., and ROGERSON, C. H. (1939), 'Feeding in infancy and subsequent psychological difficulties', *J. ment. Scien.*, vol. 85, pp. 1163–82.

SEARS, R. R., and WISE, G. W. (1950), 'I. Relation of cup feeding in infancy to thumb sucking and the oral drive', *Amer. J. Orthopsychiat.*, vol. 20, pp. 123–36.

SIMSARIAN, F. P. (1947), 'Case histories of five thumb sucking children breast fed on unscheduled régimes, without limitations of nursing time', *Child. Devel.*, vol. 18, pp. 180–84.

SPITZ, R. A. (1945), 'Hospitalism', *Psychoanal. Stud. Child.*, vol. 1, pp. 53–74.

SPITZ, R. A. (1946), 'Analclitic depression', *Psychoanal. Stud. Child.*, vol. 2, pp. 313–42.

SPOCK, B. (1946), *The Common Sense Book of Baby and Child Care*, Duell, Sloane & Pearce.

TRAINHAM, C., PILAFIAN, G. J., and KRAFT, R. M. (1945), 'Case history of twins fed on a self-demand régime', *J. Pediat.*, vol. 27, pp. 97–108.

6 Halla Beloff

The Structure and Origin of the Anal Character

Halla Beloff, 'The structure and origin of the anal character', *Genetic Psychology Monographs*, vol. 55, 1957, pp. 145–72.

Rationale and Plan of the Investigation

At this stage of personality study it is no longer necessary to justify the importance of independent investigation of Freudian hypotheses and theory; or indeed to defend the possibility of doing so by means of objective methods and statistical analysis. The present study is of such a kind. The area of the anal character was chosen for investigation for several reasons. It is one of the best-documented of the psychoanalytic concepts; it has been widely accepted as valid and applied in the description and explanation of personality, even outside the sphere of clinical analytical work; while very little study towards the objective validation of the Freudian formula has been reported.

The theory of the anal character may be presented as follows (Orlansky, 1949, p. 17):

The infant derives a great deal of erogenous pleasure from its bowel movements, and when this pleasure is inhibited by severe bowel training, the usual result is reaction formation. . . . In extreme cases . . . one becomes parsimonious, stingy, meticulous, punctual, tied down with petty self-restraints. Everything that is free, uncontrolled, spontaneous is dangerous. . . .

Broadly, it was the purpose of this project: (a) to state the psychoanalytic hypotheses in the anal area in objective terms, capable of independent confirmation or refutation, i.e. to formulate one structural and one etiological hypothesis; and (b) to investigate these statements by objective methods with statistical analysis of the data obtained, using normal subjects; or in other words to test the general validity of the analytic propositions to non-clinical data.

The experimental programme may be summarized. In detail it was planned:

1. To design a tool for the measurement of anal characteristics exhibited by adults – a paper-and-pencil, self-rating questionnaire.

2. To intercorrelate the item responses of a group of normal subjects.

3. To carry out a centroid factor analysis, the resulting factor structure being considered in relation to the psychoanalytic prediction that only one general factor should be necessary to account for the item intercorrelations.

4. To check the results of 2 and 3 by an identical analysis of rating data for the same sample of subjects on the same item topics.

5. To correlate the anal factor, if indeed one such appeared, with certain other personality measures, in order to ascertain what relation, if any, these had to the anal character.

6. To investigate the relation of the anal/non-anal responses to the age of the subject when toilet training was reported as complete by the mother, and the score of the mother of the subject on the questionnaire of anal characteristics mentioned above.

7. To draw conclusions from the statistical analysis and relate them to psychoanalytic theory.

The Psychoanalytic Definition

Virtually the whole substance of the argument of this paper is to be found in Freud's original communication *Character and Anal Erotism* (1908). He had observed that some of his patients were '. . . remarkable for a regular combination of the three following peculiarities: they are exceptionally *orderly*, *parsimonious* and *obstinate*' (p. 45). That is, there appeared three traits regularly together, that were logically quite independent.

The later papers on this topic by Freud himself (1915, 1916), Jones (1918, 1923), Abraham (1921, 1924), Ferenczi (1914) and others, do not contribute more than a closer study of the adult character and its component traits. The latter are well-known now, and we need only enumerate some of them. Great stress is laid on *Eigensinn*, that is, self-willedness, defiance, obstinacy; but which is at the same time more than obstinacy, in that it involves very much the active insistence on pursuing one's own path, and is often associated with strongly marked individuality. In addition they emphasize self-importance, procrastination, a passion for personal autonomy and self-control, punctuality, irritability, cleanliness, and quasi-sadism and hatred (as distinct from defiance).

Originally the traits were said to form one syndrome – *the* anal character. However, components said to arise from the early (expulsive) as opposed to the later (retentive) phase of the anal stage are sometimes distinguished. This polarity between the impulses to give and to retain is certainly noted even in the early paper by Jones. In his subclassification of the traits within the character he writes (1918, p. 428): 'The anal–erotic complex is genetically related to two of the most fundamental and far-reaching instincts, the instincts to possess and to create or produce respectively.' He recognizes a further principle of classification for the component traits – the mechanism of transformation from erotism to character; reaction-formation versus sublimation. '. . . . Some of them (the character traits) are of a positive nature – that is, they are sublimations which represent simply a deflection from the original aim; while others are of a negative nature – that is, they constitute reaction-formations erected as barriers against the repressed tendencies' (Jones, 1918, p. 414). It is, of course, structural problems of the independence or otherwise of components, such as we have here, that can be elucidated most elegantly by factor analysis of the relevant trait measures.

As regards etiology, the history that Freud (1908, p. 46) elucidated from his original patients was interpreted as indicating '. . . that the erotogenic significance of the anal zone is intensified in the innate sexual constitution of these persons.' The anal zone is said to lose its erotogenic significance in the course of their development and '. . . the constant appearance of this triad of peculiarities in (the patients') character may be brought into relation with the disappearance of their anal erotism' (p. 46). Originally, therefore, the importance of innate disposition for the development of the characteristics was stressed. Later papers emphasize rather the opposition of the environmental, pedagogic forces and the natural responses of the child in this sphere during the period of cleanliness training.

From the child's point of view then, the problem may be considered as twofold: he wishes to get as much pleasure out of the performance of defecation as possible; he wishes to retain control over it in opposition to the educative modifications desired by the mother. 'The process of defecation affords the first occasion on which the child must decide between a narcissistic and an object-loving attitude. He either parts obediently with his faeces, "offers them up" to his love, or else retains them for purposes of auto-erotic gratification and later as a means of asserting his own will. The latter choice constitutes the development of defiance. . . .' (Freud, 1916, p. 168.)

As Lou Andreas-Salome writes (1916, p. 254), '*Während das Erziehungswerk innerhalb der analen Sphäre dem tatsächlichen Sinn nach bald erledigt ist, bleibt sie deshalb im übertragenen Sinn dauernd bedeutungsvoll.*' (While the educational process in the anal sphere is, in the concrete sense, soon complete, it remains still, in the figurative sense continually important.)

So far the etiological statements have been general. In particular, it is said that severe toilet training (severe frustration of anal erotism) either in terms of cleanliness enforced too early or too harshly or both, will result in the development of the above-mentioned traits; permissive training, accomplished relatively late and gently will tend to encourage the development of traits opposite to those mentioned.

Even in this highly condensed summary of the psychoanalytical position, mention must be made of Abraham's opinion with respect to the pathological nature or otherwise, of the character. While acknowledging the pathological extreme to which the 'peculiarities' may go, he also recognizes the presence of the traits in 'normal' persons and indeed stresses their social value. 'They render it possible for the individual to adapt himself to the demands of his environment as regards cleanliness, love of order, and so on' (Abraham, 1924, p. 393).

It seems clear then, that this definition of the anal character and its background can be stated in two simple hypotheses, namely that a psychological, functional entity exists, corresponding to the anal character, as described by the psychoanalysts; and that anal characteristics in the adult are related to bowel training experiences in infancy.

The Experimental Literature

The early work in this area has been summarized in papers by Hilgard (1952), Orlansky (1949) and Sears (1943). Since the appearance of these reviews several more sophisticated studies have been reported, although their results still do not allow us to draw very clear conclusions.

Structural investigations

Sears (1943) reported the first structural investigation. He inter-correlated ratings of the original triad of traits (orderliness, obstinacy and parsimony); the correlations, while low, were all found to be in the expected, positive direction.

Barnes (1952) presented a factor analysis of the whole series of traits supposedly associated with fixation at all the Freudian pre-genital stages. His hypothesis that the oral, anal and phallic characters would appear as three distinct factors was not borne out; however, the first factor of meticulousness (characterized by orderliness, cleanliness, reliability, law abidance) was interpreted by him as essentially anal. He acknowledges that this leaves out the parsimonious, resentful, rigid and sadistic elements presented by clinicians. These did, however, load significantly on the second factor, called by him, overt aggression. We should prefer to interpret his result as showing that the meticulous and aggressive aspects of the character, i.e. the sublimations and reaction forma-tions, should be considered as separate entities or alternative manifestations, in so far as they appear in two orthogonal factors.

Measures of pre-genital and post-genital fixations have also been factor analysed by Stagner, Lawson and Moffit (1955), using responses to items of the Krout Personal Preference Scale. Their factors are difficult to interpret and suggest principally that the oral and phallic characters are not independent; items corresponding to them overlapped on many factors. Paradoxi-cally, their results also indicate that so-called early and late anal characteristics probably do manifest themselves independently.

The conclusions of Barnes on the one hand, and Stagner *et al.* on the other, are therefore mutually contradictory – one study dividing the character on the dimension of sublimation versus reaction-formation, and the other on early versus later stages.

With regard to the wider reference of the character, Miller and Stine (1951) have found a positive relation between anal characteristics and social acceptance by peers, in school children. While Farber (1955) has reported a highly significant relationship between anal characteristics and aggressive political attitudes, as measured by two short scales of five and four items respectively. Both these studies suggest that the anal character may have some connexions with the conforming personality.

Etiological investigations

The study of origins begins with the work of Hamilton (1929) which first showed, outside the therapeutic situation, the connexion between conscious memory for childhood anal erotism and the possession of traits which Hamilton interpreted as anal (namely stinginess or extravagance, sadism, masochism, fetichism, concern for clothes).

The relevance of comparative, anthropological evidence in this field has, of course, always been appreciated, but until recently no authoritative objective study has been available. Now Whiting and Child (1953), using the Human Relations Area Files, have gathered together all its data on child rearing practices and collated them with adult personality manifestations in the area of customs and belief systems related to illness. Their analysis is not therefore directly connected with the present problem, but may be considered from the point of view of general information about the continuity or otherwise of early experience and later personality.

Of the four principal hypotheses set up for the anal system, none could be confirmed. Judgements of socialization anxiety connected with toilet training were not found to be related to: anal explanations of illness (e.g. defecation held responsible for illness), patient responsibility for illness (i.e. number of specific acts of a person which are believed capable of making him sick), or to fear of others causing illness. Neither were judgements of initial satisfaction in the anal sphere related to anal therapeutic practices. With the cultural data used, Whiting and Child can only be said to have shown that the permanence of the results of toilet training experiences have been overemphasized, or at least, that they are not related, even suggestively to customs regarding illness.

The Investigation of the Structural Hypothesis

Hypothesis I: that a psychological, functional entity exists, corresponding to the anal character, as described by psychoanalysts

As has been indicated, the character is said to be composed of a number of traits. The decision as to the number of components to be included for investigation is, of course, to some extent arbitrary. A careful sifting of the psychoanalytic writings suggested that the following had been presented as the most salient of these: *Eigensinn* (obstinacy plus), parsimony, collecting, orderliness, cleanliness, punctuality, procrastination, quasi-sadism in personal relations, conscientiousness, pedantry, feelings of superiority, irritability, desire to domineer, desire for personal autonomy.

Using these trait names as a basis, a questionnaire was constructed – the items to measure the manifestations of the traits in terms of overt behavior and attitudes. Our hypothesis then implies that the items should intercorrelate significantly and the intercorrelations be accounted for by a single, general factor. If the matrix were not to be significant, no functional entity as represented by the items can be said to exist. If more than one factor proved significant and the factors were orthogonal, it would have to be concluded that the character is not a unity – but that some so-called components are actually independent functions.

Design of the questionnaire. As we have stated, items were prepared to correspond to the fourteen selected anal characteristics. For each trait the aim was to present a wide range of manifestations or examples, in the hope thereby to increase validity, although this would be at the expense of high reliability.

Initially a large number of items were written, and arranged in scales pertaining to the individual traits. The usual rules were followed: i.e. equal numbers of items suggesting anal and non-anal responses were arranged, the direction of the multiple-choice answer scales being balanced for direction of score. A five-point scale was presented for the subjects, although a median dichotomy was used in the statistical analysis.

From the first stage of item writing a decision as to the *a priori* anal answer was made on the basis of the literature. It is important to note that these interpretations were adhered to without change throughout the study.

Subjects for the preliminary item analysis were seventy-five residential undergraduate students (thirty-five men and forty women) in the Queen's University of Belfast. They were drawn from all departments of study.

Item analysis. (a) Distributions of responses on the five-point scale were obtained in order to arrange the dichotomous splits. Items with excessively eccentric splits were discarded; the limit being 75:25 per cent. (b) Subjects were scored for the number of anal responses, by items and by trait subscales, according to the predetermined scheme. (c) Tetrachoric correlations were computed between dichotomized subscale scores and the items within each subscale. Hamilton's (sixteen) nomograms were used for this and all other computation of tetrachoric correlations.

On the basis of the consistency analysis a selection of twenty-eight items (the two showing highest consistency with the scale total in each scale) was made, to serve as the final '*A*' questionnaire. The mean r_t for the selected items was $+0.71$, and the range $+0.93$ to $+0.51$. Table 4 presents the content of these items.

A validation technique. It is an often-stated view that self-ratings obtained in the usual way with paper-and-pencil tests, may refer essentially only to the verbal habits of the subject and therefore may have little connexion with his actual behavior. To test this hypothesis, to check the self-rating information for the experimental population, data was obtained not only from the subjects themselves but from their associates. That is, peer ratings were employed to supplement self-ratings.

Subjects for the final analysis were fifty-five men and sixty-five women undergraduates, again at Queen's University, and at a Belfast teachers' training college, all of whom had lived together in residence halls for at least one year. The testing took place in their free time in the halls and each subject received a small payment for the work involved, which took about one hour.

In order to collect the equivalent information in both the self-rating and the rating media in the most efficient way; and in order that the ratings should be tied as far as possible to objective concepts, the following scheme was devised.

Subjects were gathered together in groups of twenty, and then divided into fives by taking adjacent names in alphabetical order. (The latter procedure ensured that friends and 'enemies' were randomly distributed.) All groups were homogeneous with respect to sex. Each subject answered the questions for himself in the usual way and for the four other members of the group in the way that he thought was *true for them* (that is, not necessarily as they themselves would answer).

The administration of the questionnaire was carried out by the author in an informal atmosphere. The subjects were instructed to answer each item for all five members of their group rather than all items for one person at a time; and a short general discussion of the need for objectivity and the danger of the halo effect was presented.

In this way directly comparable scores were obtained for each subject from himself and from four peers who knew him reasonably well. For the purpose of our check on the validity of the self-ratings, the scores in the two media were now subjected to the same analysis (i.e. intercorrelation and factor analysis) with the aim of comparing the factor or factors emerging.

The statistical analysis. Self-Rating (SR) *analysis.* The twenty-eight items were scored in the usual way and a split-half consistency coefficient computed correlating the first half of the questionnaire with the second. The product-moment correlation coefficient, Spearman–Brown corrected, was found to be $+0.62$ ($N = 120$).

Table 1 shows the item intercorrelation matrix, constructed using tetrachoric correlations. From an inspection of the SR data on Table 3 it is clear that the matrix is definitely non-random and skewed in the positive direction. By the first, preliminary test our structural hypothesis is confirmed.

A centroid factor analysis was carried out on the 28×28 matrix; the procedure of Guilford (1936) being followed.

The factors obtained and their significance. There seems as yet to be no one generally accepted criterion for the significance or otherwise of centroid factors, even when rotation is not carried

129

Table 1

Intercorrelations of ' A ' Questionnaire Items (Self-Rating Medium)

	1	2	3	4	5	6	7	8	9	10	11	12	13	14	15	16	17	18	19	20	21	22	23	24	25	26	27	28
1																												
2	11																											
3	14	−25																										
4	23	29	08																									
5	32	07	14	20																								
6	10	−13	26	−04	14																							
7	21	−06	38	06	15	36																						
8	22	29	−10	19	11	11	−13																					
9	03	46	30	−09	15	−03	−05	36																				
10	−03	−01	−01	11	14	18	03	37	34																			
11	11	21	21	33	17	18	01	14	37	13																		
12	32	05	34	−10	−11	−07	29	04	20	44	09																	
13	36	02	00	03	12	28	05	28	28	19	33	17																
14	50	01	10	18	−06	34	03	39	18	30	10	02	31															
15	29	−11	01	03	23	−13	−03	−09	−12	17	14	03	13	08														
16	22	41	16	19	19	02	08	−22	23	52	25	37	36	−02	−04													
17	15	40	−01	15	05	36	06	06	−07	03	24	09	11	07	03	36												
18	16	16	16	33	−03	28	08	31	10	16	24	04	06	06	03	11	02											
19	19	05	05	22	14	28	07	−17	−07	13	08	04	07	06	00	28	43	22										
20	41	−03	15	11	−01	61	24	20	10	20	27	28	26	43	−10	−10	22	−13	13									
21	29	14	11	05	06	06	20	20	29	25	27	03	24	04	14	61	09	−22	10	09								
22	−12	14	14	19	14	−23	−19	−03	03	12	26	53	19	33	04	71	05	18	09	23	−03							
23	30	19	27	16	13	13	00	−07	−01	27	21	18	07	07	−06	02	−04	09	14	06	05	25						
24	40	19	16	10	16	−03	05	18	−06	−01	42	12	13	30	13	09	05	15	03	11	10	26	07					
25	09	28	15	27	33	−03	05	−05	−01	18	−03	11	34	13	01	71	13	21	04	15	43	27	−25	30				
26	−18	−02	−06	04	−06	05	05	01	−06	17	26	26	08	19	01	09	−08	04	26	26	10	45	−14	−04	12			
27	−03	−21	21	04	05	29	27	−01	−25	23	07	38	08	−06	09	38	15	30	33	00	12	24	−07	41	44	14		
28	−07	−18	−15	28	04	36	−08	47	−03	16	−11	13	−04	04	−05	−08	−13	11	03	24	26	22	−20	28	26	52	33	

Note: See Table 4 for item contents.

Table 2

Intercorrelations of 'A' Questionnaire Items (Rating Medium)

	1	2	3	4	5	6	7	8	9	10	11	12	13	14	15	16	17	18	19	20	21	22	23	24	25	26	27	28
1																												
2	32																											
3	37	09																										
4	20	−06	13																									
5	−25	−20	03	40																								
6	−04	19	10	10	17																							
7	−07	10	19	10	09	−03																						
8	14	52	−11	17	−33	28	−09																					
9	42	32	32	25	−21	24	−08	49																				
10	27	33	30	15	−29	27	08	27	38																			
11	−06	18	12	−02	00	57	05	15	26	31																		
12	49	24	32	00	−29	−27	05	−03	−08	−04	−18																	
13	47	28	25	17	−21	51	15	42	27	21	31	22																
14	−07	−02	−06	36	05	05	05	49	30	36	58	−23	33															
15	19	−11	−13	13	−03	03	08	24	43	03	49	04	56	38														
16	14	−02	04	06	19	37	08	07	32	56	67	17	15	63	10													
17	17	39	07	06	18	06	25	10	31	01	24	16	16	19	−17	14												
18	55	39	34	26	−22	24	21	18	27	22	08	43	06	13	16	34	13											
19	18	07	04	31	62	36	02	38	31	02	02	00	13	00	−04	10	19	01										
20	−09	01	04	25	28	23	02	25	39	16	24	11	34	06	13	13	30	00	50									
21	35	15	33	26	02	11	17	32	38	−05	25	24	30	00	15	37	41	32	26	43								
22	20	03	08	17	−13	27	26	10	25	35	25	45	41	00	06	22	−06	20	00	08	12							
23	03	21	21	24	−06	26	22	23	31	47	57	07	53	06	08	56	25	67	15	20	31	09						
24	35	36	13	04	−19	13	16	21	39	−04	46	22	43	53	19	46	13	45	10	44	30	00	19					
25	11	11	−04	04	16	23	22	21	38	21	03	03	32	32	19	39	37	32	−03	33	07	−14	02	59				
26	54	28	41	16	−27	26	13	25	20	20	43	60	51	13	05	−05	−03	51	27	21	56	50	45	30	26			
27	05	30	30	30	−06	23	22	21	20	−06	19	04	32	25	−01	20	−02	24	−02	−08	10	36	32	11	−15	33		
28	17	07	−08	09	15	−05	03	−15	−20	−06	24	32	19	−01	15	01	18	09	23	00	34	−05	−06	−17	01	35	−03	

Note: See Table 4 for item contents.

out. In this study the recent modification by Cureton (1955) of Burt's (1946–7) most often-used formula was followed. We consider it provides the most efficient and cautious guide.

Burt's formula is designed for the computation of the standard error of a particular loading on successively extracted factors. Cureton has generalized it, so that a standard error applying to the whole factor is obtained. Then following Vernon (1950), Cureton states that a factor will be significant if and only if, more than half of its loadings are greater than this standard error, denoted by a'.

Table 3

Significance of the SR and R Correlation Matrices

No. of correlations above 1 per cent level:	SR = 30 R = 65 (4)*
No. of negative correlations:	SR = 89 R = 78 (189)*

Note: Using McNemar's (1949, p. 177) approximate formula for SE of r_t and assuming p′ and q′ = $\frac{1}{2}$. $N = 120$, $n = 378$.
* Values in parentheses are the expected number on the chance hypothesis.

In the self-rating medium one general factor emerged, with twenty-two out of its twenty-eight loadings above the value of a'; for the second bipolar factor only eight of the loadings were above its a' value. Clearly, only the first factor is to be accounted for by other than chance variation. The general factor then is the only significant one to emerge.

The pattern of item loadings on Factor 1 is shown in Table 4. General discussion of the implications of this result will be deferred until after the presentation of the rating analysis.

Rating (R) *analysis.* Numerical values 1–5 were assigned to the five possible grades of answer and mean scores were computed for the rated answer of each item for each individual. That is, each subject received a score for each item which was a mean of the answers attributed to him by his four peers. The procedure then followed in every respect that described above for the SR data.

The split-half consistency coefficient here was +0·86 ($N = 120$). It will be noted that this figure is somewhat higher than the SR coefficient – a possible explanation may be that our impressions

Table 4

Self-Rating Medium, Factor I

Item no.	Loading	
16	0·677	Often in the position to say, 'I told you so.' (0·681)*
10	0·505	Takes an active part in family affairs, even to the extent of being considered 'bossy'. (0·465)
24	0·483	Enjoys the sense of power which comes from a victory of his will over other people's. (0·645)
13	0·483	Annoyed to hear people express strong opinions, because they seldom know enough about the subject being discussed. (0·613)
1	0·483	Feels that unpunctuality is one of *the* most annoying social vices. (0·490)
11	0·468	Would often get real pleasure telling people what he thought of them. (0·488)
20	0·463	Has 'off days', when friends say he must have got out of the wrong side of the bed. (0·597)
4	0·436	Agrees that it is necessary for a housewife to have everything 'just so'. (0·309)
27	0·425	Blames newspapers very much for distorting the news in order to make a better story. (0·298)
12	0·420	Does not find it difficult to see a job through to the end. (0·238)
25	0·419	Admits that sometimes revenge is sweet. (0·369)
21	0·414	Dislikes lending books and other possessions. (0·596)
22	0·411	Is often the last to give up trying to do a thing. (0·286)
14	0·394	Becomes stubborn when others interfere with his way of doing things, even when there is something in what they say. (0·525)
3	0·373	Agrees that in modern life there is an awful lot of waste of time, of energy, of money. (0·340)
19	0·372	Often spends so long working out the best way to do things, the actual doing gets delayed. (0·379)

Note: When $N = 120$, $n = 28$, $s = 1$; $a' = 0·304$.

* Figures in parentheses are the loadings on the Rating Medium Factor I.

Table 4 (*continued*)

Item no.	Loading	
9	0·366	Would not eat a biscuit which had fallen on the floor. (0·570)
18	0·330	Feels uncomfortable when looking at a crooked picture on the wall. (0·689)
26	0·329	Sets himself high standards, compared with acquaintances. (0·758)
5	0·326	Has often lost out on things because he did not make up his mind soon enough. (−0·039)
6	0·324	Although he tries to remain calm and even-tempered things do often occur which upset him. (0·515)
8	0·305	When he needs to buy something, goes on looking and looking until he finds just the right thing. (0·416)
28	0·284	Prefers to work alone rather than with a group. (0·127)
23	0·271	Agrees that 'cleanliness is next to godliness'. (0·465)
17	0·266	Agrees that a man's first duty is to make enough money to look after his family really well, personal work preferences come after this. (0·323)
2	0·256	Is often amazed at the muddles other people get into. (0·411)
7	0·220	Would rather buy a record than a ticket for a concert. (0·163)
15	0·066	Does not agree that there is usually a good reason for people being late for an appointment. (0·206)

of other people are more homogeneous than our own view of ourselves. The correlation matrix was again found to be non-random and positively skewed (see Tables 2 and 3). The centroid analysis, too, yielded again only one significant factor. On this first, general factor twenty-one item loadings were above a', while on the second factor only ten were (see Table 4).

The relationship of the Self-Rating and Rating factors. We have seen now that the results in both media are formally similar. Each of the matrices was positively skewed and significant, and further, the first general factor was sufficient in each case to account for the intercorrelations. More specifically to investigate the validity of the self-rating result, scores on the two first factors were correlated. In both media items with no appreciable loading at all (one on each factor) were ignored, and all others considered to have the same loading, i.e. they contributed one unweighted point each.

The product-moment correlation between SR Factor I and R Factor I was found to be $+0.48$ (corrected for attenuation, $N = 120$). This value is not high, but having regard to the relatively small number of subjects and the fact that the correlation is nevertheless significant beyond the 0.01 per cent level of confidence, we may conclude that the factors are basically similar.

Having established this similarity of the two results, no further description of the rating data is necessary, while we may continue with the discussion of the self-rating result, on the assumption that we have some information about actual behavior.

Conclusions. On the basis of the analysis then it may be concluded that the intercorrelations of a set of items corresponding to anal traits are essentially positive and are to be accounted for by only one general factor (see Table 3).

Further, using the initial *a priori* scoring system based on the psychoanalytic literature and without further modification of sign, all the loadings on this Factor I are positive, as shown on Table 4. All but one loading are appreciable. This single general factor confirms the first hypothesis, that the characteristics under consideration form a syndrome in a positive way. There is not evidence to suggest, for example, that the postulated early and late anal stages give rise to distinct character formations.

What then of the detailed structure of the factor, how does the pattern of item loadings correspond to the analytic picture? To some extent it seems that the character should be reinterpreted or described with different emphasis. The items with highest loadings imply traits such as: superiority, desire to domineer, quasi-sadism, irritability, conscientiousness and *Eigensinn*. This would seem to confirm Jones' stress on sadism, feelings of omnipotence, contempt for others, and the need for power over them.

The qualities of parsimony, cleanliness and collecting propensities on the other hand contribute less variance than the literature would have led one to predict.

It has been noted that the correspondence of the SR and R factors is by no means perfect. Therefore the SR factor does not perhaps warrant more specific interpretation; we would suggest only the general trend is for the items pertaining to compulsive control over others and feelings of personal superiority, as well as *Eigensinn*, to appear more salient in the anal character as manifested in normal personality than some writers have suggested.

The anal factor and introversion. As has been indicated, the anal character has been envisaged as the result of the overlearning of certain precepts connected with the cleanliness practices and values of our culture. Now the causal background of the manifest dimension of introversion–extraversion has recently been investigated, notably by Eysenck (1955). He has shown that introvert subjects are those in whom reactive inhibition is generated slowly and is dissipated quickly. From this inhibition theory it can be predicted that introverts would condition relatively quickly and this indeed is the case. The further implications are then that the introversion-extraversion dimension may be conceived as one of relative socialisation. Obsessionals providing the paradigm of the oversocialised introvert and psychopaths that of the unsocialised extravert.

From these premises certain hypotheses may be made concerning the relationship between the high '*A*' scores on the present questionnaire and measures of introversion. To this end, and at the instigation of Professor H. J. Eysenck, correlations were run between certain scores on the Guilford Test of Factors *S*, *T*, *D*, *C* and *R* and the approximate factor scores (SR) on the '*A*' questionnaire. It was hypothesized that there would be a negative correlation with *R* (rhathymia or freedom from care); and a positive one with the two measures of introversion, *S* (social introversion) and *T* (thinking introversion).

Subjects were sixty-four undergraduate students (thirty-six

men and twenty-eight women), some of whom also acted as subjects for the testing of Hypothesis II. The obtained product-moment correlations were: $+0.16$ with R; -0.06 with S; and $+0.34$ (significant at 1 per cent level) with T. With regard to the hypotheses, this result must be regarded as inconclusive.

It may be mentioned here that Barnes (1952) has reported correlations between his anal factor or factors (see p. 125) and those of the Guilford–Zimmerman test. With the meticulous anal factor no values were found to be significant, and with the aggression factor, which also contained anal components, a *positive* correlation with rhathymia is reported.

However, even if the hypotheses presented above are too crude, it is of obvious importance that the place of the anal character in the generally acknowledged dimensions of personality be known, and further exploratory correlational work must be the first step to this knowledge.

Investigation of the Etiological Hypothesis

Hypothesis II: that anal characteristics in the adult are related to bowel training experiences in infancy

For the purpose of testing this hypothesis the only feature of the coercive-permissive bowel training variable considered was the time in infancy when training had been completed. That is to say, relatively early training was considered coercive and relatively late training permissive. The reason for employing this crude measure will be obvious when it is realized that in work with adult subjects, the situation in question will have taken place about twenty years ago. Qualitative information, if available, would in these circumstances be likely to involve so much error as to make it worthless.

In defense of the validity of this reduction we would cite two other relevant studies. Huschka (1942), in her early study of this etiological problem with young children, cited physiological-anatomical evidence to show that early training (started before eight months and completed before eighteen months) must be considered coercive in that the child is physically not yet able to learn. Whiting and Child (1953), in their previously mentioned cultural study, correlated the variables of severity of socialization and age, finding the coefficient to be − 0·52 (which is said to be significant).

In the present investigation the score of the subjects on the 'A' questionnaire was related to the age at which bowel training was reported by the mother to be completed. Moreover a further relationship was considered. In order to compare the relative variance contributed by the variable considered essential by analysts, with that considered important by psychologists in general, the score on the 'A' questionnaire was obtained for the mothers of the subjects.

This design allowed for the comparison of the relative predictive powers of these two independent variables, namely, the one 'crucial' experience in infancy (measured by the age of subject when bowel training was said to be completed); and the influence of the whole attitude of the mother upon this complex of character traits (as measured by the score of the mother score, on the 'A' questionnaire).

It is possible to anticipate several results: (a) Only the time of training variable might contribute significant variance to the dependent variable, the present score of subject; (b) only the score of the mother might be significant in this connexion; (c) only the interaction term might be significant (potting × M-score); (d) any combination of these terms, or none, might prove significant. It may be noted here that the interaction hypothesis is often put forward as it provides, of course, a *rapprochement* between the holistic and the specific point of view. Miles (1954) has recently advocated this.

Subjects for this part of the study were forty-three graduate students (twenty-two men and twenty-one women) at Queen's University working for the Diploma in Education. They completed the self-rating form of the 'A' questionnaire as a routine part of class procedure. Permission to interview the mothers was obtained from the students. At the time of the visit the investigation was introduced as a study on the similarities and differences between mothers and their children.

From our point of view then the purpose of the interview was to elicit information about toilet training histories and to enable the mother to complete the questionnaire. However, for purely diplomatic reasons, the interview incorporated many other questions along the usual case-history lines about the subjects' development.

It is estimated that at least two-thirds of the mothers gave a date of completed training readily and with the impression of a relatively clear memory for this stage in the life of their child. The others were also able to give a date, but only with reference to some other event, for example, three months after the beginning of walking, the date of the latter event being remembered. Only one mother declined to make any sort of estimate. In the analysis no weighting was given with regard to the relative confidence with which the information was given.

Table 5

Analysis of Background Variables

Toilet training:	Early		Late	
M-score:	Above median	Below median	Above median	Below median
	9	11	19	9
	18	9	14	17
	12	11	17	9
	10	18	13	8
	16	10	15	7
	19	10	15	13
	19	10	13	7
	16	12	15	15
	10	9	11	12
	13	14	13	12
	(14)			(15)

Note: The Bartlett test for homogeneity of variance yielded a non-significant chi square.

Source	Sum of squares	df	Mean square	F
Between groups	104·60	3	34·87	3·52
Within groups	357·40	36	9·93	
Toilet training	9·60	1	9·60	
M-score	102·80	1	102·80	10·35
Interaction $T \times M$	1·20	1	1·20	
Within groups	357·40	36	9·93	

The data. The range of ages at which bowel training was reported as complete was found to be eight to twenty-four months, the median falling at 13·22 months. The subjects were therefore divided into an early group (complete at thirteen months and earlier) and a late group (later than thirteen months).

For the '*A*' questionnaire the mothers' median score fell at twelve answers in the anal direction with a range of six to twenty-one. The mothers were here divided into two groups of high and low scorers respectively, again at the median.

The analysis. A 2×2 analysis of variance test was run, as shown in Table 5. It will be seen that the hypothesis of random sampling from a common population must be rejected, and the data provides definite support for the inference that the score of the mother contributes the only significant variance with regard to the present score of the subjects on the questionnaire concerning so-called anal characteristics.

The product-moment correlation between mother and subject scores was found to be $+0·51$ (corrected for attenuation, significant at 0·1 per cent level); that between subject score and age at completed toilet training, $+0·05$.

Conclusions and Discussion of the Results

From our data we may claim that in factorial terms the anal character has been shown to exist; or in other terms, that the syndrome is a meaningful dimension of variation for the description of our subjects' responses. It is clear, too, that the extent to which the individual character manifests these particular components is related significantly to the degree to which the same components are exhibited by the mother. Contrary to analytic writing, however, in our sample it is not related to bowel training experiences.

It must, of course, be acknowledged that a null result for a hypothesis such as the present second, etiological one, cannot in itself be considered as showing that no relationship such as was postulated exists; but only that it has not been demonstrated in this case.

Psychoanalysts will doubtless take the latter point of view, pointing out two apparently important sources of error that may have masked the 'true' relationship that in their view exists.

1. It may be that time of completed bowel training was too crude a single measure of coercive practice. We, however, would again stress the correlation obtained by Whiting and Child (1953) between severity of training and relatively early age at training, found over a wide range of cultures.

2. The time interval between the event of training and the mothers' attempt to recall it for our benefit, was about twenty years, and hence the recall may not be at all accurate. It will be remembered, however, that the ages given for our group provided their own norms with regard to what was considered early and late respectively. Hence only differential error in the age estimation (between coercive and permissive mothers) would be relevant error here.

It is admitted that together or singly these, and indeed other factors, may have contributed enough error variance to provide the null result. However, supported by the above arguments and the general null results reported by Whiting and Child (1953) for the influence of early anal experience on later personality manifestations, we should consider that the postulated correlation between early bowel training and a high degree of anal characteristics exhibited by adults is not valid. Alternative etiological explanations must therefore be examined.

Innate, constitutional background

It may be that the factor of innately heightened erotism associated with the anal zone does play the large part in the formation of the character which Freud (1908) originally attributed to it. This would account for the variation in scores on the questionnaire, and therefore for the appearances of our factor; while at the same time producing no relationship with toilet training. Then, assuming that the individual differences in strength of initial anal erotism are an inherited feature, we may account for the correlation with the mother.

Although this specific explanation is not proven by our results, neither, of course, can our results be used logically to refute it.

Eclectic learning theory

Orlansky (1949), in his evaluation of the Freudian etiological hypotheses, presents a general cultural theory of the transmission and formation of personality traits. He has this to say about the anal character (1949, p. 20):

> Obedience, punctuality, cleanliness, hoarding and the other 'anal' character traits are certainly inculcated into the child by middle-class parents of capitalist society, this syndrome of traits being in part historically associated with the Protestant virtues which were so well rewarded during the rise of capitalism, and having also an independent culture-history of their own. In these terms, the origin of the anal character can be understood as an adjustment of the individual on the level of personality to the concrete economic and cultural conditions.[1]

From the point of view of cultural utility, it is certainly true that most of the anal traits are functional. As Orlansky has suggested, if we assume the basic premise of a competitive, materialistic society and life in cities, they lead to efficiency in group enterprise and to success for the individual. It will be noted however that certain components, such as irritability and procrastination, cannot be considered functional even with this premise. Tentatively it would have to be suggested that they represent resultant by-products of the overlearning of the other traits.

In general then it may be considered that parents will try in various degrees to inculcate anal traits into their children. Behavior conforming to these parental values will be rewarded by them, and behavior fitted to the needs of society will be further rewarded

1. Quentin Bell (1948, p. 76) has made the same point: '. . . in Holland, in England, in the Scandinavian countries, and in the United States soap and water have marched hand in hand with protestantism, commerce, expansion, industry, and a sober but spotless attire. Whether it be that the result of tireless scrubbing is pleasing to those who set industry high among the virtues, while dirt is considered shiftless, feckless, unprincipled, and insolvent, I do not pretend to say. But there would certainly seem to be some affinity between the bourgeoisie and the bath. Among the catholic peoples on the other hand and wherever a more or less feudal society persists, stinks are in evidence, but of small account, and dirt a frequent concomitant of sumptuosity.'

by it. Some empirical confirmation of this is provided by Miller and Stine (1951) in their study, referred to earlier, of social acceptance and the degree of 'pre-genitality' exhibited by children. They report that in contrast to the other traits, such as oral and phallic, children who scored high on anal traits were chosen as friends and work partners more often than low scorers and rejected less frequently. They concluded that at least during the latency period, anal characteristics are social assets.

If we consider the anal characteristics as functional and also, as Kardiner (1939, p. 44) and Orlansky do, essentially the result of obedience to cultural demands in childhood, as enforced conformity in fact; then surely the origins, significance and relationships of the so-called anal character must be considered all anew. Then, for example, the relationship of the character to what is known as the conforming personality and many of its manifestations becomes important.

The childhood background of compulsive conformers has already been postulated, even if not fully explored. Hoffman (1953, p. 383) has written:

One origin of compulsive conformity lies in childhood experiences with parents of their equivalents who are punitive, strict, coercive and dominantly overprotective. The child is punished for expressing and attempting to gratify pleasurable impulses and prevented from exploring the environment at his own pace. At the same time, he is forced to behave in the manner prescribed by his parents though alien to his own needs and perhaps beyond his capacities.

In the background then, of the anal character and the conforming personality, similar considerations have been adduced.

However, it must be immediately apparent that early conformity as it applies to our subjects does not lead to simple conformity in adult life. There is some evidence (Barnes, 1952) that a certain kind of conformity, namely law abidance, is homogeneous with anal meticulousness; but obstinacy, self-willedness and defiance are cardinal components of the character. It seems rather that conformity and self-willedness must be considered two distinct patterns of response characteristics of different individual reactions to previously enforced obedience.

Here we may cite the study of Hoffman (1953) again. Subjects were given the opportunity to shift their perceptual judgement

143

reports with reference to a pseudo group norm. Some shifted in order to conform, some persisted in their previous responses and others reacted with a shift in judgement *away* from the presented norm. It is the latter 'rebellious non-conformists' who would appear to be our anal characters with their marked individuality and resentment to outside interference, and it is unfortunate that Hoffman did not choose to investigate them as well as the conformers.

Clearly future work would profitably be concerned with the problem of the place of the anal character in relation to other personality dimensions, with its specific etiology, and then indeed with the question of a more apposite name.

Summary

The present paper is an account of an experimental investigation of the psychoanalytic theory of the anal character. The theory states that the infant derives erogenous pleasure from his bowel movements and that, when this is inhibited by coercive toilet training, a characteristic personality syndrome results. The syndrome or character is said to consist basically of three traits, parsimony, *Eigensinn* and orderliness. This triad was first pointed out by Freud. Later workers, such as Jones and Abraham, enumerated other component traits. The most salient ones are considered to be the following: punctuality, cleanliness, procrastination, quasi-sadism in personal relations, conscientiousness, pedantry, feelings of superiority, irritability, desire to domineer, desire for personal autonomy.

The analytic postulates on the subject are summarized in two hypotheses, one structural and one etiological:

I. That a psychological, functional entity exists, corresponding to the character as described by psychoanalysts.

II. That anal characteristics in the adult are related to bowel training experiences in infancy.

A questionnaire was designed to provide some measure of the attitudes, opinions and habits which are said to be manifestations of the anal character.

Hypothesis I was tested by a factor analysis of the questionnaire responses (subjects were 120 undergraduate students). One general factor emerged and no other significant factors. The structural proposition then, would seem to have been confirmed. In factorial terms, at least, the anal character may be said to exist.

A validation of this result was attempted. To check the self-rating data, peer ratings were obtained by means of the same questionnaire. Peers answered the questions in the way that they considered the ratees *should* have done. A separate factor analysis of these responses was carried out. Again only the general factor proved accountable for by other than chance variation. The correlation between the self-rating and rating factors was highly significant. It was therefore considered that the rating analysis substantiated the conclusions drawn above.

The relationship of this self-rating anal factor to measures of introversion-extraversion was investigated by means of the Guilford Test of Factors S, T, D, C and R. The correlation with T (thinking introversion) was found to be significant, those with S (social introversion) and R (rhathymia or freedom from care) negligible.

For Hypothesis II the bowel training histories of forty-three postgraduate students was investigated by means of interviews with the mothers. For the purpose of the analysis relatively early completion of training was equated with relatively coercive training. These mothers also completed the above-mentioned questionnaire. The relative predictive powers of the anal score of the mother and the age of completed toilet training, for the score of the student subject, were compared by means of a 2×2 analysis of variance. Only one term proved significant (and that beyond 1 per cent) – the questionnaire score of the mother.

From our data then we may conclude that although the anal character is a meaningful dimension of variation for the description of our subjects' attitudes and behavior, it is not related to toilet training experiences, but strongly to the degree of anal character exhibited by the mother.

These conclusions are strictly applicable only to a young, normal, Northern Ireland population, and our result must therefore be interpreted with caution. However, accepting the results, a discussion of the anal theory is then attempted – in the light of the fact that the so-called anal character would appear to have no

Psychosexual Development and Character Formation

connexion with early anal experience. Alternative etiological positions are appraised and one based on the concept of conformity is tentatively put forward.

References

ABRAHAM, K. (1921), 'Contributions to the theory of anal character', in *Selected Papers on Psycho-Analysis*, Hogarth Press, 1927.

ABRAHAM, K. (1924), 'The influence of oral eroticism on character formation', in *Selected Papers on Psycho-Analysis*, Hogarth Press, 1927.

ANDREAS-SALOME, L. (1916), '"Anal" and "sexual"', *Imago*, vol. 4, pp. 249–73.

BARNES, C. A. (1952), 'A statistical study of the Freudian theory of levels of psychosexual development', *Genet. Psychol. Monog.*, vol. 45, pp. 105–75.

BELL, Q. (1948), *On Human Finery*, Hogarth Press.

BURT, C., and BANKS, C. (1946–7), 'A factor analysis of body measurements for British adult males', *Ann. Eugen.*, vol. 13, pp. 238–55.

CURETON, E. E. (1955), 'A note on the use of Burt's formula for estimating factor significance', *Brit. J. stat. Psychol.*, vol. 8, p. 28.

EYSENCK, H. J. (1955), 'Cortical inhibition, figural after-effect, and theory of personality', *J. abnorm. soc. Psychol.*, vol. 51, pp. 94–106.

FARBER, M. L. (1955), 'The anal character and political aggression', *J. abnorm. soc. Psychol.*, vol. 51, pp. 486–9.

FERENCZI, S. (1914), 'The ontogenesis of the interest in money', in *Contributions to Psychoanalysis*, Badger.

FREUD, S. (1908), 'Character and anal eroticism', in *Collected Papers*, vol. 2, Hogarth Press, 1924, pp. 45–50.

FREUD, S. (1915), 'Three essays on sexuality', in *Complete Works*, vol. 7, Hogarth Press, 1955.

FREUD, S. (1916), 'On the transformation of instincts with special reference to anal eroticism', in *Collected Papers*, vol. 2, Hogarth Press, 1924, pp. 164–71.

GUILFORD, J. P. (1936), *Psychometric Methods*, McGraw-Hill.

HAMILTON, G. V. (1929), *A Research in Marriage*, Boni.

HAMILTON, M. (1948), 'Nomograms for the tetrachoric correlation coefficient', *Psychometrika*, vol. 13, pp. 159–67.

HILGARD, E. R. (1952), 'Experimental approaches', in E. Pumpian-Mindlin (ed.), *Psychoanalysis as Science*, Stanford University Press, pp. 3–24.

HOFFMAN, M. L. (1953), 'Some psychodynamic factors in compulsive conformity', *J. abnorm. soc. Psychol.*, vol. 48, pp. 383–93.

HUSCHKA, M. (1942), 'The child's response to coercive bowel training', *Psychosom. Med.*, vol. 4, pp. 301–8.

JONES, E. (1918), 'Anal erotic character traits', in *Papers on Psycho-Analysis*, 5th edn, Ballière, Tindall & Cox, 1948.

JONES, E. (1923), 'Hate and anal eroticism', in *Papers on Psycho-Analysis*, 3rd edn, Ballière, Tindall & Cox.

KARDINER, A. (1939), *The Individual and His Society*, Columbia University Press.

MCNEMAR, Q. (1949), *Psychological Statistics*, Wiley.

MILES, D. W. (1954), 'The import for clinical psychology of the use of tests derived from theories about infantile sexuality and adult character', *Genet. Psychol. Monog.*, vol. 50, pp. 227–88.

MILLER, D. R., and STINE, M. W. (1951), 'The prediction of social acceptance by means of psychoanalytic concepts', *J. Personal.*, vol. 20, pp. 162–74.

ORLANSKY, H. (1949), 'Infant care and personality', *Psychol. Bull.*, vol. 46, pp. 1–48.

SEARS, R. R. (1943), *Survey of Objective Studies of Psychoanalytic Concepts*, Social Science Research Council, New York.

STAGNER, R., LAWSON, E. D., and MOFFITT, J. W. (1955), 'The Krout Personal Preferences Scale: a factor analytic study', *J. clin. Psychol.*, vol. 11, pp. 103–13.

VERNON, P. E. (1950), 'An application of factor analysis to the study of test items', *Brit. J. Psychol.*, *Stat. Sec.*, vol. 3, pp. 1–15.

WHITING, J. M., and CHILD, I. L. (1953), *Child Training and Personality*, Yale University Press.

7 Gerald S. Blum and Daniel R. Miller

Exploring the Psychoanalytic Theory of the 'Oral Character'

Gerald S. Blum and Daniel R. Miller, 'Exploring the psychoanalytic theory of the "oral character"', *Journal of Personality*, vol. 20, 1952, pp. 287–304.

In these days of sophisticated discussion on how to study psychoanalytic theory we feel somewhat defensive concerning the methods we are about to describe. Not only did we confine ourselves to conventional techniques in psychology's stockpile but we used as many as we could. This approach was designed to test whether the theory *can* be phrased in operational terms amenable to traditional types of experimentation.

The topic we chose to investigate was the theory of 'oral character'. On one hand, there is sufficient agreement in the psychoanalytic literature to provide a starting point from which to formulate hypotheses. On the other, this aspect of the theory is admittedly incomplete. The combination made the area seem especially promising for experimental exploration.

Various clinical manifestations of oral passivity are summarized by Fromm (1947, pp. 62–3) in the following selected excerpts describing what he calls the 'receptive orientation':

In the receptive orientation a person feels 'the source of all good' to be outside, and he believes that the only way to get what he wants – be it something material, be it affection, love, knowledge, pleasure – is to receive it from that outside source. In this orientation the problem of love is almost exclusively that of 'being loved' and not that of loving. . . . They are exceedingly sensitive to any withdrawal or rebuff they experience on the part of the loved person. . . . It is characteristic of these people that their first thought is to find somebody else to give them needed information rather than to make even the smallest effort of their own . . . they are always in search of a 'magic helper'. They show a particular kind of loyalty, at the bottom of which is the gratitude for the hand that feeds them and the fear of ever losing it. Since they need many hands to feel secure, they have to be loyal to numerous people.

It is difficult for them to say 'no', and they are easily caught between conflicting loyalties and promises. Since they cannot say 'no', they love to say 'yes' to everything and everybody, and the resulting paralysis of their critical abilities makes them increasingly dependent on others.

They are dependent not only on authorities for knowledge and help but on people in general for any kind of support. They feel lost when alone because they feel that they cannot do anything without help. . . .

This receptive type has great fondness for food and drink. These persons tend to overcome anxiety and depression by eating or drinking. The mouth is an especially prominent feature, often the most expressive one; the lips tend to be open, as if in a state on continuous expectation of being fed. In their dreams, being fed is a frequent symbol of being loved; being starved, an expression of frustration or disappointment.

Collection of Data

Having delimited our field of investigation, we were then faced with decisions concerning subjects and specific techniques. In regard to subjects, we chose to work with humans rather than animals. Generalizations from animal behavior are largely by way of analogy. Furthermore, the complexities of interpersonal relationships cannot be fully duplicated in animal work. A second decision concerned normal versus abnormal subjects. We chose the former because of the frequently heard objection that a theory derived largely from abnormal subjects must be shown to be applicable to normals. A third decision involved the desired age level of the subjects. The selection finally centered on eight year olds, since children in the latency period have the double advantage of being relatively free of the rampant psychosexual conflicts of earlier childhood on one hand, and of crystallized adult defenses on the other. The experimental group consisted of the eighteen boys and girls in the third grade at the University of Michigan during 1948–9.

To test the hypotheses formulated from the literature, we first had to select a criterion measure of orality. This operational definition consisted of nonpurposive mouth movements recorded at various times over the three-week period of the research. Trained observers followed the children individually during eight two-minute intervals as part of a time-sampling procedure. They tallied such oral activities as thumb-sucking, licking the lips, tongue-rolling and bubbling. In addition to these routine class-room observations, the same activities were noted in an experiment on boredom tolerance (see p. 158). All children were ranked on both measures and a final average ranking computed.[1]

Data on the dependent variables were collected by the following methods: teacher ratings, time-sampling, sociometrics and experimental situations. Wherever feasible, we employed several approaches to test each hypothesis. Since the theory postulates that all individuals fall along a continuum of orality, rank-order correlations (corrected for ties) were calculated to measure the association between variable and criterion.

Testing the Hypotheses

Each of the following sections presents the statement of a hypothesis, the design worked out to test it and the subsequent results.

I. Extreme interest in food

Hypothesis. Since the oral character is emotionally involved with eating beyond the dictates of simple hunger, he will consume extreme amounts of oral supplies and evince great interest in related activities. Accordingly, positive correlations are predicted between the orality criterion (mouth movements) and variables measuring interest in food.

Methods. 1. Ice-cream consumption. Our measure of consumption of oral supplies was the amount of ice-cream eaten after hunger satiation. The children all ate lunch together. The meal, provided by the school, was dietically planned and ample for all the children. Upon conclusion of a short rest period which followed lunch, they were offered an unlimited supply of vanilla ice cream contained in one-ounce paper cups packaged especially for the study. The carton of ice-cream was placed on a table in the center of the room

1. These two measures of mouth movements correlated 0·61 with each other.

by a female graduate student who supervised the distribution of cups. Each child was allowed to take one whenever he wished. However, only one cup at a time was permitted and that in return for an empty one. No limit was placed on how much a child ate. The carton was kept in the room for the entire forty minutes devoted to arts and crafts, during which period observers recorded the exact number of cups consumed by each child. This procedure was repeated daily over three weeks. From these data averages were computed. The range in any one day's session was quite startling, varying all the way from no cups to thirty-nine for a single child. The absence of any parental complaints concerning illness or lack of appetite was a pleasant surprise in view of the inability of the observers, even at the end of the most frustrating days of the experiment, to eat more than five or six cups without discomfort.

2. Eagerness at lunch time. The regular teacher and five practice teachers were given a scale describing various kinds of behavior typical of oral children. They were asked to write the names of the children who occurred to them spontaneously as they read each of fourteen items.[2] At the completion of the form they were asked to reconsider each item and to increase all shorter lists of names to five. Among the questions was: 'Which children appear most impatient to eat at lunch time, as if eating were particularly important to them?'

2. Following is the complete list of questions: (a) Which children do you think get discouraged or give up most easily when something is difficult for them? (b) Which children do you think are most able to take care of themselves without the help of adults or other children? (c) Which children get the blues most often? (d) Which children would you most like to take with you on a two-week vacation? (e) Which children tend to ask the teacher for help most often, even when they know how to do the task? (f) Which children are most eager to have other children like them? (g) Which children display their affections most openly to the teachers? (h) Which children's feelings seem to be most easily hurt? (i) Which children seem to be always eager to help even when they are inconvenienced? (j) Which children seem to accept the suggestions of others almost without thinking twice? (k) Which children appear most impatient to eat at lunch time, as if eating were particularly important to them? (l) Which children make a special effort to get the teachers to like them? (m) Which children would you least like to take with you on a two-week vacation? (n) Which children seem most concerned with giving and receiving things?

Results. These figures strongly support the predicted association between orality (mouth movements) and interest in food.

Table 1

Mouth movements		
1. Ice-cream	0·52	$P < 0.05$
2. Eagerness at lunch time	0·51	$P < 0.05$

II. Need for liking and approval

Hypothesis. In terms of the theory, a significant relationship should be found between degree of orality and the need for liking and approval.

Methods. 1. 'Which children are most eager to have other children like them?' (Teacher item 6)

2. 'Which children make a special effort to get the teachers to like them?' (Teacher item 12)

3. Approaches to teachers for approval. (Time-sampling item)

4. Approaches to children for approval. (Time-sampling item)

5. Attention to observers. (Time-sampling item)

Viewing these correlations as a whole, the hypothesis seems to be fairly well supported. Although only two are significant beyond the 10 per cent level, all are in the positive direction.

Table 2

Mouth movements		
1. Eagerness for others' liking	0·68	$P < 0.01$
2. Efforts for teachers' liking	0·10	not significant
3. Approaches to teachers for approval	0·44	$P < 0.10$
4. Approaches to children for approval	0·24	not significant
5. Attention to observers	0·36	$P < 0.20$

III. Dependency

Hypothesis. Closely allied to the preceding hypothesis is the prediction of a positive correlation between orality and dependency.

Methods. 1. 'Which children do you think are most able to take care of themselves without the help of adults or other children?' (Teacher item 2)

2. 'Which children tend to ask the teacher for help most often, even when they know how to do the task?' (Teacher item 5)

Results

Table 3

Mouth movements		
1. Doesn't take care of self	0·50	$P < 0·05$
2. Asks teachers' help	0·10	not significant

These results tend to be equivocal, with one correlation being significant and the other not.

IV. Concern over giving and receiving

Hypothesis. Since gifts represent a form of 'supplies' to the oral character, it is predicted that concern over giving and receiving varies with degree of orality.

Methods. 1. 'Which children seem most concerned with giving and receiving things?' (Teacher item 14)

2. Generosity without promise of supplies in return. A related prediction held that oral children would be reluctant to give unless attractive supplies were forthcoming. After the distribution of ice-cream on the second gift day (see section 3 immediately following) the class was allowed to use the colored pencils in a drawing period. Shortly before the end of this session, a strange adult wearing a large, yellow badge marked 'pencil drive' entered the room and made a very stirring appeal to give as many pencils as possible to the poor children of the neighborhood. Each child then went behind a screen and secretly deposited his pencils in the slot of a colorful box marked 'pencil drive'. All the new pencils had been marked with pin points, so that the contributions of each subject were readily identifiable. Unfortunately, this coding system was of little aid since only three in the entire class gave new

pencils. The rest of the collection consisted of a variegated assortment of battered, chewed-up stumps with broken points – all without identification marks. In order to locate the pencil contributors, a new procedure was developed which provided the basis for the added experiment described in section 4 following.

3. Gifts as the equivalent of food. The term 'oral supplies' connotes, in addition to food, tokens of personal recognition. It was hypothesized that, if gifts and food are equivalent supplies, receipt of gifts should result in a diminution of ice-cream consumption for the group as a whole. On one occasion the children were each given a box of crayons; another time they received seven colored pencils which they had chosen as their most desired gift in a rating session the preceding day.

4. Guilt over not giving. The theory leads to the prediction that guilt, typically experienced as a deprivation of supplies, should bring about an increase in the consumption of ice-cream. The day after the pencil drive, the teacher agreed to deliver a stern lecture telling how ashamed she was of their stinginess. She was so effective that, before she finished, one boy blurted out that he had meant to give more new pencils and ran to the box to deposit a few. Next the teacher asked the group to retrieve their donations and observers tallied the number of pencils each pupil took back, which provided the data missing in section 2 above. Shortly afterward the ice-cream was distributed and the number of cups counted as usual.

To relieve the guilt, the pencil solicitor returned later to proclaim happily that the school drive had been 100 per cent successful. He then apologized for not having announced previously that old pencils were not wanted.

Results

Table 4

Mouth movements		
1. Concern over giving and receiving	0·46	$P < 0·10$
2. Lack of generosity	0·22	not significant

3. Gifts as the equivalent of food. On the crayon day, fourteen of the sixteen subjects decreased in the number of cups consumed

($\chi^2 = 9\cdot00$, $P < 0\cdot01$); and on the pencil day, twelve out of fifteen dropped ($\chi^2 = 5\cdot40$, $P < 0\cdot02$).

4. Guilt over not giving. While there were no significant increases in the actual amount of ice-cream consumed after the 'guilt' lecture, certain qualitative observations were noted. The five most oral children in the group sat on the table next to the ice-cream carton throughout the whole period, in contrast to their usual wandering around the room. Since they had apparently been eating up to maximum physical capacity, it was virtually impossible for them to eat significantly more cups than before. Another exceptional feature was the fact that none of the ice-cream was left over this time.

Considering the above experiments as a whole, there seems to be fair support for the hypothesis that orality is related to concern over giving and receiving.

V. Need to be ingratiating

Hypothesis. The oral character, by virtue of his never-ending search for love and approval, tends to behave towards others in a very ingratiating manner.

Methods. 1. 'Which children display their affections most openly to the teachers?' (Teacher item 7)

2. 'Which children seem to be always eager to help even when they are inconvenienced?' (Teacher item 9)

3. Going out of way to do favors. (Time-sampling item)

Results

Table 5

Mouth movements		
1. Displays affection openly	−0·28	not significant
2. Always eager to help	−0·24	not significant
3. Goes out of way to do favors	0·16	not significant

These results clearly negate the predicted association between orality and the need to be ingratiating.

VI. Social isolation

Hypothesis. According to the theory, the oral character should be infrequently chosen by his peers in view of his passivity, his excessive demands for attention and his hostility when these demands are not gratified.

Methods. In a private interview each child was asked to answer a number of sociometric questions to determine his favorites among his classmates: (a) 'Which children in your classroom do you like best?' (b) 'Which of the children in your classroom would you most like to invite to a party?' (c) 'Which teachers do you like the most?'[3] (d) 'Which children in your class are you good friends with?' Class members were then ranked according to the number of times their names had been mentioned.

Results

Table 6

Mouth movements		
1. Social isolation	0·68	$P < 0.01$

This correlation strongly supports the theoretical deduction that orality and social isolation go hand in hand.

VII. Inability to divide loyalties

Hypothesis. The theory leads to the hypothesis that the more oral child has greater difficulty choosing between two friends, inasmuch as both represent potential sources of supply.

Methods. Several days after the sociometric ratings a measure of divided loyalty was obtained. Each child was interviewed individually and asked to make a number of choices between his two best friends as noted on the sociometric ratings and also between his two best-liked teachers. The interviewer recorded decision time plus comments, actions and expressive movements. The protocols were then rated blindly by three judges for degree of indecision.

3. Included only for use in section VII.

Results

Table 7

Mouth movements		
1. Inability to divide loyalties	−0·28	not significant

The correlation of this variable with the criterion contradicts the hypothesized association between orality and the inability to divide loyalties.

VIII. Suggestibility

Hypothesis. From the theory it was anticipated that the oral child, in view of his excessive need for love and approval, would be suggestible in the presence of a potentially supply-giving adult.

Methods. 1. Upon his arrival in the testing room, the child was told: 'We have some things which we want you to help us try out in order to see if they are right for school children of your age.' The experiment consisted of three parts: tasting a hypothetical cherry flavor in candy, smelling perfume from a bottle of water and feeling nonexistent vibrations in a metal rod attached to some apparatus.

2. 'Which children seem to accept the suggestions of others almost without thinking twice?' (Teacher item 10)

Results

Table 8

Mouth movements		
1. Taste	0·50	$P < 0·05$
Touch	0·00	not significant
Smell	0·03	not significant
2. Accepts suggestions	0·11	not significant

Except for taste, suggestibility does not appear to be related to degree of orality. The discrepancy between results with taste and with the other items is most easily accounted for by the specific-ally oral quality of the taste measure.

IX. Depressive tendencies

Hypothesis. Self-esteem in the oral child is presumed to depend upon external sources of love or supplies. Therefore, the unavoidable frustration of oral demands is said to be experienced as a feeling of emptiness or depression.

Methods. 1. 'Which children do you think get discouraged or give up most easily when something is difficult for them?' (Teacher item 1)

2. 'Which children get the blues most often?' (Teacher item 3)

3. 'Which children's feelings seem to be most easily hurt?' (Teacher item 8)

Results
Table 9

Mouth movements		
1. Get discouraged	0·32	$P < 0·20$
2. Get the blues	0·05	not significant
3. Feelings easily hurt	0·13	not significant

The low correlations between mouth movements and personality characteristics relevant to depression do not support the theoretical prediction.

X. Boredom tolerance

Hypothesis. Boredom is assumed to be especially disturbing to the oral child because it signifies a lack of available supplies. Therefore he would be expected to show very little tolerance for a boring, unrewarded activity.

Methods. In this experiment the child was taken into a room where he was shown a large sheaf of papers containing lines of Xs and Os. The examiner then said: 'Your class is being compared with another class in another town to see which class can cross out the most circles.' After giving the instructions, the examiner added:

'There are several pages [the examiner leafed through all the sheets]. Don't write your name on the paper. We don't care how much you yourself can do, but how much the class can do. All right, you may begin.'

The examiner then left the room. As soon as the child began, an observer casually entered the room, sat at a distance, and recorded all the actions of the subject, such as number of mouth movements and work interruptions. The child was stopped after twenty minutes. Ranks were based on number of lines completed. As mentioned previously, this experiment also contributed to the criterion measure of nonbiting mouth movements, which were tallied throughout.

Results

Table 10

Mouth movements		
1. Boredom tolerance	0·45	$P < 0·10$

While not very high, this figure does provide some support for the prediction that orality and boredom tolerance are positively associated.

XI. Summary of results

Ten hypotheses concerning oral character structure have been tested. The results can be summarized in tabular form as in Table 11.

Table 11

Strong support	Fair support	Unsupported	Equivocal
1. Extreme interest in food 2. Social isolation	1. Need for liking and approval 2. Concern over giving and receiving 3. Boredom tolerance	1. Dependency 2. Suggestibility	1. Need to be ingratiating 2. Inability to divide loyalties 3. Depressive tendencies

The goal of this phase of the research is to check the existing status of the theory, and to make revisions wherever dictated by the evidence. The above data represent the initial tests of hypotheses deduced from the psychoanalytic literature on orality. In general, a fair number of predictions have been supported, some remain questionable, and still others are clearly not supported. Before evaluating specific hypotheses, however, we prefer to await the returns from successive attempts to measure the same variables. It is very possible that any of the significant correlations may still reflect the influence of chance factors. Too, any one of the insignificant findings may be a function of faulty experimentation rather than incorrect theory. Both of these possibilities suggest the necessity for repeated research along similar lines. Apart from the fate of specific hypotheses, the over-all results hold promise for the investigation of psychoanalytic theory by conventional psychological methods.

Related Empirical Observations

Intercorrelations of major variables

In addition to providing data concerning specific hypotheses, the study lends itself to an over-all analysis of correlations among the major variables. This supplementary approach seems worthwhile in view of the postulated communality of the variables. If each variable really measures oral passivity, the table of intercorrelations should demonstrate positive relationships beyond chance expectancy. These data, grouped according to pure oral measures, experimental situations and behavioral measures, are shown in Table 12.

From Table 13 we see that the total numbers of significant positive correlations at the 10 per cent, 5 per cent and 1 per cent levels clearly exceed the chance expectancies. These results suggest the possible existence of a general 'factor' of orality.

Comparative evaluation of methodological approaches

Table 14 presents a breakdown of the personality variables into two general types – experimental situations and behavioral measures. The number of significant correlations for each type with the major variables suggests a probable difference in their relative efficacy. It is true that the same operational variables are not measured in both types. Nevertheless, the large number of significant behavioral correlations warrants speculation concerning possible causes. Three alternative explanations come to mind. One, the experimental designs were adequate and the negative

Table 12

Intercorrelations of Major Variables

| | Pure oral measures | | | | Personality | | | | | | |
| | | | | | Experimental measures | | | | Behavioral measures | | |
	1. Ice-cream	2. Eagerness at lunch (T.R.)	3. Mouth activity (T.S.)	4. Mouth activity (B.T.)	5. Suggestibility	6. Boredom tolerance	7. Divided loyalty	8. Generosity	9. Sociometrics	10. Combined teacher ratings[1]	11. Combined time samples[2]
1		19	67‡	32	30	31	−07	−29	40	−09	43*
2			41*	50†	11	34	−18	15	44*	20	01
3				61‡	04	39	−21	19	61‡	15	55†
4					25	44*	−18	32	71‡	20	17
5						12	44*	−33	36	07	−11
6							04	25	35	10	−04
7								−33	03	04	31
8									18	45*	09
9										23	12
10											−01

1. Does not include 2.
2. Does not include 3.
$* = P < 0.10$
$† = P < 0.05$
$‡ = P_u < 0.01$

results are a contradiction of the hypotheses. This possibility does not seem very plausible in light of the positive theoretical findings with other techniques. Two, the hypotheses are valid and the designs inadequate. No evidence exists for rejecting this alternative, but the marked discrepancy between results with the two approaches, both of which were carefully designed and pretested, leads us to question the explanation. Three, the difficulty lies, not in experimental design or theory, but in unreliability inherent in the settings in which the experiments were conducted. The number of observations involved in the experiments were necessarily limited to one session, whereas the behavioral measures were usually accumulated over several time periods. Unavoidable

Table 13

Number of Significant Positive Correlations among Major Variables

Probability level	Number expected by chance	Number obtained
0·10	2·75	13
0·05	1·38	6
0·01	0·28	4

and unpredictable obstacles are bound to arise in the course of experimentation in a natural setting, such as a schoolroom, where the success of each design hinges upon the precision and co-operation of a large number of individuals.

Table 14

Personality Measures Broken Down by the Type of Approach versus Major Variables

Personality measures	Probability level	Number positive correlations expected by chance	Number obtained
Experimental situations	0·10	1·70	3
	0·05	0·85	0
	0·01	0·17	0
Behavioral measures	0·10	1·35	7
	0·05	0·68	3
	0·01	0·14	2

Cases in point are the 'love withdrawal' and 'can't say no' experiments, both of which had to be abandoned. The hypothesis in the former stated that the oral child should be highly sensitive to withdrawal of love. The 'ice-cream lady' first asked the children in the class to make drawings using themes of their own choice.

When the drawings were finished she circulated around the room, praising them all freely. Then she instructed the group to draw a house, each child individually to bring his drawing to her upon its completion. She lauded half of the drawings, and held them up before the class while commenting on their merits and naming the artists. The other half were received with casual indifference but no criticism. This was the love withdrawal procedure. Finally, she asked the class to draw a picture of a child. The aim of the experiment was to determine the effects of the withdrawal of love upon both drawings and behavior as recorded by observers.

The experiment was to have been repeated several days later, with a reversal of the treatment of the previously praised and ignored halves. In the actual administration it turned out to be impossible to maintain any kind of order in the class. The children were all excited about an Indian play which they had performed that day before the entire school, and their drum-pounding and war-whooping precluded any systematic, experimental procedure.

The 'can't say no' hypothesis dealt with the inability of the oral character to refuse requests from adults for fear of losing their approval. Nine observers entered the library while the class was listening to a fascinating record. Each observer approached a child, tapped him on the shoulder, and said in a neutral tone: 'Come with me.' The reactions to this request were later reported in detail. Like the preceding experiment this one was disrupted by an unforeseen complication. At the last minute the librarian was unable to schedule a record session when the other nine children in the group were to be asked to leave.

In contrast to the above illustrative experiments, the cumulative behavioral measures, on the other hand, were not as susceptible to unforeseen disruptions, since accidental influences on any one day tended to average out in the course of time. For example, differences occured when ice-cream was delivered late, yet this did not seriously alter the final ranking of subjects on the number of cups consumed.

From these speculations, it seems preferable that research designs, when dealing with something as complex as character structure, involve a series of measurements over a period of time.

Exploration of projective instruments

The following four projective techniques were included to explore their suitability as measures of orality: the Rorschach Test (Rorschach, 1942), Thematic Apperception Test (Murray, 1943), Blacky Pictures (Blum, 1949, 1950) and a specially constructed Story Completion Test which had been found to be significantly related to sociometric status in a previous study (Miller and Stine, 1951). Since there had been no previous applications of the techniques to this topic and age range, attempts at explicit prediction were not made.

Table 15

Correlations of Projective Methods with Major Variables

| | Pure oral measures | | | | Personality | | | | | | |
| | | | | | Experimental situations | | | | Behavioral measures | | |
	1. Ice-cream	*2. Eagerness at lunch (T.R.)*	*3. Mouth activity (T.S.)*	*4. Mouth activity (B.T.)*	*5. Suggestibility*	*6. Boredom tolerance*	*7. Divided loyalty*	*8. Generosity*	*9. Sociometrics*	*10. Combined teacher ratings*	*11. Combined time samples*
Rorschach (Objective)	28	19	20	−05	11	41	−03	−11	−13	−10	45
TAT (Objective)	−40	−58	−34	−59	01	−37	33	−21	05	−02	−05
Story Completion (Objective)	−11	−45	−29	−36	08	−20	60	−06	−11	−12	−05
Story Completion (Interpretive)	47	06	33	48	40	37	23	−34	19	−12	06
Blacky (Interpretive)	21	−23	16	25	41	−06	16	−20	28	15	21

Table 15 presents the correlations of the various projective methods with the major variables. Analysis of the projectives can be grouped under two broad headings, objective and interpretive. The Rorschach, TAT and Story Completion (Objective) were all scored by counting the number of oral references, e.g. 'food', 'hunger', 'eating', etc. The Blacky and Story Completion (Interpretive) protocols were ranked according to global impressions of oral passivity. While none of the correlations is very high, it should be noted that the 'objective' approach yielded twenty-two negative and eleven positive correlations, whereas the 'interpretive' produced only five negative and seventeen positive ($\chi^2 = 10 \cdot 19$, $P < 0 \cdot 01$). Whether this difference can legitimately be attributed to type of scoring approach can be answered only by further investigation.

Summary

This project was designed to explore the feasibility of testing psychoanalytic theory by conventional psychological methods. Hypotheses concerning the 'oral character', deduced from statements in the literature, were examined by means of teacher ratings, time-sampling, sociometrics and experimental situations conducted in a third-grade class. The operational definition of orality consisted of non-purposive mouth movements recorded by observers. The eighteen subjects were ranked on the criterion and on a series of variables related to specific hypotheses.

The resulting correlations lent strong support to hypotheses dealing with extreme interest in food and social isolation. Fair support was given to need for liking and approval, concern over giving and receiving and boredom tolerance. Unsupported hypotheses were need to be ingratiating, inability to divide loyalties and depressive tendencies; while remaining equivocal were dependency and suggestibility. Apart from the currently tentative nature of these specific findings, the over-all results were interpreted as holding promise for the investigation of psychoanalytic theory by traditional techniques.

References

BLUM, G. S. (1949), 'A study of the psychoanalytic theory of psychosexual development', *Genet. Psychol. Monog.*, vol. 39, pp. 3–99.
BLUM, G. S. (1950), *The Blacky Pictures: A Technique for the Exploration of Personality Dynamics*, Psychological Corporation.
FENICHEL, O. (1945), *The Psychoanalytic Theory of Neurosis*, Norton.
FROMM, E. (1947), *Man for Himself*, Holt, Rinehart & Winston.
MILLER, D. R., and HUTT, M. L. (1951), 'Value interiorization and personality development', *J. soc. Issues*, vol. 5, pp. 2–30.

MILLER, D. R., and STINE, M. E. (1951), 'The prediction of social acceptance by means of psychoanalytic concepts', *J. Personal.*, vol. 20, pp. 162–74.

MURRAY, H. A. (1943), *Thematic Apperception Test Manual*, Harvard University Press.

RORSCHACH, H. (1942), *Psychodiagnostics*, Huber, Bern (English translation).

THOPSON, C. (1950), *Psychoanalysis: Evaluation and Development*, Hermitage House.

THORNTON, G. R. (1943), 'The significance of rank-difference coefficients of correlation', *Psychometrika*, vol. 8, pp. 211–22.

Part Five Defence Mechanisms

The defence mechanisms are probably the most investigated of the psychoanalytic propositions, reflecting their greater susceptibility to operational definition.

The section on repression is represented by three fairly extensive studies, as the concept, according to Freud (1914, *Collected Papers*, vol. 1, Hogarth Press, 1956) 'is the foundation stone upon which the whole structure of psychoanalysis rests'. From this statement of the centrality which Freud afforded this part of his theory, it is clear that a crucial test of repression is, at the same time, a crucial test of the theory of psychoanalysis. It is true that in a later formulation of the theory of personality Freud regarded repression as one of several defence mechanisms, giving rather less weight to the concept. Nevertheless, it was always held to be the most basic means of allaying anxiety by the ego and Freud's model of the unconscious was structured around wishes which have been repressed or, in later writings, impulses which have been prevented from reaching consciousness by repression.

An adequate experimental investigation of the phenomenon of repression would thus have serious consequences, either one way or the other, for the validity of psycho-analysis.

The concept of projection is also important in the psychoanalytic system, and is, in part, the rationale for a major area of personality testing – the projective techniques. Wells and Goldstein (Reading 11) examine the evidence for this 'mechanism'.

Fixation and regression, so important in the psychoanalytic

theory of neurosis, are represented by two important research studies (Readings 12 and 13).

The mechanisms of displacement and identification are also considered, although only limited space is given to these concepts.

Repression

8 R. R. Sears

Repression

R. R. Sears, 'Repression', *Survey of Objective Studies of Psychoanalytic Concepts*, Social Science Research Council, New York, 1942, pp. 105–20.

When a parent punishes a child severely for some forbidden act, the impulse that led to the act in the first place becomes, by association, a stimulus for anxiety reactions. Since any anxiety is painful, trial-and-error behavior may be initiated with the aim of eliminating the discomfort. The number of possible solutions to this difficulty are limited, however, because the actual source of the anxiety is an impulse within the person himself. Freud described three main techniques that are used: (a) flight from any external stimuli that aid in arousing the impulse, (b) voluntary rejection of the impulse and (c) involuntary *repression* of both the impulse itself and all consciousness of its existence. These defenses against anxiety likewise prevent the occurrence of the activities originally instigated by the impulse. The essence of repression lies in the elimination from consciousness of all ideas or memories that might help to arouse the impulse and thus reactivate the painful anxiety.

In his first descriptions of repression, Freud used the term 'unpleasant' to describe the kinds of mental content that are subject to repression. This term was an unfortunate choice because of its wider meanings. Actually the anxiety that is fundamental to repression is that which was originally created by parents in punishing strongly motivated behavior. Such punishment helps to create the conscience, and when something re-arouses the anxiety later, the person may be said to suffer a threat of the loss of love.

Defence Mechanisms

Freud distinguished two kinds of repression, primal repression and after-expulsion. The description above is of the former. This elimination of impulses, however, is an active inhibitory process and other ideational contents or memories that are entirely unrelated to the repressed impulse can undergo *after-expulsion* if they are associated with the primal repression according to the ordinary laws of association. This is *repression proper*, and Freud considered that the majority of lacunae in the recall of unpleasant guilt-inducing and shameful memories was dependent on this rather than on a primal repression. Freud's best technical account of repression is in (1915a) and (1915b); a detailed and critical analysis of the concept, and of Freud's various related hypotheses, has been given by Sears (1936).

Infantile Amnesia

The earliest primal repressions are those of infancy. According to Freud (1905, pp. 36–8), the expression of both genital and pre-genital impulses is met with disapproval from parents, and hence adult efforts at recall of early sexual experiences fail. A partial amnesia is created. By the process of repression proper, i.e. by a kind of associative amnesia, most of the other experiences of the preschool years are also obliterated.

It is true that most people have scanty memories of their early years, but there is no non-analytic evidence to support the notion that repression is responsible. Indeed, the data relating to the memorial process in infancy and to the recall of childhood memories by adults lead to quite the opposite conclusions; other factors are not only of demonstrable significance, but seem to be sufficient to account for the observed facts without postulating repression at all.

Careful studies by Dudycha and Dudycha (1933a, 1933b) have shown that many college students are able to recall experiences from the third year. The average age at the time of the first remembered experience was three years, seven months and the latest 'first memory' was from the fifth birthday. A review by these authors (1941) of several other studies of childhood memories indicates that recollection of incidents from the third to the fifth year is normal for most adolescents and adults. There has been no comparison of the frequency of memories from various ages but the fact that the age of earliest memory is a research problem and that many people can recall only a few incidents from early life suggests that there is relatively poorer recall the farther back one goes in the life history. But there is in no sense any evidence of a general or complete amnesia, and the studies of Bell (1902) and Hamilton (1929) show that many adults are able to recall the details of childhood love affairs as well as other matters.

The emotions involved in such childhood memories include sexual ones accompanied by a realization of the forbidden character of the experience, anger, fear, wonder, awe, joy, shame and jealousy. Dudycha and Dudycha (1933a) report that approximately 40 per cent of 200 well authenticated memories involved fear. Some of these were fear of punishment for acknowledged misbehavior, and others were fear of animals or injury when the child's own behavior was not relevant. These authors do not report any memories of sex activity but the reports were not obtained under such conditions as might elicit such memories.

The evidence that factors other than repression are responsible for the relatively scanty recall from infancy has been well summarized by Brooks (1937, pp. 221–31). In order for an apparent decrement or deficiency of recall to be called an amnesia (loss of memory), there must be adequate evidence that the response was originally learned; the explanation of infantile amnesia, of course, assumes this. To Freud, impressed by the evident vividness of children's experiences, it seemed a truism that early emotional experiences were as well learned as the later ones of adults. This naïve assumption has long since been blasted. The fact is that no matter how the process of memorizing during infancy is measured, there is clear proof that it is far below the efficiency of that of the older child or adult. Among the kinds of memory that have been studied have been recognition memory for pictures, recall memory for movements, rote memory for concrete and abstract words, for series of digits, for nonsense syllables and for poetry. In every instance the memorizing process has proved to be poor at the earliest level and to increase by a fairly constant rate to a later period. This relative inadequacy of the memorizing process,

171

in other words, appears to parallel the relative inadequacy of recall for infantile experiences.

Crook and Harden (1931) reasoned, however, that if repression produced a general decrement in recall for the infancy period, there ought to be a positive relationship between the amount of amnesia and the amount of adult neuroticism. Child (1940) has aptly pointed out that this argument depends in part on two assumptions that are indefensible: that neuroticism and infantile repression are closely related, and that infantile amnesia is primarily a function of repression. The latter is demonstrably false and the former does violence to Freud's own reservations. Crook and Harden measured neuroticism with the Pressey X-O Test and secured, by questionnaire, two measures of infantile amnesia: the age at earliest memory and the total number of memories from the preschool years. Correlations of -0.37 and $+0.52$ were obtained, respectively, between neuroticism and number of memories and between neuroticism and age at time of first recalled experience. These results appear to give a little support to the hypothesis, but only nineteen subjects were used and the reliability and validity of the Pressey X-O Test are so poor for this purpose that the results seem of little significance.

Child repeated the experiment with 290 subjects, using the Thurstone Personality Schedule, the Clark Revision of the Schedule and the Bernreuter Personality Inventory with various subgroups. He found zero correlations between the measure of neuroticism and both measures of infantile amnesia. Further, the correlation between number of early memories and age at earliest recalled experience was only -0.36. If these are measures of the same thing, they do not appear to be very reliable.

There is no good evidence, then, (a) that there is a sharply delimited infantile amnesia, (b) that the generally poor recall of childhood experiences requires other explanation than that of poor learning or (c) that amount of infantile memory deficiency is related to adult neuroticism as this latter is measured by objective procedures.

A word needs to be said, however, concerning the investigation of childhood memories. The marked influence of hypnosis on the recovery of memories suggests that strength of motivation is an important determiner of the amount and accuracy of recall from real life experiences (Stalnaker and Riddle, 1932; White, Fox and Harris, 1940). Exceptional care must be taken to avoid falsification of memory; so far no investigation has validated objectively the early occurrences subjects report. Undoubtedly, too, the stimulus constellation used for eliciting memories is important; recalls obtained in a classroom cannot be compared with those from the analytic couch or even from the quiet retrospection of a person who actively seeks his memories.

In psychoanalysis, the continuous harping on recall, the demand to go farther back, to bring up more recollections, can be so harassing as to leave an objective observer in considerable doubt over the validity of the recalled items (cf. Landis, 1940). And yet without such effort, one can scarcely feel confidence in the completeness of recall; certainly the non-analytic studies have so far been much too little concerned with the conditions of recall to be of importance in connection with the problem of repression. There is serious need of a theoretical as well as experimental evaluation of the whole technique of free association as a method of securing recall data.

Measurement of Repression

The nature of the unpleasant

Research on feeling and memory has been stimulated largely by the concept of repression. Freud dwelt at length on the obliviscence of the unpleasant and, because experimental psychologists could measure both hedonic tone and recall, the testing of this proposition has been often attempted. Unfortunately, a goodly proportion of the investigators have not inquired too closely into the meaning of the word 'unpleasant' and much of the research that involves the relation of P and U feeling to memory is completely irrelevant to the problem of repression (cf. Sears, 1936, pp. 255–7).

Here is the reason. There are many kinds of 'unpleasant' mental content, but the kinds that initiate the repression process are rather narrowly limited. These are the ones associated with anxiety arising from interference either with the conscience (or other motives designed to preserve the parents' love), or with the maintenance of pride and self-esteem. It was through the internalization of the punitive and restrictive attributes of the parents, and the threat of the loss of love, that the repression sequence was initiated. But, by and large, parents punish only those kinds of behavior that are contra-indicated by their particular culture. In Western European and American cultures, for example, infantile as well as adolescent sex behavior is one of the most consistently punished forms of action, and hence sex is one of the most frequent sources of repression. Other motives that meet with vigorous socializing control are aggression, mastery, selfishness or egoism and religious heterodoxy. As a consequence these motives and their ideational representations are peculiarly subject to repression. In addition, of course, each individual's parents have their own nonconformist specialties for the rearing of their children, and hence repressions may be created in connexion with almost any impulse.

This situation should make it clear that when Freud refers to the 'unpleasant' he is referring to ideas or memories that relate specifically to these kinds of motives and not to words, odors or pictures that for purely esthetic reasons have taken on the character of relative unpleasantness in the adult verbal system of thinking. Indeed, many memories and external stimuli that might be rated as definitely P by an adult may well have been indirectly associated with experiences of punishment in childhood, e.g. songs, perfumes, risqué stories and such words as 'kiss', 'love' and 'romance'. They would therefore be capable of eliciting guilt or anxiety and, possibly, repression. It must be kept in mind, then, that repression would be expected to occur with reference only to those ideas associated with impulses that come into conflict with the conscience (internalized punitive attributes of the parents) and not to ideas adjudged unpleasant on some other grounds. For this reason no consideration need be given here to the literature on the comparative recallability of P and U words, odors or nonsense syllables.

Recall of experience

Of somewhat greater relevance to the theory is the group of studies designed to measure recall of real life experiences. With these there is the possibility of securing memory material that does relate to the kinds of anxiety-induced unpleasantness to which repression theory refers.

The first study of this kind was that of Wohlgemuth (1923). Following a vacation period, he had 687 children from eleven to sixteen years of age record their most pleasant and most unpleasant experiences of the preceding holidays. The task was repeated ten days and fourteen days later. The proportion of experiences forgotten was the same for both kinds but these findings are of little importance. The social conditions of the school, with a headmistress present at the experiment, made it doubtful that the children would reveal the kinds of shameful experiences to which the theory is applicable. Furthermore, the pleasant experiences were described first on each occasion and the relative amount of proactive and retroactive inhibition are unknown. The recalls, too, were not only recalls of the experiences but also of the previous written recalls.

Other experiments have uniformly found that recall of the pleasant experiences was better than of the unpleasant (cf. Moore, 1935). In all cases, however, the technique of recall permitted some doubt as to just what was being recalled, the original experience or the description of it. Meltzer (1930) secured memories of all Christmas vacation experiences from 132 college students and these were rated as P and U. Recall was better for the former on the occasion of an unexpected test six weeks later. As was the case with studies by Jersild (1931), Menzies (1935), and Waters and Leeper (1936), there is no indication that truly repressible experiences were being described in the first place. This is perhaps less true of the study by Stagner (1931). He reports that the U experiences given by his subjects, college students, were mostly ones involving conflict. This does not guarantee their relevance but seems to put them closer to the type described by Freud. Stagner had his hundred subjects give but a single experience of each kind, and in connexion with each, a list of 'redintegrative items' such as colors, odors and sounds that had been in some way associated with the original experience. Three weeks later he returned typewritten descriptions of the experiences to the subjects and required them to fill in the redintegrative items. There was a small but reliable difference in favor of better recall for the pleasant.

Perhaps the most realistic setting for this kind of experiment was that used by Koch (1930), who tested college students for the recall of school grades. She gave ten quizzes during the early part of a semester and on each occasion the students rated the obtained grade on a scale of 1 to 5, the former being very satisfactory and the latter very unsatisfactory. The papers were collected again and five weeks after the last quiz the students were asked to recall all ten grades. The '1' grades were best recalled, and whether '2' or '5' grades were second best for a particular person seemed to depend on the importance of a *bad* grade to the student, i.e. whether it was simply undesirable or constituted a real threat. In the latter case it was better remembered than the '2' grades. These results support the repression hypothesis but they show that relevance of the memory material to the immediate adjustment situation is also important in determining effectiveness of recall.

Associative repression (*after-expulsion*)

A different method of tapping real-life repressions is exemplified in studies by Flanagan (1930) and Sharp (1930). Sharp constructed lists of paired associates that were meaningless so far as each member of the pair was concerned but suggested religious or profane meanings when pronounced together, as for example: 'jeh–sus', 'tuw–hel', 'dah–mit'. The rate of learning and the immediate and delayed recall of these lists were compared with those of control lists containing neutral words, as for example: 'mih–ten', muf–ler', 'res–ler'. Flanagan used the same technique but his experimental list gave sexual meanings ('tew–bal', 'piy–nis') and his control gave rural ('gob–bal', 'har–nis'). In both experiments the control lists were more quickly learned and were better recalled after twenty-four hours than were the experimental lists. All the differences were highly reliable.

The assumption involved in these experiments is that the words having salacious or profane or religious meanings had been associated, at some time in the subjects' lives, with experiences and ideas subject to repression. By associative transfer of this repressive inhibition, these words would then be inhibited also, and the learning would be slower and recall poorer than for similar paired associates that did not evoke associative inhibition.

The results affirm the theoretical expectation, but the conditions under which the experiments were performed did not preclude the possibility that the difference was caused by embarrassment and conscious reluctance to speak forbidden words in the presence of the experimenter.

This difficulty was somewhat overcome in a later study by Sharp (1938). She obtained the case histories of a group of neurotic patients and from them selected fifteen words that referred to sources of anxiety and maladjustment for all the patients. These words were then formed into lists of paired associates by using present participles, as for example: 'feeling inferior', 'going insane', 'avoiding passion'. A control list of words that related to gratifications was also secured. Experimental and control groups of patients required approximately the same number of trails to learn the two lists, but on recall tests after two days and again after three weeks, the unacceptable words were reliably less well recalled than the acceptable ones. Sharp secured similar results with the same lists from a group of normal adults enrolled in special classes.

Since the same words were used with the normals as with the neurotics, it seemed probable that the words were tapping some sources of repression that are fairly common in people with an American background. L. B. Heathers and Sears (1943) therefore attempted to repeat the experiment with another group of normal subjects similar in scholastic and general background to Sharp's group of normals. Neither with this group, however, nor with college students were differences in recall between the two lists obtained. A number of variations in procedure were introduced but none influenced the negative findings. Whatever may have been the source of the differences between the two sets of data, it seems probable that this method is too uncertain and unreliable for extensive investigation.

Experimental Induction of Repression

The relative difficulty of measuring repressions that develop in the course of ordinary living has stimulated some effort to establish repression by artificial means in the laboratory. In an extensive exploratory study, Huston, Shakow and Erickson

(1934) took advantage of the control over verbalization provided by hypnotic amnesia to create by suggestion the kinds of emotional conflict that would eventuate in repression or other mechanisms of conflict resolution. Under hypnosis, subjects were persuaded to believe things about themselves that caused embarrassment or shame. Amnesia was then suggested for the trance events. The investigators then brought up for discussion, either in conversation or by requesting appropriate actions, the matters that had been put into a conflict context under hypnosis. Little that was immediately relevant to repression was observed, but the technique of the experiment could well lend itself to intensive study of this problem.

Another repression producing technique, the significance of which cannot immediately be evaluated, has been proposed by McGranahan (1940). He constructed a list of 100 stimulus words which included twenty or more that were normally effective in producing free associations of colors, as for example: coal (black), butter (yellow). The list was presented to two groups of college students. One group was given no special instructions and the men were simply asked to write down their associations; this was done in a group. The members of the other group were taken individually and were instructed not to give color associations to any stimulus word; if they disobeyed they were to receive a very severe shock. The degree to which each subject broke down on a pursuit-meter when shocks were administered was also measured.

McGranahan (1940) found that the threat of shock was ineffective with some subjects and they persisted in giving color associations. The SD of the shock group was even larger than that of the control. The degree to which the subjects were able to 'repress' the color associations in the experimental group correlated $+0.69$ (rho) with their resistance to shock on the pursuit-meter test as measured by lack of disruption of the task. McGranahan concluded that the ability to repress was a function of cognitive organization.

The small number of subjects, coupled with the rather startling indication of a lack of inhibitory effect of threatened punishment, suggested the desirability of a further analysis of the experimental situation. Sears and Virshup (1943) presented the same list of stimulus words to three groups of twenty-five subjects each. All

subjects were tested individually and care was taken to keep all
the procedure, except that which was experimentally varied, as
similar as possible for all groups. One group was a control;
nothing was said about color responses. A second group was
simply instructed not to give colors as associations. The third
group, intended to be the same as McGranahan's experimental
group, was warned not to give colors and was threatened with
shock; subjects were given several samples of the shock in
advance. The subjects of the control group gave colors without
hesitation but neither of the other groups resembled McGranahan's. Both instructions and threatened shock reduced color
associations somewhat, on the average, and there was no difference between the three groups in the size of the SD of the distribution of number of color responses given. This failure to
reproduce the previous experimental results may have been a
function of weaker shock, different instructions or some more
intangible factor.

In order to secure a more accurate indication of the strength
of the response words that were given by groups 2 and 3, in place
of the otherwise to be expected color associations, Sears and
Virshup had the subjects return after forty-eight hours for a
recall test of the responses given to the 100 stimulus words. It
was found that with respect to the twenty words having *least
frequent* color associations, as determined from the control
groups, there were no differences between the three groups, but
that with respect to the twenty words having *most frequent* color
associations, again as determined from the control group, twice
as many responses were forgotten in groups 2 and 3 as in group 1.
This can be interpreted in either of two ways: that the 'second
choices' (instead of color) were not so strongly attached to the
stimulus words, i.e. had not so much prior practice, and were
therefore less well recalled, or that the inhibition produced either
by instruction or threat of punishment prevented the recall.
Since the interpretation is ambiguous and McGranahan's results
are not easily reproducible, this general method of approach to
the problem of repression seems to have little to recommend it
at present.

Of more immediate relevance is the study of Rosenzweig and
Mason (1934), who created anxiety in children by making them

fail at a semicompetitive laboratory task and then tested for recall of the details of the task. The forty children were taken individually and given a series of rather simple jigsaw puzzles. Before each puzzle was presented, the child was shown a picture of how it would look when completed. Different lengths of time were allowed for the different puzzles on the pretext that they were of unequal difficulty. But the child was permitted to finish only half the puzzles and it was suggested that he had 'failed the test' on the others. The actual amount of time allowed on the completed and uncompleted puzzles was the same. After the series was finished the child was asked to recall the names of all the puzzles he had tried. In spite of the fact that the Zeigarnik effect would favor recall of the uncompleted puzzles, these were less well remembered than the completed ones.

There was additional evidence that it was the success and failure that created the discrepancy in recall scores. The authors obtained from teachers ratings of the children on the trait of 'pride'. Although these were none too reliable and the differences were not great enough to furnish critical proof, those children who rated high on pride did show a greater tendency to forget the failed puzzles than did the children who were rated low on pride. This suggests that the interference with self-esteem was the significant variable in relation to the forgetting.

Rosenzweig (1940) added further weight to this conclusion with an experiment on Harvard students. He presented puzzles under two different conditions. In one case the students were told that their intelligence was to be tested, and in the other that information concerning the relative difficulty of the puzzles was being sought. The first group was ego-involved in the situation and the second group was not. As would be predicted from the results of the previous experiment, there was greater recall of completed tasks in the ego-involved group and of uncompleted tasks in the other. In other words, the Zeigarnik effect was operative in the latter but was overcome by the selective recall of ego-maximating experiences in the former.

Various investigators have shown that artificially induced experiences of success and failure create sharp changes in the motivational and recall aspects of the learning process, and since the technique is one that lends itself readily to the laboratory, it would seem to offer considerable prospective reward to further investigation. Whether the more elaborate amnesic phenomena can be studied in such a setting is an open question, but at least the rudiments of repression may exist there. Rosenzweig's obtained differences have been relatively small, but larger groups and more refined techniques might remedy that, and hence permit investigation of the quantitative problems that Freud has already posed (cf. Sears, 1936, pp. 253–5). In any case, there seem to be no alternative techniques, to date, that give as much promise with the possible exception of induced emotional conflicts under hypnosis. The recall of real-life experiences does not permit manipulation of the variables that cause repression, except as there is a natural variation among different subjects, and the same holds true of the tapping of associative repressions (after-expulsion). With the latter technique, too, each subject must be treated with individual attention to his particular complexes and that makes quantification difficult.

Conclusions

There is little to be concluded from the experimental study of repression. In general it is possible to demonstrate that, with the required conditions crudely established, recall of either real-life or experimentally induced experiences follows the expectations suggested by repression theory. But the non-analytic data offer no refinement of the theory, no addition of relevant new variables, no streamlined techniques that promise eventual solution of the problems posed by Freud. Studies of recall of real-life experiences and efforts to tap existing repressions have been almost uniformly uninformative. Some hope may be held out for the artificial creation of repressions in the laboratory, but even these must by necessity be mild and impermanent. Indeed, the triviality of obtained differences in this field makes a most discouraging picture; and the coarseness of the experimental methods so far available for trapping the sensitive dynamics of repression does not augur well for the future.

References

BELL, S. (1902), 'A preliminary study of the emotion of love between the sexes', *Amer. J. Psychol.*, vol. 13, pp. 325–54.

BROOKS, F. D. (1937), *Child Psychology*, Houghton Mifflin.

CHILD, I. L. (1940), 'The relation between measures of infantile amnesia and of neuroticism', *J. abnorm. soc. Psychol.*, vol. 35, pp. 453–6.

CROOK, M. N., and HARDEN, L. (1931), 'A quantitative investigation of early memories', *J. soc. Psychol.*, vol. 2, pp. 252–5.

DUDYCHA, G. J., and DUDYCHA, M. M. (1933a), 'Adolescents' memories of preschool experiences', *J. genet. Psychol.*, vol. 42, pp. 468–80.

DUDYCHA, G. J., and DUDYCHA, M. M. (1933b), 'Some factors and characteristics of childhood memories', *Child Devel.*, vol. 4, pp. 265–78.

DUDYCHA, G. J., and DUDYCHA, M. M. (1941), 'Childhood memories: a review of the literature', *Psychol. Bull.*, vol. 38, pp. 668–82.

FLANAGAN, D. (1930), The influence of emotional inhibition on learning and recall, *Unpublished Master's Thesis, University of Chicago*.

FREUD, S. (1905), 'Three contributions to the theory of sex', *Nerv. ment. Dis. Monogr.*, no. 7, 4th edn.

FREUD, S. (1915a), 'Repression', *Collected Papers*, vol. 4, Hogarth Press, pp. 84–97.

FREUD, S. (1915b), 'The unconscious', *Collected Papers*, vol. 4, Hogarth Press, pp. 98–136.

HAMILTON, G. V. (1929), *A Research in Marriage*, Boni.

HEATHERS, L. B., and SEARS, R. R. (1943), Experiments on repression: II. The Sharp Technique, unpublished.

HUSTON, P. E., SHAKOW, D., and ERICKSON, M. H. (1934), 'A study of hypnotically induced complexes by means of the Luria techniques', *J. gen. Psychol.*, vol. 11, pp. 65–97.

JERSILD, A. T. (1931), 'Memory for the pleasant as compared with the unpleasant', *J. exp. Psychol.*, vol. 14, pp. 284–8.

KOCH, H. L. (1930), 'The influence of some affective factors upon recall', *J. gen. Psychol.*, vol. 4, pp. 171–90.

LANDIS, C. (1940), 'Psychoanalytic phenomena', *J. abnorm. soc. Psychol.*, vol. 35, pp. 17–28.

McGRANAHAN, D. V. (1940), 'A critical and experimental study of repression', *J. abnorm. soc. Psychol.*, vol. 35, pp. 212–25.

MELTZER, H. (1930), 'Individual differences in forgetting pleasant and unpleasant experiences', *J. educ. Psychol.*, vol. 21, pp. 399–409.

MENZIES, R. (1935), 'The comparative memory values of pleasant, unpleasant and indifferent experiences', *J. exp. Psychol.*, vol. 18, pp. 267–79.

MOORE, E. H. (1935), 'A note on recall of the pleasant vs. the unpleasant', *Psychol. Rev.*, vol. 42, pp. 214–15.

ROSENZWEIG, S. (1940), Need-persistive and ego-defensive reactions to frustration as demonstrated by an experiment on repression, unpublished.

ROSENZWEIG, S., and MASON, G. (1934), 'An experimental study of memory in relation to the theory of repression', *Brit. J. Psychol.*, vol. 24, pp. 247–65.

SEARS, R. R. (1936), 'Functional abnormalities of memory with special reference to amnesia', *Psychol. Bull.*, vol. 33, pp. 229–74.

SEARS, R. R., and VIRSHUP, B. (1943), Studies of repression: III. The McGranahan Method, unpublished.

SHARP, A. A. (1930), The influence of certain emotional inhibitions on learning and recall, *Unpublished Master's Thesis, University of Chicago*.

SHARP, A. A. (1938), 'An experimental test of Freud's doctrine of the relation of hedonic tone to memory revival', *J. exp. Psychol.*, vol. 22, pp. 395–418.

STAGNER, R. (1931), 'The redintegration of pleasant and unpleasant experiences', *Amer. J. Psychol.*, vol. 43, pp. 463–8.

STALNAKER, J. M., and RIDDLE, E. E. (1932), 'The effect of hypnosis on long-delayed recall', *J. gen. Psychol.*, vol. 6, pp. 429–40.

WATERS, R. H., and LEEPER, R. (1936), 'The relation of affective tone to the retention and experiences of daily life', *J. exp. Psychol.*, vol. 19, pp. 203–15.

WHITE, R. W., FOX, G. F., and HARRIS, W. W. (1940), 'Hypnotic hyperamnesia for recently learned material', *J. abnorm. soc. Psychol.*, vol. 35, pp. 88–103.

WOHLGEMUTH, A. (1923), 'The influence of feeling on memory', *Brit. J. Psychol.*, vol. 13, pp. 405–16.

9 Saul Rosenzweig

The Experimental Study of Repression

Saul Rosenzweig, 'The experimental study of repression', in H. A. Murray (ed.), *Explorations in Personality*, Oxford University Press Inc., 1938, pp. 472–90.

'I did that,' says my memory. 'I could not have done that,' says my pride, and remains inexorable. Eventually – the memory yields.

Nietzsche: *Beyond Good and Evil*

Introduction

'The doctrine of repression,' says Freud (1924a, p. 297), 'is the foundation-stone on which the whole structure of psycho-analysis rests. . . .' And elsewhere (1935, p. 56) he adds, 'It is possible to take repression as a centre and to bring all the elements of psycho-analytic theory into relation with it.' It was therefore natural that, when in 1930 the opportunity offered to subject analytic theory to laboratory study, the concept of repression suggested itself as a point of departure. A further and decisive inducement was the fact that certain aspects of this concept, in particular those relating to memory, seemed readily amenable to experimental procedures.

Accordingly, from 1930 to 1932 the writer was occupied almost exclusively with a series of experiments designed as a program for studying repression experimentally. A small fraction of the data thus obtained has been analysed and the results published, but the much larger part still awaits the necessary leisure. In this brief preliminary report an attempt will be made to summarize the results of the published work and to give some indication of what, at this writing, seems to be concealed in the as yet unpublished and, in some cases, only partially analysed data. The reader is asked to bear in mind the tentative character of most of the statements made here and is urged to view them as a basis for the hypothesis embracing hypnotizability, repression and frustration advanced towards the close of this paper.

The theory of repression is outlined by Freud (1924b, pp. 84–97) in an article contained in the fourth volume of his *Collected Papers*. Another theoretical discussion, written with a view to experimental investigation, has recently been published by Sears (1936). In the present context suffice it to say that repression is regarded by analysts as a mechanism of ego-defence resorted to in the face of intolerable frustrations occasioned by conflict between some positive drive and the need to preserve self-respect. In the process some *impulse* is usually denied expression and associated *ideas* or *images* are forcibly forgotten. It would seem convenient for expository purposes, and perhaps for experimental ones, to distinguish these two aspects of the process by the terms 'response repression' and 'stimulus repression', the implication being that in the simplest case, say, an insult from some important person, one could study either the fate of the anger and retaliation *responses* denied expression or the fate of the *stimulus* presentations, such as the name of the insulting person or other circumstances of the humiliating incident, forgotten. In reviewing the studies of stimulus repression it is helpful further to distinguish between the *conscious* fate of the ideas or images – their supposed inaccessibility to normal recall – and their *unconscious* fate – their supposed persistence in the mind despite the content of consciousness. The same distinction is logically possible for response repression, since one could discuss the conscious fate of impulses, particularly their accompanying sensations and images, or their unconscious fate, especially in behaviour, but the investigations of this topic are not numerous and do not require such a division. Complete proof of stimulus repression would thus require evidence of both conscious forgetting and unconscious remembering. The demonstration of a complete repression cycle would require the addition of proof that the conscious representative of the unexpressed impulse had been forgotten and that the repressed response had gained substitute expression in some form or other.[1] No doubt this analysis violates the Gestalt-like character

1. A distinction between defensive and substitutive mechanisms of reaction to frustration is thus suggested. The former group would embrace projection, displacement, isolation, etc., while the latter would include sublimation, compensation, etc. Repression would, in the light of the above exposition, belong to both groups.

of the repression process, but it is at least useful for the exposition of the experimental work in question.

Only a little of the experimentation thus far represented in the literature bears upon *response repression*. One of the rare instances of such research is Brun's (1926) on drive conflicts produced in ants. He has studied the substitutive activities resorted to after repression has become necessary as a result of conflict and thus offers evidence of sublimation and regression. Some of the research of Lewin (1935) and his associates belongs by implication in this same setting. Such work, despite its importance, bears only indirectly upon the present programme. More directly related are certain studies of *stimulus repression* in which the *unconscious fate* of the ideas or images repressed was of special concern. Malamud (1934) and Malamud and Linder (1931) have investigated dreams from this standpoint, finding that when subjects are for a brief period shown and then asked to describe from memory certain types of pictures, they omit or distort items which reappear as unconscious or repressed material in the dreams they have soon after the experimental session.[2]

Of greatest relevance in the present context is that group of studies devoted to the *conscious fate* of *stimulus repression*. This work, well reviewed by Meltzer (1930), is, however, worthless as a test of repression because, as has been elsewhere (Rosenzweig and Mason, 1934, pp. 247–8) pointed out, it fails to satisfy the necessary conditions of such a test. Either these studies have been concerned with memory for an impersonal type of unpleasant experience – sensory experience, such as odours, which the psychoanalyst does not include in his theory of forgetting – or, investigating as they should the recall of dynamically frustrating experiences, they have dealt with such episodes as occur in the everyday life of the subjects instead of producing these experiences in the laboratory itself. The latter defect involves the erroneous assumption (cf. Wohlgemuth, 1923, pp. 28–39) that pleasant and unpleasant episodes occur equally often in daily life. Studies based upon uncontrolled everyday experiences are further limited by the fact that repression may already have done its work by the time the subject makes his first report – and would hence go undetected

2. Cf. in this connexion the work of O. Poetzl and that of Allers and Teller cited by Malamud and Linder (1931).

– even if evidence of it fails to appear on subsequent reports of the same events. To test the theory of repression in its relation to the conscious fate of the stimulus properly, it is necessary to bring about under controlled conditions experiences of conative striving which come into conflict with the pride of self-respect of the subjects, e.g. experiences of failure. If it is shown that such experiences are forgotten more frequently than comparable experiences of a successful nature, evidence of stimulus repression has presumptively been obtained.

Of the studies on stimulus repression which are satisfactory from the standpoint of the foregoing criteria, two are noteworthy. Koch (1930) worked on students' recall of good and bad examination grades and obtained evidence that would appear to support the Freudian theory. Zeigarnik (1927, p. 77), investigating the recall of finished and unfinished tasks, found that the latter were much more frequently recalled than the former. Although the tasks were not in general presented as a test of personal merit, when certain of them which had, for one reason or another, been so taken were interrupted, evidence of repression incidentally appeared. It will be seen later that the main evidence of this experiment is perhaps more important for the theory of repression than the obviously relevant incidental results.

The Experimental Programme

Technique

The general features of the technique employed in the present experimental programme may now be described. Subjects were given a simulatory test of intelligence in order to produce emotional tension in them and create experiences of success and failure.[3] The test consisted of a series of jigsaw picture-puzzles each of which when completed revealed some common object, such as a ship, a house or a coat, pyrographed upon its face. The subject was permitted to study a miniature picture of each object before undertaking the corresponding task. Usually he was allowed to succeed in half of the tasks but was made to fail in the

3. For an account of some of the difficulties, such as the opinion-error, that arise when such methods of experimentally inducing need-tension are employed, cf. Rosenzweig (1933a).

other half. He was then asked to name the puzzles which had been included in the test.

The formal advantages of such a technique are readily apparent. All the tasks being of the same general type, they were characterized by a sufficient degree of uniformity to permit comparisons in recall and other aspects of behaviour on the basis of a few controlled variables. Such variables were the nature of the picture represented, the jigsaw design and the outcome of the attempt to solve the puzzles. Quantification of the results was facilitated by the fact that the puzzles could be cut into any desired number of pieces and so made roughly to vary in difficulty. Obviously, the design of the construction was also a determining factor here. Moreover, the subject's success or failure could be estimated not only on an absolute basis, according to his having or not having completed the puzzle by the time he was stopped, but even more finely according to the number of pieces he had been allowed to assemble up to that time. In view of what has already been said about the simulatory character of the intelligence tests involved in this technique, it is hardly necessary to point out that in practically every instance described in the following experiments the degree to which a subject succeeded or failed in finding the solution of a puzzle was not a function of his ability but of the experimenter's purpose. Since the subject did not in general have any advance knowledge about the norms of the test, he was at the mercy of its administrator who could, according to the requirements of the investigation, stop him at any point in the solution.

By other devices further experimental control was possible. One such device was the preparation of two sets of puzzles identical in every respect except the number of pieces into which the corresponding boards were cut. One could thus obtain two parallel series of puzzles, one relatively easy, the other relatively difficult. Similarly, one could experimentally evaluate the significance of the pictures portrayed by having puzzles with nonsense syllable facings, and one could go even further in this direction by exactly duplicating the jigsaw design of such a series of puzzles and a corresponding picture series.

The foregoing technique with its numerous manipulative possibilities is the more important in view of the difficulties which one might well expect to encounter in any attempt at quantitative research involving *units of behaviour*. Its general success and wide applicability as an experimental method may be judged from the fact that by it such varied topics as repression, projection, rationalization, the experience of duration, hedonic tone and repetition choice were all fruitfully investigated.

That the present technique actually motivated the subjects and created markedly emotional states is clear from the results. Both the behavioural notes of the experimenter and the introspective reports of the subjects abound in expressions such as 'hands tremble', 'perspires freely', 'beams', 'clearly embarrassed' and 'very excited'. This is, however, not surprising if one considers that most individuals, being insecure, are highly sensitive to examinations and are really aroused by them. Through years of patient labour in the administration of intelligence and other tests psychologists have, moreover, unwittingly educated the public to accept the present type of *laboratory* or artificial situation as a *natural* or life-like one. In the case of the technique under discussion all of the following motivational factors were thus potentially present: (a) the obstacle for mastery represented by each of the puzzles; (b) the set time within which each task had to be completed; (c) competition with other individuals whom the subjects knew or were told about; (d) critical scrutiny by the experimenter during the performance. The subjects were thus contending, in the ideal case, with an environmental problem having an unequivocal solution, with elapsing time and with a group of recognized competitors. To make matters worse, the watchful eye of the experimenter was ever upon the contest, thus helping to generate 'examination anxiety'.

Preliminary experiments

A first group of experiments on some forty summer school and regular students at Harvard and Radcliffe was designed to induce complexes through the experience of failure. Subjects were, for instance, given word lists for hedonic ratings *before* and *after* taking the so-called intelligence test. In the word list, among the names of many neutral objects, were those of the objects represented in the test. The purpose of the re-rating technique was to see whether the names of objects on which failure or success had been experienced would, unconsciously to the subjects, be affected in the second evaluation as compared with the first. In a number of cases this result was clearly obtained. In addition, a general shift in the hedonic ratings of the entire list was also occasionally found. Memory for the puzzles was tested by asking the subjects to name the tasks they had attempted. Though the opposite tendency was also disclosed, it was found that many individuals recalled a greater percentage of their successes than of their failures. Thus one Radcliffe girl who was given twelve puzzles to solve, half issuing in success, half in failure, recalled all six of the successful puzzles but only three of the equally numerous failures. This objective result gained further significance in the light of her highly agitated behaviour during the test and her explanation that the continuation of her studies depended upon her obtaining a scholarship which, in turn, depended upon her receiving a superior grade in the psychology course from which she had been recruited for this experiment. Throughout the test her mind dwelt upon the lecturer in this course: 'All I thought of during the experiment was that it was an intelligence test and that he (the lecturer) would see the results. I saw his name always before me.' Under these circumstances the fact that she forgot half of her failures while remembering all of her successes might well be provisionally construed as repression.

While such tentative results were of interest as suggestions, it soon became clear that to obtain definitive conclusions the problem of repression would have to be approached at a much simpler level and only gradually developed to the point of complexity represented by these early efforts. In keeping with this plan a preliminary study was made of the relationship between success and failure, on the one hand, and hedonic tone, on the other. While common sense takes it for granted that success is pleasant, failure unpleasant, scientific psychology requires a more detailed and critical knowledge of this association before adopting a technique in which success and failure are to be treated as equivalent to pleasant and unpleasant experiences, respectively. Accordingly, some eight experiments were carried out to study hedonic tone as a function of success and failure (cf. Rosenzweig, 1932).

Experiments on stimulus repression: conscious fate

A series of circumscribed experiments on repression were now undertaken. The first of these (Rosenzweig and Mason, 1934) was done on a group of forty crippled children, with the result that the subjects could be divided into three groups according to whether they recalled a greater percentage of the names of the successful than of the unsuccessful tasks, a lesser percentage of the former than of the latter, or an equal percentage of each. Thus far the data were obviously no more than one might expect according to the laws of probability. However, in view of the fact that the conditions under which the subjects had been working were relatively well defined, it was possible to go beyond this purely statistical finding. A first step in this direction was the discovery that the group who recalled successes better than failures was differentiated from the group who recalled failures better than successes by a more advanced average mental age and a higher average teachers' rating for the trait of pride. Of similar import but of even greater apparent validity was a correlation between the results of the present experiment and those of a previous one involving preferences in the repetition of successful and unsuccessful activities. In this earlier experiment (Rosenzweig, 1933b)[4] on the same subjects it was found that the younger ones consistently chose to repeat puzzles in which they had once had success, whereas the older ones chose to repeat puzzles in which they had experienced failure. This difference in repetition choice was associated with a difference in teachers' ratings on the trait of pride, in which the younger children had a markedly lower average than the older ones. It seemed likely by way of interpretation that the older children, because prouder, were more sensitive to failure and hence strove for self-vindication, whereas the younger children, not being wounded by failure, ignored it. The relationship of these results to the Freudian *pleasure* and *reality principles* is too obvious to require discussion. Now, in the present

4. Further experimental studies of repetition choice have since been made on groups of normal adults, normal children, feeble-minded individuals and schizophrenic patients. The results have led to the formulation of a concept of frustration tolerance – a factor both quantitatively and qualitatively variable and apparently increasing in the normal course of the individual's early development. Cf. Rosenzweig (1936).

experiment on memory it was found that those subjects who tended to recall failures had formerly preferred to repeat successes while those who tended to recall successes had preferred failures for repetition. The implication seemed to be that stimulus repression failed to occur in individuals who were still functioning naïvely in accordance with the pleasure principle; or, more parsimoniously stated, that unless failure was experienced as wounding to self-respect and requiring social vindication, there was no basis for stimulus repression and it hence did not occur. These results may thus be construed as indicating that repression is a mechanism of defence resorted to relatively late in the development of the child.

As important incidental results of the experiment it was found that (a) there was a distortion in recalling the outcome – success or failure – of the tasks attempted that ran parallel with the tendencies shown in recalling the names of the tasks; (b) with increasing age there was an increase in self-critical answers to the question, 'Do you feel that you did the puzzles well?'; (c) the experiences of relatively shorter duration were much more frequently recalled than those of longer duration, presumably because of the prevailing dynamic conditions.

A second experiment on stimulus repression (Rosenzweig, 1933c) was designed to verify the results of this first one, only now an attempt was made to control the external experimental situation so as to reproduce, with two groups of thirty adults each, the conditions which had obtained with the children by virtue of the genetic differences in their personalities. To the individuals in one of the two groups the tasks were presented as an intelligence test and under these conditions there was a tendency for the finished puzzles to be recalled more often than the unfinished ones. To the subjects in the other group, the tasks were presented in an informal spirit, the object of the appointment allegedly being to help the experimenter gain certain knowledge about the puzzles – not about the subjects – so that this information would be available for guidance in an experiment being planned for the near future. To avoid suspicion all records were kept by an assistant seated apparently with his own unrelated work at a desk on the further side of the informal study in which the session took place. Under these circumstances there was a tendency for the unfinished puzzles to be recalled more often than the finished ones. Repression thus occurred in general under the expected conditions but did not occur otherwise. It is to be observed, however, that even under the adequate external conditions repression was not exemplified in the behaviour of every subject. In fact, some of those who performed the puzzles informally gave more evidence of repression than did certain of those who did the tasks as a test. One is led to suspect in these instances an underlying personality trait strong enough to over-ride the intention of the stimulus situation.

Zeigarnik's general results that unfinished tasks informally undertaken are better remembered than finished ones are in essential agreement with the present results, but the latter also explain why she found evidences of repression only very incidentally.

In attempting to interpret the above experiment more fully the problem arises as to whether the test situation resulted in the forgetting of the failures because these conditions aroused the *pride* of the subjects and hence provided a basis for *repression* or because they *excited* the subjects and thus produced a form of *dissociation*. While it is impossible to settle this question on the strength of the present evidence, it is worth noting that Breuer and Freud (1936, pp. 6–8) were confronted with the same problem in their early attempts to account for the losses of memory they regarded as fundamental to hysteria. They pointed out that such instances of amnesia may be attributed to traumas which were insufficiently abreacted – the abreaction failing to occur either because the traumas involved humiliating circumstances which the patient did not wish to remember or because these traumas were experienced in an hypnoidal, exciting or otherwise abnormal state of consciousness. In either case 'associative elaboration' in the normal conscious state would be precluded and amnesia would thus ensue.

Control experiments related to the foregoing

It would obviously be difficult to design an experiment involving experiences of success and failure which would arouse emotional tension entailing reactions of pride without at the same time producing excitement, or vice versa, but such would be necessary to

193

differentiate between the two sets of determinants under discussion. On the whole, the evidence would tend to give the pride factors greater prima facie importance since they would usually entail excitement whereas excitement alone might well occur apart from pride reactions. Further experimentation is, however, much needed at this point.

The studies which were actually undertaken at the stage of the programme being described were designed to test some of the experimental artifacts that made even the general results just outlined questionable. Among these investigations, which need not be detailed here, were the two following: (a) an attempt to study the effect of changing the criterion of success so that a coincidence with completion would not be involved; to accomplish this end all the puzzles were carried to completion but in some cases before, in others after a previously announced time limit within which the puzzles would need to be finished in order to be scored as successes; (b) an attempt to rule out as a factor in recallability the familiarity of the objects depicted in the puzzles; to achieve this purpose puzzles with nonsense syllable facings were substituted for those with pictures.

In this same connexion may be mentioned another experimental variation involving some twenty subjects who were asked to recall the puzzles not *immediately* after their performance but *at some later period*. This experiment was intended to show the significance of delay as a factor in stimulus repression, but the obtained data are insufficiently analysed to be further discussed on this occasion.

Experiments on stimulus repression: unconscious fate

The investigations discussed thus far were all concerned with the *conscious* fate of stimulus repression. In addition, a series of experiments dealing with the *unconscious* fate of such repression was performed though the results are as yet for the most part in a raw state. One group of these studies, in which about twenty subjects participated, five in each of four different experimental situations, was intended to compare *recall* of the problems with *recognition* of their names among a long list of objects. The subjects were asked not only to pick out the objects represented in the puzzles they had attempted, but to indicate in terms of a scale the degree of vividness of their recognition. If these results should reveal a poorer recall of the failures but a more frequent and more vivid recognition of them as compared with successes – which is what a first glance at the data seems to indicate – some evidence would be available for an unconscious or dispositional persistence of the failure experiences despite their not appearing in the consciousness of the subjects on account of stimulus repression.[5]

A very tentative investigation, with only four subjects taking part, may be mentioned for its suggestive value in relation to further work on the unconscious fate of stimulus repression. In this experiment a word list was first presented for hedonic ratings; after this, certain puzzles, the names of which were represented in the word list, were attempted as a test by the subjects with varying degrees of success. The word list was then given for re-rating. This experiment thus far resembles one of the preliminary studies reported above. Its unique feature was the use of a pyschogalvanometer throughout the session to measure changes in unconscious tension. From a very rough and unreliable analysis of the data it appeared that in some instances failure on the puzzles was accompanied by changes in the GSR (galvanic skin response), and that presentation after the test of the stimulus words referring to these failures gave significant deviations as compared with the original reactions to these same words. These results, if valid, would tend to support those of the preceding experiments on recognition memory. Both sets of data indicate a dispositional persistence of certain failure experiences not subject to voluntary recall. From the preliminary results of these separate studies further work in which the recognition technique was *combined* with measurement of the GSR during the same experimental session would seem to offer considerable promise.

It is also worthy of note that the above findings are in keeping with the experiment already discussed in which unfinished tasks performed under informal conditions, rather than as a test, were better remembered than finished ones. Zeigarnik obtained substantially the same results. The significance of these findings may now be more adequately understood. If undischarged tension

5. Cf. in this connexion the interesting experiment of Lynch (1932), in which memory for pleasant and unpleasant stimuli was studied by a recognition technique.

connected with a need makes for better recall under unemotional conditions, it appears reasonable to suppose that when such undischarged tensions are repressed through pride and similar motives these tensions and their associated ideas or images will still continue more strongly in the mind than will corresponding experiences representing closed and unrepressed needs. Under these new conditions, however, the unclosed need situations will lead only a dispositional or – to use the Freudian terminology – an unconscious existence. From these considerations it becomes clear, too, why the equivalence of *incompletion* with *failure* in the experiments raises certain difficulties in such studies as the present. One must then be ever careful not to confuse the *unclosed need represented by the unfinished task* (perseveration) with the *unclosed need represented by the inhibited response*, say, of anger in the face of frustration. In keeping with this interpretation, evidence of repression obtained from experiments in which the criteria of failure is incompletion is particularly striking because under such conditions the repressive tendency can become manifest in terms of forgotten failures only after overcoming the competing perseverative tendency which would, by itself, make for the recall of the unfinished tasks. The problem inherent in this distinction underlay the control experiment described above in which success was defined by a criterion other than completion.

From these reflections to the problem of response repression in general is obviously only a short step, but until it be taken, little more can be profitably said on the present topic.[6]

The Triadic Hypothesis

One of the factors which kept cropping up throughout the preceding studies has as yet been left unmentioned. In one sense it represents the contribution of individual differences which obtruded themselves despite the systematically imposed external conditions of the experiments. But in another sense it implies a larger frame of reference than the concept of repression alone – a frame within which these individual differences are absorbed by a new set of general principles.

6. The work of Lewin and his associates on substitute activities is of special interest in this connexion. See Lewin (1935), ch. 6.

The factor in question concerns the way in which individuals seemed, according to the impression of the experimenter, to vary in their *immediate reaction to frustration or failure*. These variations in reaction appeared to correlate with subsequent predominance in recall of successes or failures. Briefly, it seemed that individuals who at the time of experiencing failure were inclined to blame the external world (e.g. the puzzles, the experimenter), a type of reaction later called 'extrapunitive', *or* to blame themselves, later called 'intropunitive', tended characteristically to recall their failures, in contradiction to the repression hypothesis; only those who tended to gloss over their failures as if inevitable and tried to rationalize them away at the time of their occurrence, a type of reaction later called 'impunitive', recalled their successes better than their failures, i.e. displayed stimulus repression. It was accordingly suggested in a former publication (Rosenzweig, 1934) that each of the types of reaction might have a special relation to memory. One could speculate that both the extrapunitive and the intropunitive reactions would entail remembering the occasion of frustration, in the former case, as if in anticipation of revenge, in the latter, as if in preparation for nursing the wounds to one's pride and 'eating one's heart out'. It could be maintained that the aggressive impulses were being preserved to be expressed later, in the former case, against outer objects, in the latter, against the subject's own self. The impunitive type of reaction, on the other hand, might be expected to entail a conscious forgetting of the occasion of frustration, as if in order to reconcile oneself – and others – to the disagreeable situation. The impunitive reaction would thus be summed up in the expression 'forgive and forget', whereas the other two types would involve neither forgiving nor forgetting. Thus the hypothesis soon arose that specific types of inadequate or subjective reaction to frustration might be found to be correlated systematically with special mechanisms of defence, repression being only one of these.

It was of interest to find after this hypothesis had arisen from the experiments that Freud's accumulating clinical experience had led him to a similar position. In a later publication (Freud, 1936, pp. 143–6) he suggests that the concept of defence which he used in his earlier theoretical papers and which was later replaced by repression, be now readopted.

I now think that it confers a distinct advantage to readopt the old concept of defence if in doing so it is laid down that this shall be the general designation for all the techniques of which the ego makes use in the conflicts which potentially lead to neurosis, while repression is the term reserved for one particular method of defence, one which because of the directions that our investigations took was the first with which we became acquainted. . . . The importance of such a nomenclature is increased if one considers the possibility that a deeper insight might reveal a close affinity between particular forms of defence and certain specific disorders, as for example between repression and hysteria. Our expectation even extends to the possibility of another important interrelationship. It may easily be that the psychic apparatus utilizes other methods of defence prior to the clear-cut differentiation of ego and id, prior to the erecting of a super-ego, than it does after these stages of organization have been attained.

The similarity between this position of Freud and that just outlined is striking though one should not overlook the fact that whereas Freud is emphasizing the special relationship between certain defence mechanisms and certain types of illness, the present hypothesis stresses a special relationship between certain types of defence and certain descriptively independent types of reaction to frustration. From the standpoint of this distinction MacKinnon's experimental work see MacKinnon, 1933) on the violation of prohibitions is more pertinent than Freud's clinical observations. MacKinnon found that non-violators and violators exhibit consistently different behaviour patterns, the former having a close resemblance to what has been here described as intropunitive, while the latter appear to be either extrapunitive or impunitive. Violators who remember their violations well may be tentatively regarded as extrapunitive, those who tend to forget their violations would appear to be impunitive. The intropunitive subjects would be too full of guilt to commit violations and hence would in the experiment have none either to remember or to forget.

Since the concept of types of reaction to frustration seemed simpler than repression and appeared to be more amenable to measurement in the presenting experimental situation, the problem of preparing a measuring instrument for such types of reaction assumed definite importance. A behavioural device accordingly constructed is described in a later section (see Rosenzweig, 1935).

A more complete description of the classification of reaction types provisionally adopted may also be found there. It should be mentioned, too, that MacKinnon and the writer are now standardizing a paper-and-pencil test which promises to help considerably in at least the gross determination of these types.

A final suggestion that has arisen from the experiments on stimulus repression refers to hypnotizability. From the clinical evidence of French psychopathology as to the *dissociability* of hysterical patients and from that of Freudian psychoanalysis as to the special relationship between *repression* and hysteria, it seemed profitable to investigate the possible association of repression as a mechanism of defence and hypnotizability as a personality trait. The availability of a measure of repression in the memory techniques made such an investigation feasible but only a preliminary study with about fifteen subjects has thus far been made. A rough analysis of the results tends to substantiate the expectation upon which the experiment was based, for the hypnotizable subjects appear to have recalled their successes better than their failures more often than did the non-hypnotizable ones.

A certain amount of reciprocal corroboration was obtained from an experiment in which a group of stutterers, sent by a physician in Boston, was compared with a group of Harvard students selected because they were active either in dramatics or in debating. By and large, the stutterers appear to have recalled their failures more frequently than did the public speakers. In view of the obsessional characteristics generally attributed to stutterers and their reputed refractoriness to hypnosis, this result is in good agreement with the hypothesis that repression is a mechanism of defence pathognomonic of hysteria only.

There thus emerges a triadic hypothesis according to which hypnotizability as a personality trait is to be found in positive association with repression as a preferred mechanism of defence and with impunitiveness as a characteristic type of immediate reaction to frustration. Non-hypnotizability would, by implication, be linked with other defence mechanisms, e.g. displacement and projection, and with other types of reaction to frustration, e.g. intropunitiveness and extrapunitiveness. Should these inter-relationships be conclusively proved by experimentation yet to be done, a notable integration of certain concepts of French psychopathology (hypnotizability and dissociation) and of Freudian psychoanalysis (repression and other defence mechanisms) would have been achieved through the use of tools (techniques for studying repression and types of reaction to frustration) made available by experimental psychology.

References

BREUER, J., and FREUD, S. (1936), *Studies in Hysteria*, New York.

BRUN, R. (1926), 'Experimentelle Beiträge zur Dynamik und Ökonomie des Triebkonfliktes (Biologische Parallelen zur Freuds Trieblehre)', *Imago*, vol. 12, pp. 147–70.

FREUD, S. (1924a), 'On history of the psycho-analytic movement', *Collected Papers*, vol. 1, New York.

FREUD, S. (1924b), *Collected Papers*, vol. 4, New York.

FREUD, S. (1935), *Autobiography*, New York.

FREUD, S. (1936), *The Problem of Anxiety*, New York.

KOCH, H. L. (1930), 'The influence of some affective factors upon recall', *J. gen. Psychol.*, vol. 4, pp. 171–90.

LEWIN, K. (1935), *A Dynamic Theory of Personality*, New York.

LYNCH, C. A. (1932), 'The memory value of certain alleged emotionally toned words', *J. exp. Psychol.*, vol. 15, pp. 298–315.

MACKINNON, D. W. (1933), 'The violations of prohibitions in the solving of problems', doctoral thesis, Harvard University.

MALAMUD, W. (1934), 'Dream analysis', *Arch. Neurol. Psychiat.*, vol. 31, pp. 356–72.

MALAMUD, W., and LINDER, F. E. (1931), 'Dreams and their relationship to recent impressions', *Arch. Neurol. Psychiat.*, vol. 25, pp. 1081–99.

MELTZER, H. (1930), 'The present states of experimental studies of the relationship of feeling to memory', *Psychol. Rev.*, vol. 37, pp. 124–39.

ROSENZWEIG, S. (1932), 'The dependence of preferences upon success and failure', doctoral dissertation, Harvard University.

ROSENZWEIG, S. (1933a), 'The experimental situation as a psychological problem', *Psychol. Rev.*, vol. 40, pp. 337–54.

ROSENZWEIG, S. (1933b), 'Preferences in the repetition of successful and unsuccessful activities as a function of age and personality', *J. genet. Psychol.*, vol. 42, pp. 423–41.

ROSENZWEIG, S. (1933c), 'The recall of finished and unfinished tasks as affected by the purpose with which they were performed', *Psychol. Bull.*, vol. 30, p. 698 (abstract).

ROSENZWEIG, S. (1934), 'Types of reactions to frustration: an heuristic classification', *J. abnorm. soc. Psychol.*, vol. 29, pp. 298–300.

ROSENZWEIG, S. (1935), 'A test for types of reaction to frustration', *Amer. J. Orthopsychiat.*, vol. 5, pp. 395–403.

ROSENZWEIG, S. (1936), 'The preferential repetition of successful and unsuccessful activities', *Psychol. Bull.*, vol. 33, p. 797 (abstract).

ROSENZWEIG, S., and MASON, G. (1934), 'An experimental study of memory in relation to the theory of repression', *Brit. J. Psychol.*, vol. 24, pp. 247–65.

SEARS, R. R. (1936), 'Functional abnormalities of memory with special reference to amnesia', *Psychol. Bull.*, vol. 33, pp. 229–74.

WOHLGEMUTH, A. (1923), *A Critical Examination of Psycho-Analysis*, London.

ZEIGARNIK, B. (1927), 'Untersuchungen zur Handlungs- und Affektpsychologie', *Psychol. Forschungen*, p. 77.

10 Vincent J. Tempone

Extension of the Repression–Sensitization Hypothesis to
Success and Failure Experience

Vincent J. Tempone, 'Extension of the repression–sensitization
hypothesis to success and failure experience', *Psychological Reports*,
vol. 15, 1964, pp. 39–45.

Byrne (1961) has conceptualized repression–sensitization as a
characteristic way in which individuals respond to threatening stimuli. Repression–sensitization is conceptualized as an
approach–avoidance continuum. At the avoidance end are
repressers who characteristically respond with blocking, denying
and repression; at the other end are individuals who respond in
an approaching, facilitating, vigilant manner. Although Byrne
offers some evidence that is relevant to the scale's validity, the
data are from correlational studies in which his scale correlates
with other measures postulating similar mechanisms.

The purpose of this paper was to extend the theoretical
network surrounding the repression–sensitization hypothesis
to success and failure conditions and to provide additional
evidence of the scale's validity as a measure of repression–
sensitization.

If repressers respond in an avoiding, denying, repressing
manner to threatening stimuli and sensitizers respond in a vigilant,
approaching, facilitating manner, then, given a threat experience,
stimuli associated with the situation should take on differential
meaning for repressers and sensitizers. Repressers should avoid
similar threat situations and stimuli associated with that situation
while sensitizers should become acutely aware of similar situations
and stimuli associated with it. On this basis, it was hypothesized
that: (a) subjected to a failure condition repressers would have
significantly higher thresholds for critical stimuli (or stimuli
associated with that condition) than sensitizers; (b) under a
success condition repressers' and sensitizers' thresholds to critical
stimuli would not differ significantly; (c) repressers' and sensitizers' thresholds would not differ significantly for neutral stimuli

(stimuli not associated with the condition) under either the success or failure condition.

Method

A series of pilot studies were run to select an appropriate condition where threat could be introduced and stimuli associated with that condition would, when presented tachistoscopically, take on a differential meaning for repressers and sensitizers. An anagram test that had been successfully used in two prior studies (Eriksen, 1954; Postman and Solomon, 1950) was selected.

Apparatus

A Keystone Overhead Projector, manufactured by the Keystone View Company of Meadville, Pennsylvania, equipped with a 1000-watt bulb and a flashometer attachment made by the Ilex Optical Company was used. The words were printed in capital letters on $4 \times 3\frac{1}{4}$ inches transparent slides and projected onto a screen 8 feet 7 inches from the projector. Ss sat approximately 9 feet from the screen.

Procedure

Byrne's R–S scale was administered to 244 University of Texas students. Scores ranged from 28 to 113, with a mean of 61·51 and a standard deviation of 18·50. This is similar to Byrne's (1961) reported distribution ($M = 62·61$, $SD = 17·51$).

Those Ss scoring in the seventy-fifth percentile and above were designated sensitizers; those in the twenty-fifth percentile and below were repressers. Confederates were selected from those scoring between these two extremes. Eighty Ss, forty repressers and forty sensitizers, were selected and assigned to one of two conditions: success or failure. Operationally, success was defined as Ss getting six out of eight anagrams correct and failure as two or fewer anagrams correct. Twelve Ss had to be discarded because they failed to meet this criterion.

The experiment was divided into two phases.

First phase. While Ss waited in experimental cubicles, confederates were briefed as to their roles. The confederate's role was to increase

S's sense of success or failure by being successful while *S* failed (failure condition) or failing when *S* was successful (success condition). From the pilot study it was known that it took *S*s a minimum of 30 seconds to 1 minute to solve the anagrams, therefore confederates were told not to solve the anagram quickly, but to wait for a signal from *E* before indicating they had the correct solution. In the success condition the confederates only had one success, *S* being successful on at least six anagrams. In the failure condition the confederates memorized the correct solutions and got a minimum of seven successes. Groups of two or four *S*s were run in each session with a one to one ratio of confederates to *S*s.

Confederates and *S*s were taken to the experimental room where they received test booklets consisting of an instruction page and one anagram on each of 8 other pages. Instructions were read to *S*s.[1] To ensure that *S*s in the success condition correctly solved six of the eight anagrams without spending more than 5 minutes on each one, they were given the hint that the first letter of each anagram was the correct first letter of the word.

*S*s worked on one anagram at a time and at the completion of the time were given the correct solution and told to circle it if they had it right or write out the word and underline it if they had it wrong; thus each *S* had equal exposure to the word.

Second phase. This phase was the same for all groups. Nineteen words were tachistoscopically presented with a Keystone Overhead Projector. The order of presentation, except for the first three practice words which were always constant, was counterbalanced. The position within the serial order was initially randomly determined.

The anagrams, their correct solutions (the critical words) and

1. Instructions read as follows: On the following pages a series of anagrams is presented. They consist of letters arranged in a scrambled order. Using only these letters, you are to rearrange the letters so that they spell an English word. You must use the exact letters that appear; you can't use a letter more than once unless it appears more than once. Your solution would be only one word, not a hyphenated word, nor should it be two or more words. After you have solved each anagram raise your hand. *Do not turn* the page to the next anagram until the instructor tells you. Here are a few examples: atc, cat; wrma, warm.

the neutral words appear in Table 1. The neutral and critical
words were matched according to word frequency and word
length. Using a 22·5 lens opening, each word was exposed twelve
times: three times at speeds of 1/100, 1/50 and 1/25 of a second,

Table 1

Anagrams, Their Correct Solution, Critical Words, Their
Matching Neutral Words and Their Frequency Values

Anagram	Critical words (correct solutions)	Frequency value*	Neutral words	Frequency value*
Tuloimr	turmoil	12	vinegar	14
Slehalc	shellac	8	pronoun	12
Gtlunto	glutton	10	outcast	12
Aplarep	apparel	37	impetus	31
Agleabr	algebra	16	lunatic	15
Maleige	mileage	36	emerald	22
Fncaita	fanatic	18	wildcat	18
Nuemalr	numeral	4	sawdust	10

* Frequency with which the word occurs in four and a half million words
according to Thorndike Semantic Count.

and once at 1/10 and 1/5 of a second and 1 second. The dependent
variable was the number of trials required to recognize the word
correctly. Prior to each presentation, E announced the trial
number. Ss were told to fixate on two cross marks on the center of
the screen. The room was darkened with black cardboard to keep
the light constant. Each S and confederate received a booklet,
which consisted of an instruction page and nineteen additional
pages on which they could record the word in the appropriate
trial number blank when they correctly recognized it.

At the completion of the experiment, Ss were indirectly
questioned as to what they thought about the experiment. Only
two Ss were in any way suspicious of the confederates and their
data were eliminated. Since Ss were recruited at the beginning of
the semester and were, for the most part, introductory psychology
students, they were experimentally naïve.

Results

The group means for critical and neutral words for repressers and sensitizers under the success and failure conditions are presented in Table 2. Inspection of Figure 1 shows that the group means for critical words are in the predicted direction. Repressers have higher thresholds than sensitizers under the failure condition. Under the success condition, differences appear negligible. Thresholds to neutral words, although lower, seem to follow the same direction as critical words.

Table 2

Mean Number of Trials for Repressers and Sensitizers to Correctly Recognize Eight Critical Words and Eight Neutral Words under Success and Failure Conditions

Groups	Success		Failure	
	Critical	Neutral	Critical	Neutral
Repressers	6·831	6·725	7·748	7·306
Sensitizers	7·281	6·944	6·917	6·719

Bartlett's chi square test for homogeneity of variance was applied. A χ^2 of 6·965 with 7 df was non-significant. It was concluded that the data offered no significant evidence against the hypothesis that the samples were drawn from populations with equal variances.

Using a ranking procedure[2] a series of t-tests were computed to determine whether repressers' and sensitizers' thresholds to the critical and neutral words differed significantly under the success and failure conditions. Under the success condition repressers' and sensitizers' thresholds to either the critical or neutral words

2. Inspection of the data revealed wide differences among Ss in threshold ability. To reduce this variability Ss in each condition were ranked according to their thresholds to the three practice words and then matched across conditions. Although Ss were matched after the experimental condition, this does not violate the assumption of independence (Edwards, 1960). Ss within conditions were treated the same way. This design merely permits one to control for intersubject variability.

did not differ significantly ($t = 0.93$, df $= 19$, n.s. for critical words and $t = 0.47$, df $= 19$, n.s. for neutral words). Under the failure condition repressers' thresholds to critical words were significantly higher than sensitizers' ($t = 2.14$, df $= 19$, $p < 0.05$); for neutral words the difference was not significant ($t = 1.35$,

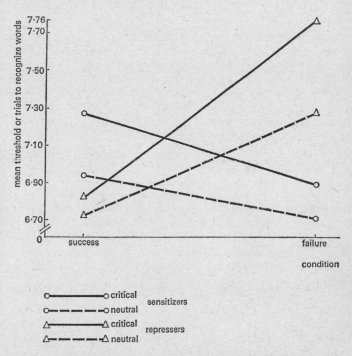

Figure 1 Mean thresholds for repressers and sensitizers to critical and neutral words under a success or failure condition

df $= 19$, n.s.). Thus all three hypotheses were supported. (a) Subjected to a failure experience, repressers had higher thresholds than sensitizers for critical words or words associated with that condition ($t = 2.14$, df $= 1/19$, $p < 0.05$). (b) Under a success condition repressers' and sensitizers' thresholds did not differ for critical words ($t = 0.93$, n.s.). (c) Repressers' and sensitizers' thresholds to neutral stimuli did not differ significantly under the

207

success or failure condition ($t = 0 \cdot 475$, n.s. under success and $t = 1 \cdot 35$, n.s. under failure).

To test the reliability of the tachistoscope as a measuring instrument, odd-even reliability coefficients for the eight critical words and eight neutral words were computed. These product-moment correlations were $0 \cdot 898$ and $0 \cdot 868$, respectively. When the Spearman–Brown correction formula was applied, $r = 0 \cdot 946$ for critical words and $0 \cdot 929$ for neutral words.

Discussion

In interpreting these results it seems unnecessary to postulate a prerecognition factor where some unconscious process perceives the threat value of the stimulus prior to the conscious perception of it and activates defense mechanisms of repression or sensitization. A more parsimonious explanation is offered by Eriksen's S–R model (Eriksen and Browne, 1956). Eriksen distinguishes between response and perception. Perception is an intervening process between the stimulus and the response. The presentation of a stimulus elicits various intervening responses. If one of these intervening responses has been followed by anxiety, the S–R connexion will be weakened. More specifically, the presentation of the stimulus ALGEBRA below threshold may present a number of cues to S. In this case these cues might be $AL----A$. These cues may elicit a number of responses: R_1; $ALBEGRA$; R_2; $ALUMINA$; $ALFALFA$. If R_1 has been followed by anxiety, in this case failure on the word algebra on the anagram test, then the occurrence of R_1 becomes the conditioned stimulus for arousal of anxiety. Even if R_1 is the strongest response in the family hierarchy, the occurence of R_1 which now serves as CS for anxiety will weaken the S_1–R_1 connexion. Since R_2 or R_3 is not followed by anxiety, their occurrence will gain in relative strength as compared to R_1. The probability of a response that has been followed by anxiety would be expected to decrease. On succeeding trials more cues would be presented. In this example the recognition of the letter G would eliminate R_2 and R_3. Even though R_1 is followed by anxiety, enough cues would eventually become available to make the word completely recognizable. The occurrence of anxiety to the partial cues presented early in the perceptual task would have enough disruptive influence to increase the recognition threshold. It would follow from this model that words which evoke anxiety would have less probability of occurrence and thus would have higher thresholds than neutral words.

Even if one accepts this interpretation, the question still remains why thresholds to neutral words, although not significantly different for repressers and sensitizers, followed the same trend and therefore seem to be influenced by the experimental condition. One explanation might be that anxiety generated by the critical words generalizes to the neutral words. Since thresholds to the neutral words are lower under success condition where it was assumed that there was little anxiety, this does not seem to be an adequate explanation. It was anticipated that, in accordance with two prior studies (Eriksen, 1954; Postman and Solomon, 1950), neutral words, although not differentiating between repressers and sensitizers, would have higher thresholds. Since Ss had no prior exposure to the neutral words, but had seen the critical words on the anagram test, it was predicted that this prior exposure would lower thresholds to the critical words. Why this effect was not present in this study awaits further investigation. If this S–R interpretation is accepted, the question still remains why anxiety is more disruptive for repressers than sensitizers. Byrne (1961) has hypothesized that repressers are less likely to verbalize negative self-descriptions to themselves or E than sensitizers. In support of this, Byrne found that sensitizers are more ready to admit faults than repressers. With faults defined as admitting to negative self descriptions on Worchel's Self-Activity Inventory (Worchel, 1957), a correlation of 0·66 ($p < 0·01$) is reported between the R–S scale and negative self-descriptions.

If high scoring Ss or sensitizers are ready to admit faults and self-devaluating statements about themselves, while repressers are reluctant to admit any faults, then self-devaluating thoughts are less anxiety arousing for sensitizers and more anxiety arousing for repressers. Stimuli associated with the self-devaluating experience (failure on the test) are more likely to be anxiety arousing to repressers than sensitizers. Therefore, the anxiety induced by the failure condition would have a more disruptive effect on repressers' thresholds to critical words than on those of sensitizers.

This study does provide empirical support for the validity of

Byrne's scale as a measure of the repression–sensitization dimension. It also suggests that future perceptual studies using the R–S scale should specify the conditions under which threshold measures are taken.

References

BYRNE, D. (1961), 'The repression–sensitization scale: rationale, reliability, and validity', *J. Personal.*, vol. 29, pp. 334–49.

EDWARDS, A. L. (1960), *Experimental Design in Psychological Research*, Holt, Rinehart & Winston.

ERIKSEN, C. W. (1954), 'Psychological defenses and ego strength in the recall of completed and incompleted tasks', *J. abnorm. soc. Psychol.*, vol. 49, pp. 45–50.

ERIKSEN, C. W., and BROWNE, T. (1956), 'An experimental and theoretical analysis of perceptual defense', *J. abnorm. soc. Psychol.*, vol. 51, pp. 224–30.

POSTMAN, L., and SOLOMON, R. L. (1950), 'Perceptual sensitivity to completed and incompleted tasks', *J. Personal.*, vol. 18, pp. 347–58.

TEMPONE, V. J. (1962), 'Differential thresholds of repressers and sensitizers under a success or failure condition', doctoral dissertation, University of Texas.

WORCHEL, P. (1957), *Adaptability Screening of Flying Personnel: Development of a Self-Concept Inventory for Predicting Maladjustment*, Randolph Air Force Base, Texas.

Projection

11 William D. Wells and Rachel L. Goldstein

Sears' Study of Projection: Replications and Critique

William D. Wells and Rachel L. Goldstein, 'Sears' study of projection: replications and critique', *Journal of Social Psychology*, vol. 64, 1964, pp. 169–79.

Background

In 1936, R. R. Sears published an experiment which showed that persons who have an undesirable trait, and who lack insight into the fact that they have that trait, assign the trait in excessive amounts to others.

Because this study seemed to demonstrate the action of a psychoanalytic 'defense mechanism' it attracted a great deal of attention. Textbook writers used it to illustrate the meaning of the term 'projection' (Hilgard, 1962; Krech and Crutchfield, 1958; Leuba, 1961; Morgan, 1961; Munn, 1961; Rogers, 1962; Smith, 1961; Wickens and Meyer, 1961; Williams, 1960); and theorists used it in work on personality dynamics (Berkowitz, 1960; Cattell, 1957; Frenkel–Brunswik, 1954).

Sears' experiment has also influenced theory and research in the areas of attitude formation and person perception (Bruner and Tagiuri, 1954; Goldings, 1954; Lehner, 1960; Taft, 1955). And, because it produced a set of positive correlations among ratings on scales measuring stinginess, obstinacy and orderliness, it has been used as evidence for the existence of an 'anal' personality syndrome (Child, 1954; Frenkel–Brunswik, 1954; Hilgard, 1962; Sears, 1943; Smith, 1961).

A study as important as this one ought to be repeated, if only to test the generality of the findings. Sears' subjects were drawn from a limited and atypical population – the members of three fraternities at one university – but users of his findings have often treated them as though they hold true for all of human nature.

Furthermore, the procedural details of the study – the rating scales, the classification system, the statistical analysis, etc. – constitute but one of a variety of ways of testing the same hypothesis. If the principles demonstrated are truly general, they ought to reappear when the data are collected and treated in other ways – provided that there is no real change in the logic of the experiment.

Two studies replicating certain features of Sears' study have been published (Lemann and Solomon, 1952; Rokeach, 1945). Both employed somewhat different methods of gathering and analysing data, and both employed subjects from somewhat different populations. Neither one replicated Sears' findings.

These failures to replicate create a problem. It may be that the original results were right and that the nonconfirming studies omitted something essential. Or it may be that the relationships Sears found are too weak to survive even minor changes in subjects or procedure. If so, it would certainly be unwise to go on assuming that his relationships demonstrate a fundamental truth about human nature.

The data reported here came from two additional attempts to reproduce Sears' findings. The first, like Sears' experiment, employed college fraternity members as subjects. The second, like the studies which did not substantiate Sears' findings, employed college coeds.

In both cases, every detail of Sears' procedure was duplicated as faithfully as possible, so that either a successful replication or a failure to confirm would be informative. A successful replication would show that the original results hold true at least for other groups of college students and would therefore increase confidence in their generality. A failure to confirm would provide additional reason to believe that Sears' findings should not be generalized beyond the exact time, place and circumstances of the original investigation.

Subjects

The fifty-seven fraternity members who participated in the study all belonged to one social fraternity at Newark College of Arts and Sciences, Rutgers University. Like most students at Newark Rutgers, they lived at home and commuted to school; so they probably did not know each other as well as Sears' subjects did. They had attended meetings, parties and other social events together for a minimum of six months before the study began. At least two-thirds had belonged to the fraternity for at least a year, and about a third had attended the same high school.

The ninety-nine coeds who participated in the study were attending Paterson State Teachers College, Newark State Teachers College or the Douglass College of Rutgers University. Students at the three colleges assembled small groups of close friends for the experiment. Eleven of the groups were groups of five, two were groups of six, two were groups of seven and two were groups of nine. The subjects within individual groups were all well acquainted.

Method

Each subject rated himself (or herself) and each member of his (or her) own group on seven-step rating scales intended to measure four 'opprobrious' traits: stinginess, obstinacy, disorderliness and bashfulness. [The form and the content of the scales are described in Sears' paper (1936, p. 152) and are discussed below.]

Subjects who were rated above average (e.g. stingier than average) on a trait by the other members of their group were classified as 'having' the trait. Subjects who were rated below average on a trait were classified as 'not having' it. Subjects who were classified as having one of the traits, and who rated themselves higher (e.g. stingier) on the trait than they rated others, were classified as 'insightful' – they had the trait and knew it. Subjects who were classified as having a trait, and who rated themselves lower (e.g. less stingy) on it than they rated others, were classified as 'non-insightful' – they had the trait and did not know it. This classification method duplicated the classification method used by Sears in his analysis.

Defence Mechanisms

The critical comparison was between the 'insightful' and the 'non-insightful' subjects. Sears found that those who had an opprobrious trait, and lacked insight into the fact that they had it, attributed the trait to others to a greater degree than those who had the trait and knew it. He interpreted this finding as a demonstration of the projection mechanism.

Sears also used the 'insightful' – 'non-insightful' distinction to subclassify subjects who were classified as *not* having the opprobrious traits. Subjects who did not have one of the traits (e.g. subjects who were rated *less* stingy than average by others) and who gave themselves lower ratings on it than they gave to other people, were called 'insightful'. Subjects who did not have the trait, and gave themselves *higher* ratings on it than they gave to others, were classified as 'non-insightful'. The ratings assigned to others by members of these two groups were also compared.

When Sears made this comparison he found that non-insightful subjects rated others as having even less of the opprobrious trait than did insightful subjects. He interpreted this finding as an indication that a process like projection occurs even when the trait is not opprobrious.

In addition, the average rating assigned *by* others was correlated with the average rating assigned *to* others – first for all subjects, then for 'insightful' and 'non-insightful' subjects separately. When Sears examined these relationships he found consistent negative correlations in the ratings made by 'insightful' subjects only. He interpreted these correlations as evidence for a mechanism he called 'contrast formation' – the more of a trait an insightful person possesses, the less of it he attributes to other people. Analogous correlations were computed from the present data.

Finally, the average ratings assigned each subject on each trait were intercorrelated. Positive and significant correlations among stinginess, orderliness and obstinacy would provide further evidence for the existence of an anal syndrome.

Results

Tables 1 and 2 show the mean ratings assigned to others by the four groups formed by Sears' criteria. Sears' data are also presented for comparison. Note that Sears' data are in standard scores, while the present data are in raw-score form.

The three sets of results are in fairly close agreement. In all these sets of data, *non*-insightful subjects who 'had' opprobrious traits (group A) tended to assign them to other people to a greater

Table 1

Mean Scores Assigned to Others

Trait	Subjects 'having' the opprobrious trait				Subjects 'not having' the opprobrious trait			
	Non–insightful A		Insightful B		Non–insightful C		Insightful D	
	n	M	n	M	n	M	n	M
Fraternity members (in raw scores)								
Stinginess	15	3·36	9	3·08	8	3·06	24	3·14
Obstinacy	5	3·58	19	3·27	14	3·30	18	3·37
Disorderliness	13	3·45	13	3·46	11	3·55	20	3·55
Bashfulness	9	3·11	16	3·11	10	3·04	22	3·15
Coeds (in raw scores)								
Stinginess	29	3·13	21	2·96	14	2·57	35	2·86
Obstinacy	33	3·45	12	2·91	12	2·83	42	3·15
Disorderliness	20	3·44	25	3·38	17	2·94	37	3·45
Bashfulness	12	3·52	30	2·79	22	2·76	35	3·20
Sears' data (in standard scores)								
Stinginess	20	0·23	22	0·02	12	−0·29	43	−0·01
Obstinacy	22	0·37	21	−0·29	12	−0·49	42	0·06
Disorderliness	11	0·16	30	−0·55	20	−0·01	36	0·42
Bashfulness	7	−0·20	20	−0·41	14	0·06	19	0·41

degree than did insightful subjects who had the traits (group B). Also, in groups C and D (the groups of subjects 'not having' the opprobrious traits according to Sears' classification), the insightful subjects tended to assign the traits to other people in greater degree than did non-insightful subjects. Thus, although between-group differences were small and often not statistically significant, a faithful duplication of Sears' procedures produced similar results.

Table 3 shows correlations between average rating received by subjects and average rating they assigned to other persons, first for all subjects and then for insightful and non-insightful subjects separately. Again Sears' results are included for comparison, and

Table 2

Tests of Significance of Differences between Ratings Assigned to Others by Members of Insightful and Non-Insightful Groups

Trait	'Having' the opprobrious trait				'Not having' the opprobrious trait			
	A–B Diff.	σ_D	df	t	C–D Diff.	σ_D	df	t
Fraternity members (in raw scores)								
Stinginess	0·28	0·17	22	1·65	0·08	0·22	30	0·36
Obstinacy	0·31	0·23	22	1·35	0·07	0·13	30	0·54
Disorderliness	−0·01	0·14	24	0·07	0·00	—	29	0·00
Bashfulness	0·00	—	23	0·00	0·10	0·11	28	0·91
Coeds (in raw scores)								
Stinginess	0·17	0·17	48	1·00	0·29	0·21	47	1·38
Obstinacy	0·54	0·26	43	2·08*	0·32	0·21	52	1·52
Disorderliness	0·06	0·17	43	0·35	0·51	0·14	52	3·64‡
Bashfulness	0·73	0·21	40	3·48†	0·44	0·15	55	2·93†
Sears' data (in standard scores)								
Stinginess	0·21	0·27	40	0·78	0·28	0·28	53	1·00
Obstinacy	0·66	0·30	41	2·20*	0·55	0·39	52	1·41
Disorderliness	0·71	0·37	39	1·92	0·43	0·21	54	2·05
Bashfulness	0·21	0·42	25	0·50	0·35	0·31	31	1·13

* $P < 0.05$.
† $P < 0.01$.
‡ $P < 0.001$.
Note: In Sears' data, PE_D translated in σ_D by formula $\sigma_D = PE_D/0.67$.

again there is fairly close agreement. As in Sears' data, the correlations between rating received by insightful subjects and rating assigned by them were generally negative, while the analogous correlations for non-insightful subjects were not. It was this set of relationships that led Sears to suggest the mechanism he called 'contrast formation'.

Table 4 shows the intercorrelations among stinginess, obstinacy and orderliness – the three traits in the 'anal syndrome'. Shown also are intercorrelations of these ratings with ratings on the bashfulness scale.

Table 3

Correlations between Mean Ratings Received from Others and Mean Ratings Assigned to Others

Trait	Whole group		Insightful subjects		Non-insightful subjects	
	n	r	n	r	n	r
Fraternity members						
Stinginess	56	0·08	33	0·00	23	0·12
Obstinacy	56	−0·19	37	−0·27	19	−0·06
Disorderliness	57	−0·13	33	−0·19	24	−0·03
Bashfulness	57	0·08	38	−0·07	19	0·22
Average		−0·04		−0·13		0·06
Coeds						
Stinginess	99	0·09	56	−0·14	43	0·32
Obstinacy	99	0·16	54	−0·09	45	0·35
Disorderliness	99	0·10	62	0·06	37	0·27
Bashfulness	99	−0·12	65	−0·27	34	0·37
Average		0·06		−0·11		0·33
Sears' data						
Stinginess	97	−0·03	65	−0·08	32	0·09
Obstinacy	97	0·01	63	−0·15	34	0·34
Disorderliness	97	−0·35	66	−0·46	31	0·13
Bashfulness	60	−0·32	39	−0·34	21	−0·22
Average		−0·17		−0·26		0·08

As far as the 'anal' traits are concerned, agreement is poor – both between Sears' data and the present data and between the data from the fraternity members and the data from the coeds. Certainly no strong evidence for an anal syndrome can be found. In fact, the simplest way to account for the relationships would seem to be in terms of a simple halo effect.

Table 4

Correlation among Mean Ratings on Four Traits

Trait	Stinginess	Obstinacy	Orderliness	Bashfulness
Fraternity members				
Stinginess	0·30	−0·38		0·56
Obstinacy		0·01		−0·16
Orderliness				−0·48
Coeds				
Stinginess	0·48	0·11		0·23
Obstinacy		0·04		−0·09
Orderliness				0·12
Sears' data				
Stinginess	0·37	0·39		—
Obstinacy		0·36		—
Orderliness				—

Discussion

Rokeach (1945) and others (Murstein, 1957; Rosenthal, 1959) have pointed out an ambiguity created by the way Sears classified his subjects. Among those 'having' the opprobrious traits, subjects were called 'insightful' if their average rating of others was *lower* than the rating they assigned to themselves, while they were called 'non-insightful' if their average rating of others was *higher* than their self-ratings. In the absence of a consistent difference in self-rating, this method of classification would automatically produce a higher average rating of others by the 'non-insightful' subjects than by subjects in the 'insightful' category.

At the other end of the scale, among those 'not having' the opprobrious traits, the method of classification would force a similar difference in the opposite direction. The same artifact could also have produced the correlations, shown in Table 3, which led to the notion of 'contrast formation'.

An additional problem is created by the format of the rating scales. Each step on each scale had a specific label. The stinginess scale, for example, read:

1. Generous, perhaps an easy mark.
2. Rather easygoing.

3. Sensible about use of possessions.
4. Cautious but not a tightwad.
5. Fairly careful about his rights as an owner.
6. Pretty tight about most things.
7. Very stingy.

Since subjects rated above average on this scale were all classi-fied by Sears as 'stingy', and since the average score on the scale was about 3·3, the group called 'stingy' in Sears' classification included some subjects who were classified by their peers as 'sensible about use of possessions', and all subjects classified as 'cautious but not a tightwad' and 'fairly careful of his rights as an owner' – as well as subjects who, according to the mean rating they received, were actually perceived as stingy.

It seems hard to justify this classification. The theory the experiment was designed to test requires that the person doing the projecting actually possesses the opprobrious trait, not some mild degree of its desirable opposite. When the present data were treated by means of Sears' method of classification, a substantial number of subjects who did not have the opprobrious trait (according to ratings by their peers) were classified as possessing it.

The same problem occurs with the ratings on the other vari-ables. In each case Sears' method of classification placed in the 'obstinate', 'disorderly' or 'bashful' category a substantial number of subjects who were rated by their peers as *not* having the opprobrious trait in question.

Sears' data were presented in standard score form; so it is impossible to be sure that they incorporated the same contra-diction. But since raters generally tend to give favorable ratings, especially when evaluating friends, it seems reasonable to suppose that a similar contradiction existed also in Sears' raw data.

Reanalysis

To find out whether a literal interpretation of the meaning of the scale steps would change the conclusions drawn from the data, all subjects were reclassified according to the following criteria: subjects who had been given ratings of 5, 6 or 7 by at least 50 per cent of their peers were classified as having the opprobrious trait.

(All the scales were oriented so that scores of 5, 6 or 7 were un-favorable.) Subjects who were given ratings of 1, 2 or 3 by at least 50 per cent of their peers were classified as having the desirable trait at the opposite end of the rating scale.

Table 5

Mean Scores Assigned to Others
(Subjects reclassified)

Trait	Non–insightful C			Insightful D			
	n	M	σ	n	M	σ	Diff.
Fraternity members							
Stinginess	9	3·53	0·57	35	3·07	0·46	0·46†
Obstinacy	16	3·41	0·40	22	3·31	0·29	0·10
Disorderliness	8	3·68	0·19	13	3·57	0·30	0·11*
Bashfulness	9	3·13	0·40	31	3·08	0·24	0·05
Coeds							
Stinginess	18	3·04	0·59	72	2·86	0·58	0·18
Obstinacy	12	3·24	0·98	65	3·07	0·74	0·17
Disorderliness	20	3·57	0·59	44	3·28	0·56	0·29*
Bashfulness	27	3·23	0·72	52	3·09	0·58	0·14

* $P < 0.05$ by simple analysis of variance.
† $P < 0.01$ by simple analysis of variance.

Since it seemed desirable to limit the analysis to subjects who were perceived by their peers as actually possessing the traits, subjects who were not rated on one side or the other of the scale by at least 50 per cent of the raters were dropped from the analysis.

Subjects who were given ratings of 1, 2 or 3 on a trait by at least 50 per cent of their peers – and who gave themselves a 1, 2 or 3 rating – were reclassified as 'insightful'; subjects who were given ratings of 1, 2 or 3 by at least 50 per cent of their peers, and gave themselves a 4, 5, 6 or 7, were reclassified as 'non-insightful'. A similar subclassification was made of subjects rated by their peers at 5, 6 or 7. If their self-ratings agreed with the peers' verdict, they were called 'insightful'. They were called 'non-insightful' otherwise.

This method of classification all but demolished the A and B categories – the categories of subjects 'having' the opprobrious traits according to their peers' ratings. The demolition was so nearly complete that not enough As and Bs remained to permit meaningful analysis.

Table 6

Correlations between Mean Ratings Received from Others and Mean Ratings Assigned to Others
(Subjects reclassified)

Trait	Whole group		Insightful subjects		Non-insightful subjects	
	n	r	n	r	n	r
Fraternity members						
Stinginess	44	0·13	35	0·28	9	−0·58
Obstinacy	42	0·02	26	0·01	16	0·15
Disorderliness	23	−0·21	16	−0·02	7	−0·74
Bashfulness	41	−0·14	32	−0·13	9	−0·36
Coeds						
Stinginess	94	0·10	71	0·08	23	−0·01
Obstinacy	90	0·15	67	0·06	23	0·15
Disorderliness	71	0·10	46	0·23	25	−0·20
Bashfulness	86	−0·11	53	−0·17	33	−0·11

Note: The correlation data in Table 6 include ratings by subjects in the A and B categories. These subjects had been excluded from the data in Table 5 because the subgroups they formed were too small to permit meaningful analysis.

However, the new classification method left sizeable groups of Cs and Ds. These were subjects who, according to peer opinion, had traits at the desirable ends of the rating scales. The Ds were 'insightful' in that they also gave themselves desirable ratings, and the Cs were 'non-insightful' in that they did not.

This new classification (Table 5) reversed Sears' finding. The average rating assigned to others by the 'non-insightful' subjects was regularly, and in a few cases significantly, higher than the average rating assigned to others by subjects in the 'insightful' category. Table 6 shows that the new classification also destroyed the pattern of negative correlations which had led to the concept of 'contrast formation'.

This finding is similar to results reported by Rokeach (1945). Rokeach used a rating scale quite different from the scales used by Sears, but when he followed Sears' method of analysis he found a pattern in the data similar to the pattern Sears had found. When he reanalysed the data by a method which eliminated the spurious correlation, the pattern disappeared.

Taken together, Rokeach's results and the present results intensify doubts about the advisability of accepting and making use of Sears' original conclusions. If 'projection' and 'contrast formation' are names for ways humans generally behave, confirming evidence should not perish so easily. It ought to present itself when the data are submitted to any reasonable analysis.

The present results also force much the same conclusion with respect to the correlations Sears found among the traits of the 'anal syndrome'. Even in Sears' data the correlations were low. In the present data several of them reversed. The evidence does not suggest the presence of a clear-cut and dependable trait cluster.

Concluding Discussion

These findings underscore the rule that research results should not be treated as established fact until they have been confirmed by repetition. The original study appeared when psychological interest in psychoanalytic mechanisms was high. The results were widely accepted, and were perpetuated through repeated mention in secondary sources. Published studies which cast doubt upon the generality and the validity of the findings were almost ignored. Now, after the study has influenced theory and research for twenty-five years, the weight of negative evidence has become all but decisive.

Summary

Sears' classic study of projection was replicated twice – once with a group of college fraternity members serving as subjects, and once with a group of college coeds. In both cases the results agreed with Sears' results when the data were analysed according to Sears' method. However, when the data were reanalysed with a method which eliminated a possibly spurious correlation, the results reversed. The implications of this reversal, and the relations between it and the findings of other studies of projection, are discussed.

In an additional analysis of data from his projection study, Sears had intercorrelated ratings on scales intended to measure obstinacy, stinginess and orderliness, and had found evidence for an 'anal syndrome'. A similar analysis of data from the present study produced no evidence of an anal trait cluster.

References

BERKOWITZ, L. (1960), 'The judgemental process in personality functioning', *Psychol. Rev.*, vol. 67, pp. 130–42.

BRUNER, J. S., and TAGIURI, R. (1954), 'The perception of people', in G. Lindzey (ed.), *Handbook of Social Psychology: Vol. 2. Special Fields and Applications*, Addison-Wesley.

CATTELL, R. B. (1957), *Personality and Motivation Structure and Measurement*, World Books.

CHILD, I. L. (1954), 'Socialization', in G. Lindzey (ed.), *Handbook of Social Psychology: Vol. 2. Special Fields and Applications*, Addison-Wesley.

FRENKEL-BRUNSWIK, E. (1954), 'Contributions to the analysis and synthesis of knowledge', *Proc. Amer. Acad. Arts Scien.*, vol. 80, pp. 271–350.

GOLDINGS, H. (1954), 'On the avowal and projection of happiness', *J. Personal.*, vol. 23, pp. 30–47.

HILGARD, E. R. (1962), *Introduction to Psychology*, Harcourt, Brace & World, 3rd edn.

KRECH, D., and CRUTCHFIELD, R. S. (1958), *Elements of Psychology*, Knopf.

LEHNER, G. F. J. (1960), 'Some relationships among personal adjustment of self-ratings self-scores, and assigned "average" scores', *J. Psychol.*, vol. 50, pp. 333–7.

LEMANN, T. B., and SOLOMON, R. L. (1952), 'Group characteristics as revealed in sociometric patterns and personality ratings', *Sociometry*, vol. 15, pp. 7–90.

LEUBA, C. L. (1961), *Man: A General Psychology*, Holt, Rinehart & Winston.

MORGAN, C. T. (1961), *Introduction to Psychology*, McGraw-Hill, 2nd edn.

MUNN, N. L. (1961), *Psychology*, Houghton Mifflin, 2nd edn.

MURSTEIN, B. I. (1957), 'Studies in projection: a critique', *J. proj. Tech.*, vol. 21, pp. 129–36.

ROGERS, D. (1962), *The Psychology of Adolescence*, Appleton-Century-Crofts.

ROKEACH, M. (1945), 'Studies in beauty: II. Some determiners of the perception of beauty in women', *J. soc. Psychol.*, vol. 22, pp. 155–69.

ROSENTHAL, R. (1959), 'The experimental induction of the defense mechanism of projection', *J. proj. Tech.*, vol. 23, pp. 357–64.

SEARS, R. R. (1959), 'Experimental studies of projection: I. Attributions of traits', *J. soc. Psychol.*, vol. 7, pp. 151–63.

SEARS, R. R. (1943), 'Survey of objective studies of psychoanalytic concepts', *Soc. Scien. Res. Coun. Bull.*, no. 51.

SMITH, H. C. (1961), *Personality Adjustment*, McGraw-Hill.

TAFT, R. (1955), 'The ability to judge people', *Psychol. Bull.*, vol. 52, pp. 1–23.

WICKENS, D. D., and MEYER, D. R. (1961), *Psychology*, Holt, Rinehart & Winston, 2nd edn.

WILLIAMS, G. W. (1960), *Psychology: A First Course*, Harcourt, Brace & World.

Fixation and Regression

12 O. H. Mowrer

An Experimental Analogue of 'Regression' with Incidental Observations on 'Reaction-Formation'

O. H. Mowrer, 'An experimental analogue of "regression" with incidental observations on "reaction-formation"', *Journal of Abnormal and Social Psychology*, vol. 35, 1940, pp. 56–87.

I

Two extremely interesting experimental demonstrations of 'regression' in the rat have already been published and it may therefore seem unnecessary to report another instance of this same phenomenon. On the basis of evidence already available, there can be scarcely any question of the reality of regression in human beings or, as the two studies just cited show, of the possibility of its occurrence in animals well below man in the evolutionary scale. Since neither of these studies, however, was apparently conducted with an altogether satisfactory understanding of the theory of regression as it has been developed clinically, they have served in certain respects to obscure rather than to clarify the fundamental nature of regression and the conditions of its occurrence. The present study represents an attempt to eliminate some of this ambiguity. Although animal experimentation along these and related lines may eventually have something new and useful to contribute to human psychopathology, that day apparently still lies in the future. In the meantime, it would seem to behoove those who look forward to making such contributions to acquire the greatest possible familiarity with those theories and principles that have already been derived from careful clinical inquiry at the human level. If clinical concepts are to be taken over and applied carelessly in animal experiments, the results obtained can be expected to be correspondingly confused and meaningless.

Since regression is pre-eminently a psychoanalytic concept and since no one has superseded Freud as a theorist in this field, it is appropriate to turn to him for an authoritative statement of this principle. This writer, it so happens, is not a formal systematist, and it is accordingly necessary to extract his purely theoretical views, piecemeal as it were, from the context of his extensive clinical and popular writings. This is not to say, however, that his theoretical formulations are inexplicit, contradictory, or any less comprehensive and complete than the limitations of logic and empirical observation necessitate in a new and difficult field of inquiry.

In a technical paper that appeared in 1916, Freud introduced the topic of regression as follows:

When we investigate psychoneurotic conditions, we find in each of them occasion to comment upon a so-called *temporal regression*, i.e. the particular extent to which each of them retraces the stages of its evolution. We distinguish two such regressions – one in the development of the ego and the other in that of the libido. In sleep, the latter is carried to the point of restoring the primitive narcissism, while the former goes back to the state of hallucinatory wish-fulfilment.

At a later point in the same article, Freud also distinguished between 'the previously mentioned temporal or developmental regression' and what he then termed 'topographical regression'. In subsequent writings, however, he has made comparatively little use of this latter term, employing instead the term 'repression'. Writing in 1920, Freud said:

[In the present discussion] we have not been using the word '*regression*' in its general sense but in a quite specific one. If you give it its general sense, that of a reversion from a higher to a lower stage of development in general, then repression also ranges itself under regression; for repression can also be described as reversion to an earlier and lower stage in the development of a mental act. Only, in repression this retrogressive direction is not a point of any moment to us; for we also call it repression in a dynamic sense when a mental process is arrested before it leaves the lower stages of the unconscious. Repression is thus a topographic-dynamic conception, while regression is a purely descriptive one.

226

As is well known, Freud worked out most of his psychological principles on the basis of observations concerning the sex life of neurotic human beings, but, as in the case of regression, many of his findings have a much wider application. Consequently, it is understandable why it should be in this setting that one finds Freud's most trenchant formulations regarding regression, which, however, because of the dynamic character of all psychoanalytic concepts, are necessarily intertwined with other principles which must also be given at least incidental consideration.

In a paper that appeared in 1912, Freud presented a detailed statement of his conception of regression in the etiology of neurotic illness and posited that its occurrence or non-occurrence is primarily contingent upon two factors: *fixation* and *frustration*. According to the view developed at that time and subsequently held with relatively little modification, the erotic life (libido) of civilized human beings passes through several more or less discrete stages in its development from the so-called narcissism of infancy to the genital heterosexuality of normal adult life. Because of the continuing pressure of the socializing and educational forces in modern society (plus the changing needs of the child, produced by physical maturation), each of the intermediate stages is successively achieved and then abandoned for the next higher level of adjustment, until the final adult goal is reached. If, however, for any of several possible reasons, this development process does not go forward in the usual way and the individual never advances beyond one of the intermediate stages, there results what may be called *absolute* fixation. This is a phenomenon that actually occurs in the lives of some persons and is assumed to provide the basis for the sexual perversions. But since there is here no question of a *return* from a later to an earlier mode of adjustment, the problem of regression is not, of course, involved.

On the other hand, in the lives of persons who do make the prescribed step-by-step transitions in their sexual development (however falteringly), the habits that are acquired and reinforced at each successive stage necessarily have a certain strength or intensity (cathexis) that is more or less enduring; and it is the varying strength of such habits that determines the extent to which *relative* fixation may be said to have occurred at any given

227

point. This phenomenon, in contra-distinction to absolute fixation,[1] is of special significance for the understanding of the mechanism of regression; for it is presumably the specific nature and extent of the relative fixations in an individual's life-history which determine the pattern of regression ('choice of neurosis') that will occur if, subsequently, a superimposed mode of adjustment or habit system meets with an insuperable obstacle (i.e. if *frustration* occurs) and if there is relatively little opportunity for further *progression* (i.e. for the development of still other new habits). In other words, the greater the strength of a relative fixation, other things equal, the greater the tendency for regression to occur to the level of that fixation when subsequently acquired habits (in the same impulse-need-system) are thwarted, punished or otherwise prevented from functioning effectively and bringing the customary satisfaction.

Of the various passages in which Freud has described the principle of regression, perhaps none is more vivid or instructive than the following, which, for additional reasons that will later become evident, is worth quoting in full.

The second danger [besides that of absolute fixation] in a development by stages such as [that of the libido] we call *regression*; it also happens that those portions which have proceeded further may easily revert in a backward direction to these earlier stages. The impulse will find occasion to *regress* in this way when the exercise of its function in a later and more developed form meets with powerful external obstacles, which thus prevent it from attaining the goal of satisfaction. It is a short step to assume that fixation and regression are not independent of each other; the stronger the fixations in the path of development the more easily will the function yield before the external obstacles, by regressing on to those fixations; that is, the less capable of resistance against the external difficulties in its path will the developed function be. If you think of a migrating people who have left large numbers at the stopping-places on their way, you will see that the foremost will

1. Freud holds that, although sharply distinguishable at the conceptual level, there is in actual practice a continuum between absolute and relative fixations. He says: 'There exist, therefore, two extremes – "inhibited development" and "regression" – and between them every degree of combination of the two factors.' (It should be noted, incidentally, that *absolute* and *relative fixation* are not Freudian terms, but their introduction seems warranted as an aid to clear theoretical exposition.)

naturally fall back upon these positions when they are defeated or when they meet with an enemy too strong for them. And again, the more of their number they leave behind in their progress, the sooner will they be in danger of defeat.

The writer goes on to say that a clear conception of the relation between fixation and regression is fundamental to the understanding of the psychoanalytic theory of the neurosis, for, as already indicated, regression or a tendency to regression is assumed to lie at the basis of all symptom-formation. When, under the stress of a need that has been denied its customary form of gratification, regression occurs or is in danger of occurring, anticipation of the penalties that were originally effective in bringing about the required habit progression to this particular level of gratification is, according to psychoanalytic theory, sure to be reactivated;[2] and it is precisely this reactivation of old anticipations of punishment which provides the anxiety that is so constant and so conspicuous a feature of every neurosis. It is for this reason that regression is so likely to be pathogenic. In this connexion, Freud says:

I think that you will be soonest reconciled to this exposition of fixation and regression of the libido if you will regard it as preparatory to a study of *aetiology* of the neuroses. . . . People fall ill of a neurosis when the possibility of satisfaction for the libido is removed from them – they fall ill in consequence of a 'frustration', as I called it. . . . This of course does not mean that every frustration in regard to libidinal satisfaction makes everyone who meets with it neurotic, but merely that in all cases of neurosis investigated the factor of frustration was demonstrated.

The libido is [thus] blocked, as it were, and must seek an escape by which it can find an outlet for its cathexis (charge of energy) in conformity with the demands of the pleasure-principle: it must elude, eschew the ego. The fixations upon the path of development now regressively transversed . . . offer just such an escape. In streaming backward and re-'cathecting' these repressed [abandoned] positions, the libido withdraws itself from the ego and its laws; but it also abandons all the training acquired under the influence of the ego. It was docile as long as satisfaction was in sight; under the double pressure

2. The connexion between punishment (or threat of punishment) and education (habit progression) has been discussed at length in a previous publication. It is here taken for granted and will be given only incidental consideration in the subsequent pages of this paper.

of external and internal frustration it becomes intractable and harks back to former happier days.

You see that this escape of the libido under the conditions of conflict [frustration] is rendered possible by the existence of fixations. The regressive cathexis (with libido) of those fixations leads to a circumventing of the repressions [inhibiting anxieties] and to a discharge – or a satisfaction – of the libido, in which the conditions of a compromise have nevertheless to be maintained. By this detour through the unconscious and the old fixations the libido finally succeeds in attaining to a real satisfaction, though the satisfaction is certainly of an exceedingly restricted kind and hardly recognizable as such.

In thus retrogressively resorting to earlier modes of gratification, the individual, however, commonly re-encounters *old* anxieties; and it is the coexistence of *both* pain- and pleasure-giving functions in the symptomatic acts of the psychoneuroses that gives them much of their apparent mystery, unintelligibility and tenacity. The paradox is rendered all the more dramatic by the fact that the individual in whom old sources of pleasure are being reactivated is likely to know nothing, consciously, of this aspect of the process and to experience only the painful component. As Freud says, 'the person concerned is unaware of the satisfaction and perceives this that we call satisfaction much more as suffering, and complains of it.'

Taken, then, in its most general, abstract form, regression – or, to use a somewhat more descriptive term, habit regression – is a relatively simple concept. As the preceding discussion shows, it is merely the converse of habit *progression*, which may be defined as the development of a new mode of need-gratification as a consequence of disruption of or interference with a previously established mode of adjustment. If, after habit progression has occurred, the more recently acquired mode of adjustment is in turn disrupted, one of two results may be expected: still further habit progression or return to an earlier mode of adjustment, i.e. habit *regression*.

In contrast to its conceptual simplicity, regression as it actually occurs in the case of any given human being is likely to be a relatively complicated affair. First of all, the behavior that appears when a given level of adjustment is regressed to is almost never exactly the same as the behavior that occurred previously, before this level of adjustment was abandoned. Changes in physical size and appearance, altered status in the community or family, acquisition or loss of habits not directly affected by the regression, re-arousal of anxieties that were used to produce habit progression, and a number of other factors may so confuse any given instance of regression as to render it almost unrecognizable as such. Yet another complication arises from the fact that in many cases neurotic symptoms appear, not because regression has actually occurred, but because it is merely in danger of occurring. Finally, regression at the human level is not something that ordinarily transpires before the eyes of the clinical observer but has to be reconstructed on the basis of the testimony of the affected individual or of other persons.

From the point of view of exemplifying the concept of regression and of giving it objective specificity, it is, therefore, a real advantage to be able to produce instances of this phenomenon under the controlled and reproducible conditions of the laboratory. Beginnings have been made in the study of experimentally induced regression in children, but such work, whether with children or adults, has severe limitations. Animals can, of course, be much more freely manipulated and modified from the point of view of their basic behavior in an experimental setting than can human beings, and their use in this connexion is clearly indicated. At the present stage, however, the usefulness of animals in such research is probably mainly pedagogical, in the sense that it provides a more general opportunity for first-hand contact with clinically discovered phenomena than does the clinic itself and supplies paradigms that may be especially useful as aids to the clearer conceptualization of the psychological principles involved. Special care should apparently be exercised at present not to interpret such experimentation as constituting 'tests' of the validity of the concept of regression, or of any other psychological principle derived from clinical investigation at the human level. If comparable findings are obtained in animals lower than man, a certain presumption is established in favor of the validity of the observations at the human level; but, on the other hand, failure to obtain comparable findings does not demonstrate the invalidity of the human observations. It is, therefore, as an 'analogue' of human regression that the animal behavior

231

reported in the next section is presented and not as a rigorous, experimental attempt to determine whether the theory of regression, as developed psychoanalytically, is 'true or false'.

II

During the course of an investigation undertaken for a different purpose, it was discovered that by slightly altering conditions, something analogous to human regression could be produced in the white rat. The apparatus being employed at that time and later taken over without modification for the present study, consisted of a box-like compartment, $5 \times 10 \times 36$ inches, the front side of which was made of glass, with the floor consisting of a grill of transverse stainless-steel rods (0·084 inch in diameter), spaced 0·375 inch apart. The top was hinged so as to act as a door through which rats could be put into and taken out of the apparatus. At the right-hand end of the compartment thus formed was a brass pedal, 2×4 inches, hinged at the bottom and normally held in a vertical position by a spring attached to an arm that extended horizontally in the rear. This arm made an electrical contact that was broken whenever the pedal, which moved very easily, was pressed. By means of a 5000-ohm, wire-wound potentiometer, the sliding arm of which could be slowly rotated by a constant-speed motor and an electromagnetic clutch arrangement, an alternating current (60 cycles, 115 volts at source) could be impressed on the steel rods forming the grill. This current built up linearly from zero intensity until, at the end of 2·25 minutes, it reached a maximum intensity, after which it remained constant until the pedal was pressed, at which time the potentiometer would reset (due to release of the clutch) and the current on the grill would drop to zero. As soon as the pedal was allowed to return to normal position, the current would again automatically build up.[3]

3. The mechanical details of this apparatus will be described more fully in a later publication. In order to protect the rat from receiving a tetanizing shock in the event of a marked drop in bodily resistance (as, for example, due to its feet becoming moist with urine), a 10,000-ohm fixed resistance was placed in series with the grill and the leads from the potentiometer. The strength of the current impressed on the grill when the motor-driven

When a rat (never before subjected to shock) was placed in this apparatus for the first time and the alternating current was allowed to build up, there was usually an initial period of about 60 seconds during which the shock appeared to be subliminal. There then appeared minor signs of agitation, such as sniffing at the grill, lifting of individual feet, 'sitting up', moving the head to and fro, and so forth. As the current became stronger, the agitation became progressively more violent, culminating in jumping, squealing, biting at the grill, clawing at the walls and random running about. Under these circumstances the average rat would, through chance, hit the pedal and thereby turn off the shock within 3 to 6 minutes after its onset. This first, wholly fortuitous escape from shock created a noticeable tendency for the animal to stay at the pedal end of the apparatus; and when the shock next became liminal,[4] the resulting agitation consequently occurred primarily in this vicinity. On the second trial, the animal usually hit the pedal within 2 to 4 minutes and very commonly 'froze' as soon as it did so, in precisely the position that it happened to be in at the instant when the shock went off (reminding one of the game of 'Statue' played by children). On the third presentation of the shock, the amount of random movement that occurred before the pedal was pressed and the shock terminated was relatively limited. Learning, in other words, was fairly precipitous. By the time an animal had had ten presentations of shock, random agitation had virtually disappeared and the pedal-pressing reaction had become prompt and specific. Between trials, after the pedal habit was well established, the rat would usually sit (often on its haunches facing the pedal) in a position that was expedient for making the next pedal reaction.

----

potentiometer was at maximum setting was adjustable by means of a second (manually operated) potentiometer of the same specifications, in tandem with the first, which, however, was set so as to give the type of behavior described in the following paragraph and was not changed during the course of the present study.

4. On the second and for a few subsequent presentations of the shock, the limen seemed to be considerably lowered, agitated behavior being observable as soon as 30 to 40 seconds after the current started to build up. This 'sensitization' effect has been studied quantitatively and will be discussed separately.

In the early stages of learning, escape from shock by pressing the pedal would often be immediately followed by several additional, highly energetic repetitions of this act, not infrequently accompanied by biting of the metal frame surrounding the pedal. This behavior naturally delayed the shock from building up again. Reactions that seemed to be definitely anticipatory also occurred occasionally, some seconds after the last pedal reaction was made but before the shock had again actually become liminal (as judged by other behavior). These reactions likewise caused the shock-presenting apparatus to reset at zero, but they were not counted as learning trials. In order for a reaction to count as a trial, a minimum of 30 seconds had to elapse between reactions.

In the present study, five Wistar albino male rats, 6 months old and experimentally naïve, were subjected to ten learning trials daily for three successive days under the conditions just described. These animals will be referred to collectively as the control group and designated individually as C1, C2, C3, C4 and C5. Complete records of learning performance were kept for each of these rats, but they are of no special relevance here and need not be reproduced.

Five comparable animals, constituting the experimental group (E1, E2, E3, E4 and E5), instead of being treated as were the members of the control group, were first submitted to the following procedure. On each of six successive days they were put individually into the apparatus, with the shock-terminating pedal covered with a metal curtain. The shock was then allowed to build up to maximum intensity and remain there for 15 minutes. At the end of this time the shock was turned off by the experimenter and the rat removed from the apparatus. Under these conditions all the animals discovered that if they sat quietly on their hind legs, holding their fore-paws well above the grill, they received comparatively little shock.[5] The result was that after

5. The relatively low voltage of the current made this effect possible. If a much higher voltage had been used, such that the total amount of current flowing through the rat would have remained approximately constant regardless of changes in the rat's resistance, then the smaller the area of contact with the grill the greater the concentration, or density, of current in the affected areas and the greater the subjective intensity of the shock. Under the latter conditions, sitting on the hind legs would have been more, instead of less, painful than crouching on all fours.

two or three 15-minute sessions in the apparatus, the rats would take this position as soon as the shock became sensible and would maintain it, with only occasional interludes of random activity, until the shock was turned off. This reaction of sitting quietly on the hind legs in order to lessen (though not entirely escape) the shock will be designated as Habit A, in contrast to the pedal-pressing reaction, which will be designated as Habit B.

On the day following the six days of training in Habit A, the animals in the experimental group were put into the apparatus, with the metal curtain removed, and the pedal therefore made available to them for the first time. Within 10 minutes or less time some of the animals showed enough random activity to result in their pressing the pedal. But some of the animals persisted in Habit A so consistently that they did not press the bar in this length of time and had to have their toes pinched slightly by means of a slender rod that was inserted below the grill, in order to break up the Habit-A type of adjustment and bring about a renewal of random activity. In this way all the animals in the experimental group were eventually made to press the pedal, after which Habit B (the pedal habit) was learned fairly rapidly, though not so rapidly as it had been learned by the control group. This difference was obviously due to the lingering tendency on the part of the former group to meet the shock situation by means of Habit A, a tendency which was not present in the latter group; but since Habit B was a definitely superior mode of adustment (permitting the rat to escape the shock completely instead of only partially), it eventually superseded Habit A in all cases. By the end of three days of training in Habit B (thirty trials in all), the animals in the experimental group were quite as proficient in executing it as were the animals in the control group. That is to say, after equal amounts of training in Habit B, the animals in the two groups behaved in an indistinguishable manner in this situation. This fact, nevertheless, does not mean that they no longer differed. As will be shortly noted, the fact that their historical antecedents were different caused them to act quite differently under changed conditions.

To summarize the procedure up to this point, the five animals in the control group and the five animals in the experimental group were given equal amounts of training in Habit B, with only this difference, that the latter were first required to learn Habit A and were then made to abandon it and *progress* to Habit B, whereas the animals in the former group learned *only* Habit B.

Table 1

Trials	Control group					Experimental group				
	C1	C2	C3	C4	C5	E1	E2	E3	E4	E5
1	59	87	98	92	95	73	186	149	88	73
2	64	94	116	95	75	45	128	277	300	108
3	75	91	128	90	101	157	300	102		78
4	125	74	124	108	120	300		300		78
5	120	110	121	111	69					63
6	92	134	160	137	86					108
7	123	141	86	118	153					75
8	124	118	121	107	75					84
9	113	90	82	98	182					69
10	120	65	105	118	83					108

The entries represent the time (in seconds) that the individual members of two groups of rats delayed, after the onset (at zero intensity) of a gradually increasing electric charge on the grill on which they stood, before pressing a pedal to cause this charge to drop to zero, the pedal being also for the first time in their experience electrically charged. It will be noted that the pedal-pressing reaction to the grill shock, referred to as Habit B, persisted in all the rats in the Control Group for all ten trials, despite the 'frustrating' shock on the pedal. On the other hand, in four out of five of the animals in the Experimental Group, Habit B was abandoned after one to three contacts with the pedal (a delay of 300 seconds being the criterion of abandonment). Upon abandoning Habit B, the rats in the experimental group 'regressed' to Habit A.

On the day following the completion of training in Habit B, the animals in both groups were put into the apparatus with the pedal accessible as usual, except for the fact that whenever they touched it they received a slight shock from its surface.[6] This, a new element in the situation, created a type of conflict. In order to terminate the mounting grill shock, the rat, in other words, had to submit to at least a momentary additional shock from the

6. The current used to produce this shock was derived from a Muen-zinger-Walz constant-current apparatus and was adjusted to 0·03 milli-amperes.

pedal. Instead of Habit B now functioning without hindrance, as it previously had, a definite obstacle was placed in the way of its free performance. Under these conditions, the animals in the control group continued to execute Habit B for ten trials (cf. section V). On the other hand, four of the five animals in the experimental group promptly 'regressed' to Habit A (see Figure 1, 1A). The difference in behavior in this connexion is clearly shown in Table 1, which, taken with the accompanying legend, is self-explanatory.

III

Before discussing the supplementary observations on 'reaction-formation' made in connexion with the experiment just described, it is desirable to consider the behavior here reported in somewhat greater detail. It is believed that the basic psychological mechanisms underlying this behavior are comparable in all essential respects to those involved in the phenomenon of regression as it is defined psychoanalytically and that by making this parallelism explicit certain problems can be seen somewhat more clearly than when viewed only against the complex background of clinical observations.

Upon first encountering a given form of noxious stimulation (grill shock),[7] the rats in the experimental group in the present study made a characteristic adjustment to it (Habit A). This adjustment represented a *first fixation*. It was not, however, an entirely adequate solution to the problem, and when a new, more completely satisfactory type of adjustment was made available, the animals (in some instances with a little prodding) fairly quickly *progressed* to it (Habit B). This new adjustment constituted a *second fixation*. Now, however, when an 'external obstacle' (shock on pedal) was placed in the way of this latter type of behavior, i.e. when a *frustration* was introduced, the impulse to terminate the grill shock by means of Habit B was thrown into *conflict* with the impulse to avoid the pedal shock. Since the margin of advantage that Habit B had previously had

7. This may be thought of as analogous in function to libido (erotic drive) in Freud's discussion of regression in human beings (section I).

over Habit A was now eliminated (in four of the five animals), Habit A became the preferable (less 'painful') mode of adjustment and was reverted to. In manifesting this regressive change, moreover, the behavior of the rats here employed further paralleled the behavior commonly observed in human beings under similar circumstances in that a very elementary type of 'symptom' (reaction-formation) also emerged. This feature of their behavior will be returned to subsequently.

The first major point to be emphasized in the present connexion is that the regressive behavior here reported was *historically* determined. Since the animals in the control group did not abandon Habit B when its previously unhampered execution was interfered with, it follows that the animals in the experimental group did so, under externally identical circumstances, solely for the reason that their *past experiences* had been different.[8] In other words, because they had first learned, and later abandoned, a given type of adjustment (Habit A), they were *predisposed* to return to it, in a way that the animals in the control group were not, when the subsequently acquired adjustment (Habit B) was interfered with.[9] As the passages cited in section I indicate, this view of the historical determination of regression is completely consonant with psychoanalytic theory. Freud has unremittingly stressed the role of prior fixations in the causation of regression,

8. It can scarcely be supposed that this dissimilarity of behavior was due to 'constitutional' differences. Genetically these animals, coming from a highly inbred strain, were practically identical, and the two groups were, moreover, formed by purely random selection.

9. This finding may seem to have an obvious moral for education. If 'stable personalities' are desired, then let children be taught only one mode of adjustment to any given need. In other words, 'bad habits', if allowed to form, not only have to be overcome before 'good habits' can be established, but they more or less permanently weaken the 'good habits'. Therefore, establish the 'good habits' in the first place. Although this is good advice in so far as it is practical, the fact is that human needs and human abilities do not develop hand in hand. The infant has most of the basic needs that the adult has, but he has vastly different potentialities for fulfilling these needs in 'good' (i.e. socially approved) ways. He must, therefore, necessarily be allowed to develop and engage, often for months or even years, in habits that are 'bad' in the sense that they must ultimately be given up for 'better' ones. This is a dilemma that must be kept constantly in mind in the training of children.

and the term itself carries a similar implication. A person cannot 'go back' to something with which he has had no previous experience.

In a challenging paper, Lewin has, however, taken the position that regression is not historically determined. He says:

The theory of regression indicated [here] is entirely unhistorical. According to it, the regressive behavior would occur under the described circumstances even if the person in question were created as an adult Golem. In other words: even a person without childhood who never experienced child-like behavior should regress to child-like behavior very different from what has actually happened in the history of the individual.

According to this writer, the personality of a normal adult is 'more differentiated' than that of a child. This so-called differentiation ('number of sub-parts within the person') tends to break down under 'high pressure', i.e. the personality becomes less complexly structured. 'In other words: a person under pressure should "regress" to a more "primitive" level at least as far as his degree of differentiation is concerned.' Lewin adds that this 'primitivation' occurs not because of the continuing latent existence of specific habits or patterns of adjustment (fixations) that have been overt at an earlier point in the individual's life-history, but because the personality is more or less destructured, as a result of a traumatic factor (abnormal 'tension', 'high pressure' or some other strain within the personality). If, for example, a bunch of toy blocks is arranged so as to form a house and if the house is then pushed over, the resulting un-structured mass of blocks is more 'primitive'; this change in complexity of organization represents 'regression', even though the blocks had never before been in such a disorganized state. According to Lewin, it is sheer coincidence that the personality of the child and of the adult who has 'regressed' is, in both cases, relatively undifferentiated.

In his study of reasoning in schizophrenic human adults, Cameron concludes that the intellectual changes occurring in this type of mental disorder involve simple 'disorganization' and 'confusion' rather than regression, as many writers currently believe. This conclusion agrees with Lewin's re-definition of regression in ahistorical terms, but Lewin's views in this connexion are not supported by the main body of clinical observation, nor by the findings of the present, admittedly analogical investigation. Personality de-structuralization, of the kind posited by Lewin, may indeed occur, but it seems distinctly dubious to propose that the behavioral changes of the kind that are commonly referred to as 'regressive' and believed to be historically determined also fall into this category.

In addition to the question as to whether regression is or is not historically conditioned, yet another issue arises here. In the two studies cited at the outset of this paper, Hamilton and Krechevsky, and Sanders have taken the position that regression represents 'a reversion to an earlier, well-established mode of behavior, and persistence in that mode despite the relative inefficiency of that behavior in solving the problem confronting the organism. Further, regression has been assumed to arise when the individual is placed in a strong emotional situation.' These writers thus indicate, first of all, their acceptance of the orthodox psychoanalytic view that regression is a function of past experience. Their second point, that the mode of behavior regressed to in any given case is relatively 'inefficient', involves assumptions that will be returned to in the next section. For present purposes, major interest attaches to their contention that the *precipitating* cause of regression (as contrasted to the predisposing cause, i.e. fixation) is a 'strong emotional situation'. This latter proposition conforms to the popular notion that 'mental breakdowns' are caused by severe emotional experiences or 'shocks', but it is not in keeping with the analytic view in such matters, according to which the precipitating cause of regression is *frustration*, which in turn is defined as a relatively specific interference with an established mode of need-fulfilment. In other words, 'emotional situations' are pathogenic, i.e. lead to regression, only when they constitute such an interference. Failure to make this essential distinction impairs the relevancy of the otherwise admirably designed experiments of the writers cited.[10]

10. In reporting a series of studies aimed primarily at other problems, Miller and collaborators have assigned frustration its proper role in relation to regression as psychoanalytically conceived. They have secured evidence demonstrating: (a) that interference with a thoroughly established maze

O. H. Mowrer

In the experiment reported by Hamilton and Krechevsky, rats first learned that they could obtain food either by turning to the right or to the left at the choice point on a simple T-maze, but that they could do so more quickly (due to a shorter path) by turning to the right. When this *right*-turning habit was well established (occurring in 90 per cent of the trials), conditions were altered so that a *left* turn now resulted in their getting to the food more quickly. The right-turning habit consequently began to disappear and to be superseded by a new left-turning habit. At this stage the animals were divided into a control group and an experimental group, and in the case of the latter animals 'a strong electrical shock was administered at a point just before the bifurcation'. 'Upon introduction of shock the experimental group, *as a group*, showed a decided tendency to revert to its former right-turning behavior.' The control group, on the other hand, continued, as might have been expected, to show left-turning behavior with gradually increasing regularity. The shock just before the choice point was regarded in this experiment as providing a 'strong emotional situation'; and since it resulted in a reduced tendency to perform a subsequently acquired habit, this change was taken as evidence of the statement that regression occurs 'when the individual is placed in a strong emotional situation'.

The inadequacy of this analysis is indicated by the experiment reported by Sanders. In her study rats were trained to run down an initial common path, take a U-shaped detour to either the right or to the left, and then come back into a final common path, at the end of which they obtained food. Definite preferences were

habit through non-reward results not only in a retrogressive change from few to many errors (blind-alley turns) but also in a reversion to the particular *patterning* of errors observed early in the initial learning period; (b) that interference, through non-reward, with the habit of running down a straight alley for food reinstates an earlier gradient of speed of running; and (c) that this type of frustration also produces a return of earlier random activity (sniffing about, grooming, etc.) accompanied, however, by a form of 'energization' (aggression?) that makes this activity more vigorous than it originally was. Although the role of frustration in the production of regression is demonstrated admirably in these studies, it is didactically unfortunate that the particular situations employed were of such a nature that the role of fixation was not also clearly illustrated.

shown by individual rats for one or the other of the alternative routes, which preferences were assumed to be 'unlearned', 'ontogenetically lower', possibly 'inherited'. This 'natural tendency' to select a given route was then strengthened by introducing a differential temporal delay in the final common path, consisting of only 5 seconds if the preferred path were taken but of 90 seconds if the non-preferred path were taken. Training was continued until thirty-six of forty trials were 'in the direction of the natural tendency'. At this point the procedure was reversed, the long delay in the final common path occurring if the previously preferred path were taken and the short delay occurring if the previously non-preferred path were taken. The latter procedure was continued until all animals had altered their behavior to the extent of now selecting the formerly non-preferred path in thirty-six of forty trials. At this juncture an electric shock was introduced just before each animal reached the choice point, near the end of the initial common path. As a consequence, all five of the rats used in this study reverted to the originally preferred route, although this route was now not 'adaptive by any objective standard' since it continued to involve the longer delay in the final common path. On the basis of this finding, Sanders concluded that 'regression has an emotional basis', although a second experiment with the same animals showed that if they were shocked in an unrelated compartment, but immediately before they were put into the maze, no regression occurred. The latter finding leads Sanders to add the qualification that although 'regression has an emotional basis . . . this emotionality must be very closely integrated with the situation'.

Martin, using the same type of apparatus previously employed by Hamilton and Krechevsky, has likewise recently reported failure to obtain regression by shocking rats outside the experimental situation proper, thus giving further grounds for the inference, suggested by Sanders' findings, that electrical shock (emotional disturbance) *per se* does not produce this phenomenon.

It is impossible to say precisely why it is that in both the Hamilton and Krechevsky experiment and the Sanders experiment, regression occurs only if shock is administered just before the choice point, not if administered in a spatially unrelated situation; but the present writer entertains a strong suspicion that this fact is in some way dependent upon the character of the *anticipatory reactions* in progress as the animal approaches this point. Anyone who has watched rats run a familiar maze has observed their tendency to hug the wall on the side of their next anticipated turn. Such a tendency is probably one of the best objective measures in animals of what is known in human beings as 'intent'. It is well established that if a person (especially a child) is punished merely for *intending* to do something, the punishment is quite as effective in inhibiting the intended act as is punishment administered during or after the act. On the other hand, if a person is simply subjected to a painful type of stimulation before a given intention is formed (and if no connexion is established through the speech process), such a penalty will have no specific deterring effect. Similarly in the case of rats in a maze: if they are shocked before a given 'intention' has formed, i.e. before certain anticipatory reactions are in progress, there will be no inhibition of the act for which the anticipatory reactions are appropriate.[11] Although it is realized that this hypothesis, when applied to the experiments in question, raises certain unsettled issues, it points the way for further investigation and serves as a tentative means of bringing the results of these experiments into line with the conception of regression which holds that its precipitating cause is a *specific frustration* (habit interference) rather than a generalized emotional disturbance.

IV

In the experiments just cited, the authors take as one criterion of regression the 'relative inefficiency' of the habit that is reverted to. If, as in these experiments, the habit reverted to involves the use of a spatially or temporally longer path to food than does the abandoned habit, it may appear that there is indeed an objective basis for comparing the 'efficiency' of the two habits. As various writers have pointed out, however, the concept of 'efficiency' always has an ultimately subjective reference. In what sense can a shorter pathway connecting two points in space be

11. Evidence presented by Miller in another connexion lends strong support to this assumption.

said to be 'more efficient' than a longer pathway, except in the sense that the margin of gains over losses is greater *for the rat* in one case than in the other? Under the simplest conditions, the loss would be locomotor effort (increased fatigue stimulation) and the gain would be food (reduced hunger stimulation). With amount of food obtained per run (on either path) constant and with the effort exerted unequal, then the short path is, in this *subjective* sense, more 'efficient'. Theoretically, if none of the factors in this situation was altered, the habitual use of the short path would never be abandoned.

The fact is, however, that at a particular point in both of the investigations under discussion the short path *was* abandoned. How did this change come about? According to the present analysis, it could have occurred only because the margin of gains over losses was altered in such a way as to make it 'more efficient', in the subjective sense, for the rat to take the long path. In these investigations the food received at the end of a run remained constant, and the relative lengths of the two pathways remained constant. What changed? As already indicated, it is the present writer's conviction that in order to obtain the effect reported by the authors cited, the short pathway must have taken on anxiety-arousing potentialities (due to the electric shock) which it did not formerly possess and which were not acquired (at least, not in the same degree) by the long path. If such can be assumed to be the case, the advantage in using the short path would thereby have been destroyed, and it would have then become 'more efficient' to take the longer path; i.e. the margin of gains over losses would have been reversed, with a corresponding shift in behavior, which was 'regressive' but not 'inefficient'. Only by arbitrarily restricting interest to the food-getting function can the regressed-to behavior be characterized as 'inefficient'. Such an atomistic approach is obviously unrealistic and can be pursued to no advantage.[12]

When the results of the experiment described in section II of the present study were first publicly reported, Dr Saul Rosenzweig raised the question as to whether the abandonment of

12. The writer is assuming no one will hold that the regression observed in these experiments had a 'structural' basis, i.e. was produced by differential damage to the neural mechanisms mediating the two habits.

Habit B (pedal pressing) and the return to Habit A (sitting on the hind legs) was really a regression, or simply an 'intelligent, adaptive reaction to a change in external circumstances'. He emphasized the view that real regression always involves giving up one mode of adjustment that is relatively 'good' for one that is 'not so good'. He summarized his point by saying that had he been a rat in the experimental situation described, he would have done just what the rat did but that he would not have felt that he had 'regressed'. Dr Rosenzweig did not, in other words, consider the habit that was reverted to any less 'efficient' than the habit that was abandoned, and suggested that the change was not, therefore, genuinely regressive.

The writer fully agrees, as may be surmised from the preceding discussion, that it was *not* less 'efficient' for the rats (experimental group) that had learned Habit A, as well as Habit B, to revert to Habit A when an electric charge was put on the pedal (thereby interfering with Habit B); but it is not so easy to concede that this change in behavior cannot, for this reason, be legitimately regarded as a regression. As already pointed out, this type of change seems to possess all the essential attributes needed to qualify as regression in the traditional psychoanalytic sense; and it may help in clarifying the issue to recall that one of the distinctive contributions of psychoanalysis has been to break down the dichotomy between 'normal' and 'abnormal', 'adaptive' and 'maladaptive'. According to psychoanalysis, all behavior – including even the most rampant and maddest of psychoneurotic symptoms – is adaptive in the basic sense that the individual who is doing the behaving is trying to diminish his discomfort and tensions, thereby obeying the all-inclusive 'pleasure-principle'. Living organisms do what they have to do and can; from the point of view of their own psychic economy every act represents the most 'efficient', most 'adaptive' behavior that is psychically possible under the circumstances.[13]

13. This somewhat dogmatic statement raises a recondite psychological problem. How does one account for such apparent violations of the pleasure-principle as 'deliberate' postponement, or even permanent renunciation, of gratifications that are immediately available (in the objective sense) and the self-infliction of injury or the solicitation of such treatment from others? This issue has, however, been dealt with in two other papers and will not be discussed at this time.

It is not difficult to see why there should be a strong inclination to assign a negative value judgement to regressive behavior. Human regressions are commonly in a direction *opposite* to that of the educational, socializing forces of the group; regression, under these conditions, is antisocial (counter-cultural) and as such is regarded *by other persons* as 'bad', i.e. from their point of view 'undesirable'. This fact may prompt the group to take such retaliatory action toward the regressing individual (social dis-approval, segregation, etc.) as will prevent the regressed-to mode of adjustment from being as satisfactory as it otherwise might be; but it is still the 'lesser of two evils', from the individual's stand-point. If such were not the case, the regressive adjustment would be abandoned.[14]

If, therefore, in the experiment described in section II, the mode of adjustment (Habit A) that was regressed to when Habit B (pedal pressing) was interfered with was necessarily 'better' from the rat's point of view, and if it is scarcely meaningful to speak of a rat's behavior as being either 'good' or 'bad' in the social sense (particularly in a situation that did not simultaneously involve other rats), then there would appear to be no grounds for holding that this adjustment was in any psychologically significant sense

14. 'Better' adjustments than the one regressed to may, of course, be theoretically possible in a given situation, but the actual behavior of any particular human being is always limited, not by an all-wise Providence, but by that individual's own perceptions, knowledge and intelligence, i.e. by his existing habit systems and his capacity and opportunity for new learning. (To take an example at the animal level, it was theoretically entirely possible in the conflict situation described in section II, with electric shock on both the grill and the pedal, for the rat to turn over and lie on its fur-covered back, thereby completely escaping all shock. But this behavior is not in the reaction repertoire of ordinary rats and did not, therefore, come within the range of adjustmental alternatives in this situation.) The essence of many types of psychotherapy consists of an attempt to enlarge the patient's repertoire, or range, of relief-bringing (satisfying) behavior, either by 'advice' (instruction) or by placing him in situations in which new learning is demanded (occupational therapy, change of environment, etc.). The psychoanalytic approach, on the other hand, rests on the assumption that most behavior limitations (neurotic incapacities) are due, not so much to simple habit deficits, as to internal conflicts (inconsistent habits) involving anxieties that are not 'realistic'. The therapeutic goal of analysis, therefore, is to remove these anxieties and thereby free the individual for effective, satisfaction-bringing action.

inferior, considering the changed character of external circumstances. It was, to be sure, a less-preferred adjustment *before* the shock was put on the pedal, a fact clearly shown by the alacrity with which the rats 'progressed' from Habit A to Habit B when the pedal was for the first time made available to them (without shock on it). The mere fact, however, that in one situation a given type of adjustment (Habit A) may be inferior to another (Habit B) does not mean that, with altered circumstances (shock on pedal), the former may not become superior. In the field of *habit dynamics*, functional values are relative, not absolute; and much confusion can apparently be avoided if this fact is kept continually in mind.

In the light of the foregoing discussion, the supplementary experiment, reported below, may seem superfluous – and in the writer's estimation it is, in so far as the validity of this discussion is concerned; but it was nevertheless carried out, mainly as a matter of curiosity, and also partly in the hope that it might further point up some of the issues previously raised. It will be recalled that Dr Rosenzweig questioned the justification for calling the reversion from Habit B to Habit A in the above experiment a 'regression', on the grounds that, with the alteration in external circumstances (introduction of shock on pedal), Habit A, which had previously been abandoned for Habit B, ceased to be an inferior type of adjustment and became the superior adjustment; and going from an inferior to a superior adjustment was not be to regarded as a 'regression'. The writer's reply has been, in effect, that behavioral changes are always *progressive* in the dynamic sense[15] and that regression has

15. This statement must be qualified in two respects. In the first place, it applies only to behavioral changes that are relatively stable, that involve, as it were, at least a temporary dynamic equilibrium. It obviously does *not* apply to behavioral changes that involve mere random, unorganized, unrewarded striving. The second point is that although regression is most clearly, unambiguously definable in the genetic sense, it may also conceivably be defined, in the dynamic sense, as a disruption (due to failure of reward or conflict) of a patterned, well-organized type of adjustment to the given situation, with ensuing recourse to random, unorganized behavior. But since random behavior is always a prelude (save in *Gestaltheorie*) to the establishment of a stable habit, regression, defined in this dynamic sense, is also a genetic regression. Cf. Wells' discussion of the *genetic, dynamic* and *social* aspects of regression.

meaning, therefore, only in the *genetic* sense; and since Habit A was genetically prior to Habit B, then the change noted *was* a regression.

The supplementary experiment here referred to was carried out as follows.[16] Five experimentally naïve rats were put individually into the apparatus previously described, and the electric shock on the grill (floor) was allowed to build up. The pedal at the end of the apparatus was available from the outset as a means of escape from the grill shock, but it was also kept continuously charged with the same intensity of electric current previously used to produce regression in the experiment already reported. Under these conditions four of the five rats readily acquired the pedal-pressing response (Habit B), despite the presence of shock on the pedal, and executed it with relatively little evidence of conflict for ten trials per day on each of three successive days. At the end of this time the experiment was discontinued, with no indication that the picture would have changed had it been carried on indefinitely. The fifth animal hit upon and then abandoned the Habit-B type of response to the grill shock after two trials on the first day and manifested instead a Habit-A type of adjustment. On the second day this animal completed ten Habit-B responses, but on the third day, after four Habit-B responses, again resorted to Habit A. In short, the results thus obtained show that in four of the five rats tested, the Habit-B type of adjustment was consistently preferred to the Habit-A type of adjustment, under the conditions stated, while in one animal the choice was unstable.

These results indicate, in other words, that for rats with no previous training ('fixation') in the performance of either Habit A or Habit B, the latter is the favored adjustment. This finding might, therefore, be taken as an answer to Dr Rosenzweig's query as to whether the reversion from Habit B to Habit A under the conditions previously described was indeed regressive, in the sense of involving a change from a 'good' to a 'less good' habit. Have we not, in the experiment just described, a four-to-one vote in favor of the 'goodness' of Habit B, as judged by five 'unbiased' rats? Was not, therefore, reversion from Habit B to Habit A in the other experiment an instance of 'true' regression, in that

16. The writer is indebted to Dr Neal Miller for proposing the particular form of this experiment.

the rats which manifested this behavior did something that four out of five other rats, by the testimony of their own behavior, branked as 'crazy', i.e. opposed to the self-interest of 'right-thinking' rats in general?

The dilemma is easily resolved by making explicit some of the implied steps in this line of reasoning. In the experiment last performed, what was done, in effect, was to try to set up a social standard by which to judge the 'normality' of rat behavior in a given situation. Instead of using a *human* social norm, which would have been patently unwarranted, a *rat* norm was established instead; and then the behavior of other rats was compared and contrasted therewith. Since the behavior of these other rats was found to be *different*, it was judged, therefore, as 'abnormal', in this case, 'regressive'. What was overlooked here – but is fortunately well known because of the experimentally controlled character of the situation – is that the life-histories of the two groups of rats were different in one important detail, namely, that one group had been previously fixated on Habit A whereas the other group had not. The characteristically different types of reaction on the part of the two groups of rats in externally identical situations were, therefore, neither more nor less 'normal' for one group than for the other.[17] The difference merely shows, again, the force and cogency of the argument previously advanced, that regression is historically conditioned (by the presence or absence of prior fixations) and that it is primarily in the *genetic* sense that this concept has greatest usefulness and meaning.[18]

17. In another study the point has been stressed that apparently the sole basis for calling many types of behavior 'abnormal', in both human beings and the lower animals, is that they are simply not understood by the observer. The problem is rendered especially acute in human beings by virtue of the fact that their life histories are so exceedingly variable, and yet these variations are rarely well known to the observer (or even to the individual himself).

18. It goes without saying, of course, that in the experiments here reported the picture would have been very different had a sufficiently intense shock been used on the pedal to have prevented *all* rats from pressing it in order to escape the grill shock. Naturally, the intensity of the shock was standardized somewhat below this point. The relation of intensity of shock in this situation to the type of reaction produced further emphasizes the

V

As early as 1908, Freud alluded to the principle of 'reaction-formation', yet it is only within relatively recent years that he and other psychoanalytic writers have particularly stressed its significance. This state of affairs has been part of a more general shift of emphasis in analytic theory, the outcome of which has been to elevate anxiety to a position of preeminent importance as 'the fundamental phenomenon and the central problem of the neurosis'. According to this latter conception, all symptomatic acts are to be viewed as serving in one way or another as 'mechanisms of defence' against this phenomenon. Representing a return to a theoretical position tentatively advanced in 1894 and then abandoned, this interpretation was revived by the elder Freud in 1926 and has recently been further elaborated by Anna Freud. The latter lists ten 'mechanisms of defence', as follows: regression, repression, isolation, undoing, projection, introjection, turning against the self, reversal, sublimation and reaction-formation. It is therefore in this setting, as one of a variety of related mechanisms, that reaction-formation will be discussed and exemplified.

Like all other psychoanalytic principles, reaction-formation is regarded as pathological only when it functions with unusual force or frequency. In its simplest, least dramatic forms, it involves nothing more, for example, than the tendency on the part of a student who is especially fond of playing bridge to avoid his bridge-playing friends at the time of an impending examination. The paradox is that he avoids them precisely for the reason that he likes them, but the paradox disappears when it is realized that he also fears the consequence of indulging his liking, at least at this particular time. The student's avoidance of his friends under these circumstances thus represents an attempt to minimize the

---

relativity of effects in the study of habit dynamics. In passing it may be mentioned that the nature of the results obtained in a situation of this kind can also probably be significantly influenced by the relative amount of training given in the performance of particular habits (strength of fixation) and, somewhat less certainly, by the age of the animals employed. The possible role of age was only hinted at in some preliminary experimentation and has not been definitely established.

prospect of failing the examination; it is, in short, a 'defence' against anxiety. The tendency for an inebriate to make wide detours in order to avoid passing a familiar bar when trying to support a resolution to be temperate is another illustration of the same mechanism.

Of the various passages in which Freud refers to reaction-formation, the following, constituting an incidental comment on the infantile neurosis of a five-year-old boy, sets forth the essential features of this phenomenon perhaps most clearly.

Thus we have a conflict springing from ambivalence – a firmly founded love and a not less justified hatred, both directed against the same person. His [little Hans's] phobia must be an attempt to resolve this conflict. Such conflicts due to ambivalence are very common; we are acquainted with another typical outcome of them in which one of the two contending trends, usually the tender one, becomes enormously augmented, while the other disappears. Only the excessiveness of the tenderness and its compulsive character betray the fact that this attitude is not the only one present, and that it is ever on its guard to keep the contrary attitude suppressed, making it possible to construe a train of events which we describe as repression through *reaction-formation*.

The element of conflict in such a situation emerges, not only from the love-hate ambivalence *per se*, but also from the knowledge (often unverbalized) that overt expression of hostility would result in 'loss of love' (punishment, deprivation, isolation, etc.). Anticipation of such a loss arouses anxiety, and in the attempt at 'defence' against the latter the most elaborate efforts may be made to conceal and deny the component of hostility. How can the defence be managed better than by continual testimony, in word and act, of affection and solicitude? But the trained eye detects this subterfuge, this intensification of one type of behavior by the very strength of an opposing impulse.[19] Anna Freud describes as follows the form that reaction-formation may take in a little girl who is highly ambivalent toward her mother:

A child who has been aggressive toward her mother develops an excessive tenderness towards her and is worried about her safety; envy

19. The Queen in *Hamlet* (III, ii, 240) shows a nice appreciation of this mechanism in her famous remark: 'The Lady doth protest too much, methinks.'

and jealousy are transformed into unselfishness and thoughtfulness for others. By instituting obsessional ceremonials and various pre-cautionary measures she protects the beloved person from any out-break of her aggressive impulses, while by means of a code of exag-gerated strictness she checks the manifestation of her sexual impulses [which would be disapproved by the mother no less than aggression].

Particularly common as the basis of compulsive behavior in both children and adults, reaction-formation is not, however, always easy to demonstrate convincingly from clinical material. Although (like regression) relatively simple as an abstract con-cept, it is likely in any actual case – save in such elementary examples as first given above – to seem complicated and obscure, especially in situations in which other interpretations are logically possible. It is all the more fortunate, therefore, that what seem to be good experimental analogues of this phenomenon as it appears in human beings can be produced by the use of animals in the laboratory.

It has already been remarked that instances of reaction-formation were observed in connexion with the study of regres-sion reported in section II. It will also be recalled that after the animals in the experimental group had acquired Habit A and then abandoned it for Habit B, a shock was put on the pedal involved in executing Habit B; and that the shock, after a few (one to three) repetitions of the pedal response under these conditions, caused Habit B to be in turn abandoned, with a reversion to Habit A. This breakdown of Habit B and regression to Habit A, although relatively precipitous, did not, however, occur without evidence of conflict in these animals. Even more pronounced in the animals in the Control Group, this conflict took the following form. After Habit B was well established in these animals, they customarily sat very near the pedal after pressing it, in readiness for the next presentation of shock from the grill. When, however, shock was put on the pedal, their behavior was noticeably altered. After discovering that the pedal was charged, these animals would frequently *retreat* from the pedal end of the apparatus soon after they began to feel the grill shock, i.e. as soon as they began to have an impulse to press the pedal. In effect, they were thus *running away from the pedal because they wanted to go toward and touch it*; they were, in other words, manifesting a simple but presumably genuine type of reaction-formation. A more precise, though less dramatic, statement of the causal sequence here involved would be that these rats ran away from the pedal because of anxiety, which was aroused by the tendency to touch it. In this sense the reaction-formation was indeed a defence against (flight from) anxiety. But since the grill shock continued to mount, its motivational value soon exceeded that of the anxiety and overcame the rat's 'pedal phobia', driving the animal back to the pedal and compelling it to press it.

In other words, in this situation a state of conflict, or 'ambivalence', was generated, in which there were recurrently competing impulses, the one an impulse to approach and press the pedal (and thereby escape the grill shock), the other an impulse *not* to press the pedal (and thereby avoid an additional shock from it). In the absence of grill shock, there was no impulse to press the pedal, nor fear of it, and therefore no need to flee from it. As the grill shock mounted, however, this fear of the pedal recurred, and the animal sought to dissipate it by running away from the pedal; but since complete escape was impossible and since the grill shock continued to mount, the fear of the pedal was eventually exceeded by the intensity of the grill shock, and the animal (having no Habit A to regress to) was forced to return to and press the pedal.

The records reproduced in Figure 1 show some interesting instances of this type of behavior. Before these records can be completely intelligible, however, a brief explanation is due as to how they were obtained. First of all, it should be mentioned that the grill constituting the floor of the apparatus used in this work was 'free floating', to the extent that the two metersticks forming the side-rails of the grill were extended approximately another meter at the left-hand end and were there pivoted on a fulcrum, while the right end, not similarly extended, was supported by a system of springs. A thread connected to the right end of the grill communicated with an optical lever which caused a beam of light to register on a piece of moving photographic paper any significant movement on the part of a rat while on the grill. If the rat was at the right end of the grill (near the pedal), the beam of light was deflected toward the left side of the paper (upper side in Figure 1), and, if the rat moved to the opposite end of the grill,

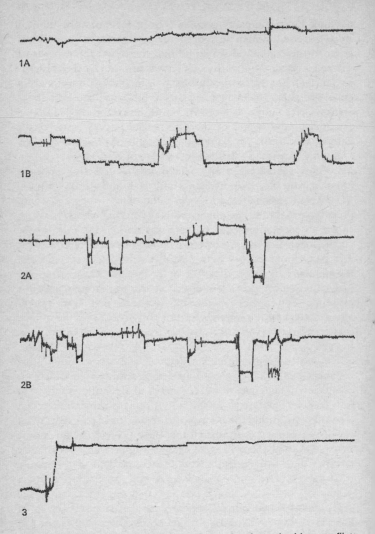

Figure 1 Records showing instances of 'reaction-formation' in a conflict situation in rats

the beam moved to the right (lower) side of the paper. Agitated behavior at any one location on the grill registered simply as rapid transverse oscillations of the beam. The recording system was critically damped to prevent after-vibration. The transverse white lines on the records represent seconds, with 5-second intervals accentuated by somewhat wider white lines.

Records 1A and 1B in Figure 1 are continuous and show the step-by-step development of reaction-formation in one of the animals (C4) used in the control group in the experiment on regression during the session in which shock was for the first time placed on the pedal. It will be noted that the first depression of the pedal, with resulting elimination of the grill shock (represented by the sudden drop of the oblique white lines, indicating grill-shock intensity), occurred without any apparent agitation on the part of the rat (see the irregular black line, made by the light beam controlled by the vertical movements of the grill). The second pedal-pressing reaction was preceded by a slight amount of agitation, as indicated by the oscillations of the light beam just before the shock-indicator drops to zero. Before the third reaction, the rat moved away from the pedal a little distance (slight drop in the black line at beginning of record 1B), and then, after a pause, returned to the pedal and pressed it. This was the first of a series of responses that seemed to involve unmistakable instances of reaction-formation. As the grill shock built up a fourth time, the rat retreated from the pedal end of the apparatus relatively early and remained at the opposite end until the shock had reached an unusually high intensity, at which point the rat returned to the pedal and, after considerable conflict, pushed it. Almost exactly the same thing happened on the fifth presentation of the shock. Somewhat similar behavior also occurred on the five following presentations of grill shock (not shown).

Records 2A and 2B, obtained from another member (C3) of the control group, show a slightly different pattern of behavior, but the phenomenon of reaction-formation is no less clearly manifested. On the presentation of grill shock first shown in record 2A (which had been preceded by two initial trials), this animal remained at the pedal end of the apparatus until the shock had become quite intense, then fled to the opposite end of the apparatus, remained there in some conflict for eight or ten seconds, but finally returned to the pedal and pressed it without ado. This pattern of behavior is duplicated, with minor variations, on the three subsequent presentations shown in these two records. On the last of these the rat showed considerable intermittent agitation as the shock built up but stayed at the pedal end of the apparatus (save for an incomplete excursion toward the opposite end) until the shock reached maximum intensity (indicated by the flat, non-ascending portion of the white line). At this point the animal dashed to the other end of the apparatus, remained there for a brief period, returned to the pedal, hesitated a while longer, and then finally pushed it. But that action did not end matters. For some reason, perhaps because of the unusual duration and intensity of the grill shock on this trial, the rat continued violently to push and bat at the pedal for a considerable time after the grill shock was turned off. This is indicated by the failure of the grill shock to start building up and also by the break in the black line at the top of the record (made by a beam of light reflected from a second optical lever attached to the pedal).

Record 3 portrays the behavior of one of the rats (E1) in the experimental group at the point when it 'regressed'. At the extreme left of this record, the grill shock is seen approaching maximum intensity, with the rat at the non-pedal end of the apparatus (indicating reaction-formation). After the shock had reached and maintained maximum intensity for 10 or 12 seconds, the animal came, somewhat falteringly, toward the pedal and pushed it. This, however, was the animal's last pedal reaction. It is to be noted that, as the next presentation of shock built up to and then remained at maximum intensity, there was not the slightest tendency toward reaction-formation. It was as if the rat had 'decided' not to push the pedal again but instead to sit on its hind legs and 'take' the shock, i.e. 'regress'. Since the pedal was dangerous only when there was a temptation to touch it, there was now no reason to fear or flee from it.

These more or less fortuitous observations on reaction-formation are, so far as the writer is aware, the first that have been published concerning this phenomenon in animals. Other instances have undoubtedly been noted in prior experimentation and can probably be multiplied indefinitely by specifically planned attempts to produce them.

Summary

The five major divisions of this paper may be characterized as follows:

Section I reviews the concept of 'regression' as it has been developed psychoanalytically and restates it in the terminology of the psychological laboratory.

Section II describes an experiment in which 'frustration' of one mode of adjustment, Habit B, caused regression in one group of rats to a previously practiced ('fixated') mode of adjustment, Habit A, but did not lead to regression in another group of rats that had not practiced Habit A before acquiring Habit B.

In section III the hypothesis that regression is 'historically conditioned' (by the presence or absence of prior fixations) is supported and contrasted to an ahistorical interpretation of this phenomenon; the view that 'emotional disturbance', rather than specific frustration, is the precipitating cause of regression is also discussed and criticized.

Section IV is devoted to a consideration of the social, dynamic, and genetic implications of regression. It is concluded that from the definitional standpoint the genetic aspect of this phenomenon is basic.

In section V the psychoanalytic concept of 'reaction-formation' is defined and exemplified by human illustrations and by behavior manifested by rats in connexion with the study of regression.

13 Roger G. Barker, Tamara Dembo, Kurt Lewin and M. Erik Wright

Experimental Studies in Frustration in Young Children[1]

Roger G. Barker, Tamara Dembo, Kurt Lewin and M. Erik Wright, 'Experimental studies of frustration in young children', in T. M. Newcomb and E. L. Hartley (eds.), *Readings in Social Psychology*, Holt, 1947, pp. 283–90.

Frustration occurs when an episode of behavior is interrupted before its completion, i.e. before the goal appropriate to the motivating state of the individual is reached. It is well established that frustration has widely ramifying effects upon behavior; the behaving person is not like a rolling billiard ball that remains motionless when its movement is stopped. However, what these effects are and how they are produced have not yet been determined. To frustration has been attributed most of what is valued and deplored in individual and group behavior: delinquency, neurosis, war, art, character, religion. This, however, is speculation. It is of greatest importance that these questions be removed from the realm of speculation, that the conditions of frustration be conceptualized, that its degree and effects be measured and that systematic experimental studies be made. It is with these problems that the studies here reported are concerned. They constitute an effort to measure the degree of frustration and its effects upon intellectual and emotional behavior and social interaction.

This has been done by comparing the behavior of children in a non-frustrating play situation with their behavior in a frustrating play situation. Children were observed on two occasions: first, in a standardized playroom under conditions of unrestricted free play; second, in the same room with the same toys, but with a number of more attractive, but inaccessible, toys present. The latter were provided by replacing a wall of the original room with

1. Prepared by the authors from data more fully reported in Barker, Dembo and Lewin (1941) and Wright (1943).

a wire-net partition through which the subjects could easily see the fine toys but through which they could not move. The subjects were children who attended the preschool laboratories of the Iowa Child Welfare Research Station. They ranged in age from two to six years.

Two series of experiments were performed. In the first series, by Barker, Dembo and Lewin, thirty children were studied individually with the objective of determining some of the effects of frustration on intellectual and emotional behavior. In the second series, by Wright, seventy-eight entirely different children were taken in pairs with the main emphasis upon the effects of frustration on social behavior. The second series of experiments served, also, as a check upon the first so far as effects on intelligence and emotion were concerned.

The Non-Frustrating Situation

On the floor of the experimental room in the non-frustrating play situation there were three squares of paper, each twenty-four by twenty-four inches. A set of standardized play materials was placed on each square. After entering the experimental room with the child or pair of children, the experimenter demonstrated the toys and gave complete freedom to play. The child (or children) was left to play for a thirty-minute period. During this time the experimenter, as if occupied with his own work, sat at his table in the corner and made records of the behavior occurring.

The Frustrating Situation

Three parts of the frustration experiment can be distinguished in the temporal order of their occurrence: the pre-frustration period, the frustration period and the post-frustration period.

In the pre-frustration period the dividing partition was lifted so that the room was twice the size it had been in the non-frustrating situation. The squares were in their places, but all toys except the crayons and paper had been incorporated into an elaborate and attractive set of toys in the part of the room that had been behind the partition. In all cases the children showed great interest in the new toys and at once started to investigate them. Each child was left entirely free to explore and play as he wished. If, after several minutes, the child had played with only a limited number of toys, the experimenter demonstrated the others. The experimenter returned to his place and waited until the child had become thoroughly involved in play; this took from five to fifteen minutes. The pre-frustration period was designed to develop highly desirable goals for the child which he could later be prevented from reaching. This was a prerequisite to creating frustration.

The transition from pre-frustration to frustration was made in the following way. The experimenter collected in a basket all the play materials which had been used in the non-frustrating free-play session and distributed them, as before, on the squares of paper. He then approached the child and said, 'Now let's play at the other end,' pointing to the 'old' part of the room. The child went or was led and the experimenter lowered the wire partition and fastened it by means of a large padlock. The part of the room containing the new toys was now physically inaccessible, but it was visible through the wire-net partition. With the lowering of the partition, the frustration period began. This part of the experiment was conducted exactly as was the non-frustrating session. The experimenter wrote at his table, leaving the child completely free to play or not as he desired. The child's questions were answered, but the experimenter remained aloof from the situation in as natural a manner as possible.

Thirty minutes after the lowering of the partition, the experimenter suggested that it was time to leave. After the experimenter had made sure that the child was willing to leave, the partition was lifted. Usually the child was pleasantly surprised and, forgetting his desire to leave, joyfully hurried over to the fine toys. If the child did not return spontaneously, the experimenter suggested his doing so. The lifting of the partition at the end of the frustration period was designed to satisfy the desire of the child to play with the toys and to obviate any undesirable after-effects. The child was allowed to play until he was ready to leave.

Both the non-frustrating and frustrating situations produced two general kinds of behavior: occupation with accessible goals and activities in the direction of inaccessible goals. We shall call the first *free activities* and the second *barrier and escape behavior*. Playing with the available toys, turning on the light and talking with each other or with the experimenter are examples of free activities. Trying to leave the experimental situation and attempting to reach the inaccessible toys behind the barrier or talking about them are examples of barrier and escape behavior.

A subject could be involved in more than one activity simultaneously, e.g. he might ask to have the barrier raised while swinging the fish line. In these cases we speak of *overlapping situations*. A type of overlapping situation of special importance occurred when play and non-play activities took place simultaneously. We have called this *secondary play*. *Primary play*, on the other hand, occurred when the subject seemed to give play his complete attention.

Sample Record

A part of a record is given below to acquaint the reader with the sequence and content of the course of events. This is the type of material with which we had to work.

Subject 22 is a girl fifty-three months old. Her I.Q. is 122. Each unit of action is numbered consecutively. At the end of each unit the length in seconds and the constructiveness rating are given. Constructiveness rating is discussed in the section immediately following.

Non-frustrating situation

1. Subject: 'Here,' to the experimenter, 'you make me something from this clay.' She takes the clay to Square 1 and asks, 'Where are the other things?' (Referring to toys present in another experiment.) 'I want you to play with me.' The experimenter continues recording. (45; 2)

2. Subject throws clay onto Square 2. 'This is an elephant.' Then, finding a small peg on the floor, 'Look what I found. I'll put it at his eyes.' Looks at it. Makes elephant sit up. (70; 6)

3. Subject starts to draw. 'I'm going to draw a picture. Do you know what I'm going to draw? That will be a house. That is where you go in.' (45; 7)

4. Someone moves in another room. Subject: 'Who is that?' (10)

5. Subject goes to Square 1, shakes phone, and examines it. Manipulates phone, pretends conversation but does not use words. 'How do. . . .' are the only words that experimenter can distinguish. (30; 5)

6. Subject sits on chair and looks around. 'I guess I'll sit here and iron.' Repeats, then says gaily, 'See me iron.' (45; 5)

Frustration situation

1. Subject watches experimenter lower the partition. She asks, 'I will not play on the other side again?' Experimenter answers, 'You can play here now.' Subject faces the experimenter for about fifteen seconds with hands behind her neck. (25)

2. Subject looks around. (5)

3. Subject goes to Square 3 and examines sailboat and fish pole. (15; 2)

4. Subject stands at Square 3 and looks at barrier. (5)

5. Turning to the play material on Square 3, Subject takes the fish line and dangles it about sailboat. (20; 2)

6. Subject goes to the barrier and reaches through the meshes of the screen. (5)

7. Subject turns around, looks at the experimenter, laughs as she does so. (15)

8. Subject goes to Square 3, takes the fish pole, and returns to the barrier. She asks, 'When are we going to play on that side?' Experimenter does not answer. Then, in putting the fish pole through the barrier, Subject says, 'I guess I'll just put this clear back.' She laughs and says, 'Out it comes!' Takes pole out again. (35; 2)

9. Subject walks to experimenter's table. (10)

10. Subject goes to Square 2 and manipulates clay. (10; 2)

11. From Square 2 she looks at the objects behind the barrier and says, 'I do like the balloon.' Then she asks, 'Who put that house there?' Experimenter answers, 'Some of my friends.' (35)

Constructiveness of Play

From this example, the reader will gain an impression of the richness of the play which occurred. It is possible to use such manifold material for many purposes. In the first experiments we were most interested in phases of the play related to the intellectual aspects of the child's behavior. For this purpose we made an analysis of the play activities on the basis of their constructiveness. One can distinguish variations in the type of play on a continuum ranging from rather primitive, simple, little-structured activities to elaborate, imaginative, highly developed play. We speak in the former case of low constructiveness; in the latter,

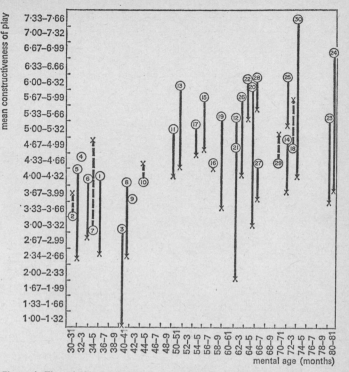

Figure 1 The relation between mean constructiveness of play and mental age in the non-frustrating and frustrating play situations. The mean constructiveness of primary and secondary play in the non-frustrating situation is indicated by circles. The mean constructiveness of play in the frustrating situation is indicated by crosses. Change in the constructiveness of play from the non-frustrating to the frustrating is designated by solid lines when constructiveness decreases in frustration, and by broken lines when it increases. The absence of a cross indicates no change in constructiveness

of high constructiveness. In our first experiment, constructiveness was rated on a seven-point scale (2 to 8) devised to be applicable to play with all the toys. Examples of its use are given in the preceding sample record. The mean constructiveness of play for an experimental session was determined by assigning the proper scale value to each play unit, multiplying by the duration of the unit, summing these values for the whole record, and dividing by the total time of play during the session. The mean constructiveness ratings had an estimated reliability coefficient of 0·88. Their validity as an indicator of intellectual level is indicated by a correlation with mental age of 0·73.

Results

Average constructiveness of play in the non-frustrating and frustrating situations

The mean constructiveness of the play of each child in the non-frustrating and frustrating situations is shown in the correlation chart. These data include all play, both primary and secondary. The mean constructiveness of play in the non-frustrating situation is 4·99 and in the frustrating situation 3·94. The mean regression in constructiveness of play is 4·39 times its standard error. Stated in terms of mental-age equivalents, i.e. in terms of the regression of constructiveness upon mental age, the mean regression amounts to 17·3 months of mental age. Twenty-two of the subjects regressed in the constructiveness of their play, three did not change and with five subjects the constructiveness of play increased in frustration.

These data establish rather definitely the fact that a frustrating situation of the kind considered here reduces, on the average, the constructiveness of play below the level upon which it normally occurs in a non-frustrating, free-play situation. Further analysis showed that regression in the constructiveness of play occurred when only primary play and only play units of the same length in the non-frustrating and frustrating situations were compared.

These results indicate that frustration not only affects actions involved in achieving inaccessible goals, such as attempts to find roundabout routes or aggression against physical or social barriers, but that it may also affect behavior not directly frustrated or involved in overcoming the frustration. The findings show the importance of the total situation for promoting or hindering a child's creative achievement, and they suggest that the level of intellectual functioning is dependent upon the immediately existing situation.

Roger G. Barker, Tamara Dembo, Kurt Lewin and M. Erik Wright

Measurement of strength of frustration

The technical arrangements of the experiment were planned to create frustration and non-frustration. Inevitably, these results were not secured in all cases, inasmuch as we had control over only the immediate, experimental situation and not over the expectations and attitudes which the children brought to the experiment. In some instances frustration occurred in the non-frustration situation and in others there was no frustration in the frustration situation. In addition, all degrees of strength of frustration occurred. Thus far in the analysis we have proceeded as if the technical arrangements had functioned with all subjects as was intended. The data have been classified according to the intention of the experimenters rather than according to the psychological realities of the situations for the subjects. We turn now to an analysis of some quantitative differences in the dynamic properties of the existing psychological situations.

We have taken as a measure of strength of frustration the proportion of the total experimental period occupied by barrier and escape behavior. Inasmuch as we are here concerned with the *changes* in strength of frustration from the non-frustration to the frustration situations, we have limited ourselves to a consideration of the *difference* in the amount of time occupied with barrier and escape actions in the two settings. Using this difference as a measure of increase in frustration, it turned out that twenty subjects were relatively strongly frustrated and ten subjects relatively weakly frustrated.

Considering these two groups of subjects, we find that there is a highly significant reduction in the constructiveness of play in the case of the strongly frustrated subjects amounting to 1.46 ± 0.15 constructiveness points when both primary and secondary play are considered, and 1.11 ± 0.15 constructiveness points when primary play alone is included. The first is equivalent to a regression of twenty-four months' mental age, the latter to a regression of nineteen months' mental age. With the weakly frustrated subjects, on the other hand, there is a small and not statistically significant reduction in constructiveness, amounting to 0.23 constructiveness points for primary and secondary play and 0.12 points for primary play. All subjects showing an increase in

265

constructiveness of play in frustration fall in the weakly frustrated group.

From these results it is clear that regression in level of intellectual functioning is determined by dynamic situational factors that are subject to measurement.

Emotion

Pari passu with the shift in constructiveness of play there occurred a change in emotional expression. In frustration there was a marked decrease in the happiness of the mood (e.g. less laughing, smiling and gleeful singing); there was an increase in motor restlessness and hypertension (e.g. more loud singing and talking, restless actions, stuttering and thumb sucking); and there was an increase in aggressiveness (e.g. more hitting, kicking, breaking and destroying). The changes were greater with the strongly frustrated than with the weakly frustrated subjects.

Social interaction in the non-frustrating and frustrating situation

In order to describe the changes in social interaction from non-frustration to frustration, it was first necessary to distinguish various types of social behavior. Five main categories of social interaction were differentiated:

Cooperative actions included those in which both children strove towards a common goal and helped each other to achieve that goal.

Social parallel behavior covered activities in which both children, separately, pursued almost the same goals but watched each other closely.

Sociable actions were those in which the goal seemed to be maintenance of the social contact itself.

Social matter-of-fact interactions were impersonal contacts made primarily for information about ownership or other property rights.

Conflict actions occurred when children were aggressive towards each other; acts of aggression ranged in intensity from verbal teasing to physical violence.

The most typical form of social interaction in the non-frustration situation was friendly in character; 67·2 per cent of all social interaction was spent either in cooperative or sociable behavior. However, 14·9 per cent of the time was spent in inter-child conflict.

There were two important shifts in social behavior from non-frustration to frustration: cooperative behavior increased from 38·2 per cent to 50·4 per cent of total interaction, and social conflict decreased from 14·9 per cent to 6·9 per cent. These changes are significant at the 2 per cent and 1 per cent levels, respectively. There were no statistically significant changes in the amount of time spent in sociable, social parallel or matter-of-fact social interactions. The two shifts which occurred point toward increased interdependence and unity under the influence of frustration.

Table 1

Percentage of Hostile and Friendly Behavior toward the Experimenter which Occurred as Social and Solitary Action

| Situation | Hostile | | Friendly | |
	Social	Solitary	Social	Solitary
Non-frustration	99	1	26	74
Frustration	82	18	51	49

Strength of friendship and social interaction

On the basis of their behavior in the nursery school, eighteen of the pairs of subjects were judged to be strong friends and twenty-one weak friends. The strong and weak friends resembled each other very closely in their social interaction in the non-frustrating situation. However, the changes in social behavior in frustration were more marked for the strong friends than for the weak friends. Cooperativeness increased and conflict decreased significantly for these subjects while they did not change significantly for the weak friends. When the weak and strong friends were compared with each other in the frustrating situation the strong friends were found to exhibit significantly more cooperative behavior and significantly less conflict behavior than the weak friends.

Under the relatively calm, stable conditions with low level of emotional tension that existed in the non-frustrating situation, the social behavior of strong and weak friends was not observably

267

different. When the environmental surroundings became precarious, however, when frustration occurred, and when there was a heightening of emotional tension, the influence of the preexisting friendship relation became apparent. A greater cohesiveness and unity tended to occur under stress with the strong friends than with the weak friends.

In non-frustration, the contacts with the experimenter were predominantly friendly: 80 per cent of all experimenter-directed behavior was of this nature. A marked change took place in frustration. There was a 30 per cent rise in the amount of hostile action towards the experimenter and a 34 per cent decrease in friendly approaches. Although friendly contacts were still more frequent than hostile ones, the situation in frustration could no longer be characterized as predominantly friendly. It will be noted from the tabulation above that hostile actions against the experimenter were predominantly social in character in both nonfrustration and frustration, while friendly actions were not predominantly social. This suggests that the children may have felt more powerful and able to cope with hostile forces when in social contact than when alone. This interpretation is supported by the fact that in non-frustration there was a great amount of solitary, friendly contact with the experimenter, while in the frustrating situation, where the power of the experimenter had become much stronger, the proportion of friendly, solitary actions toward the experimenter decreased, and the proportion of friendly social action increased. It appears that under frustration the children needed social support to make even a friendly approach to the powerful, implicitly hostile adult.

In general, only when the individuals combined did they feel strong enough to attack the superior adult power. We should expect that the stronger and more cohesive the group, the more capable they would feel of challenging the power of the experimenter. This interpretation is substantiated by the data on hostile actions toward the experimenter in the frustrating situation. The strong friends showed more hostile action against the experimenter than did the weak friends (47 per cent and 31 per cent respectively) and the difference was even more marked when direct physical attack on the experimenter was considered: 26 per cent for the strong friends and 4 per cent for the weak friends.

Furthermore, only the strong friends went so far as to hit the experimenter with blocks, tear his records, throw him off his chair, scratch at him, etc. The weak friends stopped at touching the experimenter while calling him names.

Discussion

The main findings of the studies reported may be summarized as follows: Frustration, as it operated in these experiments, resulted in an average regression in the level of intellectual functioning, in increased unhappiness, restlessness and destructiveness, in increased intra-group unity and in increased out-group aggression. The amount of intellectual regression and the amount of increase in negative emotionality were positively related to strength of frustration. The degree of intra-group unity and of out-group aggression were positively related to strength of friendship. These findings present important and difficult problems for social-psychological theories.

Theory in science has two main functions: to account for that which is known, and to point the way to new knowledge. It does this by formulating hypotheses as to the essential nature of the phenomenon under consideration. The fruitfulness of a theory lies in the unknown facts and relations it envisions which can then be tested, usually by experiments. A fruitful theory gives birth, as it were, to new knowledge which is then independent of its theoretical ancestry.

The main results of the present experiments were predicted on the basis of a theory. Originally the experiments were designed to test the hypothesis that strong frustration causes tension which leads to emotionality and restlessness, to de-differentiation of the person, and hence to behavioral regression. These results were obtained. It is probable that not only the changes in the constructiveness of play, but also the greater cohesiveness of the strong friends under frustration can be interpreted as regression. In the non-frustrating situation the social interactions of the strong and the weak friends did not differ, but under the tensions created by frustration the previously existing, fundamental structure of interpersonal relations was revealed. De-differentiation of the person from diffusing tension would be expected to reduce the variety and complexity of both intellectual and social behavior and leave the strongest structures intact. In the case of the strong friends, this basic structure was one that led to a friendly, cooperative interrelation.

However, the experiments suggest that other factors probably enter also. In the frustrating situation, the subject's future time perspective and security were shattered by the superior power of the experimenter. This could easily have two results: first, to interfere with long-range planning, and this would certainly result in lowered constructiveness of play; second, to lead to a mobilization of power by the subject directed at increasing his security. Counter-aggression on the part of the subjects was clear in the shift towards hostility in their relations with the experimenter. It seems likely that the greater cohesiveness occurring in the frustrating situation is one aspect of the efforts of the subjects to increase their power *vis-à-vis* the experimenter. This is particularly likely in view of the predominantly social character of all hostile actions against the experimenter, and the greater hostility of the strong friends.

References
BARKER, R. G., DEMBO, T., and LEWIN, K. (1941), 'Frustration and regression: an experiment with young children', *Univ. Iowa Stud. child Welf.*, vol. 18, no. 1.
WRIGHT, M. E. (1942), 'Constructiveness of play as affected by group organization and frustration', *Char. Personal.*, vol. 11, pp. 40–49.
WRIGHT, M. E. (1943), 'The influence of frustration upon the social relations of young children', *Char. Personal.*, vol. 12, pp. 111–22.

Displacement

14 Neal E. Miller

Theory and Experiment Relating Psychoanalytic
Displacement to Stimulus–Response Generalization

Neal E. Miller, 'Theory and experiment relating psychoanalytic
displacement to stimulus–response generalization', *Journal of
Abnormal and Social Psychology*, vol. 43, 1948, pp. 155–78.

Diverse Origin of the Two Concepts

The concept of displacement comes from the clinic, that of
generalization from the laboratory. The experiments and hypotheses to be described in this paper were devised in an attempt to
relate these two concepts and to begin the formulation of a
theory of displacement in terms of principles of learning.

Freud was led to the concept of displacement by applying the
free association method to the analysis of material appearing in
dreams (1920, 1927). Though the mechanism of displacement
seems to be especially operative in the realm of dreams, other
examples are easier to expound. A problem child is a nuisance
because he pinches, bites and scratches his little playmates at
school and harasses the teacher in a variety of ingenious ways.
Investigation reveals that in all probability the fault lies not in
the playground situation at school but rather in the home situation. He hates his foster parents. Formerly, he attempted to pinch,
bite and scratch these foster parents, but was forced to desist.
Later he commenced to plague his schoolmates in this manner.
After the home situation is cleared up, the trouble on the playground disappears. This transfer of aggression from the home
situation to the school is called displacement.

A more familiar example is that of the man who, when
severely frustrated at the office by business or professional rivals

and unable to revenge himself directly, may come home and make scapegoats of members of his family.

According to an hypothesis especially elaborated upon in *Frustration and Aggression* (Dollard *et al.*, 1939) and refined in later publications (Miller, 1939; Miller and Dollard, 1941; Sears, 1941), the irrational component of latent aggression against out-groups which easily flares into outbursts of race persecution and war is produced by the mechanism of displacement rather than by an instinct of aggression. According to this hypothesis, the out-groupers may be not only the target for the direct aggression which they arouse by competition with the in-groupers, but also may be the scapegoat for strong aggression which is first aroused by friction within the in-group, then suppressed by in-group taboos and conveniently displaced to members of the out-group.

Finally, displacement is involved in transference which is a crucial factor in psychoanalytic therapy. In transference the patient irrationally displaces to the analyst love and hate which have their real origin elsewhere.

The concept of generalization grew out of the work in Pavlov's laboratory. In a typical experiment a hungry dog is placed in a soundproof room and harnessed to a device which electrically records the dripping of his saliva (Pavlov, 1927). Then a tone of a specific pitch is sounded a number of times always immediately followed by food until the dog has been conditioned to salivate to the sound of the tone alone. Next the dog is presented for the first time in the training situation with tones of different pitches and it is found that he salivates immediately to these new tones also. This transfer of the response from the original to the new tones is called generalization. It is further found that the more similar the new tone is to the pitch of the originally conditioned one, the larger is the response to the new tone. This greater transfer the more similar the new tone is called a gradient of generalization.

From the out-group aggression and the analysis of the bizarre dreams of Freud's patients to the electric recording of the salivation of dogs in Pavlov's soundproof laboratory seems to be a huge leap. The following experiments were designed to cast the first rope of a slender bridge across that chasm.

Experiment on Object Displacement or Generalization

In the first stage of the first experiment albino rats were trained to strike at each other.[1] They were placed two at a time in an enclosure, the floor of which was a grid. Through this grid they were given an electric shock sufficiently strong to keep them active. Their random acts were observed through a glass window

Figure 1 Rats trained to strike at each other. Albino rats were trained by trial and error to commence striking each other as soon as a mild electric shock was turned on. The experimenter reinforced this behavior by turning off the shock as soon as the animals commenced striking vigorously in the way they do at the beginning of a fight

on one side of the enclosure. When they by chance happened to approach each other in a sparring position similar to that used by rats in fighting, the shock was abruptly turned off. Thus the act of sparring was rewarded by escape from shock. After a minute without shock the current was turned on again and the animals given another trial. As training progressed, they were

1. This experiment was performed with the assistance of Miss Maritta Davis.

required to strike at each other before the shock was turned off. Training was continued till the habit of striking was thoroughly established. Figure 1 shows two animals that have learned by trial and error to commence striking each other vigorously as soon as the shock is turned on.

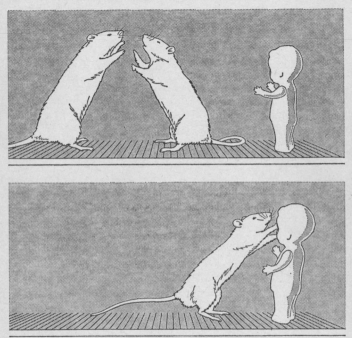

Figure 2 Striking displaced from other rat to doll. When two rats were placed in the apparatus along with the doll, they struck at each other as soon as the electric shock was turned on; when placed in the apparatus one at a time they struck at the doll. (The apparatus used in the experiment had a grid floor twelve inches square. The apparatus here is much narrower)

After this training, the animals were given test trials in which a small celluloid doll was placed in the arena along with each pair of rats. As can be seen in the upper part of Figure 2, the animals struck at each other when the shock was turned on, and not at the doll. In different test trials, the animals were placed *one at a time* in the same apparatus. Under these conditions they tended to strike at the doll when the shock was turned on. This is illustrated in the lower part of Figure 2.

Twelve animals were trained and given both tests. For half of them the first test was the one with the other rat and the doll both present, for the other half, the one with the doll alone. When another rat was present only one of the twelve struck at the doll, and this one then immediately turned to strike at the other rat. If the tendencies to strike the other rat and the doll were equally strong, half of the animals would be expected to strike at each. Instead, eleven out of the twelve animals struck at the other rat. Using chi-square corrected for discontinuity, it can be calculated that a difference of this size would be expected by chance less than one time in a hundred. Therefore, we may conclude that when another rat and the doll were both present, the stronger tendency was to strike at the other rat.

When the animals which had been trained to strike the other rat were placed into the arena alone with the doll and given an electric shock, six of them knocked it down by striking at it; the other six pushed it over in various irrelevant ways such as bumping it head on in the course of running around the cage. In order to show that the tendency to strike the doll when no other rat was present was produced by the previous training to strike at another rat (i.e. would not have been produced by electric shock without this training), a control group of twelve untrained animals was tested one at a time under exactly similar conditions. Only one out of the control group struck at the doll before knocking it down in various irrelevant ways. By means of chi-square corrected for discontinuity it was calculated that a difference of this size in favor of the experimental group would be expected by chance less than five times in a hundred. This indicates that the tendency to knock the doll down by striking at it was a function of previous training to strike at another rat.

Similarity between Object Displacement and Stimulus Generalization

When rats trained to strike the other animal were prevented from doing this by the absence of that animal, they tended to strike the doll. Viewed in Freudian terms this might be taken to indicate displacement. If one can call the original response of striking the other rat aggression, then this aggression has been displaced to the doll which might be called a scapegoat. However, it is not necessary to go this far; it will be safer to say that some pattern of response, as yet undesignated, has been displaced from the other rat to the doll.[2]

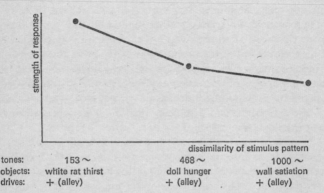

tones:	153 ∼	468 ∼	1000 ∼
objects:	white rat thirst	doll hunger	wall satiation
drives:	+ (alley)	+ (alley)	+ (alley)

Figure 3 The parallel between displacement and generalization. The strength of the direct responses to the stimulus pattern involved in the original learning is represented by the first point on the left; the strengths of the weaker displaced, or generalized, responses are represented by the other two points. The particular values selected to illustrate a gradient of generalization in this diagram are from a typical experiment on the generalization of a conditioned galvanic skin response to tones of different pitches (Hovland, 1937)

But exactly the same phenomenon may be described equally as well in stimulus-response terms as transfer of training, or, in other words, generalization. This is clearly illustrated in Figure 3. The first data are from a typical experiment on conditioning (Hovland, 1937). A tone of the pitch of 153 double vibrations

2. In classroom demonstrations the author has repeatedly shown that if animals are trained to bite a rubber tube as soon as an electric shock is turned on and then tested with shock but without the tube being present, they are (a) more likely to bite other objects similar to the tube than to bite grossly dissimilar objects, and (b) much more likely to bite such objects than are animals given an electric shock without any previous training of any kind.

per second is presented to college students and always followed by electric shock until a conditioned galvanic skin response has been established. Then this tone and other tones are presented without shock. The largest response is to the tone originally conditioned, the next largest to the most similar tone and the smallest to the least similar tone. This is a gradient of generalization.

The experiment on displacement may be analysed in exactly the same way. The response of striking was originally established to the stimulus of another rat, the partner. Thus the stimulus of the partner will evoke the strongest response and, assuming the doll to present a different stimulus pattern, it will evoke a weaker response. Therefore, when a rat is confronted simultaneously with the stimuli of the partner and the doll, the stronger response to the partner will win out and he will strike at the partner rather than at the doll. When the partner is absent, however, the stimulus of the doll is more similar to the original stimulus than is the stimulus of the wall. Hence, the stimulus of the doll evokes the stronger response; the rat strikes at the doll rather than at the wall.

Another experiment (Miller and Bugelski, 1948) on human subjects has been analysed in a similar way. In this experiment it was found that subjects who had been angered by frustrations imposed upon them by members of their own country expressed less favorable attitudes toward faraway foreigners who could not possibly have been responsible for their plight. In this case one may assume that the members of the out-group were sufficiently similar as stimulus objects to the members of the in-group so that the response of aggression generalized from the one to the other.

Drive Generalization or Displacement from Hunger to Thirst

Transfers from one external stimulus to another have been dealt with. According to psychoanalytic observations, however, displacement may occur not only from one external object to another, but also from one drive to another. Thus a person presenting the symptom of excessive eating or drinking may be found not to be suffering directly from hunger or thirst, but rather from the mounting tension of a thwarted sex drive (Coriat, 1921;

277

Hochman, 1938; Saul, 1944). Translated into stimulus–response terms, this would seem to mean that the stimulus patterns of the different drives are similar enough so that generalization from one drive to another occurs. As a tentative hypothesis it may be assumed that displacement is a general phenomenon not limited to sex, aggression and anxiety.

Figure 3 illustrates the way in which drive displacement may be produced by generalization. It is assumed that thirsty animals have learned to run down an alley to drink water, and are then given tests in this alley under three different conditions of drive: thirsty, not thirsty but hungry, neither thirsty nor hungry. The stimuli in these test situations have varying degrees of similarity to those involved in the original learning. The first, thirst plus alley, is identical. The second contains as identical elements all the stimuli in the alley and some from the hunger drive, which it is assumed is not completely distinctive from thirst. The third contains only the identical elements involved in the alley. The way in which this parallels the sequence of tones of different pitches is illustrated in Figure 3. When the animals are tested without either thirst or hunger, the stimuli in the alley will be expected to mediate some generalization of the responses of running and drinking; when they are not thirsty but hungry, more generalization should occur.

An experiment was performed to test these expectations.[3] Thirty thirsty animals were trained to run down an alley six feet long to drink water from a tube supplied by a burette graduated in tenths of a cubic centimeter. Motivated by a forty-five-hour water deprivation,[4] the animals were given five trials a day every other day to a total of fifty trials. After this training, they were deprived of water for another forty-five hours and then all given water in their cages for one hour. At the end of this period they were lured over to the water bottle till they would consistently turn away and refuse to drink. Half of them had been deprived of food and so were hungry; the other half received wet food and were not hungry.

3. This experiment was performed with the assistance of Miss Inez Aaronson.

4. Because this experiment was run during the summer when the humidity in New Haven is usually high, the drive was only fairly strong.

Figure 4 presents the results of the hungry and non-hungry groups when tested in the alley immediately after having refused water in their cages. It can be seen that, exactly as demanded by the hypothesis, both groups show a tendency to run the alley and even to drink, and that the hungry group manifests the stronger

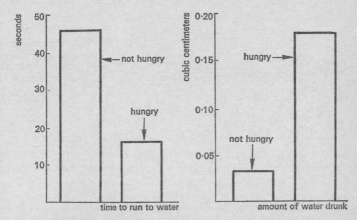

Figure 4 Effect of hunger on water-getting habit of non-thirsty animals. Thirsty rats were trained to run an alley to secure water. Then they were completely satiated on water in their home cages and it was found that they would run down the alley faster and drink more if tested when hungry than if tested when not hungry

response by requiring less time to run the alley and by drinking more water. A statistical analysis indicates that the difference in running time and in amount of water drunk would be expected by chance less than two times in a hundred and three in a thousand, respectively. This demonstrates that hunger and thirst have a certain functional equivalence, which may be called either generalization or displacement.[5]

5. *Technical notes:* In this experiment the generalization may have been facilitated by the fact that, since thirsty animals stop eating dry food, they may have been somewhat hungry as well as thirsty while they were being trained to run the alley for water. To the extent that this was true, the hunger drive would be a stimulus element common to the training and testing situation during the non-thirsty tests of the experimental and not during these tests of the control group.

The faster running and more drinking of the hungry group was deduced

279

It seems likely that a similar type of drive interaction is relevant to the development of the human sex drive. Freud maintains that during infancy sex is an anaclitic drive (*Anlehnungstrieb*), dependent on the more primary drives involved in the nursing and care of the child. In the light of the results of the experiment which has just been described, it seems likely that, as the sex drive begins to emerge in the child, there should be some tendency for it to motivate responses which have been successful in satisfying other drives and for these responses to be directed toward the stimulus object which had been most frequently involved in satisfying those drives, namely, the mother.

Confirmation of Additional Deductions

The principle of generalization was useful in predicting these results. Additional stimulus–response principles should also be applicable to the same situation. During the original training,

---

from the principle of generalization; it is also in line with Hull's (1943) postulate 7, which states: 'Any habit strength ($S^H R$) is sensitized into reaction potentiality ($S^E R$) by all primary drives active within an organism at a given time, the magnitude of this potentiality being a product obtained by multiplying an increasing function of $S^H R$ by an increasing function of D.'

Kendler (1945) has demonstrated a possibly similar facilitating effect of weak thirst on habits established by using food as a reward for hungry animals. He used resistance to extinction as his measure of habit strength and had both the relevant and irrelevant drives present during both the training and extinction. In his experiment, as well as in one by Siegel (1946), stronger thirst apparently interfered with the habit. This seems to be in line with the fact that hungry animals will not eat dry food when they are very thirsty. In the present experiment the effect of hunger on a thirst-motivated habit was chosen for study (instead of the opposite relationship) in order to avoid any interference of this kind which might possibly override the effect being studied. It should also be kept in mind that in Kendler's and Siegel's experiments the two drives were both present during training and testing, while in the present one the irrelevant drive was absent during training (or possibly weakly present because the thirst tended to stop the animals from eating dry food) and the relevant drive was absent during testing. It seems likely that the weaker effects of the irrelevant drive will be less likely to be masked when the stronger effects of the relevant one are absent.

the responses of running and drinking were reinforced by a reduction in the strength of the thirst stimulus. During the test trials, however, thirst is already reduced to a minimum so that little, if any, reduction and hence little, if any, primary reinforcement can occur. Thus a succession of such non-reinforced trials

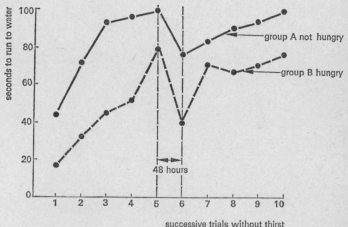

Figure 5 Experimental extinction and spontaneous recovery measured by running time during a series of trials with water present but thirst absent. Animals trained to run for water and tested when not thirsty showed experimental extinction by a progressive increase in time scores and spontaneous recovery by a decrease after a forty-eight-hour interval and resatiation. The animals with an irrelevant drive, hunger, ran faster than those without it

should, according to the principle of experimental extinction, produce a decrement in the strength of response. If this decrement is indeed produced by extinction it should be subject to spontaneous recovery, that is, a rest interval should partially restore the strength of response. After the rest interval a second succession of non-reinforced trials will, of course, be expected to produce a second decrement in the response.

The data in Figure 5 demonstrate that both extinction and recovery occur. A succession of non-thirsty trials produces a decrement in response indicated by longer running times. An interval of one day produces recovery despite the fact that the animals have been thoroughly satiated again in their cages. A second succession of trials produces a second extinction. In Figure 6 it can be seen that the same pattern applies to the amount of water consumed, first extinction indicated by less drinking,

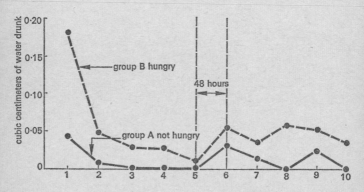

Figure 6 Experimental extinction and spontaneous recovery measured by amount of water drunk during a series of trials after satiation on water. Animals trained to run down an alley for water and then allowed to drink water in the home cage until they consistently refused it, showed experimental extinction by a progressive decrease in the amount of water drunk in the alley, and spontaneous recovery by an increase. The animals with an irrelevant drive, hunger, drank more than those without it

then recovery, then some further extinction. These data indicate that the principles of extinction and recovery apply not only to situations where non-reinforcement occurs by virtue of absence of the appropriate reward to be consumed but also where non-reinforcement occurs by virtue of absence of the appropriate drive to be reduced.

Finally, it should be noted that the tendency for the hungry animals to run faster and drink more than the non-hungry ones persists through all of the ten trials.

Generalization or Displacement from Pain and Fear to Hunger

It is perhaps not surprising that there should be transfer between the particular stimuli of hunger and thirst, but would there be any generalization between two stimuli which might appear to be far more dissimilar, such as hunger and fear? There is some clinical evidence for such a dynamic relationship. With some people overeating seems to be motivated by fear; they worry themselves fat.

The next experiment determines whether responses originally established on the basis of hunger will generalize to pain and fear.[6] In addition to verifying the clinical observations, this experiment avoids a source of ambiguity in the interpretation of the preceding one. In that experiment it might be argued that the sole reason for the better performance of the hungry animals was that they were not inhibited by the effects of a full stomach. When either pain or fear is used in the test for drive generalization, this type of explanation is impossible.

The response originally established on the basis of hunger was running on a T-maze and turning in the correct direction to get food. The painful stimulus was an electric shock of one second's duration and five milliamperes strength, held constant by a vacuum tube device. In the first stage of the experiment hungry rats were trained on a T-maze to turn in the correct direction to get a pellet of wet food. In order to make the choice as distinctive as possible, a sixty-watt desk lamp was suspended one meter above the end of the right-hand arm of the T. The maze was made of elevated strips of wood six centimeters wide. From the start to choice point was twenty-five centimeters, and from there to the end of each arm, fifty centimeters. So that electric shock could be administered as a painful stimulus in the second stage of the experiment, all the pathways had been boiled in paraffin and were wrapped with a grid of stainless steel wires spaced one centimeter apart.

Twenty-three male albino rats were used. For twelve the reward was on the end of the right arm of the maze, for eleven, on the

6. This experiment was performed with the assistance of Mr Jacob Goldstein.

left. The animals were given three trials a day. So that their hunger drive would be at a high level on the next day, they were given only dry food without water for an hour after each day's run. Then the food was removed and the water restored. Training was continued until the animal had reached a criterion of nine correct turns out of ten.

After reaching this criterion, the animals were put through a preliminary experiment which involved one test trial on the maze when satiated, four days of retraining, and another test trial on the maze when satiated. For half of these animals the first test was immediately after having received an electric shock (five milliamperes for one second) on a grid away from the maze and the second test was without shock; for the other half these procedures were reversed. The results were in line with theoretical expectations. When satiated the animals were slowed down, but they did run and take the correct turn. These results were highly reliable. After just having received shock they were not slowed down as much as when tested without shock. This difference could have been produced by chance one time in ten.

In order to secure a more clear-cut difference between the shock and non-shock groups the animals were given four additional days' retraining, satiated as before, and given a series of tests with shock administered directly on the maze. After satiation all animals were given one trial without shock. Then twelve of them received five trials on which immediately after being placed at the starting point they received an electric shock lasting for one second *irrespective of what they did on the maze*. After this they received another non-shock test. Trials were given at fifteen-minute intervals. As a control eleven animals received similar trials without shock.

Complete satiation was accomplished before the test by placing the hungry animal for one hour in a cage containing wet food. After that the experimenter placed the animal with a supply of wet food on one of the elevated perches used to hold the rats between training trials and left it there until it had turned away three consecutive times from additional wet food offered on a spoon.

The results are presented in Figures 7 and 8. It can be seen that in the control group, which did not receive shock, the response of

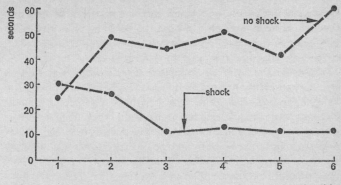

Figure 7 Effect of pain on the speed of performance of a habit established by hunger. Hungry animals were trained to run a T-maze for food and given a series of test trials when completely satiated. For one group an electric shock of one second's duration was introduced on trials two through six. The animals receiving this shock ran faster than those without it

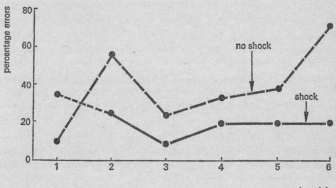

Figure 8 Effect of pain on the accuracy of a habit established by hunger. Hungry animals were trained to make the correct run on a T-maze to secure food. Then they were given six test trials when completely satiated. For one group an electric shock, which lasted for one second no matter what the animal did on the maze, was administered on trials two through six. The animals with this shock made fewer errors than those without it

running correctly to food when satiated occurred at first and then tended to extinguish.[7] In both the time and error scores the difference between the first and sixth trials would be expected by chance less than one time in a thousand.

The experimental group, on the first trial, which was without shock, was slightly but not significantly poorer than the control. On the second trial, during which the experimental animals received their first shock, they ran faster and made fewer errors than the controls. On this trial the differences in either time or errors would be expected by chance only two times in a hundred. By the sixth trial the differences had increased to a point where they would be expected by chance less than two times in a thousand.

The number of errors made by the animals in the experimental group was not only smaller than that of the controls; it was also reliably less than the 50 per cent which would be expected by chance. Thus the shock elicited the habit previously learned on the basis of hunger rather than mere random running. This demonstrates generalization from hunger to pain.[8]

When the animals that had just received the series of shocks on the maze were given an additional test trial without shock, they continued to make fewer errors and run faster than the controls. The differences are of a magnitude to be expected by chance less

7. The definite tendency of the control animals in this and the preceding experiment to perform the habit for a few trials after being thoroughly satiated is different from the results reported by Koch and Daniel (1945). It seems possible that the lack of performance after satiation in their experiment may have been produced by the fact that while they used hard dry pellets as a reward during training, they satiated their animals with wet mash which seems to be a more preferred food. Since they used a different type of habit, bar pressing, differences in the stimuli and responses may also have been involved. Anderson (1941), using a maze, one trial a day, and allowing his animals to recover from their hunger more gradually so that they were not over-stuffed, reports very considerable persistence of maze running despite satiation.

8. This generalization may be based indirectly on stimuli produced by similar states of muscular tension elicited by both drives, rather than upon common elements directly present in the drives themselves. In other words, one of the reasons the animals make fewer errors when shocked may be that their tense, fast running creates cues which make the situation more like that in which they learned the maze while hungry.

than two times in a hundred and one in a thousand, respectively. This demonstrates that the habit generalized from hunger to pain could also be maintained by fear.

Prevention by Absence versus Inhibition by Conflict

In all of these experiments the animals were prevented from performing the direct response during the test for displacement by the absence of an appropriate goal. In the first experiment animals trained to escape shock by striking at another rat were prevented from doing this by the absence of that rat. In the second experiment, hungry animals were prevented from eating by the absence of food, and in the third, there was no way to escape a one-second shock on the maze.

In clinical examples of displacement the direct response is also sometimes prevented by absence of the appropriate object, as when one is angered by a message left by the chief but unable to say anything to him because he has already left town.

In many other cases, the direct response is prevented not by absence of the appropriate object, but by conflict; the chief is physically present but direct aggression against him is prevented by fear and then displaced to the office boy. In order to parallel this situation in the tests for striking displaced to the doll, the experimenter would have had to leave both rats in the compartment, but teach one of them to bite so severely that the other would avoid striking at it.

But if the other rat and the doll are similar enough for striking to generalize from one to the other, the avoidance preventing striking will also be expected to generalize. Similarly, the fear inhibiting aggression should tend to generalize from the chief to the office boy. It is obvious that if the inhibiting responses generalize as much as (or more than) the responses which they inhibit, the latter will be just as inhibited in the new displacement situation as they were in the original direct one. Therefore, displacement can occur only if the tendencies opposing the occurrence of the response generalize less strongly than the response itself. In other words, in order to be able to deduce displacement in this type of situation, one must assume that the gradient of generalization falls off at a faster rate for the inhibiting tendencies than for the responses which they inhibit.

Such an assumption is made plausible by the fact that experimental work on conflict (Miller, 1944) has demonstrated that if a hungry animal is first trained to find food at the end of an alley and then given an electric shock there, the tendency to avoid that place is weakened by distance more than the approach to food which it inhibits. In other words, the spatial gradient of avoidance is steeper than that of approach. The present assumption is that an analogous difference exists in non-spatial dimensions of stimulus generalization. This has not been experimentally tested.

Basic Assumptions and Deductions

Let us summarize and then proceed to further implications. Five assumptions are needed to deduce the tendency for displacement to occur in situations in which the direct response to the original stimulus is prevented by conflict. These are: (a) that the direct response to the original stimulus generalizes to other similar stimuli, with the amount of generalization becoming smaller the less similar the stimuli; (b) that the response which conflicts with the occurrence of the direct response to the original stimulus also generalizes to other similar stimuli, becoming weaker the less similar the stimuli; (c) that the gradient of generalization of the conflicting response falls off more steeply with dissimilarity than does that of the original response which it inhibits; (d) that when two or more incompatible responses are simultaneously excited, the one with the greatest net strength will be the one which will occur; and (e) that the net strength of a response will be its strength minus that of any response incompatible with it which is excited at the same time. The first three of these assumptions have already been discussed; the fourth is a general assumption in behavior theory (Hull, 1943), and the fifth involves a type of complex response interaction which has not yet been subjected to experimental analysis. In addition to these assumptions, two more will be useful in dealing with other aspects of the problem. One of these is (f) that an increase in the drive involved in either type of gradient will raise the over-all height of that gradient. Evidence supporting such an assumption has been secured by Judson

Brown (1942). The final assumption is (g) that gradients of generalization approximate the form of negative growth curves. This is much more specific than the first two assumptions and is needed only for certain of the deductions. Professor Hull (1943) has found a similar assumption useful in dealing with other types of data.

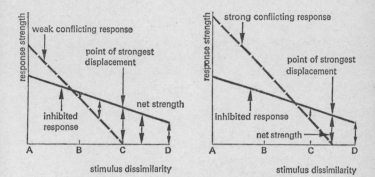

Figure 9 Displacement produced by greater steepness in the gradient of generalization of the conflicting response (assuming linearity). It can be seen that displaced responses can occur and that the strongest displaced response will be expected at an intermediate point, C, in the diagram on the left. Increasing the strength of the conflicting response weakens the strongest displaced response and causes it to be elicited by less similar stimuli, those between C and D in the diagram on the right. Although straight lines were used in order to simplify these diagrams, Figure 10 shows that the deductions are not dependent upon the assumption of linearity

The operation of the factors involved in these assumptions is illustrated graphically in Figures 9, 10 and 11. It can be seen that these assumptions do more than account for the mere fact that displacement can occur; they allow one to make the following specific deductions:

1. *When the direct response to the original stimulus is prevented by the absence of that stimulus, displaced responses will occur to other similar stimuli and the strongest displaced response will occur to the most similar stimulus present.* This follows directly from the first assumption and is illustrated in Figure 3, p. 276. It is also

illustrated by the solid line representing the inhibited response in Figure 9, if all the other features of that diagram are ignored.

Corollary: If the direct response to the original stimulus is prevented by the absence of that stimulus and the situation is such that responding to a given stimulus is incompatible with responding to other stimuli, the response will be most likely to be made to the most similar of the stimuli present. This corollary and the ones to the following deductions deal with object choice. For example, other things equal, a girl who is prevented from marrying her sweetheart by his death and who has completely recovered from her grief and other possibly negative factors, will be expected to prefer the suitor who is most similar to him, ideally his identical twin. This follows from the preceding deduction and assumption 4.

2. *When the direct response to the original stimulus is prevented by conflict, the strongest displaced response will occur to stimuli which have an intermediate degree of similarity to the original one.* In the diagram on the left side of Figure 9, these are the stimuli at point *C*; it can be seen that those which are more similar, *B*, or less similar, *D*, elicit responses of weaker net strength.

Corollary: If the direct response to the original stimulus is prevented by conflict and the situation is such that responding to a given stimulus is incompatible with responding to other stimuli, the displaced response will be most likely to occur to stimuli which have an intermediate degree of similarity to the original one. Thus a girl who is prevented from marrying her sweetheart by a violent quarrel would be expected to prefer someone not completely similar but not completely different. This follows from the preceding deduction and assumption 4.

3. *If the relative strength of the inhibitory response is increased, the point of strongest displacement will shift in the direction of stimuli which are less similar to the original one eliciting the direct response.* This is illustrated by the comparison between the two parts of Figure 9. With weak inhibition, the strongest net response occurs at point *C*; with stronger inhibition it occurs between *C* and *D*.

Corollary: If the direct response to the original stimulus is prevented by conflict and the situation is such that responding to one stimulus is incompatible with responding to others, the stimulus

responded to will be less similar the stronger the inhibition involved.
In other words, the more unhappy the girl's experience with her
previous lover, the less similar should be her choice of a second
object. This follows the preceding deduction and assumption 4.

4. *If the strength of the drive motivating the direct response to the
original stimulus is held constant, the strength of a displaced
response will be weaker than the direct response to the original
stimulus would be if it were not prevented by the absence of that
stimulus or by conflict with any inhibition.* This follows from the
first assumption, which is that the gradient of generalization has
a downward slope.

5. *If the strength of the drive motivating the direct response to the
original stimulus is held constant, the strength of the displaced
response will be greater when the direct response to the original
stimulus is prevented by the absence of that stimulus (provided
other very similar stimulus objects are present) and progressively
weaker the stronger the inhibition involved.* This follows from the
fact that inhibition weakens the response and causes the strongest
net response to occur to dissimilar stimuli which are at a lower
point on the gradient of generalization. Thus it can be seen that
the net strength of the response at the point of strongest displacement is less on the right side of Figure 9.

*Corollary: If the inhibition is strong enough so that the two
gradients do not cross, no displaced response will occur.*

Note: A comparison of Figures 9 and 10 shows that all of the
foregoing deductions and corollaries may be derived equally well
from either the assumption that the gradient of generalization
is linear or that it is a negative growth curve.

6. *If the drive motivating the direct response to the original
stimulus is increased, the strength of all displaced responses will be
increased.* This follows from assumption 6 and is illustrated in
Figure 11.

7. *If the strength of the drive motivating the direct response to the
original stimulus is increased, it will be possible for increasingly
dissimilar stimuli to elicit displaced responses.* This should occur
irrespective of whether the direct response was prevented by
absence or conflict. It follows from assumption 6 and may be
illustrated by introducing a response threshold (and extrapolating
the curves) in Figure 11. If a response threshold is introduced

parallel to and above the base line of this figure, it is obvious that the lower of the two solid curves will fall below this threshold before the upper one does.

8. *In situations in which the direct response to the original stimulus is prevented by conflict, increasing the strength of the drive to the inhibited response will shift the point of strongest displace-*

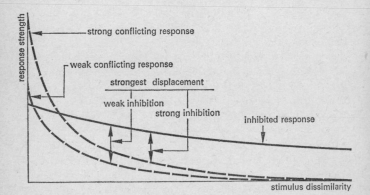

Figure 10 Effect of strength of conflicting response upon displacement (assuming that gradients of generalization are negative growth curves). Increasing the strength of the conflicting response weakens the strength of the displaced responses and causes the point at which the strongest displaced response is elicited to be moved to stimuli which are less similar to those originally eliciting the direct response. Figure 9 shows that these same effects will also be produced by linear gradients; the only difference is that when the gradients are curvilinear the conflicting responses are above zero strength at the point at which strongest displacement is elicited

ment in the direction of stimuli which are more similar to the original one eliciting the direct response. This is illustrated in Figure 11; it is the only one of the deductions which does not hold for the assumption of linear gradients as well as for that of growth curves.

Corollary: Increasing the drive to the inhibited response will shift object choice in the direction of stimuli more similar to the original one eliciting the direct response.

In order to simplify the exposition, the foregoing deductions have used generalization gradients which were represented as either linear or as negative growth curves. These deductions are not, however, limited to the assumption of these particular forms of gradients. Within the range of stimuli included in the generalization gradient, deductions 1 and 4 will hold for any

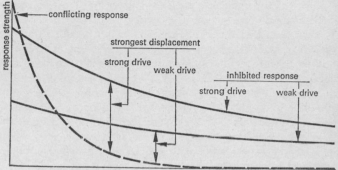

Figure 11 Effect of strength of drive upon displacement (assuming that gradients of generalization are negative growth curves). By raising the height of the whole gradient of generalization, increasing the strength of the drive motivating the inhibited response will increase the strength of the strongest displaced response and cause the points at which the strongest displaced response is elicited to be moved in the direction of the stimuli more similar to those originally eliciting the direct response. The second of these effects is the only one of those illustrated in these diagrams which would not be produced by linear gradients

form of curve which has a negative slope throughout. For all such curves, deductions 5, 6 and 7 will also hold provided that any increase in the strength of response produces some increase in the height of all points and, if the curve intercepts the base line, moves this intercept farther out to the right. The second deduction will hold for any monotonic curves which have negative slopes throughout, cross only once and cannot go below the base line of zero. The third applies to the same types of curves as the second provided that, when the strength of the response to the original stimulus is increased, (a) if the gradient is linear or convex, some increase is produced in the height of all points and

293

the point at which it intercepts the base line is moved out farther, and (b) if the gradients are concave, the amount of absolute increase at any point is some positive function of the original height of the curve at that point. The eighth deduction requires the same stipulations as the third but does not hold for linear or convex gradients.

A few of the implications of these deductions will be briefly discussed. According to the first deduction, displacement caused by absence of the appropriate stimulus object should follow the pattern of stimulus generalization, with the strongest responses being to the most similar stimuli present. According to the second deduction, displacement caused by conflict should follow a different pattern, with the strongest responses occurring to stimuli of an intermediate degree of similarity. Since many clinical cases are of the latter type and seem to follow that pattern, this difference may have been one of the factors tending to prevent investigators from identifying displacement with generalization. It is interesting to note that this difference is not incompatible with the assumption that generalization is the primary process involved. In fact, it was deduced as a factor which emerges from the interaction of the gradients of generalization of two competing responses.

The last three deductions (6, 7 and 8) become especially important in the light of the fact that there seem to be many situations in which the prevention of the direct response to the original stimulus causes the drive motivating that response to continue to mount because the displaced responses are either less efficient or completely ineffective in reducing that drive. Under such circumstances it will be possible for the displaced response to be stronger than the direct one was before its prevention caused the drive to mount. This is illustrated in Figure 11.

Finally, in addition to a mounting drive, it seems possible that the strength of a displaced response may be increased by two factors of a somewhat different kind. In the first place, the conflict between the direct response and the responses inhibiting it may cause tension producing strong stimuli which have the dynamogenic effect of facilitating whatever response finally does occur, much as locking the hands and pulling strongly in opposite directions will facilitate the knee jerk. Such an effect of conflict has been posited by Miller and Stevensen (1936) and measured by Finger (1941). In the second place, it is possible that, when generalized to a different stimulus situation and probably also modified by response generalization, the two competing tendencies may no longer be as incompatible as they were in the original situation. In that case certain elements of the two generalized responses may summate instead of conflicting. Compromise responses of this type have been discussed in somewhat more detail in a previous article (Miller, 1944).

Factors Influencing the Relative Steepness of Gradients

It seems possible that the gradient of generalization for the inhibiting response may be steeper than that of the inhibited one in some types of situations but not in others. In this case one would expect displacement to occur in some types of situations but not in others. In order to predict when displacement will occur, one would have to know what factors are responsible for the relative steepness of the two gradients. It seems likely that there are at least two such factors: (a) learning and (b) the degree to which the drive involved is dependent on external cues.

Experiments on discrimination show that the steepness of gradients of generalization can be modified by learning. If aggression against the scapegoat is not punished, this will extinguish the generalized inhibition and steepen that gradient. Similarly, if the expression of aggression against the scapegoat is rewarding, this will strengthen the generalized aggression and flatten that gradient. Under these conditions the greater steepness of the gradient of inhibition could be the result of a learned discrimination.

Another factor influencing the relative steepness could be the degree to which the drive motivating the response is dependent upon external cues. If the motivation is an acquired drive, such as fear of a given situation, it will be most strongly aroused by the cues in that situation, and less strongly aroused by other similar cues. Therefore, when the subject is confronted with cues which are somewhat similar to the original ones, the gradient of generalization will have a double effect: it will weaken not only the specific responses involved (for example, withdrawal) but also the fear motivating these responses. This double effect will cause the strength of the inhibiting response to fall off more rapidly. On the other hand, if the drive is a primary one, more dependent upon physiological factors, it will be less influenced by the cues and hence its strength will be more nearly the same in different stimulus situations. The factor of generalization will operate only on the tendency to respond and will not also affect the strength of motivation. Therefore, whenever the drive motivating the direct response to the original stimulus is relatively less dependent upon external cues than the one motivating the inhibiting response, the gradient of generalization of the direct response should not be as steep as that of the inhibiting response.

Deduction of the Functional Difference between Consciously and Unconsciously Determined Behavior

According to Freud, the unconscious is the unverbalized. To quote him (Freud, 1915, pp. 133–4):

It strikes us all at once that now we know what is the difference between a conscious and an unconscious idea. The two are not, as we supposed, different records of the same content situated in different parts of the mind, nor yet different functional states of cathexis in the same part; but the conscious idea comprises a concrete idea plus the verbal idea corresponding to it, whilst the unconscious idea is that of the thing alone. . . . Now, too, we are in a position to state precisely what it is that repression denies to the rejected idea in the transference neuroses – namely, translation of the idea into words which are to remain attached to the object.

Thus, according to Freud, the effects of memory traces of events occurring before the age at which the child learned to talk are automatically unconscious. Material that once was conscious becomes unconscious when the verbal part of the response pattern is repressed. (See also Sears, 1936.)

In man, according to stimulus-response theory, it is primarily the verbal responses (with some assistance from other stimulus-producing responses) which mediate the higher mental processes (Hull, 1943; Miller and Dollard, 1941).[9] Therefore, the absence

9. Saying that verbal and other stimulus-producing responses play an essential role in the higher mental processes does not deny the fact that the

of these verbal responses should make unconsciously determined behavior less intelligent than that which is conscious. This is exactly what Freud has observed. The therapeutic effect of making the unconscious conscious arises from the fact that conscious behavior is more intelligent.

A more thorough discussion of the details of this difference, the way repression is learned, and the implications for psychotherapy is being prepared by the author in collaboration with John Dollard. The present discussion will be limited to the problem as it affects displacement.

According to stimulus–response theory, learning to respond with highly distinctive names to similar stimulus situations should tend to lessen the generalization of other responses from one of these situations to another since the stimuli produced by responding with the distinctive name will tend to increase the differences in the stimulus patterns of the two situations. Increased differentiation based on this mechanism has been called acquired distinctiveness of cues (Miller and Dollard, 1941).

On the other hand, if the individual learns to respond to two quite different situations with the same verbal response, the stimuli produced by this response will be a common element mediating an increased amount of generalization from one situation to the other. This has been called acquired equivalence of cues (Miller and Dollard, 1941), or secondary generalization (Hull, 1943).

The removal of all verbal responses by repression, therefore, will be expected to have a dual effect: (a) in cases where similar objects or situations are labeled differently, repression will remove the basis for acquired distinctiveness and increase the

---

organism must possess certain greater capacities, the exact nature of which is still unknown, before such responses can operate in this way. The anatomical locus of these verbal thoughts and other stimulus-producing responses – whether they involve peripheral contractions of vocal cords or central activities within the brain – is unimportant as long as they are learned in the same way that saying a word is and can serve as cues in the same way that hearing oneself say a word does. They will be called stimulus-producing responses whenever they seem to have the functional properties of stimuli and to obey the laws of responses (Miller and Dollard 1941).

amount of primary generalization; and (b) in cases in which different objects or situations are given the same name, repression will remove the basis for acquired equivalence and thus decrease the amount of secondary generalization. In other words, there should be more primary and less secondary generalization in the unconscious.

The function of the mechanisms for acquired equivalence and acquired distinctiveness is to allow the patterns based on the innate characteristics of cues to be refined in the light of experience and thus to become better adapted to the particular conditions of a specific environment. In the social life of man, the importance of these mechanisms is enormously magnified by the influence of culture. The discriminations and generalizations which have been found useful through generations of trial and error are imbedded in the language which is taught to each new member of society. For example, in our society, where discriminating different stages in the ripeness of coconuts is not important, we have only two phrases, green and ripe coconuts, while among the Cook Islanders in Polynesia, in whose economy they play a paramount role as a source of food, drink and fiber, there are twelve distinctive words and phrases each describing a different stage in the maturity of this nut (Hiroa, 1932). Learning to use these words to describe the state of the coconut correctly will be expected to be of great assistance in subsequent behavior where these discriminations are important.

Since socially important discriminations are facilitated by giving different names to the situations or objects which should be discriminated, the removal of these verbal responses by repression should interfere with the discrimination and allow primary generalization to occur wherever the stimuli in the situations are superficially similar. This generalization will be maladaptive and is likely to be called displacement. In other words there should be more displacement in the unconscious. Freud's observations indicate that this is exactly what occurs.

Similarly, socially acceptable generalizations are likely to be facilitated by the habit of applying the same words to those aspects of the two situations which are functionally equivalent. Adaptive generalizations mediated in this way are, however, not referred to as displacement, but as insight or reasoning. They

298

should be greatly reduced when the verbal responses are removed by repression.

The process can become more complicated when, as is usually the case, some verbal responses are removed and others remain. For example, Mr Johnson, a somewhat neurotic and intensely ambitious middle-class social climber moved into an upper-class neighborhood near the Bartletts, an upper-class family with whom he had previous business contact. The Bartletts were the only family who gave any recognition of Johnson's arrival in the neighborhood and the whole program of obtaining social acceptance seemed to depend on them.

But on the few occasions when the Bartletts invited the Johnsons over it was all too clear that their role was more one of entertainers than of guests. Painful snubbing aroused fierce aggression, which Mr Johnson did not dare express because it would completely ruin his best chance for mobility. The overt responses of performing the aggressive acts and saying the bitter words were therefore suppressed. But even saying the words to himself caused so much anxiety that he was motivated to stop saying such words to himself and, whenever he stopped, was strongly reinforced, by a drop in the intense anxiety which they elicited. Thus he became unable to say to himself that he was angry at Mr Bartlett, or, in other words, repressed his anger.[10]

One day Mr Johnson saw the Bartlett dog running across one of his newly planted flower beds. In addition to the mild aggression which the sight of an ordinary dog doing this would be expected to arouse, he thought of it as the Bartlett dog and the mental stimulus of these words aroused burning anger which, however, was not labeled as anger at Bartlett. Feeling very angry, he picked up a large stone and threw it violently at the dog.

In this case Mr Johnson's anger was aroused by a verbal response, thinking of the Bartletts when he saw their dog. Since

10. This repression was probably dependent on patterns which had been established during infancy when his helplessness made him subject to stronger drives.

The stimulus–response description of the way in which repression is motivated and reinforced was worked out in collaboration with John Dollard. For experimental evidence that a reduction in the acquirable drive of anxiety can serve as a powerful reinforcing agent, see Miller (1948).

this particular verbal response was not repressed, it could mediate the generalization of anger from Mr Bartlett and his snubs to his dog. Since no verbal response of the type, 'I am sore at Bartlett,' occurred, Mr Johnson was not conscious of the source of the aggression. If he had said to himself, 'I am sore at Bartlett,' throwing the large rock so violently at the dog would have seemed illogical as a result of his previous training to respond to words grouped into sentences of this kind and unfair in the light of his social training to limit punishment to those labeled as deserving it.

In this case it is not the single word as a stimulus which is crucial but rather the subject–verb–object relationship of a group of words. Though sentences are obviously responded to in this way, the details of how responses to patterns of this kind are learned have not yet been thoroughly studied.

To summarize, the repression of verbal responses specifying the source of aggression may remove a basis for discrimination and allow the illogical generalization, or displacement, of that aggression to be mediated by a different verbal response which is not repressed. In the illustration, displacement was facilitated by the fact that Mr Johnson was conscious of the fact that it was the Bartlett dog but unconscious of the fact that he was angry at Mr Bartlett.

Summary

1. Pairs of albino rats were trained by trial and error to commence striking at each other, like they do when fighting, as soon as an electric shock was turned on. This behavior was reinforced by turning off the shock when the animals started striking vigorously. In test trials they were placed in the apparatus along with a celluloid doll. When tested in pairs they struck at each other, but when no other rat was present, they struck at the doll. In psychoanalytic terms this might be described as displacement and in stimulus–response ones as generalization from the other rat to the doll.

2. On the assumption that the stimulus patterns involved in the different drives are not completely dissimilar, it was deduced that a certain amount of generalization, or displacement, should

occur from one drive to another. This deduction was confirmed by the following experiments. (a) Rats motivated by thirst and rewarded by water were trained to run down a short alley. They were then completely satiated on water in their home cages and tested in the alley under one of two conditions: hungry or not hungry. Those tested with the irrelevant drive of hunger ran faster and drank more water than those tested without it. (b) Hungry rats were trained to take the correct turn on a T-maze in order to secure food and tested after being completely satiated away from the maze. Those tested with an electric shock on the maze, which lasted for one second irrespective of what they did, ran faster and made fewer errors than those tested without this irrelevant drive. The fear persisting after a series of shocked trials caused the experimental animals to continue to run faster and more accurately than their controls.

3. In both of the above studies, experimental extinction was observed during a series of trials with reward present but drive absent. When the animals in the first study were satiated and tested again after an interval of forty-eight hours, spontaneous recovery was indicated by an increase in the speed of running and in the amount of water consumed.

4. In a further analysis, the situation in which the direct response to the original stimulus-object is prevented by the absence of that object was contrasted with the one in which the direct response to the original stimulus is prevented by conflict. It was shown that displacement would be expected in the latter type of situation only if the gradient of generalization of the conflicting responses is steeper than that of the responses which they inhibit. On the basis of this and other stimulus–response assumptions, the following deductions were made. (a) When the direct response to the original stimulus is prevented by the absence of that stimulus, displaced responses will occur to other similar stimuli and the strongest displaced response will occur to the most similar stimulus present. (b) When the direct response to the original stimulus is prevented by conflict, displaced responses can occur and the strongest displaced response will occur to stimuli which have an intermediate degree of similarity to the original one. (c) If the relative strength of the inhibitory response is increased, the point of strongest displacement will shift in the

Defence Mechanisms

direction of stimuli which are less similar to the original one eliciting the direct response. (d) If the strength of the drive motivating the direct response to the original stimulus is held constant, the strength of the displaced response will be weaker than the direct response to the original stimulus would be if it were not prevented by absence and/or if no conflict were present. (e) If the strength of the drive motivating the direct response to the original stimulus is held constant, the strength of the displaced response will be greater when the direct response to the original stimulus is prevented by the absence of that stimulus (provided other very similar stimulus objects are present) and progressively weaker the stronger the inhibition involved. (f) If the drive motivating the direct response to the original stimulus is increased, the strength of all displaced responses will be increased. (Thus, if the displaced response is less effective than the direct one in reducing the drive, it may continue to mount so that the displaced response becomes stronger than the original direct one.) (g) If the strength of the drive motivating the direct response to the original stimulus is increased, it will be possible for increasingly dissimilar stimuli to elicit displaced responses. (h) In situations in which the direct response to the original stimulus is prevented by conflict, increasing the strength of the drive to that response will shift the point of strongest displacement in the direction of stimuli which are more similar to the original one eliciting the direct response.

5. It was deduced that the gradient of generalization for the conflicting response should tend to be steeper than that for the direct one when: (a) the direct response is punished and the displaced one is not, and/or (b) the drive motivating the direct response to the original stimulus is relatively less dependent upon external cues than the one motivating the conflicting response.

6. A stimulus–response analysis of the difference between consciously and unconsciously determined behavior indicated why the latter should be less adaptive and exhibit more displacement.

302

References

ANDERSON, E. E. (1941), 'The externalization of drive: III. Maze learning by non-rewarded and by satiated rats', *J. gen. Psychol.*, vol. 59, pp. 397–426.

BROWN, J. S. (1942), 'The generalization of approach responses as a function of stimulus intensity and strength of motivation', *J. comp. Psychol.*, vol. 33, pp. 209–26.

CORIAT, I. H. (1921), 'Sex and hunger', *Psychoanal. Rev.*, vol. 8, pp. 375–81.

DOLLARD, J., *et al.* (1939), *Frustration and Aggression*, Yale University Press.

FINGER, F. W. (1941), 'Quantitative studies of "conflict": I. Variations in latency and strength of the rat's response in a discrimination-jumping situation', *J. comp. Psychol.*, vol. 31, pp. 97–127.

FREUD, S. (1915), 'The unconscious', in *Collected Papers*, vol. 4, Hogarth Press.

FREUD, S. (1920), *A General Introduction to Psychoanalysis*, Boni & Liveright.

FREUD, S. (1927), *The Interpretation of Dreams*, Allen & Unwin, and Macmillan, New York.

HIROA, T. R. (1932), 'Ethnology of Ranihiki and Rakahanga', *B. P. Bishop Museum Bull.*, vol. 99, pp. 98–136.

HOCHMAN, S. (1938), 'Mental and psychological factors in obesity', *Med. Rec.*, vol. 148, pp. 108–11.

HOVLAND, C. I. (1937), 'The generalizations of conditioned responses: I. The sensory generalization of conditioned responses with varying frequencies of tone', *J. gen. Psychol.*, vol. 17, pp. 125–48.

HULL, C. L. (1943), *Principles of Behavior*, Appleton-Century-Crofts.

KENDLER, H. H. (1945), 'Drive interaction: I. Learning as a function of the simultaneous presence of the hunger and thirst drives', *J. exp. Psychol.*, vol. 35, pp. 96–109.

KOCH, S., and DANIEL, W. F. (1945), 'The effect of satiation on the behavior mediated by a habit of maximum strength', *J. exp. Psychol.*, vol. 35, pp. 167–87.

MILLER, N. E. (1939), 'Experiments relating Freudian displacement to generalization of conditioning', *Psychol. Bull.*, vol. 36, pp. 516–17.

MILLER, N E. (1941), 'The frustration-aggression hypothesis', *Psychol. Rev.*, vol. 48, pp. 337–42.

MILLER, N. E. (1944), 'Experimental studies of conflict', in J. McV. Hunt (ed.), *Personality and Behavior Disorders*, Ronald Press.

MILLER, N E. (1948), 'Studies of fear as an aquirable drive: I. Fear as motivated and fear-reduction as reinforcement in the learning of new responses', *J. exp. Psychol.*, vol. 38, pp. 89–101.

MILLER, N. E., and BUGELSKI, R. (1948), 'Minor studies of aggression: II. The influence of frustrations imposed by the in-group on attitudes expressed toward out-groups', *J. Psychol.*, vol. 25, pp. 437–42.

Defence Mechanisms

MILLER, N. E., and DOLLARD, J. (1941), *Social Learning and Imitation*, Yale University Press.

MILLER, N. E., and STEVENSON, S. S. (1936), 'Agitated behavior of rats during experimental extinction and a curve of spontaneous recovery', *J. comp. Psychol.*, vol. 21, pp. 205–31.

PAVLOV, I. P. (1927), *Conditioned Reflexes*, Oxford University Press.

SAUL, L. J. (1944), 'Physiological effects of emotional tension', in J. McV. Hunt (ed.), *Personality and the Behavior Disorders*, Ronald Press.

SEARS, R. R. (1936), 'Functional abnormalities of memory with special reference to amnesia', *Psychol. Bull.*, vol. 33, pp. 229–74.

SEARS, R. R. (1941), 'Non-aggressive reactions to frustration', *Psychol. Rev.*, vol. 48, pp. 343–6.

SIEGEL, P. S. (1946), 'Alien drive, habit strength, and resistance to extinction', *J. comp. Psychol.*, vol. 39, pp. 307–17.

Identification

15 Paul Mussen and Luther Distler

Masculinity, Identification and Father–Son Relationships

Paul Mussen and Luther Distler, 'Masculinity, identification and father–son relationships', *Journal of Abnormal and Social Psychology*, vol. 59, 1959, pp. 350–56.

By identifying with his parents, i.e. endeavoring 'to mold (his) own ego after the fashion of one that has been taken as a model' (S. Freud, 1949, p. 63), the child begins to acquire his parents' personality characteristics, behavior, values, motivations and attitudes. Two of the major consequents of the processes of identification are the development of the super-ego, or conscience, and the acquisition of behavior and personality characteristics appropriate to his own sex (sex-typing).

It has been hypothesized that both boys and girls form their first identification with a female, the mother, because she is likely to be the most gratifying and affectionate person with whom the child has contact (Mowrer, 1950; Sears, Maccoby and Levin, 1957). Continued identification with the mother is appropriate for a girl, for she must acquire feminine personality characteristics and interests, but the boy 'must shift to a masculine identification, sometime in his early years, if he is to develop normally masculine personality' (Sears, Maccoby and Levin, 1957, p. 373).

According to psychoanalytic theory, the boy's shift to identification with his father begins during the Oedipal phase of development and is motivated by fears and anxieties related to his hostility toward that parent. By identifying with his father, the boy's fears of counter-aggression are reduced and, at the same time, he vicariously obtains his mother's attention and affection. This is the defense mechanism that has been called 'identification with the aggressor' (A. Freud, 1937) and 'defensive identification' (Mowrer, 1950).

In contrast to this, the developmental hypothesis states that identification with the father depends on a positive, affectionate relationship between father and son (Mowrer, 1950; Payne and Mussen, 1956). If the father is an important source of nurturance, reward and satisfaction, his responses and characteristics acquire secondary reward value and the boy imitates his father's behavior in order to 'reproduce bits of the beloved and longed for parent' (Mowrer, 1950, p. 615).

Although the two hypothesized explanations of the dynamics underlying identification with the father seem to be vastly different from each other, there is some supportive evidence for each of them. The validity of the developmental identification hypothesis has been tested in a number of recent studies (Levin and Sears, 1956; Payne and Mussen, 1956; P. Sears, 1953; Sears, Maccoby and Levin, 1957; Sears, Pintler and Sears, 1946). Thus in one study, five-year-old boys with warm and affectionate fathers (as judged by home interviews) showed stronger father identifications than did boys with 'cold' fathers (P. Sears, 1953). It has also been reported that adolescent boys who perceive their fathers as nurturant (according to projective tests) are more likely to identify strongly with this parent than are boys who do not perceive their fathers as rewarding (Payne and Mussen, 1956). Moreover, certain characteristics of boys generally regarded as consequents of identification with the father – sex-typed behavior such as aggression (Levin and Sears, 1956), masculine interests and attitudes (Payne and Mussen, 1956), and highly developed conscience (Sears, Maccoby and Levin, 1957) – tend to be associated with favorable father–son relationships.

The hypothesis of defensive identification is a complex one that is difficult to investigate empirically. However, there are extensive clinical observations indicating that, as this hypothesis would predict, many children attempt to reduce their anxieties by adopting the aggressive characteristics of individuals whom they perceive as threatening to them (A. Freud, 1937; Mowrer, 1950).

It is quite possible, of course, that the two hypothesized identification processes are not mutually exclusive but may function together to facilitate the boy's shift from a feminine to a masculine identification (Sears, Maccoby and Levin, 1957). This view is consistent with that of the role theorists who equate identification with the father with 'father role playing' (Brim, 1958; Cottrell, 1942; Parsons, 1955). These theorists maintain that identification, or role-playing, depends on the *power* of the identificand – a combination of his reward value *and* his threat or punishment potential. More specifically:

Given two ... persons with whom one interacts and who differ in power over the actor (the identifier), i.e. differ in the degree to which they control rewards and punishments for the actor, one would predict that the actor would adopt many of the characteristics of the powerful as contrasted to the less powerful other person. This follows from the fact that it is more important to the actor to predict the behavior of the powerful figure, that he is motivated more strongly to take his role (i.e. to identify), that rewards and punishments are more impressive and the learning consequently better (Brim, 1958, p. 3).

The present paper reports the results of an investigation that attempted to evaluate the validity of the three hypothesized explanations of identification – developmental, defensive and role-playing. It was assumed that, for young boys, appropriate sex-typing of interests is an indication of identification with the father, and that amount of identification can be estimated from the degree of sex-typing. The rewarding-nurturant and threatening-punitive qualities of the father were evaluated in terms of the child's *perceptions* of the father, rather than in terms of the father's actual behavior, the criterion used in some previous studies (Levin and Sears, 1956; P. Sears, 1953; Sears, Maccoby and Levin, 1957).

There were several central questions. How do boys who are strongly identified with their fathers, i.e. highly masculine in their interests, perceive their fathers: as basically nurturant and rewarding, as would be predicted from the developmental identification hypothesis, or as punitive and threatening, in accordance with the defensive identification hypothesis? Or are they viewed as powerful agents of both reward and punishment, as the role-playing hypothesis of identification maintains?

Method

Subjects

According to psychoanalytic theory and observational data, the late preschool period is a critical time in the boy's shift from feminine to masculine identification. For this reason, it seemed best to use kindergarten boys as Ss for this investigation.

Initially, thirty-eight white five-year-old boys in two kindergarten classes of a predominantly middle-class public school[1] were given the IT Scale for Children (ITSC), a projective test of sex-role preference (Brown, 1956). The test consists of thirty-six picture cards depicting various objects, figures and activities commonly associated with masculine or feminine roles. The child is given a card with a figure drawing unstructured as to sex and referred to as IT. He is then presented with groups of pictures of toys and with paired choices of activities, and asked to choose what IT would like.

'In using IT the assumption is made that the child will project himself or herself into the IT-figure on the basis of his own or her own sex-role preference, and will attribute to IT the child's own role preference.' (Brown, 1956, p. 5). The possible range of scores on the test is from zero, an exclusively feminine score, to 84, an exclusively masculine score.

The ten boys with the highest scores (range 79–84, with a mean of 83) and the ten boys with the lowest scores (range 30–63, with a mean of 53) were selected for further study.[2] The two groups

1. The authors wish to express their appreciation to A. B. Campbell, Assistant Superintendent of Schools of Berkeley, C. B. Johnson, Principal of the Jefferson School, and C. B. Holmes and E. P. Light, kindergarten teachers, for their cooperation in this study.

2. While the Ss were selected only on the basis of masculinity score on the ITSC, there is some suggestive evidence that those scoring low on the test were also somewhat more feminine in personality characteristics. Their teachers rated the Ss on twenty scales of personality characteristics, adapted, with slight modifications, from the Fels Child Behavior Scales. These characteristics were: aggression, affection, cheerfulness, competition, conscience, curiosity, emotional control, gross activity, friendliness, gregariousness, kindness, leadership, obedience, patience, physical apprehensiveness, quarrelsomeness, sensitivity, shyness, suggestibility and tenacity (Richards and Simons, 1941).

The two groups of Ss differed significantly (at approximately the 0·02

were matched in socioeconomic status, each of them having the same number of upper-lower, lower-middle and upper-middle class boys. Ten of the Ss, 5 high scorers and 5 low scorers, came from one kindergarten class, and 10 from the other.

Measures of parent–child relations. Between one and four weeks after he had taken the ITSC, each of the twenty boys was tested individually in a structured doll-play session. Early in the session the child familiarized himself with three easily manipulated dolls, representing a mother, a father and a boy doll, and some very simple toy furniture, which were on a low table in the testing room. S was told that these were to be used in a story-telling game in which the examiner would make up the first part of the story and S would complete it.

The examiner then presented, with appropriate manipulations of the dolls, a series of nine incomplete, family situation stories, and the child was asked to complete each one in play. The stories were structured in such a way that the child could depict either or both parents as nurturant and/or punitive. Five of the incomplete stories follow:

1. The child wants a certain toy. He can't reach it. He goes into the living room to get help. Both Mommy and Daddy are busy reading. What happens?

3. The child lives on a very busy street. Mommy and Daddy told him never to cross the street alone. The child is playing in the front yard, and Mommy and Daddy are not there. A friend is on the other side of the street playing with his new bike. The child wants to cross the street very much. What happens?

---

level) on four of the twenty scales. The low scorers rated significantly higher than the highly masculine on: gross activity, friendliness, cheerfulness and gregariousness. The latter three characteristics are, according to sociological analyses of sex role, specifically assigned to the expressive or feminine role (Brim, 1958; Cottrell, 1942; Parsons, 1955). The relatively high ratings of gross activity among those low in masculinity may also reflect group differences in these social characteristics. Significant positive correlations between the gross activity scale and the cheerfulness and gregariousness scales have been reported previously (Richards and Simons, 1941). Apparently, the child who is expressive, outgoing, and cheerful is quite likely to be seen as more active.

4. The child is having fun playing with his toys. Mommy and Daddy say, 'It's time to go to bed now.' The child says, 'I don't want to go to bed now.' Then the child throws a toy on the floor and it breaks. What happens?

5. The child is getting ready to go to school. He has a knot in his shoelace. He can't fix it. What happens?

8. Let's pretend the little boy had a bad dream. Now the little boy wakes up from his bad dream, screaming. He calls for Mommy or Daddy. Which one does he call for, Mommy or Daddy? Then what happens?

If the child failed to respond to one of the stories or said 'I don't know,' the story was repeated or the question rephrased. If *S* did not mention the parents in his play, the examiner asked 'What did Mommy or Daddy say or do?' When the child did not designate a specific parent in his response, the examiner inquired 'Who did that, the Mommy or the Daddy?' Each doll-play session was completely recorded.

Scoring the doll-play responses

The major hypotheses with which the study was concerned dealt with the relationship between boys' masculinity scores and their perceptions of their fathers. The structured doll-play situation, however, permitted evaluations of the child's perceptions not only of his father but also of his mother and his parents as a unit (when mentioned without specific designation of mother or father) as nurturant and/or punishing. The assumption underlying the use of this technique is that the boy's responses in doll play reveal his own feelings about his parents' treatment of him.

Each story was scored for the presence of nurturance or punishment by the father, mother or 'they' (parents undifferentiated). The stories were scored without the scorer's knowledge of the child's ITSC score.

The following scoring categories were used:

Father Nurturance (FN) score was the total number of stories in which the child character in the stories received help, comfort, attention or reassurance from the father (e.g. 'his Daddy gets it for him' in response to story 1 described above).

A Mother Nurturance (MN) score was derived by counting the number of stories in which the mother was depicted as nurturant.

(For example, in response to the story about the dream, 'He calls his Mommy and she says it's just a dream and he can sleep with her.')

They Nurturance (TN) score was the number of stories in which the parents as a unit were nurturant. (For example, S, in response to story 3: 'They help him cross the street.' E: 'Who helps, Mommy or Daddy?' S: 'His Mommy and Daddy.')

Total Nurturance (TotN) score was the sum of the MN (Mother Nurturance), FN (Father Nurturance) and TN (They Nurturance) scores.

The total number of stories in which the father, mother or 'they' disciplined, spanked, criticized or admonished the child in the story constituted, respectively, the Father Punishment (FP), Mother Punishment (MP) and They Punishment (TP) scores.

Total Punishment (TotP) score was the sum of the FP (Father Punishment), MP (Mother Punishment) and TP (They Punishment) scores.

It should be noted that a given story could be scored for more than one variable. For example, if the mother in the story spanked the child and later comforted him, the story would be scored both Mother Punishment (MP) and Mother Nurturance (MN).

The total number of stories involving relationships with the father, either nurturant or punitive (i.e. FN plus FP) constituted the Father Power (FPow) score. Analogously, Mother Power (MPow) was the sum of the Mother Nurturance (MN) and Mother Punishment (MP) scores.

Results

The three theoretical formulations of the dynamics underlying the shift from feminine to masculine identification, outlined above, could be evaluated by determining the relationships between masculinity status and perceptions of parents, as measured by the child's responses in doll play. If the developmental hypothesis is valid, highly masculine boys would perceive their fathers as more rewarding and affectionate or, operationally, would have higher Father Nurturance (FN) scores than boys with low masculinity scores. On the basis of the defensive identification hypothesis, however, it would be predicted that boys who were most strongly identified with their fathers – as this is reflected in their highly masculine interests – would regard their fathers as more threatening and punitive, i.e. would have higher Father Punishment (FP) scores than boys whose father identifications are weak. The role-playing hypothesis of identification offers a third prediction. According to this theory, boys with strong tendencies to play the father role or to identify with the father would feel that their fathers were powerful figures and important sources of both rewards and punishments. In terms of the variables of this study, this would mean that highly masculine boys would have higher Father Power (FPow) scores than boys who have not achieved strong masculine identifications.

Since responses to the structured doll-play situation were scored for perceptions of the mother and 'they' (parents as a unit) as nurturant-gratifying and/or punitive-threatening, it was also possible to assess the relationships between these variables and strong or weak sex-typing among five-year-old boys.

Table 1

Mean Scores of Boys' High and Low Masculinity Groups on Family Perception Variables

Variable	High masculinity group	Low masculinity group
Mother Nurturance (MN)	2·1	1·7
Father Nurturance (FN)	3·7	2·2
They Nurturance (TN)	0·8	0·7
Total Nurturance (TotN)	6·6	4·7
Mother Punishment (MP)	1·2	1·5
Father Punishment (FP)	2·8	2·1
They Punishment (TP)	0·2	0·7
Total Punishment (TotP)	4·2	4·3
Mother Power (MPow)	3·3	3·2
Father Power (FPow)	6·5	4·3

Table 1 presents the mean scores of the high and low masculinity groups on all the doll-play scores.

In view of the facts that the number of Ss in each group was small and that the distributions of scores on these variables were non-normal, U-tests (Mann and Whitney, 1947) were employed to compare rank transformation scores on all doll-play scores of Ss scoring high and low on the ITSC. The results of these tests and their significance levels are summarized in Table 2.

Table 2

Differences Between High and Low Masculinity Groups on Family Perception Variables

Variable	U	p	Group with higher scores
Mother Nurturance (MN)	45·5	ns	—
Father Nurturance (FN)	23·5	0·02	highs
They Nurturance (TN)	48·5	ns	—
Total Nurturance (TotN)	16·0	0·004	highs
Mother Punishment (MP)	44·0	ns	—
Father Punishment (FP)	30·5	0·06	highs
They Punishment (TP)	34·0	0·07	lows
Total Punishment (TotP)	47·0	ns	—
Mother Power (MPow)	49·5	ns	—
Father Power (FPow)	18·5	0·007	highs

It is obvious from this table that the two groups of Ss differ significantly in many of their perceptions of their families. Compared with boys low in masculine identification, as measured by the ITSC, those who were high in this characteristic perceived themselves as receiving more Total Nurturance (TotN) (i.e. more nurturance from all sources combined). Evidently, this difference is primarily attributable to differences in one major component of TotN, the perceptions of father's nurturance, for the two groups differ significantly in Father Nurturance (FN) scores but not in the Mother Nurturance (MN) or They Nurturance (TN) scores.[3]

This finding seems clearly consistent with the developmental identification hypothesis. It supports the prediction, made on the basis of this hypothesis, that young boys are more likely to

3. While the use of t-tests was not entirely warranted because of the non-normality of the doll-play scores, these tests were applied to the data of Table 1. The results were very similar to the U-test results, i.e. the high and low masculinity groups differed significantly from each other in the variables FN ($P = 0·01-0·025$), TotN ($P = < 0·01$), FP ($P = 0·01-0·025$), FPow ($P = < 0·005$) and almost significantly in TP ($P = 0·05-0·10$).

identify strongly with their fathers, and thus to acquire masculine interests, if they perceive their fathers as highly nurturant and rewarding.

The data also appear to lend support to the second, or defensive identification, hypothesis, which predicted that high masculine identification would be related to views of the father as threatening and punitive. Highly masculine boys tended to attribute more punishment to the fathers in their doll-play stories than boys low in masculine identification did, although the difference between the two groups in the father punishment score was not quite as marked as the difference in the father nurturance variable.

The third, or role-taking, hypothesis states that the degree of identification and, consequently, sex-role learning varies with the amount of the child's interaction with the identificand and the degree to which the latter has power over him, i.e. controls both his rewards and his punishments. The data of the present study seem to be fully in accord with this hypothesis, since the low and high masculinity groups differ markedly in Father Power (FPow) scores, the high identifiers giving a significantly greater number of these responses. This finding is exactly what would be anticipated, since this score is composed of the FN and FP scores, and the highly identified group scored significantly higher in each of these.

The high and low masculinity groups were not significantly different in any of the variables related to perceptions of the mother. However, compared with those scoring low on the ITSC, high scorers tended to perceive their parents as a unit as less punitive, i.e. tended to have lower They Punishment (TP) scores ($P = 0.07$). This would seem to be further confirmation of the findings of another study which concluded that adolescent 'boys' who feel comfortable in their relationships with their parents adopt more of their father's behavior and attitudes than boys who experience less favorable parent–child relationships' (Payne and Mussen, 1956, p. 361).

It may be that the boy who scores high in They Punishment (TP) views his family milieu as hostile and unfriendly. While he may not feel that either parent is particularly threatening, he may feel generally rejected, unwanted and unimportant. In so far as this is true, the child may be expected to attempt to avoid intensive interactions with his parents. Under these circumstances, he should not identify strongly with his father, and consequently, should not acquire highly masculine interests.

Discussion

The data of the present study indicate that for boys, sex-typing of interests is more directly related to their perceptions of their fathers than to perceptions of their mothers. This finding is in accord with the findings of previous studies (Levin and Sears, 1956; Payne and Mussen, 1956; Sears, Maccoby and Levin, 1957) as well as with an assumption underlying all three of the identification hypotheses outlined above; namely, that the acquisition of masculine interests, attitudes and patterns of behavior is primarily determined by the boy's interactions with his father.

Some of the findings of this study lend support to the defensive identification hypothesis; others seem to support the developmental hypothesis. Since the two hypotheses generate predictions that are in some respects diametrically opposed, there are also data that are inconsistent with both hypotheses. Thus, since the developmental hypothesis postulates that identification with the father is dependent upon nurturant rewarding interactions with that parent, the finding that boys also identify with punitive, threatening fathers must be inconsistent with this hypothesis. Conversely, the finding that boys are more likely to identify with a nurturant father is inconsistent with the view of defensive identification or identification with the aggressor.

A high level of masculine identification does not appear to depend on any one specific type of father–son relationship. From the child's point of view, the significant factor seems to be the father's *salience* – his importance in the child's life – rather than the particular techniques he uses in dealing with his child. Thus, as a group, boys who have made substantial father-identifications – reflected in their strongly sex-typed interest – perceived their fathers as both more nurturant *and* more punitive. Hence, masculine sex-role identification cannot be attributed exclusively to either the reward value or the threat potential of the father.

For these reasons, it seems to us that the role theory of identification is most fully consistent with – and most adequately integrates – the present data. The two groups were clearly differentiated on the Father Power (FPow) score, indicating that, compared with the other group, the highly masculine boys had – or at least perceived that they had – more intensive interactions with their fathers. This is exactly what is predicted by the role theory of sex-role identification, which maintains that more interaction with another individual, e.g. the father, leads to greater assimilation of his role.

Moreover, role theory states most explicitly that an individual is most likely to assimilate the role of, or identify with, individuals he sees as powerful. From the child's point of view, the most powerful individual is probably the one who most effectively controls his rewards and punishments. In this way, the theory implies that both reward and punishment strongly influence the course of role learning.

It follows from these postulates of role theory that the boy should be most strongly motivated to imitate or to practice his father's role frequently if he has a great deal of interaction with his father and sees him as a powerful source of rewards and punishments. Under these circumstances, the child gets extensive experience playing the father's role and adopts more of the father's characteristics, including those connected specifically with his sex-role. Our data are substantially in accordance with these theoretical predictions. The highly father-identified Ss – those who had adopted masculine interests and behavior – did in fact perceive their fathers as more interactive with them and as major providers of rewards *and* punishments.

There is also a psychoanalytic hypothesis which these data seem to confirm. In summarizing psychoanalytic writings on identification, Bronfenbrenner (1958) notes that one of the 'syndromes of parent–child relationship . . . predisposing the child to incorporate or introject the parent' is 'a relationship based on conditional love, in which the parent, willfully or unconsciously, withholds expression of affection as the price of conformity' (p. 128). This means that the boy is most likely to identify with his father if his feelings toward him are affectionate, while the father's love is given conditionally. According to this hypothesis, high nurturance from the father, together with the threat of withdrawal of his love (high FP) would lead to strong father identification. This prediction seems to be verified by the finding that highly masculine boys have relatively high FPow scores, indicating a high degree of combined father nurturance and father punishment.

The findings may also be conceptualized in terms of general behavior theory. Among those with whom the preschool boy has intimate associations, the father is the one who has the most adequate knowledge of appropriate masculine behavior. If there is a high level of father–son interaction (high FPow scores), the father should frequently, and fairly regularly, reward the son's sex-appropriate responses and punish sex-inappropriate responses when they occur. Consequently, the boy's masculine responses should be relatively rapidly and effectively strengthened, while his sex-inappropriate responses become extinguished. In short, vigorous application of both rewards and punishments by the father facilitate the son's shift from feminine to masculine identification.

On the other hand, the condition of relatively little father–son interaction implies sporadic, and at best ineffective, rewards and punishments by the father. Under these circumstances, the shift in identification may be a difficult one, and the child's acquisition of sex-typed interests and behavior may be considerably retarded.

It seems that the father's use of *both* reward *and* punishment is his most effective method of 'teaching' his son masculine behavior. It must be emphasized, however, that the high masculine and low masculine groups also differed significantly in the individual variables relating to perceptions of father reward and father punishment. From this it may be inferred that sex-appropriate behavior may be 'taught' primarily by rewarding appropriate responses *or* punishing inappropriate responses. In short, from the child's point of view, the important factor is the salience of his relationship with his father, not the particular techniques that the father uses in handling him.

Of course, the present data refer *only* to masculinity of interests. Other possible long-range consequents of different processes of identification cannot be evaluated. For example, it is quite possible that boys who learn their sex roles primarily as a result of being punished or threatened by their fathers differ in many ways (e.g. in personality characteristics, self-conceptions or basic motivations) from those who achieve their masculine identifications by means of developmental identification or through learning based on some combination of reward and punishment by the father. As the data stand, however, we can only state that five-year-old boys may shift from feminine to masculine identification, as measured by the acquisition of masculine interests, as a result of either developmental or defensive identification processes or, as role theory suggests, by some combination of the two.

Summary

The IT Scale for Children (ITSC), a test of sex-typing of interests, was administered to thirty-eight white, middle-class, kindergarten boys. The ten Ss scoring highest in the test were assumed to have developed the highest degree of male role identification, while the ten scoring lowest were considered the least strongly identified with this role.

In order to determine the relationship between parental perceptions and degree of masculine identification, each of the twenty boys was tested in a structured doll-play situation. During the session, the child completed, in play, nine incomplete stories involving parent–child relations. Responses were scored in terms of the amount of nurturance, punishment and power (nurturance plus punishment) attributed to the mother, father and parents as a unit.

The study was designed to evaluate three hypothesized processes of identification – developmental, defensive and role-taking. Analysis of the data provided evidence consistent with all three hypotheses. As predicted from the developmental identification hypothesis, young boys who were strongly identified with the male role perceived their fathers as more rewarding and nurturant ($P = 0.02$) than their weakly identified peers did. According to the defensive identification hypothesis, the strongly father-identified boys perceive their fathers as more punitive and threatening. This hypothesis was also supported ($P = 0.06$). Boys high and low in masculinity were also clearly differentiated on the Father Power score ($P = 0.007$). This finding indicates that those who have made substantial male identifications view their fathers as powerful sources of *both* reward and punishment, and is in accordance with role theory, which maintains that the child is most likely to assimilate the role of an individual with whom he has intensive interactions, especially if this individual is powerful. To the present authors, it seems that role theory, with its explicit emphasis on the importance of both reward and punishment in role-learning, best integrates all these data.

References

BRIM, O. G., Jr (1958), 'Family structure and sex role learning by children: a further analysis of Helen Koch's data', *Sociometry*, vol. 21, pp. 1–16.

BRONFENBRENNER, U. (1958), 'The study of identification through interpersonal perception', in R. Tagiuri and L. Petrullo (eds.), *Person Perception and Interpersonal Behavior*, Stanford University Press, pp. 110–30.

BROWN, D. D. (1956), 'Sex role preferences in young children', *Psychol. Monog.*, vol. 70, no. 14 (whole no. 421).

COTTRELL, L. S., Jr (1942), 'The analysis of situational fields in social psychology', *Amer. soc. Rev.*, vol. 7, pp. 370–83.

FREUD, A. (1937), *The Ego and the Mechanisms of Defence*, Hogarth Press.

FREUD, S. (1949), *Group Psychology and the Analysis of the Ego*, Hogarth Press.

LEVIN, H., and SEARS, R. R. (1956), 'Identification with parents as a determinant of doll play aggression', *Child Devel.*, vol. 27, pp. 135–53.

MANN, H. B., and WHITNEY, D. R. (1947), 'On a test of whether one or two random variables is stochastically larger than the other', *Ann. math. Stat.*, vol. 18, pp. 50–60.

MOWRER, O. H. (1950), *Learning Theory and Personality Dynamics*, Ronald Press.

PARSONS, T. (1955), 'Family structure and the socialization of the child', in T. Parsons and R. F. Bales (eds.), *Family, Socialization, and the Interaction Process*, Free Press.

PAYNE, D. E., and MUSSEN, P. H. (1956), 'Parent–child relations and father identification among adolescent boys', *J. abnorm. soc. Psychol.*, vol. 52, pp. 358–62.

RICHARDS, T. W., and SIMONS, M. (1941), 'Fels Child Behavior Scale', *Genet. Psychol. Monog.*, vol. 24, pp. 259–309.

SEARS, P. (1953), 'Child rearing factors related to playing of sex-typed roles', *Amer. Psychol.*, vol. 8, p. 431 (abstract).

SEARS, R. R., MACCOBY, E. E., and LEVIN, H. (1957), *Patterns of Child Rearing*, Row, Peterson.

SEARS, R. R., PINTLER, M. H., and SEARS, P. (1946), 'Effect of father separation on preschool children's doll play aggression', *Child. Devel.*, vol. 17, pp. 219–43.

Part Six
Unconscious Motivation and Dreaming

The Readings in this Part deal with the important notion of unconscious motivation and the meaning of dreams.

In Reading 16 by Rycroft the idea is put forward that what Freud described as characteristics of the unconscious or id are better thought of as the grammar of an unconscious, non-verbal language. A study by Erickson attempts to demonstrate experimentally the psychopathology of everyday life – which is postulated to result from the working of unconscious forces.

Freud's book *The Interpretation of Dreams* (1900; Hogarth Press, 1953) was regarded by him as his best work; and dreaming as 'the royal road to the unconscious' was an important tool in his uncovering of unconscious conflicts in the treatment of his patients. Two papers examine the validity of Freudian hypotheses concerning dreams in the light of contemporary research into sleep and dreaming.

16 Charles Rycroft

Causes and Meaning

Charles Rycroft, 'Causes and meaning', in *Psychoanalysis Observed*, Constable, 1966, pp. 7–22.

When this volume was first suggested its provisional title was *Objections to Psychoanalysis* and it was to have been included in the *Objections* series, in previous volumes of which churchmen, both Anglican and Catholic, and humanists have discussed critically their own beliefs. It soon became apparent, however, that the choice of this title was based on a false analogy, since it assumed that psychoanalysis is a 'belief' in the sense that Christianity and humanism are, and that analysts are the priests and theologians of a new religion – a view to which no analyst could be expected even to appear to subscribe.

The title *Objections to Psychoanalysis* also begged an important question, since one of the unsolved problems about analysis is precisely its logical and metaphysical status; and to have assumed in the title that it is an ideology would have precluded at the outset discussion of what sort of an animal psychoanalysis really is, whether it is a religion, as some of its critics assert, a science, as most of its practitioners claim, or an art, a craft, one of the humanities, a form of semantic theory – or even something *sui generis*, a new phenomenon which eludes classification into any of the traditional categories.

It therefore seemed better to abandon the idea of *Objections to Psychoanalysis* and start afresh by inviting a number of persons who have been in close intellectual and professional contact with psychoanalysis, whether as practitioners themselves, like Dr Lomas, Dr Storr and myself, or as workers in related fields, like Mr Geoffrey Gorer in social anthropology and Mr Wren-Lewis in theology and industrial science, to discuss psychoanalysis in the form in which they have themselves encountered it.

My own contribution should be read as an overture which

introduces some but not all of the themes which are developed in the four main essays; that of cure being elaborated by Dr Storr, that of cause and meaning by Dr Lomas in his essay on Freudian and existentialist analysis, that of the analyst as an authority on sex and child care by Mr Geoffrey Gorer, and that of psycho-analysis, science and religion by Mr Wren-Lewis. All four essays were, however, written independently of my Introduction and of one another and combine to form a conspectus of psychoanalysis today, of its place in the world, and of its prospects and poten-tialities, which is both more detailed and more panoramic than could have been achieved if it had been observed through a single pair of eyes.

In this context psychoanalysis is to be understood in its wider meaning to include all 'psycho-dynamic' theories and therapies, regardless as to whether they emanate from Freud or Jung or elsewhere. Although the Freudian professional organizations regard the term 'psychoanalysis' as one which refers solely to their own theory and practice, and although the Jungians and Adlerians call themselves analytical and individual psychologists respectively in the hope of differentiating themselves from the Freudians, these distinctions have never caught on even among the well-informed laity, which has always been more impressed by the similarities of the schools than by their differences.

In England, too, the attempt to reserve the term 'psycho-analysis' for Freudian theories has been rendered absurd by two local developments: the emergence of Kleinian analysis which claims to be Freudian and is yet disowned by many Freudians but received sympathetically by many Jungians, and the close personal relations existing between individual Freudians and Jungians which has resulted in a number of Jungian analysts having become analysands of Freudians and vice versa. The picture is further complicated by the existence of the existentialists, who certainly belong to the movement of thought begun by Freud but who reject many of his basic premisses.

Throughout this book, therefore, psychoanalysis, unless specifically qualified, should be taken to refer to all those theories and therapies – whether Freudian, Jungian or existentialist – which assume the existence of unconscious mental processes, which concern themselves with the elucidation of motives and which make use of transference – and which can be differentiated from the organic school of psychiatry and from behaviourism (learning theory) by the fact that they regard subjective experience as a central object of study and not as an awkward contaminant which has to be either ignored or eliminated.

When I first became an analyst it seemed to me that the idea of applying the scientific method to psychological phenomena was a perfectly straightforward matter and that there were no particular difficulties about regarding unconscious wishes or infantile complexes as causes of which present-day conscious symptoms were the effect, or in assuming that if a patient became aware of the unconscious and infantile determinants of his symptoms, these would vanish; and, indeed, even today I frequently have clinical experiences which can readily be understood in this way.

But, and it is a big but, these experiences only occur with a certain type of patient and under certain conditions. They occur with patients who are basically healthy and whose personality neither the therapist nor the patient feels inclined to call into question, and they occur only if both the patient and his nearest and nominally dearest wish him to lose his symptoms. In other words the patient loses his symptoms only if two conditions are fulfilled: firstly, that he understands their origin, and secondly, that his conscious wish to lose his symptoms is greater than his wish to retain the *status quo* in his personal relationships. For instance, if a married man is impotent or sexually perverted, his recovery depends not only on his understanding of the origin of his disability but also on whether his wife really and truly welcomes his recovery, and on whether, if she doesn't, he feels prepared to overcome her reluctance or, if that seems impossible, to make alternative arrangements. Whether he does feel prepared to do either will depend on many more factors than the unconscious determinants of his symptoms: it will be influenced by his conscious values, his religious attitudes, his general feelings towards his wife, his assessment of her mental stability, etc.

I am really making three points here. Firstly, symptoms are not solely an individual matter, they have a social nexus and function and change in one person may be contingent on changes in others. Secondly, in patients other than straightforward psychoneurotics, analysis involves consideration of the whole personality including his conscious values. And thirdly, conscious as well as unconscious motives play a part in the maintenance of neuroses.

The last point raises the question as to whether conscious motives can be regarded as causes. Although there are, it seems to me, no difficulties about regarding unconscious 'wishes', 'motives' and 'causes' as synonymous, particularly when the 'effect' being considered is a symptom which is alien to the patient's personality, it is much more difficult to maintain that they are interchangeable ideas when applied to conscious phenomena. Once any mental process or group of ideas becomes conscious it becomes part of the whole complex of thoughts, feelings, wishes, values and aspirations which constitute the personality, and one of the characteristic functions and activities of the personality is making decisions. Although a neurotic cannot decide to become potent or to lose a fear of crowds, and his symptoms are therefore the effect of forces and ideas of which he knows nothing, the healthy person (and the neurotic in healthy and unaffected parts of his life) spends much of his time deciding whether or not to do things that he wishes to do or feels he ought to, and his decisions are influenced not only by the strength of his own wishes and principles but also by his estimate of the likely effects of his actions on himself later and on those around him. It would seem indeed that one of the functions of consciousness is to enable decisions to be made, and the idea that all conscious decisions are strictly determined by unconscious forces seems to imply that all deciding is an illusion and that consciousness has no function – which is unlikely. A more probable hypothesis is that consciousness transmutes instinctual drives in such a way that the outcome of any act of decision is *not* solely determined by the relative strength of the instinctual forces involved.

Although this latter assumption is one which could be used to retain the notion of unconscious causation in a psychology which took account of conscious motives – and is indeed so used by the American school of psychoanalytical ego-psychology (Hartmann, 1958, 1964) – it is not in fact the assumption which Freud made when he propounded his principle of psychic determinism. Freud's aim was to establish a 'scientific psychology' and he hoped to be able to do so by applying to psychology the same principles of causality as were in his time considered valid in physics and chemistry. As a young man his own teachers in physiology had held that it was inadmissible to explain the working of the human body by reference to principles other than those which could be derived from physics and chemistry, and as a result they rejected all vitalist biological theories. Freud's grand design was to adopt the same attitude towards the working of the mind, and he believed that his discovery of unconscious mental forces made his project attainable. If, he argued, all mental activity is the result of unconscious mental forces which are instinctual, biological and physical in origin, then human psychology could be formulated in terms of the interacting of forces which were in principle quantifiable, without recourse to any vital mental integrating agency, and psychology would become a natural science like physics (Jones, 1953).

However, the principle of psychic determinism remains an assumption, and one which Freud made out of scientific faith rather than on evidence, and I know of no instance in Freud's writing of his claiming to have predicted in advance the outcome of any choice or decision made by a patient. Indeed, when describing the causes of neuroses, he more than once repudiated the idea that it is possible to predict whether a person will develop a neurosis or, if he does, what kind of neurosis it will be. All he claimed was that in retrospect it is possible to assert that such-and-such an event or situation in childhood had been the cause of the neurosis; a procedure which is more reminiscent of a historian than of a scientist.

He did however claim, and successfully claim, to be able to demonstrate that choices made by patients are not arbitrary and that they can be understood as revealing and characteristic manifestations of their personality. For instance, in his *Introductory Lectures* (1916–17a) Freud describes how he asked a womanizing male patient to tell him the first female name that came into his head. The man did so, producing a name which was not that of any of the many women he knew, but was very similar to Freud's nickname for him. Now, Freud does not claim to have predicted this name – indeed he describes himself as having been as surprised by it as the patient was – but he saw immediately its similarity to the patient's name, and this did not surprise him, since he had already appreciated that the man was not a great lover of women, but a narcissist.

What Freud did here was not to explain the patient's choice causally but to understand it and give it meaning, and the procedure he engaged in was not the scientific one of elucidating causes but the semantic one of making sense of it. It can indeed be argued that much of Freud's work was really semantic and that he made a revolutionary discovery in semantics, namely that neurotic symptoms are meaningful disguised communications, but that, owing to his scientific training and allegiance, he formulated his findings in the conceptual framework of the physical sciences. In some aspects of his work Freud saw this himself clearly. His most famous work he entitled *The Interpretation of Dreams* (1900) not *The Cause of Dreams* and his chapter on symptoms in his *Introductory Lectures* is called *The Sense of Symptoms* (1916–17b). He was also well aware that many of his ideas had been anticipated by writers and poets rather than by scientists.

The idea that psychoanalysis is not a causal theory but a semantic one is not original. It has been propounded in America by T. Szasz in his *Myth of Mental Illness* (1962), in which he argues that the idea that the neuroses are diseases with causes is a social fiction which is outgrowing its usefulness, and in England by James Home in his paper 'The concept of the mind' (1966). It is also held in different forms by the existentialists. But it is not orthodoxy, and the majority of Freudian analysts disclaim it entirely. They thereby lay themselves open to attack from critics like Professor Eysenck who see quite clearly that psychoanalysis cannot satisfy the canons of those sciences which are based on the experimental method but who believe that if they can demonstrate its inadequacy as a causal theory, they have proved that it is nonsense (Eysenck, 1953, 1965). To my mind, one of the merits of the semantic view of analysis is that it completely undercuts the Eysenck–Psychoanalysis controversy by showing that both parties are not only, as Eysenck himself has said, arguing from different premises but from wrong premises. On their side the analysts are claiming that analysis is what it is not, and, on his, Eysenck is attacking it for failing to be what it has no need to claim to be.

And both parties are assuming that it is only the physical sciences which are intellectually respectable. It is perhaps relevant here, that for very different historical reasons, both psychology and medicine are faculties which suffer from an inferiority complex in relation to science.

Recognition of the semantic nature of psychoanalytical theory would also undercut the tendency of analysts to engage in futile controversy as to whether the cause of neurosis is to be found in the first three months or years of life, or whether the fundamental cause of neurosis is constitutional envy of the mother's breast or is to be found in the Oedipal phase of childhood or in the infant's sensitivity to environmental impingements, and enable them to concentrate on improving their techniques for getting into communication with those who have become alienated for whatever reason.

There is, of course, one type of neurosis which undoubtedly does have a cause, and this is the traumatic neurosis which occurs after a totally unexpected shock, but this is precisely the neurosis which does *not* fit into psychoanalytical theory, and one of its symptoms, the traumatic dream in which the shocking experience is relived, provides the one example of a dream which is not amenable to analytical interpretation. Freud evidently regretted this, since in his last book, *An Outline of Psychoanalysis* (1940), he wrote of the traumatic neuroses: 'their relations to determinants in childhood have hitherto eluded investigation'.

It does, of course, remain possible that all the neuroses might be explained as similar to the traumatic neuroses, in that they could be seen as responses to specific pathological and unsatisfactory childhood experiences, though it is worth noting that Winnicott, the English analyst who has been most persistent in tracing the origin of neuroses to environmental failures in early childhood, has also found it necessary to introduce the distinction between a 'true' and a 'false' self. But 'true' and 'false', like the 'authentic' and 'inauthentic' of the existentialists, are semantic and evaluative concepts, not scientific, causal ones. Perhaps the principle of psychic determinism applies to the 'false self', while the 'true self' has free will (Winnicott, 1958).

Preoccupation with the idea of causality has led analysts into the position of giving advice and making recommendations about matters on which, to my mind, they only appear to be experts. If, so the argument runs, neurosis is the result of infantile traumata and deprivation, then it could be prevented by parents caring for their children better, and analysts have therefore come to regard themselves, and to be accepted, as experts on the upbringing of children. Both in this country and more particularly in America, a literature exists which contains advice on such matters as how and when infants should be weaned, how the births of children should be spaced, when and whether they should be punished, and even on how parents should love their children, the authority for such advice apparently deriving from psychoanalysis. Now although much of this advice is probably as wise as advice emanating from other sources, it tends in fact to derive from paediatric and child-guidance experience, and much of it is open to objections of three kinds.

Firstly, the idea that children should be treated lovingly and humanely is one that does not require any scientific, medical or psychological backing and can be arrived at without reference to psychoanalysis or, indeed, any other body of knowledge.

Secondly, loving is not an activity which can be engaged in on advice, since its essence is sincerity and spontaneity.

And thirdly, much of the trauma and suffering endured by children is unavoidable. It is really no use saying that children should not be separated from their parents and need their full-time love and attention up to such-and-such an age, when the facts of human existence are such that no parent can guarantee to remain alive for the requisite number of years after becoming one, or even that he or she will go on loving the other parent for so long. As a result much of this sort of advice is both sentimental and perfectionist and may even, on occasion, be harmful, since it may encourage parents to be insincere out of a sense of guilt or duty. It may also induce a sense of guilt in parents who, through no fault of their own, have to bring up children under difficult and unsatisfactory conditions. Many of our patients are the offspring of tragedy, not of faulty child-rearing.

The idea that neurosis is caused by lack of love in childhood can also lead analysts into priggishness. If neurosis is the result of parental deprivation then perhaps analysis is a form of replacement-therapy and the effective agent in treatment is the analyst's concern, devotion and love. But this view of the matter leaves unexplained why the analyst should consider himself to be the possessor of a store of *agape* or *caritas* so much greater than that of his patients' parents. Analysts who hold that their capacity to help patients derives from their ability to understand them, and that this ability depends on their knowledge of the language of the unconscious, are really being more modest. The claim to possess professional expertise does not contain a concealed claim to moral superiority over the laity.

If psychoanalysis is recognized as a semantic theory not a causal one, its theory can start where its practice does – in the consulting room, where a patient who is suffering from something in himself which he does not understand confronts an analyst with some knowledge of the unconscious – i.e. who knows something of the way in which repudiated wishes, thoughts, feelings and memories can translate themselves into symptoms, gestures and dreams, and who knows, as it were, the grammar and syntax of such translations and is therefore in a position to interpret them back again into the communal language of consciousness. According to the scientific analyst this can only be done by elucidating and reconstructing the history of the illness and of its infantile origins, but even he agrees that this is useless unless the analyst has made contact (*rapport*) with the patient, and it seems to me that it makes better sense to say that the analyst makes excursions into historical research in order to understand something which is interfering with his present communication with the patient (in the same way as a translator might turn to history to elucidate an obscure text) than to say that he makes contact with the patient in order to gain access to biographical data. In the former he is using the past to understand the present, in the latter he is using his biographical research to legitimize his *rapport* with the patient by formulating it in terms of a theory about the causes of neurosis. Furthermore, as the conditions of analytical work make it inconceivable that any analyst, or even group of like-minded analysts, will ever encounter a representative sample of any particular neurosis and as, indeed, the validity of particular neurotic diagnostic categories is open to doubt, since neuroses are in a sense personal creations, such research is in any case methodologically suspect.

There is, however, a form of research which not only can be done by analysts but is indeed done by all analysts regardless of whether they consider themselves research workers or not. This is research into the private languages of patients and of the ways in which their cryptic and disguised utterances and gestures can be understood and translated back into common and communicable language. This is research in exactly the same sense that linguistic research is. An analyst encountering a new patient is in a position surprisingly similar to that of a linguist who encounters a community which speaks an unfamiliar language. To get his bearings he explores how much language they have in common, listens to him and by locating the contexts in which initially incomprehensible utterances occur and referring back in his own mind to other languages he knows, he gradually learns his patient's language, and makes himself familiar with his imagery and style of thought and feeling.

If he is not theoretically minded he will leave it at that, in the same way as some people who have a gift for languages may learn to speak them without ever acquiring an interest in grammar and linguistic theory. His research will then increase his own insight and clinical competence but will not be communicated to anyone who does not come into direct contact with him as patient, pupil or colleague. The late John Rickman, who would, I suspect, have agreed with much of this essay, often used to remark that much that is valuable in psychoanalysis is handed on not in learned papers but by verbal tradition.

If, on the other hand, he is theoretically minded, he will formulate the language-patterns he has learnt, will relate them to those he has previously encountered or which have already been described in the literature, and will write clinical and theoretical papers. To continue the linguistic analogy, diagnosing a patient as suffering from hysteria or obsessional neurosis is like locating a language as belonging to a particular family, while general analytical theory is analogous to general language theory. The basic principles of the language theory applicable to dreams, verbal imagery and physical gestures have already been formulated by Freud in his *Papers on Metapsychology* (1915) where the grammar and syntax of the unconscious is stated in terms of the primary processes (condensation, displacement, etc.) and in the analytical literature on symbolism.

Here again I must disclaim originality. The idea that what Freud described as characteristics of the unconscious or id is better thought of as the grammar of an unconscious, nonverbal language is to be found in, for instance, Erich Fromm's *The Forgotten Language* (1952) and Tauber and Green's *Prelogical Experience* (1959), though neither of these are books which I would endorse in their entirety.

The statement that psychoanalysis is a theory of meaning is incomplete and misleading unless one qualifies it by saying that it is a *biological* theory of meaning. By this I mean that psychoanalysis interprets human behaviour in terms of the self that experiences it and not in terms of entities external to it, such as other-worldly deities or political parties and leaders, and that it regards the self as a psychobiological entity which is always striving for self-realization and self-fulfilment. In other words, it regards mankind as sharing with the animal and plant world the intrinsic drive to create and recreate its own nature. Part of the resistance among analysts to the idea that psychoanalysis may be a semantic theory derives from the fact that the concept of meaning is felt to have both religious and political overtones. Freud himself dismissed the problem of meaning by asserting that anyone who questions the meaning of life is ill. By this he can, I think, only have meant that living itself gives meaning to life and that this is doubted only by those who have become to some measure self-alienated, and who as a result have recourse to religious or ideological theories of meaning as a 'secondary construction', an attempt to restore the lost sense of meaningfulness by deriving it from some source external to the self. This was, I suspect, the real basis of his antagonism to religion. For him, religion was a cosmology, its central notion being a God who was outside the universe and who had created it. As a scientist, he realized that the traditional Judaic-Christian cosmology was no longer tenable, and he therefore interpreted religion as an illusion which those who needed it created for themselves in order to preserve the childhood illusion of being absolutely protected and loved by a father. However, in interpreting religion as a neurosis, as a defence against anxiety and feelings of helplessness, he was himself applying a theory of meaning, since he made sense of it to himself by ascribing to it a function in the lives of those who believe it and one with which he could himself empathize (Freud, 1927).

Recent developments in theology, however, make it very doubtful whether cosmology can be regarded as the central religious idea or whether belief in a God 'out there' is the essence of the religious attitude. Although we can have no idea of what Freud personally would have made of Bonhoeffer's 'religionless Christianity', or of Zen Buddhism, or of statements like Guntrip's (1961) 'the fundamental therapeutic factor in psychotherapy is more akin to religion than to science, since it is a matter of personal relationship . . . religion has always stood for the good object relationship', there would seem to be no necessary incompatibility between psychoanalysis and those religious formulations which locate God within the self. One could, indeed, argue that Freud's id (and even more Groddeck's it, 1950), the impersonal force within which is both the core of oneself and yet not oneself, and from which in illness one becomes alienated, is a secular formulation of the insight which makes religious people believe in an immanent God: if this were so, psychoanalysis could be regarded as a semantic bridge between science and biology on the one hand and religion and the humanities on the other. This was what I had in mind at the beginning of this essay when I listed as one possible answer to the problem of psychoanalysis's metaphysical status, the possibility that it might be something *sui generis* which could not be fitted into any of the traditional categories.

References
EYSENCK, H. J. (1953), *The Uses and Abuses of Psychology*, Penguin Books.
EYSENCK, H. J. (1965), *Fact and Fiction in Psychology*, Penguin Books.
FREUD, S. (1900), *The Interpretation of Dreams*, standard edn, vols. 4 and 5, Hogarth Press, 1953.
FREUD, S. (1915), *Papers on Metapsychology*, standard edn, vol. 14, Hogarth Press, 1957.
FREUD, S. (1916–17a), *Introductory Lectures on Psychoanalysis*, lecture 6, standard edn, vol. 15, Hogarth Press, 1963.
FREUD, S. (1916–17b), *Introductory Lectures on Psychoanalysis*, lecture 17, standard edn, vol. 16, Hogarth Press, 1963.
FREUD, S. (1927), *The Future of an Illusion*, standard edn, vol. 21, Hogarth Press, 1961.

FREUD, S. (1940), *An Outline of Psychoanalysis*, standard edn, vol. 23, Hogarth Press, 1964.

FROMM, E. (1952), *The Forgotten Language*, Gollancz.

GRODDECK, G. (1950), *The Book of the It*, Vision Press.

GUNTRIP, H. (1961), *Personality Structure and Human Interaction*, Hogarth Press.

HARTMANN, H. (1958), *Ego Psychology and the Problem of Adaptation*, Imago.

HARTMANN, H. (1964), *Essays of Ego Psychology*, Hogarth Press.

HOME, H. J. (1966), 'The concept of the mind', *Intern. J. Psychoanal.*, vol. 47, pp. 42–9.

JONES, E. (1953), *Sigmund Freud: Life and Work*, vol. 1, Hogarth Press. Abriged edn, Penguin Books, 1964.

SZASZ, T. S. (1962), *The Myth of Mental Illness*, Secker & Warburg.

TAUBER, E. S., and GREEN, M. R. (1959), *Prelogical Experience*, Basic Books.

WINNICOTT, D. W. (1958), *Collected Papers*, Tavistock.

17 Milton H. Erickson

Experimental Demonstrations of the Psychopathology
of Everyday Life

Milton H. Erickson, 'Experimental demonstrations of the psychopathology of everyday life', *Psychoanalytic Quarterly*, vol. 8, 1939,
pp. 338–53.

Introduction

The experiments reported below were conducted for the most
part in the presence of a seminar of graduate students held in
New Haven under the leadership of Dr Sapir during the spring of
1933. In addition, a few experiments which were performed elsewhere are included.

The subject who was used for many of these demonstrations
had frequently before volunteered for similar purposes. He knew
nothing, however, of the plans for these experiments; they
represented situations which were entirely new and problems
with which he had never before been confronted.

In his approach to such demonstrations, this subject customarily reacted in a way which was fairly characteristic for many
others. Ahead of time he often appeared to be resentful and
anxious, or over-eager about the impression which he and the
experimenter would make. Suddenly, however, with the beginning
of the lecture or demonstration, he would seem to shift the
responsibility completely and to lapse into an attitude of complete comfort with loss of all tension and worry.

Following one of the demonstrations described below the
subject told the experimenter that his shift in mood had been even
more marked than usual. The night before the lecture he had
been unable to sleep and had felt more than ordinarily resentful
that on so important an occasion no rehearsal or preparatory
discussion had taken place. He had even developed some nausea
and diarrhea. All of this nervousness had disappeared completely,
however, as he entered the lecture room on the morning of these
experiments.

Milton H. Erickson

Unconscious Determinants of the Casual Content of Conversation

The subject was brought into a state of profound hypnosis, during which he was instructed that after awakening he would (a) notice Dr D. searching vainly through his pockets for a package of cigarettes; (b) that he then would proffer his own pack, and (c) that Dr D. absent-mindedly would forget to return the cigarettes whereupon the subject would feel very eager to recover them because he had no others. He was further told that (d) he would be too courteous to ask for the cigarettes either directly or indirectly but that (e) he would engage in a conversation that would cover any topic except cigarettes although at the time his desire for the return of the cigarettes would be on his mind constantly.

When he was awakened the subject saw that Dr D. was looking for cigarettes. He thereupon courteously offered his own and at the same time became involved in a conversation during which Dr D., after lighting the cigarette, absent-mindedly placed the pack in his own pocket. The subject noted this with a quick glance, felt his own pockets in a somewhat furtive manner as if to see whether or not he had another pack, and showed by his facial expression that he had no others. He then began chatting casually, wandering from one topic to another, always mentioning in some indirect but relevant fashion the word 'smoking'. For example, he talked about a boat on the bay at New Haven, commenting on the fact that the sight of water always made him thirsty, as did smoking. He then told a story about how the dromedary got one hump and the *camel* two. When the question of travel was raised he immediately pictured the pleasure he would derive from crossing the Sahara Desert rocking back and forth comfortably on a *camel*. Next he told a tale of Syrian folk-lore in which again a camel played a role. When he was asked to tell something interesting about patients he told of taking a patient to see a marathon dance which the latter enjoyed immensely while he himself was reminded by the antics of the dancers of a circus where one would see elephants, hippopotami and *camels*. Asked what he would like to do, he commented on the pleasant weather and said that there was nothing more glorious than paddling in a canoe or floating at ease on the water, smoking.

Manifestations of Unconscious Ambivalent Feelings in Conversation about a Person

During hypnosis the subject was told that he admired and respected Dr D. very much but that unconsciously he was jealous of him and that because of this jealousy there would be a cutting edge to complimentary remarks which he would make. He was further told that after awakening a conversation would be started with Dr D. in which he would take part. The subject was then awakened and the conversation begun.

The topic of traveling and its contribution to personal education was mentioned. The subject immediately brought up the fact that Dr D. had studied both in the Middle West and in the East and that, having traveled abroad as well, he might well be called cosmopolitan. He himself, he added, would like to travel and get a cosmopolitan education but in the last analysis that was what was being done by any old tramp who traveled from one part of the country to another by stealing rides on freight cars. There followed a discussion of human behavior as it reflected local environments during which the subject remarked that the man who had traveled showed a broader knowledge and better understanding of people and of cultural things; he added, however, that the same thing might possibly be said of any resident of east-side New York.

Lapsus Linguae and Unconscious Irony

During hypnosis the subject was instructed that after he awakened Dr D. would begin talking to him about some abstruse subject in which he was not at all interested, and that although he would actually be profoundly bored he would try to appear interested. He was told that he would want very much to close the conversation, that he would wish for some way of shutting off this interminable flow of words, that he would look around him in the hope of finding some distraction, and that he would feel that Dr D. was terribly tiresome. He was then awakened, whereupon Dr D. began the conversation. Although the subject appeared to be politely attentive, Dr D. would occasionally say, 'Perhaps you're not interested?' The subject would reply with excessive emphasis, 'Oh, yes, certainly, I'm very much interested.' Now and then he would interrupt Dr D., trying to pin him down to some definite point for discussion, but each time this effort was evaded. At length the subject began glancing about the room and was noted casually to observe an open door. Finally he interrupted Dr D. saying, 'Excuse me, I feel an awful draft,' and got up to close the door. As he did so he was asked what he was doing. He replied, 'The air seems to be awful hot ['hot air!']; I thought I would shut off the draft.' When the hypnotist pretended not to understand and asked him what he was doing the subject replied, 'Why, I just shut the bore.' His remark was then repeated by the hypnotist for the benefit of those in the audience who had not heard it. When the subject heard his statement given as 'shutting the bore' he started visibly, seemed tremendously embarrassed, and with much urgency turned to Dr D. saying, 'Did I say that? I didn't mean that. I just meant I closed the door.' He was very apologetic in his whole manner and bearing.

Unconscious Resentment Expressing Itself in Masked Forms through a Smoke-Screen of Overcompensatory Courtesy

The subject was told during hypnosis that he felt antagonistic, resentful and jealous of Dr D., and that this emotional state would persist after he was awakened. He was also told that after awakening he would try to be courteous and acquiescent toward Dr D. in every way and would appear to be willing to do anything requested of him.

After being awakened the subject seemed to be entirely at ease; he responded courteously to some casual remarks addressed to him by Dr D. Presently Dr D. asked him if he would mind changing his seat. The subject replied certainly not, that he would be delighted, but that *he* was quite comfortable where he was; if, however, it would make *Dr D.* more comfortable, he would be delighted to change his seat. The request was repeated, whereupon the subject arose and asked Dr D. to designate the precise chair in which he was to seat himself. He walked over toward the designated chair but asked Dr D. if perhaps a certain other chair might not serve even better since the reason Dr D. had given for his request was that he was not quite in full view of the audience.

When Dr D. insisted that the designated chair was the better one the subject, with great courtesy, still questioned, seeming nevertheless most willing to do precisely what was desired and to be hesitant only about seating himself before he was absolutely certain of Dr D.'s wishes. After much insistence by Dr D. that he seat himself the subject agreed that the chair indicated was precisely the one that he ought to sit in and proceeded to do so; but as he did so he moved the chair about six inches to one side and shifted its position so that it faced in a slightly different direction. Immediately upon seating himself he turned and politely asked, 'Is this the way you would like to have me?' After a few moments of casual conversation Dr D. found fault with his position and asked him if he would mind taking his original chair. He rose promptly, said that he would be delighted to sit anywhere that Dr D. wished but that perhaps it would be better if he sat on the table, and offered to move the designated chair to any desired spot, suggesting some clearly unsuitable positions; finally, when urged insistently to sit in the chair he again had to move it.

Ambivalence: Manifestations of Unconscious Conflict about Smoking in the Distortion of Simple, Daily Smoking Habits

During profound hypnosis the subject was instructed to feel that he wanted to get over the habit but that he felt it was too strong a habit to break, that he would be very reluctant to smoke and would give anything not to smoke, but that he would find himself compelled to smoke; and that after he was awakened he would experience all of these feelings.

After he was awakened the subject was drawn into a casual conversation with the hypnotist who, lighting one himself, offered him a cigarette. The subject waved it aside with the explanation that he had his own and that he preferred Camels, and promptly began to reach for his own pack. Instead of looking in his customary pocket, however, he seemed to forget where he carried his cigarettes and searched fruitlessly through all of his other pockets with a gradually increasing concern. Finally, after having sought them repeatedly in all other pockets, he located his cigarettes in their usual place. He took them out, engaged in a brief conversation as he dallied with the pack, and then began a search for matches which he failed to find. During his search for matches he replaced the cigarettes in his pocket and began using both hands, finally locating the matches, too, in their usual pocket. Having done this, he now began using both hands to search for his cigarettes. He finally located them but then found that he had once more misplaced his matches. This time, however, he kept his cigarettes in hand while attempting to relocate the matches. He then placed a cigarette in his mouth and struck a match. As he struck it, however, he began a conversation which so engrossed him that he forgot the match and allowed it to burn his finger tips whereupon, with a grimace of pain, he tossed it in the ash tray. Immediately he took another match, but again introduced a diverting topic by asking the audience in a humorous fashion if they knew the 'Scotch' way of lighting a cigarette. As interest was shown, he carefully split the match through the middle. One half of the match he replaced in his pocket in a time-consuming manner and tried to light his cigarette with the other half. When it gave too feeble a flame he discarded it and had to search for the second half. After striking this another interesting topic of conversation developed and again he burned his fingers before he made use of it. He apologized for his failure to demonstrate the 'Scotch' light successfully and repeated the performance, this time holding the flame in such a way as to ignite only a small corner of the cigarette from which he succeeded in getting only one satisfactory puff. Then he tossed the match away and tipped the cigarette up so that he could see the lighted end. He started to explain that that was how the 'Scotch' light was obtained and noted that only one small corner of the cigarette was lit. He smiled in a semi-apologetic manner and explained that he had really given a 'Jewish' light to the cigarette, whereupon the lighted corner expired. He made a few more humorous comments, and as he talked and gesticulated appropriately he rolled the cigarette between his fingers in such a fashion that he broke it, whereupon he put it aside and took another. This time a member of the audience stepped up and proffered him a light, but as the lighted match drew near to the tip of his cigarette the subject sneezed and blew it out. He apologized again and said he thought he would light his own cigarette. While taking out his matches he commented on the vaudeville trick of rolling cigars from one corner of the mouth to the other and proceeded to demonstrate how he could roll a cigarette in that fashion, which he did fairly successfully. However, in doing so he macerated the tip of the cigarette and had to discard it. He took another, holding it in his mouth while he reached for his matches, started a conversation, and took the cigarette out so that he could talk more freely. It was observed that he took the cigarette out with his hand held in the reverse position to that which he usually used, and after completing his remarks he put the dry end of the cigarette in his mouth, exposing the wet end. He then tried to light this, held the match to the tip in the proper fashion, puffed vigorously, finally got a puff of smoke and then blew out the match. Naturally the wet end of the cigarette did not burn satisfactorily and quickly went out. He looked at it in amazement and in a semi-embarrassed manner mumbled that he had lit the wrong end of the cigarette; he then commented that now both ends of the cigarette were wet, and discarded it for another. After several similar trials he finally succeeded in lighting the cigarette. It was observed that although he took deep puffs he tended to let his cigarette burn undisturbed, and that instead of smoking it down to a reasonable butt he quickly discarded it.

A little later while smoking the subject attempted to demonstrate the violent gestures of a patient and in so doing knocked off the burning tip. Then while lighting another cigarette he became so interested in talking that he lit the cigarette in the middle rather than at the tip and had to discard it. As usual he showed profound embarrassment at seeming so awkward.

(On other occasions when the subject had demonstrated this phenomenon, he would finally complete the demonstration by selecting a cigarette in a strained and laborious fashion and then, obviously centering all of his attention upon the procedure of lighting it, would hold his hand tensely as he lit the match, applying it with noticeable rigidity to the cigarette and holding it there so long and puffing so repeatedly that all doubt was removed concerning the actual lighting of the cigarette, whereupon his whole manner and attitude would relax and he would appear to be physically comfortable.)

Unconscious Convictions of Absurdities with Rationalization
in Support of the Belief in Them

During hypnosis the subject was instructed that he was about to
be reminded by the hypnotist of something he had known for a
long time, that he had known it both as a result of his own experience and from reading about it in authoritative books. This, he
was told, was the fact that 'all German men marry women who
are two inches taller than they are.' A state of absolute emotional
and intellectual belief in this was suggested and he was warned
that he might be called upon to defend this statement. He was
told that he had read of this in a book written by Dr Sapir in
which the reference occurred on page forty-two. He was informed
that he would know this not only in the hypnotic state but also
when awake. The subject was then wakened.

During the course of a casual conversation mention was made
of the peculiar customs of various nations and peoples. Remark-
ing that he was reminded of a peculiar custom among the Ger-
mans, the subject went on to describe the suggested phenomenon
in a matter-of-fact way. When his statement was challenged he
expressed obvious surprise that anybody should doubt it. He
argued that it was entirely reasonable, that customs established
originally from some simple purpose could be perpetuated by
future generations until, regardless of their absurdity, they were
looked upon as rational and commonplace. From this statement
he proceeded to draw a social parallel to the attitude of Mussolini
regarding compulsory marriage, arguing in a logical, orderly and
reasonable fashion. When this failed to convince the doubters he
drew upon personal experience, citing examples with a casual,
simple, matter-of-fact and convincing manner, and calling upon
others in the group to verify his statements. When they failed
to do so and cited contrary instances he smiled agreeably and
stated that every rule had its exception and that the failure of the
German in the audience to confirm his observation was characteristic of the well-known tendency to overlook the obvious in
familiar situations. When he was asked whether any authority
in the field was known to hold such a belief he promptly stated
that he had read the same observation in a book by Dr Sapir
entitled, *Primitive Peoples and Customs*. When he was asked where

in the book it was described he smiled in a deprecating fashion and remarked that it had been so long since he had read the book that he could not be sure of the page but that, as he recalled it, it seemed to be between pages forty and forty-five – forty-four, perhaps; this despite the fact that the hypnotist had specified page forty-two. He was then asked by a member of the audience what chapter it was in; he stated that as far as he recalled it was chapter two. Asked for the chapter heading, he explained that he had read the book so long ago he really could not recall it. When a member of the audience then stated that such a belief was contrary to all common sense the subject, in amazement and with some embarrassment, asked rather urgently, 'Surely you would not dispute a man as famous and distinguished as Dr Sapir?', nodding his head toward Dr Sapir. His whole manner was suggestive of intense surprise at such arrogant disbelief.

Automatic Writing: Unconscious Obliteration of Visual Impressions in Order to Preserve an Hypnotically Ordered Amnesia

During hypnosis the subject was instructed that on awakening he would engage in a casual conversation and that as he did so his hand would begin writing, but that he would have no knowledge of what he was doing.

After he had written some incomplete sentences he was asked what he was doing by others in the audience. With some amazement he explained that he had been talking to Dr D. When he was informed that while talking to Dr D. he had also been writing, he immediately pointed out that this could not have been since he had been holding a cigarette in his right hand. (He had actually transferred the cigarette from his left to the right hand upon completing the writing.) As the audience continued to insist he pointed out that he had had no pencil and nothing to write on, in addition to the fact that *he knew* he had not been writing and that the audience must have been mistaken. His attention was then called to a pencil and some paper on the table; he seemed surprised to see the paper and pencil and insisted that he had not had anything to do with either. He was asked to examine the paper to see if there were not some automatic writing on it, or at least writing. He picked up the paper, glanced at the top sheet, shook his head and began slowly to thumb over each sheet, examining the papers over and over again on both sides and finally restoring the pile to its original state. He said that he had found no writing on any of the sheets. His attention was called to the top sheet which he was asked to examine. He looked it over carefully at the top, turned it over and examined it, seemed to be in doubt as to whether or not he had taken the top sheet and took the second sheet; he examined that, put it away, and glanced at the third sheet; he then seemed to feel that possibly he *had* had the top sheet in his hand, so he re-examined that very thoroughly and carefully and then, still holding it right side up, declared hesitantly, as if he hated to dispute with the audience but felt compelled to disagree, that there was no writing on the paper. One of the audience called his attention to the particular part of the paper on which there was writing. He glanced at it, looked back at his informant in a puzzled way and then re-examined that part of the paper. After turning it over somewhat doubtfully and glancing at it he turned it right side up again. He then began holding it so that the light struck it obliquely and finally declared, still in a puzzled fashion, that there *really* was no writing on the paper. Finally he was given the suggestion by the hypnotist that there *was* writing and that he would see it. He glanced back at the paper in surprise and then an expression of amusement and amazement spread over his face as he saw the writing apparently for the first time. He commented on the juvenility of the handwriting, disowning it. When asked to tell what it said he showed much interest in reading the characters but appeared to have a certain amount of difficulty in deciphering the writing. The last word was incomplete; he read it, spelled it and stated that it seemed to be only part of a word. When he was asked to guess what the word was he promptly reread the sentence in order to get the context, but was unable to guess. He then wanted to know why the writing had not been finished and was informed by the hypnotist that if he would just watch the pencil on the table it would suddenly lift up in the air and begin writing the rest of the word. He looked doubtfully at the hypnotist and then said, 'Why, it's lifting up', seeming to have no realization that his own hand was picking up the pencil and holding it poised in position to write. Gradually his hand began forming letters. He was asked what the pencil was writing, to which he replied. 'Wait – wait; let's see'; he appeared to be entirely absorbed in the supposed phenomenon of a pencil writing alone. The hypnotist watched the writing, which was proceeding very slowly, and soon realized that the word in question was 'delicious'. The hypnotist then announced this to the audience while the subject was writing the last four letters and finished by the time the subject had finished writing. The subject looked up upon completing the word and said, 'It's delicious', and then read the sentence to see if the word was relevant to the meaning. Apparently he had not heard the observer announce the word to the seminar.

'Crystal' Gazing: Hallucinatory Vividness of Dream Imagery Embodying Anger Displaced from Hypnotist on to Dream Person

In a somnambulistic state the subject was instructed that he was to gaze at the wall and that as he did this the wall would become distant, far-away, foggy and blurred, and that gradually a dark point would appear which would become more and more elaborate, that movement would enter the scene and that soon he would see a well-known and emotionally stirring moving picture.

The subject began these observations with faint interest and considerable difficulty at first but gradually a profound change in his manner and attitude occurred as he was seen to watch the moving images with intense interest. He resented any inquiries as to what he was seeing and gave the impression that he did not want to be distracted from the scene. Now and then he would turn slightly to ask, 'Did you see that? Watch.' The moving scene was from Rasputin and the Empress, showing the stumbling and falling of the Czarevitch, to which the subject showed appropriate emotional reactions. He went on to describe the sequence of events in proper chronological order. When the demonstration had gone far enough he was told that the picture was changing. He disregarded this; when the hypnotist insisted, he declared that he did not want to listen now, that the hypnotist should wait until the picture came to an end. He was obdurate about accepting any suggestions concerning the changing of the picture. The suggestion was then tried of speeding up the movie, making it go faster and faster. When this was done it was possible to shift the scene to a hospital picture which he described as one in which *a nurse shouted loudly at a patient*. Here he manifested great resentment toward the nurse for doing this, apparently hallucinating the nurse's voice. The incorporation into the hallucinatory image of his anger against the experimenter and the child-like and fear-laden exaggeration of his impression of loud and angry voices because of his own inner anger were all very evident.

Implantation of a Complex

During hypnosis the subject was instructed to recall having had dinner at Dr D.'s home on the previous day. He was then told that the hypnotist would review a certain series of actions which had occurred on the previous day, and that the hypnotist would refresh his memory of certain things that the subject had done which he regretted intensely and which constituted a source of much shame to him. Thereupon he was told to remember how during the course of the afternoon he had stood by the fireplace, leaning against the mantel while talking to Dr D. about various subjects, when his eye happened to fall upon a package of cigarettes lying behind the clock on the end of the mantelpiece. The tale went on that Dr D. had noticed his glance and had proceeded to tell the subject that the package of cigarettes was a sentimental keepsake of his marriage, that he and his wife had received this package of cigarettes on their wedding day and had preserved it unused ever since. As Dr D. added various romantic elaborations the subject had not paid much attention because he was really rather bored by the sentimental story. After fingering the package, Dr D. had replaced it at the other end of the mantelpiece; but the subject had not paid any attention to this either. Shortly after this Dr D. and his wife had left the room for a few minutes. During their absence the subject noticed that he was out of cigarettes and glanced about the room to see if his host had some. Noticing a pack of cigarettes at the other end of the mantelpiece, he thought that his host would have no objections to his helping himself. He stepped over and took this pack of cigarettes from the mantelpiece, opened it, extracted a cigarette, lit and smoked it. Not until he had finished smoking did he realize that this was the very pack of cigarettes which Dr D. had placed at the end of the mantelpiece instead of returning to its original hiding place behind the clock. The subject was then reminded of how distressed he had felt, of his sense of being in a quandary as to what he ought to do, of how he had hastily closed the pack and had replaced it behind the clock and had then decided that he had better put it where Dr D. had placed it, but how before he could do this his host had returned so that he had been forced to carry on a casual conversation with this burden on his mind. Furthermore he was told that even now and after awakening this burden would still be on his mind.

The subject was roused and after a few brief remarks Dr D. offered him a cigarette. The subject started, glanced furtively first at Dr D. and then at the hypnotist and finally in a labored fashion reached out and accepted the cigarette, handling it in a gingerly manner. Dr D. began an innocuous conversation, but the subject paid little attention to what was said and asked Dr D. what he thought about sentimentality, uttering the word 'sentimentality' in a tone of disgust. He then stated that he himself was not sentimental and that he tended to dislike people who were sentimental and maudlin. He stated that he hoped that Dr D. was not sentimental, that he did not impress the subject as being sentimental. Dr D. made another attempt to change the topic of conversation but the subject persisted with his own line of thought. He raised a hypothetical question about a man who owned an old homestead and who, as a result of the economic depression, had lost much money and was in a quandary about the necessity of selling it. He went on to talk of the burning of the house, of the house going up in smoke, and various allied topics. He then talked of guilt feelings, how everybody stole, how he himself had stolen; he wanted to know how Dr D. would feel about anybody who had stolen unwittingly. Another attempt by Dr D. to change the trend of the conversation failed. The subject then told of having once stolen a cigar which belonged to a man who had kept it for sentimental reasons. He said he had taken the cigar and smoked it without realizing that it was a keepsake, and that he had felt very badly about it and wondered about the possibility of replacing it so that the sentimental man would not be angry with him. In a defensive manner he then expressed a high regard for a person's feelings and contended that, nevertheless, people should not think too hard of others who had unwittingly violated some of their sentimental values. After this he stated that not only had he stolen the cigar but he had even stolen cigarettes (pause), a pack of cigarettes. As he said this he glanced in a particularly furtive manner at Dr D. and also at the hypnotist, and seemed very ill at ease. He told about having smoked a cigarette and having enjoyed it, but that it had left a bad taste in his mouth afterwards and that even though he had stolen the cigarettes long ago he could not get them off his mind, that they still troubled him though common sense told him it was nothing to be concerned or worried about.

The Assumption of Another's Identity under Hypnotic Direction, with Striking Unconscious Mimicry and the Assumption of Unconscious Emotional Attitudes

During hypnosis the subject was informed that after awakening *he* would be Dr D. and that Dr D. would be Mr Blank, and that in the role of Dr D. he would talk to the pseudo Mr Blank. Additional suggestions which the subject fully accepted were given to complete the trans-identification. After the subject was awakened a conversation was begun. The pseudo Mr Blank questioned him about his work in the seminar, as though he were Dr D.; the subject responded by giving an excellent talk about his experiences in the seminar and his reactions to the group, talking in the phraseology of Dr D. and expressing the personal attitudes of Dr D. A chance conversation with Dr D. on the previous day had supplied him with a great deal of information which he utilized fully. It was noted also that he adopted Dr D's mannerisms in smoking and that he introduced ideas with certain phrases characteristic of Dr D. When the pseudo Mr Blank challenged his identity the subject contradicted 'Mr Blank' politely and seemed profoundly amazed at 'Mr Blank's' remarks. Then suddenly, with an expression of dawning understanding, he turned to the hypnotist saying 'He's in a trance, isn't he?' and thereafter was only amused at 'Mr Blank's' remarks. 'Mr Blank' then questioned the subject about his 'wife', to which the subject responded in a way that would have been natural for the real Dr D. When asked about children he assumed an expression of mild embarrassment and replied, 'not yet, but you never can tell.'

'Mr Blank' then began talking to the hypnotist in his ordinary fashion, at which the subject again seemed tremendously surprised. With a puzzled look on his face he suddenly leaned over and tested 'Mr Blank' for catalepsy. When he found none his face was expressive of some concern; he promptly whispered to the hypnotist, 'He's coming out of the trance,' but was relieved when the hypnotist assured him that it would be all right if this happened.

Finally, when an attempt was made to rehypnotize him in order to restore his own identity, the subject displayed the emotional attitude of resistance toward the induction of hypnosis which would have been entirely characteristic of the real Dr D. The subject seemed actually to experience the same emotional responses that Dr D. would have had at such a time. Finally, because he appeared to be entirely resistive to simple suggestion, it was necessary to induce hypnosis by indirect methods.

This rather astonishing result offers a technique for the experimental investigation of the phenomena of identification, and of the unconscious incorporation of parental emotions by children.

18 Kenneth Z. Altshuler

Comments on Recent Sleep Research Related to
Psychoanalytic Theory

Kenneth Z. Altshuler, 'Comments on recent sleep research related to
psychoanalytic theory', *Archives of General Psychiatry*, vol. 15,
1966, pp. 235–9.

In the last ten years the study of dreams has ceased to be an
exclusive realm of the clinical practitioner. The work of Dement
and Kleitman in 1957 and the rapidly increasing number of their
colleagues ever since confirmed beyond question the coincidence
of rapid eye movements (REM), low voltage, fast electroencephalogram (stage 1 EEG) and visual dreams, and led to the recognition of dreams as universally occurring cyclical phenomena,
biologically rooted in man's genetic neurophysiological endow-
ment. Dream periodicity and length have been determined in
various age groups, and the limits to which they may be influenced are being defined by studies of drugs, interruption or
deprivation of dreams, and the like. One pathological entity,
narcolepsy, had been clarified as a possible derangement of the
mechanism underlying the REM state, while studies of identical
twins, with and without mental illness, are defining the im-
mediacy of genetic influence on dream cycles (Dement, 1960;
Dement and Kleitman, 1957; Dement, Rechtschaffen and
Gulevitch, 1964; Fisher, 1965; Gresham, Webb and William,
1961; Kehoe and Brink, 1964; Ornitz, Kitvo and Walter,
1965; Oswald *et al.*, 1963; Rechtschaffen and Maron, 1964;
Rechtschaffen *et al.*, 1963; Roffwarg, Muzio and Dement, 1966;
Whitman, Pierce and Maas, 1960; Whitman *et al.*, 1961).

There remains the psychoanalytic hypothesis of dreams that
must be brought into harmony with the data or modified accordingly. The well-known hypothesis is that dreams serve the specific
function of guarding sleep against disruption by anxiety-laden
or anxiety-evoking unconscious impulses. By disguised expression of the wish in a sleep-protecting compromise between wish
and defense, the dream uniquely serves the purposes of drive

discharge during sleep. In this formulation the dream begins with an unconscious wish striving towards expression becoming screened behind (transferred) a harmless preconscious day residue (Freud, 1900).

Certain phenomena seem to support this view. The increasing body movements prior to a REM period suggest an organism disturbed (Kamiya, 1961). In the REM period itself there are cortical discharge rates approaching those of wakefulness, and an abrupt increase and shift to irregularity in respiratory rhythm, accompanied by higher systolic blood pressure and a more rapid and irregular pulse (Evarts, 1960, 1962; Snyder *et al.*, 1964). Vivid and dramatic picture stories related to the directional scan of the eye movements, and cycles of penile erection that parallel the REM periods, are likewise interpretable as an active mastery process in the face of libidinal upsurge (Fisher, Gross and Zuch, 1965; Roffwarg *et al.*, 1962). There are in addition the striking findings of dream deprivation experiments. As dreams are interrupted, the number of starts increase to the point where ultimately no sleep is possible without dreaming, unless drugs are used as a dream-suppressing adjunct (Dement, 1960; 1964). Personality changes have been noted in some subjects with prolonged deprivation of dreams, and animals with the pontine REM sleep center destroyed die inexplicably after several weeks (Jouvet, Jouvet, Valtz, 1963). Thus, a physiological necessity for dreaming is suggested, and enthusiastic clinicians have sometimes leaped at this evidence as striking confirmation of the theory.

On the other hand, the galvanic skin reflex, a measure that is reduced in states of arousal or tension, is increased during REM periods (Hawkins *et al.*, 1962). Amphetamine, a drug that promotes wakefulness, *reduces* REM time instead of calling forth an increase to master the waking tendency (Rechtschaffen, 1964; Rechtschaffen and Maron, 1964). A decrease in REM time is also effected by such diverse drugs as alcohol, the phenothiazines, barbiturates and, perhaps, imipramine, while lysergic acid diethylamide (LSD-25) or γ-hydroxybutyrate administration evokes an increase (Freud, 1900; Green, 1965; Gresham, Webb and William, 1961; Muzio, Roffwarg and Kaufman, 1964; Oswald *et al.*, 1963; Whitman *et al.*, 1961). More important for the theory is the finding that anxious subjects on the first night in a sleep lab will often skip the first REM period entirely instead of increasing the amount of REM time; and the missed period is replaced usually by stage 2 sleep rather than wakefulness as would be expected had the anxiety broken through (Dement, 1964; Rechtschaffen, 1964). Moveover, states of instinctual hunger or satiation (thirst, hunger)(Bokert, 1965; Dement and Wolpert, 1958; Rechtschaffen, 1964) influence the length of REM time not at all and its content minimally; and while external stimuli may be incorporated into ongoing dreams, stimulation at other times in the cycle does not evoke REM periods and visual dreams (Rechtschaffen, 1964; Zung and Wilson, 1961). Furthermore, excitement in manifest content seems unrelated to the degree of changes in heart or respiratory rate, and exciting dreams may well occur in relation to cycles of lowered metabolism[1] rather than level of anxiety (Knopf, 1962; Verdone, 1963). Indeed, as Dement has pointed out, if the dream's purpose is to preserve sleep it fails miserably, since far more than half of all REM periods are interrupted by brief periods of wakefulness (Dement, 1964). Equally striking, if visual dreams arise in response to anxiety-evoking instinctual tensions, is their regular appearance on a clock-bound schedule of ninety minutes. Clearly, anxiety-laden instinctual wishes and the safeguarding of sleep cannot be prime causes or causes sufficient for visual dreams. At most, the wish expressing, drive reduction function may make use of or become associated secondarily with a preexisting biological cycle that it does not govern or control.

There remains the issue of what goes on during non-REM sleep (NREM). First impressions that NREM was almost devoid of content soon proved to be wrong. Careful inquiry brought reports of recalled mental activity in up to 50 per cent of awakenings during NREM sleep (Foulkes, 1962; Kamiya, 1961; Rechtschaffen, 1964), albeit generally of a more abstract, thought-like, non-visual quality. Surely Freud's famous 'Autodidasker' dream was one of this type (he recalled only the word), yet it provided as rich a yield as visual dreams when subjected to analysis. Moreover, pavor nocturnus, the terrifying inchoate nightmares of childhood, may occur during NREM sleep and so do similar abrupt and frightened awakenings in adults (Dement, 1964).

1. As indicated by rectal temperature.

In enuresis too the event usually occurs during NREM sleep, though the typical dreams may be elaborated subsequently in the mixed atmosphere of dampness, discomfort and conflicting motivation (Pierce, 1961; Scott, 1964). Somnambulism also occurs in the deeper stages of sleep. While the most recent work suggests that somnambulism is unaccompanied by dreams, there is little doubt that psychological disturbances bear on the precipitation or frequency of episodes, and motivational factors may yet be being worked on or given expression during them as affirmed by earlier investigators (Davidson, 1945; Jackson, 1954; Kales *et al.*, 1966; Riser *et al.*, 1962; Sandler, 1945; Simmel, 1942; Sours, Frumkin and Indermill, 1964). Finally, deep sleep (stage 4) is conserved in the same way as is stage 1 REM, and if individuals are deprived of both, the stage 4 is compensated for first, even at the further expense of stage 1 (Agnew, Webb and Williams, 1964).

It has been posited that the thought-like activity of NREM sleep is limited to the working over of preconscious day residues in preparation for the visual dream, while the visual dream guards sleep during REM periods and it alone serves the purpose of drive discharge (Fisher, 1965). If enuresis, somnambulism, pavor nocturnus and the autodidasker experience are motivationally expressive, the hypothesis would seem unlikely. It is also uneconomical, for it requires ancillary theories and leads to internal contractions. What guards sleep during NREM periods, or is there no conflict then? Why are some anxieties (the first night effect) met by a decrease of REM, and others (the process of psychotic breakdown) by increased REM in an occasional case and no particular change most of the time. Why replace a drive discharge period with a preparation, no discharge period when anxiety mounts as in the first night effect?

It is more parsimonious and in keeping with the data to assume that conflictual and analysable mental activity is not confined to REM periods, but occurs throughout the night – as indeed it does throughout the day. What *is* different is the mode of representation and clinical availability. During the day unconscious mental activity may be perceived in slips of the tongue, forgetting and the like, but similar conflict resolving adaptive compromise is subtly evident in all behavior, whether it be mannerisms, choice of occupation or mate, or whatever. Mental activity in general may also be said to be influenced by, limited, or fashioned about early and continuing unconscious conflicts.

REM periods have been reported in neonates and perhaps the fetus, and certainly predate actual dreaming (Roffwarg, Muzio and Dement, 1966). It has also been suggested that the 'eye wobbles' may enforce the occurrence of visual dreaming, rather than the other way around. If this is so, all that is left to the dreamer is the choice of images, in turn determined by those conflicts currently in ascendance. In view of all these findings, the unique position of visual dreams may be only in their clinical usefulness rather than as guardians of sleep or in any *special* role in drive discharge. That is, as obligatory concomitants of a physiological cycle, they cast ordinary adaptive mental activity in perceptual symbols that are most amenable to analysis.

It was Freud's hope that his theoretical constructs would some day be replaced by biological understanding. Because of this heritage, perhaps, few if any analysts have felt it necessary to describe the disordered mentation of uremia of other toxic biological states in terms of id–ego and super-ego balance. In such cases the intangible metaphor yields to the palpable toxin, and structural psychic considerations become superfluous.

Recently it has been suggested that the dream itself is based on the accumulation of a neurohumoral substance which is periodically disposed of (metabolized) in order to re-establish normal levels. Interference with this disposition would be the cause for repeated dream starts under conditions of dream prevention, and the ultimate appearance of personality changes of a decompensatory nature (Dement, 1964; Fisher and Dement, 1963).

It has already been documented that metabolic conditions of sleep and wakefulness are different: exchange transfusions from sleeping to waking animals will induce sleep (Mounier and Hosli, 1964), and work in our own laboratory has confirmed that patterns of energy exchange are distinct for waking and sleeping, with particular variations during dream periods being to a certain extent discriminable (Brebbia and Altshuler, 1965). Many chemicals suppress dreaming and an occasional one increases it. Following the neurohumoral idea, the dream could be conceptualized as a kind of 'normal toxic psychosis', in which a naturally occurring superabundance of metabolite is periodically reduced.

On the basis of recent chemical and electrical work in mapping networks of neurons that evoke sleep and neuronal activity during various stages of sleep, Hernández-Peón has hypothesized that a hypnogenic system from the front of the brain overlaps and suppresses hypothalamic centers for positive and negative reinforcement; these centers can be stimulated from below (spinal impulses, noise, pain, etc) and from above (the cortex). If motivation is pleasure or unpleasure as mediated through these centers and associated with certain impulses, it may be this motivational system that is active during sleep and shapes our dreams. That is, as the energetic suppression of punished impulses is itself suppressed by the hypnogenic system, punished impulses may be released and imbedded on the images activated during this stage of sleep (Hernández-Peón, 1964; 1966.).

As the remaining pieces of the puzzle are gradually teased apart and put together, some variation of this or the neurohumoral theory will probably hold true. The mechanics and physiodynamics of dreaming will finally be identified and placed within a biological framework. With this conception, the idea of the dream as primarily a motivated regression to an earlier phase (perception) may be dropped, and the need lessened for increasingly refined arguments – more and more distant from the items of clinical data – on the structural dispositions of id, ego and super-ego as causal in dreams.

There is no suggestion in this that the structural hypothesis be abandoned as a whole, or that regression be minimized as a descriptive term in analytic vocabulary. Fisher, a pioneer in dream experiments, early questioned the usefulness of 'regression to perception' as an explanatory concept (Fisher, 1957), and there is no substantive data to the effect that such regression to perception could in any way serve as a vehicle for drive deduction.

Should the suggested theories pan out, they may parallel and confirm some of the intuitive and basic tenets of psychoanalytic theory having to do with motivational conflict, dynamics, continuity of behavior and repression. Yet a good part of psychoanalytic theory as a theory of mind will remain for some time outside of biological structure, and the new discoveries do not validate all these concepts. While the new structural theories are not interchangeable with the analytic structural model of id, ego and super-ego, the basic confirmations they afford may free us to re-examine other aspects of analytic theory in their light, as suggested above in regard to the role of regression.

The structural model in psychoanalysis was developed to meet certain dilemmas of topography. As Gill has shown incisively, it failed to do so, especially in regard to the problem of repressed and repressing forces being in the same system (Gill, 1963). He detailed a number of alternatives in structural theorizing that encompassed the difficulties equally well, the final selection by any theory builder being essentially a fielder's choice. He also emphasized the functional inseparability of impulse-defense units, arranged hierarchically in unconscious and conscious, or moving from id to ego and super-ego. White (1963) alluded to similar problems that arise when the structural and libidinal models are over-extended to the point where streams of energy fuse, defuse, precipitate to form defenses, become blocked and re-fuse, until the imagery is impossible to follow and 'dances before the eyes'. As most recently re-emphasized by Beres (1965), the structural hypotheses are metaphors meant to bear on the understanding of function. As loose metaphorical aids to conceptualization they are of value; as personified structures whose formation and course are used in causal explanations, they are tautologic.

If the biology of dreaming is explained and the closeness of biological impulses to motivational centers of pleasure, pain and REMs demonstrated, much of psychoanalytic theory will immediately be on firmer ground. There is no urgency to press the findings further to fit our preconceptions in a premature effort to resolve mind–brain dualism. Rather some of the rigid superstructure of psychoanalytic theory should give way to the greater open-mindedness of what Chamberlain (1890) long ago called the principle of multiple working hypotheses, in use by analysts daily in practice. The emphasis may then shift once more from the biological construction of the dream, from the actual myriad of superimposed images that fire furiously during REMs and that perhaps reflect the diminished suppression of punishment centers of motivation, to the dream as it is constructed by the dreamer, the secondary elaboration when – awake once more – the automatic suppression (repression) is reactivated. The images of the

REM periods themselves appear to be obligatory. Perhaps the mechanisms of primary process thinking are not responsible for the images, but are called into play along with secondary process thinking when the waking dreamer attempts to make sense out of the images forced upon him. That is, the dreamer, as he awakens, may organize the events he has experienced. What he selects would depend on his mental set and the conflicts in current life; the manner of organization, on all his previous experience. While this as much as anything could be responsible for associational chains that are derivable from dream imagery, it does not imply causality in the imagery itself. A more open-minded approach may allow the dream story from REM periods and the fragment of thought in NREM phases to stand equal, though undistinguished, beside the slip of the tongue, the motivated lapse of memory, and all other pieces of behavior, as adaptive efforts to cope with present conflict by an organism etched through years of training into an individual defensive configuration, with anxiety-induced blind spots, forbidden craving and preferred defensive warps.

Summary

The data of recent studies in dream research suggest abandonment of the idea that the visual dream is more distinguished than any other behavior for its role in drive discharge and homeostatic maintenance. Rather it is unique in its mode of representation of conflict that is active, discernible and being worked over in all behavior. The haste to resolve Cartesian dualism must also be made slowly. Recent work parallels and confirms the basic ideas of psychoanalysis, but the structures involved are not interchangeable with the structural analytic hypothesis. The confirmation afforded should provide a firm base from which to freely re-examine our always tentative theory, bearing in mind the oneness and adaptive function of the organism, and bound in the range of working hypotheses only by the data observed.

References

AGNEW, H. W., WEBB, W. B., and WILLIAMS, R. L. (1964), 'The effects of stage four sleep deprivation', *EEG clin. Neurophysiol.*, vol. 17, p. 58.

BERES, D. (1965), 'Structure and function in psychoanalysis', *Intern. J. Psychoanal.*, vol. 46, p. 53.

BOKERT, E. (1965), The effects of thirst and a related stimulus on dream reports, *Paper Read at Association for the Psychophysiological Study of Sleep*, Washington.

BREBBIA, D. R., and ALTSHULER, K. Z. (1965), 'Oxygen consumption rate and electroencephalographic stage of sleep', *Science*, vol. 150, p. 1621.

CHAMBERLAIN, T. C. (1890), 'The method of multiple working hypotheses', *Science* (old series), vol. 15, p. 92. (Reprinted in *Science*, vol. 148, 1965, p. 754.)

DAVIDSON, C. (1945), 'Disturbances in the sleep mechanism', *Psychoanal. Quart.*, vol. 14, p. 478.

DEMENT, W. C. (1960), 'The effect of dream deprivation', *Science*, vol. 131, p. 1705.

DEMENT, W. C. (1964), 'Experimental dream studies', in J. H. Masserman (ed.), *Science and Psychoanalysis*, Grune & Stratton, vol. 7.

DEMENT, W. C., and KLEITMAN, N. (1957), 'Cyclic variations in EEG during sleep and their relation to eye movements, bodily motility, and dreaming', *EEG clin. Neurophysiol.*, vol. 9, p. 673.

DEMENT, W. C., and WOLPERT, E. A. (1958), 'The relationship of eye movement, bodily motility, and external stimuli to dream content', *J. exp. Psychol.*, vol. 55, p. 543.

DEMENT, W. C., RECHTSCHAFFEN, A., and GULEVITCH, G. (1964), 'A polygraphic study of the narcoleptic sleep attack', *EEG clin. Neurophysiol.*, vol. 17, p. 608 (abstract).

EVARTS, E. V. (1960), 'Effects of sleep and waking on spontaneous and evoked discharge of single units in visual cortex', *Fed. Proc.*, vol. 19, p. 828.

EVARTS, E. V. (1962), 'Activity of neurons in visual cortex of the cat during sleep with low voltage fact EEG activity', *J. Neurophysiol.*, vol. 25, p. 812.

FISHER, C. (1957), 'A study of the preliminary stages of the construction of dreams and images', *J. Amer. Psychoanal.*, vol. 5, p. 5.

FISHER, C. (1965), 'Psychoanalytic implications of recent research on sleep and dreaming', *J. Amer. Psychoanal.*, vol. 13, p. 197.

FISHER, C., and DEMENT, W. C. (1963), 'Studies on the psychopathology of sleep and dreams', *Amer. J. Psychoanal.*, vol. 119, p. 1160.

FISHER, C., GROSS, J., and ZUCH, J. (1965), 'A cycle of penile erections synchromous with dreaming (REM) sleep', *Arch. gen. Psychol.*, vol. 12, p. 29.

FOULKES, W. (1962), 'Dream reports from different stages of sleep', *J. abnorm. soc. Psychol.*, vol. 65, p. 14.

FREUD, S. (1900), *The Interpretation of Dreams*, Basic Books, 1955.

GILL, M. (1963), 'Topography and systems in psychoanalytic theory', *Psychol. Issues Monog.*, vol. 10.

GREEN, W. J. (1965), 'The effects of LSD on the sleep–dream cycle: an exploratory study', *J. nerv. ment. Dis.*, vol. 140, p. 417.

GRESHAM, S. C., WEBB, W. B., and WILLIAM, R. L. (1961), 'Alcohol and caffeine: effect on inferred visual dreaming', *Science*, vol. 140, p. 1226.

HAWKINS, D. R., *et al.* (1962), 'Basal skin resistance during sleep and dreaming', *Science*, vol. 136, p. 321.

HERNÁNDEZ-PEÓN, D. R. (1964), 'Attention, sleep, motivation, and behavior', in R. Heath (ed.), *The Role of Pleasure in Behavior*, Harper & Row.

HERNÁNDEZ-PEÓN, R. (1966), 'A neurophysiological model of dreams and hallucinations', *J. nerv. ment. Dis.*

JACKSON, D. D. (1954), 'An episode of sleep walking', *J. Amer. Psychoanal. Assn*, vol. 2, p. 503.

JOUVET, M., JOUVET, D., and VALTZ, J. (1963), 'Étude du sommeil chez le chat pontique et sa suppression automatique', *CR Soc. Biol.*, vol. 157, p. 845.

JOUVET, M., *et al.* (1961), 'Effects du 4-butyrolactone et du 4-hydroxybutyrate de sodium sur l'EEG et le comportement du chat', *CR Soc. Biol.*, vol. 155, p. 1313.

KALES, A., *et al.* (1966), 'Somnambulism: psychophysiological correlates', *Arch. gen. Psychol.*, vol. 14, pp. 586.

KAMIYA, J. (1961), 'Behavioral, subjective, and physiological aspects of sleep and drowsiness', in D. W. Fiske and S. R. Maddi (eds.), *Functions of Varied Experience*, Dorsey Press.

KEHOE, M. J., and BRINK, E. (1964), 'Studies on identical twins: 1. A comparative study of the sleep patterns, incidence and content of dreams of four pairs of identical twins', paper read at American Psychiatric Association, Philadelphia.

KNOPF, N. E. (1962), 'A study of heart and respiration rates during dreaming', unpublished master's dissertation, University of Chicago.

MOUNIER, M., and HOSLI, L. (1964), 'Dialysis of sleep and waking factors in the blood of rabbits', *Science*, vol. 146, p. 796.

MUZIO, J., ROFFWARG, H., and KAUFMAN, R. (1964), 'Alteration in the young adult human sleep EEG configuration resulting from d-LSD-25', paper read at Association for the Psychophysiological Study of Sleep, Palo Alto.

ORNITZ, I., KITVO, E. K., and WALTER, R. D. (1965), 'Dreaming sleep in autistic twins', *Arch. gen. Psychiat.*, vol. 12, p. 77.

OSWALD, I., *et al.* (1963), 'Melancholia and barbiturates: a controlled EEG, body and eye movement study of sleep', *Brit. J. Psychol.*, vol. 109, p. 66.

PIERCE, E. M., *et al.* (1961), 'Enuresis and dreaming', *Arch. gen. Psychiat.*, vol. 4, p. 166.

RECHTSCHAFFEN, A. (1964), 'Discussion of Dement's paper: experimental dream studies', in J. H. Masserman (ed.), *Science and Psychoanalysis*, Grune & Stratton, vol. 7.

RECHTSCHAFFEN, A., and MARON, L. (1964), 'The effect of amphetamine on the sleep cycle', *EEG clin. Neurophysiol.*, vol. 16, p. 430.

RECHTSCHAFFEN, A., VOGEL, G., and SHAIKUN, G (1963), 'Interrelatedness of mental activity during sleep', *Arch. gen. Psychiat.*, vol. 9, p. 536.

RECHTSCHAFFEN, A., *et al.* (1963), 'Nocturnal sleep of narcoleptics', *EEG clin. Neurophysiol.*, vol. 15, p. 599.

RISER, M., *et al.* (1962), 'De certains aspects du somnambulisme', *Toulouse med. J.*, vol. 4, p. 429.

ROFFWARG, H. P., MUZIO, J. N., and DEMENT, W. C. (1966), 'Ontogenetic developments of the human sleep dream cycle', *Science*.

ROFFWARG, H. P., *et al.* (1962), 'Dream imagery: relationship to rapid eye movements of sleep', *Arch. gen. Psychiat.*, vol. 7, p. 235.

SANDLER, S. A. (1945), 'Somnambulism in the armed forces', *Ment. Hyg.*, vol. 29, p. 236.

SCOTT, J. (1964), 'Sleeping and dreaming in enuretic children', paper read at Association for the Psychophysiological Study of Sleep, Palo Alto.

SIMMEL, E. (1942), 'Neurotic disturbances of sleep', *Intern. J. Psychoanal.*, vol. 23, p. 65.

SNYDER, F., *et al.* (1964), 'Changes in respiration, heart rate, and systolic blood pressure in human sleep', *J. appl. Physiol.*, vol. 19, p. 417.

SOURS, J. A., FRUMKIN, P., and INDERMILL, R. R. (1964), 'Somnambulism: clinical and dynamic significance in adolescence and adulthood', *Arch. gen. Psychiat.*, vol. 9, p. 400.

VERDONE, P. P. (1963), 'Variables related to temporal reference of manifest dream content', unpublished doctoral dissertation, University of Chicago.

WHITE, R. W. (1963), 'Ego and reality in psychoanalytic theory', *Psychol. Issues Monog.*, vol. 11.

WHITMAN, R. M., PIERCE, C. M., and MAAS, J. W. (1960), 'Drugs and dreams', in L. Uhrs and J. Miller (eds.), *Drugs and Behavior*, Wiley.

WHITMAN, R. M., *et al.* (1961), 'Drugs and dreams: II. Imipramine and Prochlorperazine', *Comp. Psychiat.*, vol. 2, p. 219.

ZUNG, W. W., and WILSON, W. P. (1961), 'Response to auditory stimulation during sleep', *Arch. gen. Psychiat.*, vol. 4, p. 548.

19 Terry Pivik and David Foulkes

'Dream Deprivation': Effects on Dream Content[1]

Terry Pivik and David Foulkes, '"Dream deprivation": effects on dream content', *Science*, vol. 253, 1966, pp. 1282–4.

The finding (Aserinsky and Kleitman, 1955; Dement and Kleitman, 1957b) that dreaming is associated with a random, low-voltage electroencephalogram (EEG) pattern (ascending EEG stage 1) in conjunction with intermittent bursts of conjugate rapid eye movements (REMs), and that this pattern recurs four or five times during a typical night's sleep (Dement and Kleitman, 1957a), has prompted renewed interest in the possible functional significance of dreaming. Experimental attempts to assess the importance of dreaming for human subjects have employed a method of dream deprivation, in which subjects are awakened at the onset of each episode of ascending stage 1 sleep and are thus prevented from experiencing the organismic state in which dreaming occurs. Early studies employing this method found progressively decreasing latencies to the recurrence of dream periods on deprivation nights, a compensatory increase in this stage of sleep on uninterrupted recovery nights following the deprivation treatment, and increased anxiety, irritability and appetite during the deprivation period. These results were interpreted as a 'build-up of a pressure to dream' (Dement, 1960).

More recently, however, failure to observe the reported behavioral changes with human subjects (Kales *et al.*, 1964; Snyder, 1963) and demonstration of the sleep-cycle effects of dream deprivation in intact and chronic pontile cats (Jouvet, 1965), have led to the interpretation that the supposed effects of the deprivation of a psychological experience are actually the effects of the deprivation of a physiological stage of sleep with

1. The authors have modified their conclusions in a later paper 'Effects of "dream deprivation" on dream content: an attempted cross-night replication', *J. abnorm. Psychol.*, vol. 73, 1968, pp. 403–15

some unknown biological significance (Dement, 1965). While it may ultimately prove impossible to distinguish the effects of the deprivation of this stage of sleep from the effects of dream deprivation, the present study shows that the nature of dream content, as well as of the sleep cycle, is affected by the selective deprivation of ascending EEG stage 1. In particular, the content of a dream elicited following such deprivation is intensified as a result of this manipulation.

Each of twenty male subjects slept in quiet, darkened laboratory rooms for two non-consecutive nights. Ten of the subjects were among low scorers (repressers, those who react to threatening stimuli with avoidance defenses such as denial) and ten among high scorers (sensitizers, those who react to threatening stimuli with approach defenses such as intellectualization) on Byrne's Repression–Sensitization Scale (1963) of the Minnesota Multiphasic Personality Inventory (MMPI). The subjects selected represented the top and bottom fifth of the distribution of test scores of male volunteers from an introductory psychology class.

Continuous EEG and electro-oculogram (EOG) recordings were taken during the night. Electromyogram recordings were also taken from the submental region, as a sharp drop in tonus of neck and chin muscles generally precedes the onset of ascending EEG stage 1 by a minute or so and can be used as a signal of such onset (Berger, 1961; Kales *et al.*, 1964). Ascending EEG stage 1 onset was determined by the appearance of a random, low-voltage EEG pattern accompanied by rapid eye movements, or a sudden drop in submental muscle tonus, or both. On experimental nights, the first four REM periods were interrupted at the first sign of ascending stage 1 onset. On control nights, four awakenings were made during non-REM sleep so as not to interfere with the occurrence of REM sleep. The fifth REM period on experimental nights and the third one on control nights were allowed to proceed for five minutes, after which awakenings were made for retrieval of dream content. Half of the repressers and half of the sensitizers, selected at random, were run in the order experimental–control, while the remaining subjects were run in the reverse order. The elimination of REM sleep and the progressive shortening of the periods between 'attempts at' REM sleep on experimental nights necessitated the use of the third, rather than the fifth, REM period on control nights to achieve rough comparability of sleep time preceding (and time of night of) the content-retrieval awakenings on the two nights. Even so, control-night awakenings were almost invariably made later in the night and after more sleep (68·6 minutes more, on the average) than were the comparable experimental night awakenings. This situation worked against the hypothesis of increased dream intensity following dream deprivation, since it has been shown that dream intensity increases over the course of the night (Foulkes, 1966, pp. 92–5). While the experimental design may also seem in some sense to favor the hypothesis under test, in that a 'later' REM period is used on experimental than control nights (fifth versus third), it should be noted that experimental-night control awakenings were elicited from the first sustained episode of REM sleep on that night, the other four REM periods having been terminated by an awakening at the first sign of their onset. Initial control-night content awakenings were thus made during the third sustained episode of REM sleep on that night.

On deprivation and pseudo-deprivation awakenings, the light was turned on in the subject's room, and the experimenter entered and took readings of strength of grip from a dynamometer which the subject was to squeeze four times from a prone position. Subjects had been told that the purpose of the study was the investigation of associations among stage of sleep, strength of grip and mental content, and were thus unaware that the deprivation of REM sleep was the actual purpose underlying awakenings on which dynamometer readings were taken on experimental nights.

That the experimental-night awakenings produced a deprivation effect on the sleep cycle is evident in the briefer intervals of non-REM sleep between the onset of REM episodes on experimental than on control nights (Table 1). The dynamometer technique of producing complete arousal rules out the possibility that such results reflect incomplete arousal rather than the effects of selective sleep deprivation.

The dreamlike fantasy (Df) scale of Foulkes, Spear and Symonds (Foulkes, 1966, pp. 189–90) was used in all analyses of the content-awakening interviews. This is an eight-point scale with a value of O assigned to 'No recall, feels mind was blank', and a value of 7 assigned to 'Recall of content which was perceptual, hallucinatory and bizarre'. Two judges, both completely naïve with respect to subject or treatment variables, rated the dream reports with high agreement (reliabilities of 0·88 and 0·95, respectively, for experimental- and control-night reports). Two-rater averages were used in all analyses of Df ratings.

Table 1

Effect of Deprivation Awakenings on Length of Inter-REM Intervals (The Intervals are Measured in Minutes)

Inter-REM Intervals				
Interval 0–1	Interval 1–2	Interval 2–3	Interval 3–4	Interval 4–5
Experimental night				
91·85	60·85	18·15	21·45	19·22
Control night				
90·05	80·35	66·11		
Probability				
n.s.*	0·005	0·001		

* Not significant.

The effects of deprivation awakenings on dream content are summarized in Table 2. Considering all subjects, it is evident that dreams were more intense on experimental nights than on control nights. This intensification of the dreaming process was observed for twelve of the sixteen subjects who had different Df scores on experimental and control nights and was statistically significant.[1]

1. All probability values reported in this paper are one-tail, since the alternative to the null hypothesis is, in every case, specific as to direction. Tests of sleep-cycle effects of deprivation and of represser–sensitizer differences in both sleep cycle and dream content are attempted replications of earlier published findings. In addition, results in the same direction as our finding of increased dream intensity following 'dream deprivation' were obtained in an unpublished study of Rechtschaffen and Foulkes, but their results, obtained under somewhat different conditions than ours, did not attain statistical significance. Student's *t*-test was used to evaluate sleep-cycle and eye-movement effects, and the Wilcoxon matched-pairs signed-ranks test for the dream content effects of the deprivation variable. The Wilcoxon rank-sum test was employed in evaluating represser–sensitizer differences in dream context.

Four subjects showed no change in Df ratings from control to experimental nights, and four a decrease in dream intensity following deprivation. Although an equal number (six) of repressers and sensitizers had higher Df scores on the experimental night than on the control night, the deprivation effects were significant only for repressers, whose experimental- versus control-night mean difference in Df ratings was roughly three times as large as that for sensitizers.

Table 2

Effect of Deprivation Awakenings on Dream Content as Rated on the Eight-Point Dreamlike Fantasy Scale (Df Ratings of 0 to 7)

Repressers	Sensitizers	p (R v. S)	All subjects
Both nights			
5·60	5·78	0·10	5·69
Experimental night			
6·50	6·10	n.s.*	6·30
Control night			
4·70	5·45	0·06	5·08
E v. C (p)			
0·05	n.s.*		0·025

* Not significant.

R, repressers; S, sensitizers; E, experimental; C, control; p, probability.

Examination of the EOG patterns during REM periods preceding content-retrieval awakenings further revealed that a larger percentage of 2·5-second intervals of such periods contained one or more eye movements on experimental nights than on control nights (28·3 per cent versus 21·7 per cent, respectively, $p < 0.025$). This effect also was significant for repressers (25·3 per cent on experimental nights versus 18·5 per cent on control nights, $p < 0.025$) but not for sensitizers (31·3 per cent on experimental nights versus 24·9 per cent on control nights; difference not significant). The close correspondence between differences in pre-wakening eye movement frequency and differences in the intensity of subsequently reported dreams parallels earlier findings that active dreams are preceded by more eye movement than are passive ones (Berger and Oswald, 1962).

Our sensitizer subjects scored high on MMPI pathology scales (for example, an average score three standard deviations above the general population mean on the MMPI schizophrenia scale), while the repressers had essentially normal MMPI profiles. The sensitizers had, in the absence of the deprivation treatment, more intense dream content than did the repressers – a duplication of Foulkes and Rechtschaffen's (1964) observation that high MMPI-scoring subjects have dreams of greater intensity than do more normal subjects. Sensitizers also had, in the absence of deprivation, briefer REM periods than did repressers (mean summed control-night REM time for the first two REM periods was 45·6 minutes for repressers and 33·0 minutes for sensitizers, $p < 0.025$) – a duplicate of Monroe's (1965) observation that high MMPI-scoring subjects have briefer REM periods than do more normal subjects. These two results provide an additional strand of evidence in support of the hypothesis that lessened amounts of dreaming are associated with an intensification of the dreaming process.

These results suggest that the term 'dream deprivation', as more clinically oriented investigators have suspected all along (Fisher, 1965), may still have some validity. Interference with the stage of sleep in which dreaming occurs, either by experimental manipulation or by spontaneously generated reductions in REM sleep, does seem to increase subsequent dream intensity, that is, the selective deprivation of ascending EEG stage 1 has immediate experimental, as well as the heretofore observed sleep-cycle, effects.

These results are also consonant with the Freudian conception of dreaming as a safety valve, which played a large role in earlier interpretations of the effects of dream deprivation. The dream content of sensitizers, whose safety valve is somehow always partially capped, and that of repressers under the capping effects of experimental deprivation, both exhibit intensification. In general, our results seem to indicate that the less a person dreams, the more intense are his dreams.

References

ASERINSKY, E., and KLEITMAN, N. (1955), *J. appl. Physiol.*, vol. 8, p. 1.

BERGER, R. J. (1961), *Science*, vol. 134, p. 840.

BERGER, R. J., and OSWALD, I. (1962), *Science*, vol. 137, p. 601.

BYRNE, D. (1963), *Psychol. Rep.*, vol. 13, p. 323.

DEMENT, W. (1960), *Science*, vol. 131, p. 1705.

DEMENT, W. (1965), in *Aspects Anatomo-Fonctionnels de la Physiologie du Sommeil*, Centre National de la Recherche Scientifique, Paris, pp. 571–611.

DEMENT, W., and KLEITMAN, N. (1957a), *EEG clin. Neurophysiol.*, vol. 9, p. 673.

DEMENT, W., and KLEITMAN, N. (1957b), *J. exp. Psychol.*, vol. 53, p. 339.

FISHER, C. (1965), *J. Amer. psychoanal. Assoc.*, vol. 13, p. 271.

FOULKES, D. (1966), *The Psychology of Sleep*, Scribner.

FOULKES, D., and RECHTSCHAFFEN, A. (1964), *Percept. mot. Skills*, vol. 19, p. 983.

JOUVET, M. (1965), in *Aspects Anatomo-Fonctionnels de la Physiologie du Sommeil*, Centre National de la Recherche Scientifique, Paris, pp. 397–449.

KALES, A., HOEDMAKER, F., JACOBSON, A., and LICHTENSTEIN, E., (1964), *Nature*, vol. 204, p. 1331.

MONROE, L. J. (1965), Unpublished Manuscript, University of Chicago.

SNYDER, F. (1963), *Archiv. gen. Psychiat.*, vol. 8, p. 381.

Part Seven Conclusions

Farrell deals with three questions in Reading 20: (a) How successful have been the attempts to confirm (and disconfirm) the propositions of psychoanalytic theory by non-analytical means? (b) How much has this work done to establish or modify psychoanalytic theory? (c) What, in general, are its value and its prospects?

20 B. A. Farrell

The Scientific Testing of Psychoanalytic Findings and Theory[1]

B. A. Farrell, 'The scientific testing of psychoanalytic findings and theory', *British Journal of Medical Psychology*, vol. 24, 1951, pp. 35–41.

I speak today as an outsider. I am neither a psychoanalyst nor a psychologist. I belong to that group in our community known as 'professional philosophers'. Since I was asked to speak as a philosopher, I hope you will all know what to expect. I shall confine myself to trying to bring a little order into this field by making a few 'methodological' remarks. I am conscious that my remarks may be a little naïve and ignorant.

First of all, what are we supposed to be talking about? Let me clear this question out of the way by showing how I find the very title of this symposium confusing and productive of philosophical conflict. To begin with, it is a little odd to talk about 'testing' a finding. It is more usual to talk of corroborating a finding or failing to do so. It is more natural to speak of 'testing' a hypothesis. And when we speak of 'testing a theory', it would be correct to say that what we are doing is to test important or characteristic propositions of the theory. But if a social anthropologist were to set out to discover whether the key proposition from psychoanalytic theory about Oedipal development was true or not, it would be queer to say that the anthropologist was 'testing this proposition' of the theory. It would be more natural to say that he was making some observations to 'verify' it, or 'establish' it, or 'confirm' it. What is worse, however, is that we are asked to discuss the 'scientific' testing of psychoanalytic findings. This request only makes sense if we are able to contrast 'scientific

1. This paper is printed almost exactly as it was delivered. Its main purpose was to show how some order could be introduced into this field. Therefore, it does not purport to cover all relevant experimental and other work; and it certainly makes no attempt to deal with recent items. I wish to record gratefully that my chief single obligation is to Sears (1943).

testing' with the 'unscientific testing' of psychoanalytic findings. But what, pray, does this 'unscientific testing' look like? Obviously the only relevant candidate is 'testing by a therapist'. So if we are to make sense out of the title, we have to say that the methods used by a clinician to investigate a proposition of psychoanalytic theory are 'unscientific', in contrast with the scientific methods of, for example, Kleemeier (1942) on the experimental analogues of regression, or Goldman (1948) using questionnaires and factor analysis on the formation of oral character. In view of this, the title will be liable to annoy the analysts and generate a fruitless argument over their alleged unscientific procedure.

I shall try to avoid all this by using some of the fairly standard terminology and distinctions employed by contemporary logicians. Given a proposition of psychoanalytic theory, I shall say that this can be confirmed or disconfirmed. A rough division, with many marginal cases, is drawn between experimental and observational confirmation; and the word 'testing' tends to be restricted to experimental confirmation. A proposition can be confirmed in one of two ways – directly or indirectly. It is confirmed directly when we use observational and/or experimental procedures to establish it. It is confirmed indirectly when we deduce an empirical consequence (or consequences) from it, and then establish this consequence (or consequences) directly. Suppose, for example, we are given the proposition about Oedipal development. If we try to confirm this by having a look at the development of children, and seeing whether they exhibit Oedipal behaviour, then we would be trying to confirm it directly. If, however, we try to confirm it indirectly, we would have to do so by deducing, for example, that if children do go through this period, and if there is no irremovable amnesia, then we should expect that, under suitable circumstances (e.g. in analysis), the person should be able to recall his Oepidal attitudes. So, when analysts point to the recall of Oepidal material by adults in analysis in support of the proposition about Oedipal development, they are doing something quite respectable – they are helping to confirm this proposition indirectly. A general snag, of course, is that a confirmation (or disconfirmation) process may be anything from strong to weak, depending on a variety of factors. These are too cumbersome to mention here, but it is these factors that lead us to object in the familiar ways to a putative process of confirmation (or disconfirmation). Thus, we tend to say: 'But is this *really* an exception?' or 'Surely these results are only suggestive?' or 'No, no, these findings can be interpreted quite differently', or 'The results of questionnaires about the castration complex are just irrelevant', and so on and so forth. This snag (namely that confirmation or disconfirmation may be strong to weak) applies to all the sciences, but particularly to psychology with its complex material. It helps to explain why it is apt to be so difficult conclusively to establish, or refute, a psychological hypothesis.

Suppose, next, that we do disconfirm a particular proposition of a theory. This will supply *a* reason for rejecting the proposition and modifying the theory. But whether we do reject the proposition and modify the theory depends *also* on the strength of the theory. Roughly, the stronger the theory the less upsetting or disturbing the single disconfirmation, and vice versa. The strength of a theory is determined (roughly) by three things: (a) the range and variety of empirical consequences that can be derived by means of it; (b) the conceptual economy and rigour of the theory; (c) the absence of alternative theories of comparable power. For instance, suppose I observe my five children very carefully, like Valentine, and conclude that no Oedipal phenomena are manifested. This direct disconfirmation may not by itself be very upsetting – if it is the case that psychoanalytic theory (with the help of the Oedipal proposition) entails a large and varied range of empirical consequences. This is, of course, just what *is* often claimed for psychoanalytic theory. It is said that by means of it, and it alone, we can 'explain' phenomena like the Oedipal stories in analysis, various pathological phenomena, the phenomena of romantic love, the universal incest taboo and various crucial features of personality development and formation. Consequently, the disconfirmation of any one of the propositions of psychoanalytic theory may not by itself be sufficient to make us reject the proposition and modify the theory. Moreover, the question is often so complicated in any given instance that the decision whether to reject the proposition and modify the theory is no routine matter and may take years to settle.

I presume therefore that we are concerned with at least three questions today.

Conclusions

1. How successful have been the attemps to confirm (and disconfirm) the propositions of psychoanalytic theory by non-analytical means?

2. How much has this work done to establish or modify psychoanalytic theory?

3. What, in general, are its value and its prospects?

1. My thumbnail comment on this work will pick out what are, I hope, *some* of the important items. Unfortunately, I shall have to ignore work on personality formation (e.g. Kardiner *et al.*, 1945), because of time and my own inability as yet to assess it. I shall distinguish between the propositions of psychoanalytic theory about genesis and the propositions about so-called 'dynamics'; that is to say, between propositions about, for example, infantile sexuality and its development on the one hand, and propositions about, for example, regression and repression, on the other. The non-analytic confirmation of the genetic propositions is predominantly direct, of the 'dynamic', indirect. (Please forgive my crude formulation of all these propositions.)

Consider the genetic propositions first. As far as I can judge, the following are some that have been confirmed to some extent, strongly to weakly:

Infants obtain pleasure from oral stimulation (Halverson, 1938; Levy, 1928).

Infants obtain pleasure from genital stimulation (Halverson, 1940; Levy, 1928; Sears, 1943).

Manual masturbation is more frequent among pre-school boys than girls (Koch, 1935).

Small children exhibit extensive pre-genital play (Isaacs, 1933; Malinowski, 1927).

The over-all picture is one of general support for the psychoanalytic account of erotogenesis. But the work done does not cover the whole account. As far as I am aware, it fails to cover, for example, the propositions about anal erotism, infantile narcissism, the substitutability of the erotogenic zones and the unity of the sexual impulses out of partial ones. The work on the distortions of sexuality has produced so confused a picture that there is nothing useful and brief that I can say about it.

The following are some of the propositions of psychoanalytic theory that have been disconfirmed, strongly to weakly:

Every small boy presupposes in all persons a genital like his own (Conn, 1940; Hattendorf, 1932).

All small boys think that a girl's lack of a penis is the result of injury (Hattendorf, 1932).

All small girls have penis envy and wish to be boys (cf. Valentine, 1942).

All children exhibit sexual attraction and attachment for the cross-sex parent, and sexual jealousy of the parent of the same sex. (Let us call this the Oedipal proposition, for short.) (Valentine, 1942.)

All children go through a latency period during later childhood (Malinowski, 1927).

In short, what has been disconfirmed here are certain key propositions about sexual development. What appears to have happened is that Freud used his clinical data to produce universal generalizations, and so overlooked how much learning can influence sexual development, and how greatly cultural diversities can determine the sort of thing that is learnt.

Now consider some of the 'dynamic' propositions.

When a person breaks down, there is a tendency for him to do so by regressing to an earlier mode of sexual adjustment – either of object or erotogenic zone. If one considers this proposition as a constituent of adjustment theory, then it would be reasonable to expect the following proposition to be the case 'Where breakdown occurs without regression of object or drive, there is a tendency for regression of what Sears (1943, 1944) calls "instrumental act" to occur.' According to Mowrer (1940), Sears and others, experimental work has directly confirmed this proposition. According to Maier and others (Maier and Klee, 1941, 1943; Maier, Glaser, and Klee, 1940) it has not.

Regression is a function of fixation. (Pardon in particular this crude formulation.) If we assume that Sears and others are correct, then this proposition has been indirectly confirmed so far with rats – where 'fixations' are defined by means of 'habit strength', and the criterion of the latter is the degree of resistance to change (Martin, 1940; O'Kelly, 1940a, b).

Where aggressive behaviour towards the external sources of frustration is prevented, aggressive behaviour may be self directed or displaced. The second part of this proposition, i.e. about displacement, has been directly confirmed by the study of democratic and autocratic groups (Lewin, Lippitt and White, 1939), and indirectly confirmed by Miller (1948) and Mowrer (1940) on rats. *Infantile and pre-school amnesia is the result of repression, both primal and repression proper.* This appears to have been disconfirmed in various ways. (a) If it were true, then we should not be able to recall experiences that occurred between the third and fifth years. But this is a normal capacity (Dudycha and Dudycha, 1941). (b) If it were true, then there should be no memories before some one period of life. But no such period has been discovered. (c) If it were true, then we should not be able, in particular, to recall our early affective experiences. But this can be done (Bell, 1902; Hamilton, 1929). (d) If it were true, it would follow that certain material was originally learnt by the child, and *then* repressed. But it is doubtful whether there is any evidence for this, and it appears to be incompatible with what we do know about the inefficiency of early childhood learning (cf. Brooks, 1937).

There is a strong tendency to forget ideas associated with anxiety (*in Freud's sense*). This proposition is confirmed to some small extent by work on the recall of real life and experimentally induced experiences (Koch, 1930; Rosenzweig, 1938; Sharp, 1938).

The upshot of this work is generally to confirm the dynamic propositions. This confirmation is meagre, in that the propositions confirmed are so few and bald when compared with the richness of psychoanalytic theory. What is worse, these attempts at confirmation use terms like 'fixation', 'displacement', to refer only to the experimental analogues of fixation, displacement, etc., *not* to fixation, displacement, etc. as clinically understood. This means that the confirmation of psychoanalytic propositions is weak because the clinical phenomena may be produced by factors that are not present in the experimental situation.

2. How much has this observational and experimental work done to establish or modify psychoanalytic theory?

Psychoanalytic theory certainly gets some support from the work on the dynamic propositions, however weak this support may be. We appreciate this when we realize how awkward it would have been if the experimental analogues with animals had not been confirmed. The results, however, of this work are con-silient with the results on the experimental neuroses. And the *joint* support provided by these two lines of work – on the 'dynamic' propositions and the experimental neuroses – strikes me as quite impressive. For the experimental induction of neuro-sis has shown how the similarity between animal and human con-flicts is even greater than one would have dared to hope – the animals exhibiting (amid wide individual differences) anxiety, fixations, compulsions, rituals, sexual aberrations, etc., and even showing under treatment the analogue of 'transference' (Masser-man, 1943, 1946). This combined work leaves it quite clear that, however vague and turgid psychoanalytic theory may be, future development will be on the lines suggested by its clinical insights.

Now let us ask: is the disconfirmation of the genetic proposi-tions of psychoanalytic theory disturbing enough to oblige us to modify the theory? Consider the proposition about Oedipal development. Psychoanalytic theory is weak at this point in the following respects: (a) Oedipal material is not always produced under analysis by patients of whom one would otherwise expect it (Dicks, 1947). (b) The theory makes the assumption that Oedipal stories by adults are *ipso facto* veridical. This will not do in view of the admitted importance of fantasy. Once we admit this, how do we draw the line between the veridical and non-veridical adult story? (c) We are not obliged to postulate Oedipal development in order to account for improvement and cure. There are other alternatives current, for example, the hypothesis that improvement is due to some features of the analytic situation here and now (as Dr Ezriel has emphasized). That is, we can equally well derive the empirical consequence of improvement from a psychoanalytic theory that does not contain the Oedipal proposition, but some other instead. (d) Similar remarks apply to the claim that it is only by means of a psychoanalytic theory containing the Oedipal proposition that we can derive the wide range of empirical consequences that is in fact obtained in this way. It is not difficult to see in general how a non-Oedipal psycho-analytic theory can be combined with adjustment theory to enable us to derive these same consequences. (Cf. Malinowski,

1927, on incest, Mead, 1928, on romantic love, Hull, 1939, on symptoms.)

In short, psychoanalytic theory is weak at this point in the respects just mentioned. So the direct disconfirmation of the Oedipal proposition becomes much more disturbing. The same applies, *mutatis mutandis*, to the other genetic propositions of psychoanalytic theory that were disconfirmed, as well as to the one about infantile amnesia.

There is, however, one source of strength for a psychoanalytic theory containing the Oedipal proposition. This lies in the absence of an alternative, plausible hypothesis to account for the Oedipal data produced in adult analysis. Alternatives like suggestion, the thaumaturgy of words, and fantasy making seem severally and jointly insufficient. For instance, fantasy making will not do because it merely raises the further question of why the fantasy work should take the form of Oedipal stories. Psychoanalysts are naturally reluctant to modify the theory by rejecting the Oedipal proposition until they can replace it by a better. Speaking as an outsider, my judgement is that, on balance, the disconfirmation of the Oedipal and the other genetic propositions *is* good enough to require a modification of psychoanalytic theory. A modified and acceptable genetic account will issue, no doubt, from the co-operation of various parties – analysts, social anthropologists, child psychologists, learning theorists and experimentalists.

3. Lastly, a word on the value and prospects of this work on psychoanalytic propositions and theory.

I think the value is quite considerable in at least two different ways. (a) An essential job of the clinician is to apply with skill generalizations about human beings to the individual case, in the light of the given data about him. The so-called objective psychologist is interested to obtain these generalizations by investigating individuals and abstracting from the full specificity of any given case. What this work on psychoanalysis has done is to make clearer how complementary are the efforts of the psychologist and the clinician; what is involved in the attempt to confirm the generalizations applied by the clinician; how difficult it is to confirm them; and how worth while it would be to do so. (b) Psychoanalytic theory is, *qua* theory, unbelievably bad. I have not the time to specify its ghastly blemishes. This experimental and observational work has helped to show up these blemishes, and to make clearer to all concerned just what a good scientific theory should look like. I suspect that one of the factors producing the present co-operation between analysts and others has been the methodological lesson this work has driven home. This indirect result is perhaps the most important contribution this work has yet made.

About its prospects. With the caution that I do not fancy myself as a prophet, my hunch is that some of the promising lines of development are these: observational work on real life situations (e.g. on the Lewin model); more and better observational work on the development of *individual* children, and in *different* communities (Meyer Fortes has shown me, in conversation, how poor is some of the anthropological work that has been done); the study of personality formation, a task that the Americans are pursuing with such energy at present; experimental and observational work on the technique of free association (e.g. in the sort of way that Dr Ezriel is proposing to do); attempts to verify specific propositions of the psychoanalytic theory of neurosis – instead of just attempting to set up experimental analogues. As far as I can tell there is nothing in past experience to suggest that the general prospects of *this* work are better or worse than the prospects of work in any *other* part of the psychological field. When I am in an optimistic mood, I like to think that while the first half of this century has seen psychoanalysis firmly entrenched in the scientific household, the second half will make a respectable woman out of her – to the benefit of all concerned. If this happens, we shall *ipso facto* also succeed in making the clinician less unreliable and the ordinary psychologist more helpful when they both try to *understand* you and me.

References
BELL, S. (1902), 'A preliminary study of the emotion of love between the sexes', *Amer. J. Psychol.*, vol. 13, pp. 325–54.
BROOKS, F. D. (1937), *Child Psychology*, Houghton Mifflin.
CONN, J. H. (1940), 'Children's reactions to the discovery of genital differences', *Amer. J. Orthopsychiat.*, vol. 10, pp. 747–54.
DICKS, H. V. (1947), *Clinical Studies in Psychopathology*, Edward Arnold, 2nd edn.

Conclusions

DUDYCHA, G. J., and DUDYCHA, M. M. (1941), 'Childhood memories: a review of the literature', *Psychol. Bull.*, vol. 38, pp. 668–82.

GOLDMAN, F. (1948), 'Breastfeeding and character-formation', *J. Personal.*, vol. 17, pp. 83–103.

HALVERSON, H. M. (1938), 'Infant sucking and tensional behavior', *J. genet. Psychol.*, vol. 53, pp. 365–430.

HALVERSON, H. M. (1940), 'Genital and sphincter behavior in the male infant', *J. genet. Psychol.*, vol. 56, pp. 95–136.

HAMILTON, G. V. (1929), *A Research in Marriage*, Boni.

HATTENDORF, K. W. (1932), 'A study of the questions of young children concerning sex; a phase of an experimental approach to parent education', *J. soc. Psychol.*, vol. 3, pp. 37–65.

HULL, C. L. (1939), 'Modern behaviorism and psychoanalysis', *Trans. N.Y. Acad. Scien.*, set II, vol. 1, no. 5.

ISAACS, S. (1933), *Social Development in Young Children*, Routledge.

KARDINER, A., *et al.* (1945), *The Psychological Frontiers of Society*, Columbia University Press.

KLEEMEIER, R. W. (1942), 'Fixation and regression in the rat', *Psychol. Monog.*, no. 54.

KOCH, H. L. (1930), 'The influence of some affective factors upon recall', *J. gen. Psychol.*, vol. 4, pp. 171–90.

KOCH, H. L. (1935), 'An analysis of certain forms of so-called "nervous habits" in young children', *J. genet. Psychol.*, vol. 46, pp. 139–70.

LEVY, D. M. (1928), 'Finger sucking and accessory movements in early infancy', *Amer. J. Psychiat.*, vol. 7, pp. 881–918.

LEWIN, K., LIPPITT, R., and WHITE, R. K. (1939), 'Patterns of aggressive behavior in experimentally created "social climates"', *J. soc. Psychol.*, vol. 10, pp. 271–99.

MAIER, N. R. F., GLASER, N. M., and KLEE, J. B. (1940), 'Studies of abnormal behavior in the rat. III. The development of behavior fixations through frustration', *J. exp. Psychol.*, vol. 26, pp. 521–46.

MAIER, N. R. F., and KLEE, J. B. (1941), 'Studies of abnormal behavior in the rat. VII. The permanent nature of abnormal fixations and their relation to convulsive tendencies', *J. exp. Psychol.*, vol. 29, pp. 380–89.

MAIER, N. R. F., and KLEE, J. B. (1943), 'Studies of abnormal behavior in the rat. XII. The pattern of punishment and its relation to abnormal fixations', *J. exp. Psychol.*, vol. 32, pp. 377–98.

MALINOWSKI, N. (1927), *Sex and Repression in Savage Society*, Routledge.

MARTIN, R. F. (1940), '"Native" traits and regression in rats', *J. comp. Psychol.*, vol. 30, pp. 1–16.

MASSERMAN, J. H. (1943), *Behavior and Neurosis*, Chicago University Press.

MASSERMAN, J. H. (1946), *Principles of Dynamic Psychiatry*, Saunders.

MEAD, M. (1928), *Coming of Age in Samoa*, Penguin Books edn., 1943.

MILLER, N. E. (1948), 'Theory and experiment relating psychoanalytic displacement to stimulus–response generalisation', *J. abnorm. soc. Psychol.*, vol. 43, pp. 155–78.

MOWRER, O. H. (1940), 'An experimental "analogue" of regression with incidental observations on "reaction formation"', *J. abnorm. soc. Psychol.*, vol. 35, pp. 56–87.

O'KELLY, L. I. (1940a), 'An experimental study of regression. I. Behavioral characteristics of the regressive response', *J. comp. Psychol.*, vol. 30, pp. 41–53.

O'KELLY, L. I. (1940b), 'An experimental study of regression. II. Some motivational determinants of regression and perseveration', *J. comp. Psychol.*, vol. 30, pp. 55–95.

ROSENZWEIG, S. (1938), 'The experimental study of repression', in H. A. Murray (ed.), *Explorations in Personality*, Oxford University Press, Inc.

SEARS, R. R. (1943), *Survey of Objective Studies of Psychoanalytic Concepts*, Social Science Research Council, New York.

SEARS, R. R. (1944), 'Experimental analysis of psychoanalytic phenomena', in J. McV. Hunt (ed.), *Personality and the Behavior Disorders*, Ronald Press.

SHARP, A. A. (1938), 'An experimental test of Freud's doctrine of the relation of hedonic tone to memory revival', *J. exp. Psychol.*, vol. 22, pp. 395–418.

VALENTINE, C. W. (1942), *The Psychology of Early Childhood*, Methuen.

Further Reading

Abstracts

1. 'An experimental approach to dream psychology through the use of hypnosis', Leslie H. Farber and C. Fisher, *Psychoanalytic Quarterly*, vol. 12, pp. 202–16.

A method is presented for the study of dreams and other unconscious processes by hypnosis. In hypnosis certain subjects have more awareness of the meaning of dream language than in the waking state. This awareness is influenced by the relationship between hypnotist and subject. The similarity of this relationship with other interpersonal relationships was pointed out, as well as the possibility of using this method for the study of transference. A number of experimental dreams, evoked by both sexual and non-sexual dream stimuli, are presented and their special characteristics discussed. The results obtained illustrate the great plasticity of the dream language and argue against too narrow interpretation of symbols.

2. 'Breastfeeding and character formation', Frieda Goldman-Eisler, *Journal of Personality*, vol. 17, 1948, pp. 83–103; vol. 19, 1950, pp. 189–96. *Journal of Mental Science*, vol. 97, 1951, pp. 765–82.

An intercorrelation table based on the trait scores of a hundred subjects was computed and submitted to a factor analysis. Two factors were extracted.
Factor I corresponded in most aspects to the syndrome of oral pessimism as described by psychoanalysts, and correlated 0·694 with the previously derived type pattern. It was, however, poorly saturated with impulsion, aggression and autonomy, which psychoanalysts consider to be important traits of oral character. It was significantly related to early weaning.
Factor II was highly saturated with impulsion, aggression and autonomy. It was not significantly related to early weaning.
Individuals who had high scores on factor II and who had been weaned early had significantly higher scores on factor I (oral pessimism) than the rest of the sample.
A suggestion to be investigated emerges that the concurrence in an individual of early weaning and of the characteristics of impulsiveness-aggression-autonomy, as defined in factor II, may possibly promote the development of oral pessimism.

3. 'Mechanisms of defense and readiness in perception and recall', D. W. Forrest and S. G. M. Lee, *Psychological Monographs*, vol. 76, 1962, no. 4.

An experimental attempt to link both forgetting and 'perceptual defense' as possible criteria for repression. The occurrence of the latter was predicted by intra-subject discrepancy scores on various 'needs' (H. A. Murray). No evidence for perceptual defense as repression was found but forgetting of specific motivational stimuli by individual subjects was predicted at significant levels of confidence. Conclusions reached: (a) that 'perceptual defense' is a result of output blocking rather than of input – ('verbal rather than visual'); (b) that Freud's theory of repression receives some confirmation from the recall half of the experiment.

4. 'Infant care and personality', H. Orlansky, *Psychological Bulletin*, vol. 46, 1949, pp. 1–48.

This paper reviews some of the empirical data bearing on the theory that various features of infant care determine adult personality. Orlansky's conclusion is largely negative, and he has been led to substitute a theory which emphasizes, instead, the importance of constitutional factors and of the total cultural situation in personality formation; the importance of post-infantile experience is also indicated. To the criticism that this paper stops where it should start, with the definition of specific situations which can be calculated to produce specific psychological effects upon individuals with certain constitutions, Orlansky states that he can only agree.

5. The chapter 'Freud's psychodynamics' in E. R. Hilgard's *Theories of Learning* (Methuen, 1958) is a useful drawing of parallels between psychoanalytic theory and conventional interpretations of learning.

6. A paper by G. Bergmann in *Mind*, vol. 52, 1943, pp. 122–40, discusses with reference to the history of ideas, the relationship between psychoanalysis and experimental or academic psychology.

7. An important paper, 'The scientific methodology of psychoanalysis' by David Rapaport, in M. M. Gill (ed.), *The Collected Papers of David Rapaport* (Basic Books, 1967), deals with methodology and its relation to psychoanalysis, the question of what is and what is not scientific methodology, the concepts of science and psychoanalysis.

8. In the chapter 'psychoanalysis as a developmental psychology' in the same book, Rapaport explores some of the basic concepts of psychoanalysis as a developmental psychology; he attempts to demonstrate that the core of psychoanalysis as a developmental psychology is the concept of instinctual drives and drive restraining factors, to clarify the relation between instinctual drives and experience and to reconsider the developmental relation between archaic and ordered forms of thought.

9. In Part 8 of *Cross-Cultural Studies* (ed. D. R. Price-Williams, Penguin, 1969) in the Penguin Modern Psychology Readings series, there are several excellent studies of Freudian hypotheses, namely 'A cross-cultural linguistic analysis of Freudian symbols' (L. Minturn, 1965); 'Social

influences in Zulu dreaming' (S. G. M. Lee, 1958); 'A primitive slip of the tongue' (G. A. Devereux, 1957); 'Socialization process and personality' (J. W. M. Whiting, 1961); 'The Oedipus complex hypothesis' (W. N. Stephens, 1962); 'The effects of sudden weaning on Zulu children' (R. C. Albino and W. J. Thompson, 1956); 'Projection and displacement: a cross-cultural study of folk-tale aggression' (G. O. Wright, 1956).

Bibliography

R. C. Albino, 'Defences against aggression in the play of young children', *British Journal of Medical Psychology*, vol. 27, 1954, pp. 61–71.

G. Bergmann, 'Psychoanalysis and experimental psychology', *Mind*, vol. 52, 1943, pp. 352–70.

G. S. Blum, *Psychoanalytic Theories of Personality*, McGraw-Hill, 1953.

L. H. Farber and C. Fisher, 'An experimental approach to dream psychology through the use of hypnosis', *Psychoanalytic Quarterly*, vol. 12, 1943, pp. 202–16.

H. Feigl and M. Scriven (eds.), 'The foundations of science and the concepts of psychology and psychoanalysis', *Minnesota Studies in the Philosophy of Science*, vol. 1, University of Minnesota, 1956.

D. W. Forrest and S. G. M. Lee, Mechanisms of defense and readiness in perception and recall, *Psychological Monographs General and Applied*, vol. 76, 1962, no. 4.

F. Goldman-Eisler, 'Breastfeeding and character formation', in C. Kluckhohn and H. A. Murray (eds.), *Personality in Nature, Society and Culture*, Cape, 2nd edn, 1953.

E. Hilgard, 'Freud's psychodynamics', *Theories of Learning and Instruction*, University of Chicago Press, 1965.

S. Hook (ed.), *Psycho-Analysis, Scientific Method and Philosophy*, New York University Institute of Philosophy, 1959.

E. Kris, 'Psychoanalytic propositions', in M. H. Marx (ed.), *Psychological Theory*, Macmillan, New York, 1951, pp. 322–51.

P. Madison, *Freud's Concept of Repression and Defense. Its Theoretical and Observational Language*, University of Minnesota Press, 1961.

J. P. McKee and Marjorie P. Honzik, 'The sucking behavior of mammals: an illustration of the nature–nurture question', in L. Postman (ed.), *Psychology in the Making*, Knopf, 1963.

M. Nachmansohn, 'Concerning experimentally produced dreams', in D. Rapaport (ed.), *Organisation and Pathology of Thought*, Columbia University Press, 1951, pp. 257–87.

H. Orlansky, 'Infant care and personality', *Psychological Bulletin*, vol. 46, 1949, pp. 1–48.

E. Pumpian-Mindlin (ed.), *Psycho-Analysis as Science*, Basic Books, 1952.

S. Rachman (ed.), *Critical Essays on Psychoanalysis*, Pergamon, 1963.

D. Rapaport, 'The scientific methodology of psychoanalysis', in M. M. Gill (ed.), *The Collected Papers of David Rapaport*, Basic Books, 1967.

A. A. Salama and J. McV. Hunt, '"Fixation" in the rat as a function of infantile shocking, handling and gentling', *Journal of Genetic Psychology*, vol. 105, 1964, pp. 131–62.

I. G. Sarason (ed.), *Psychoanalysis and the Study of Behavior*, Van Nostrand, 1965.

R. R. Sears, *Survey of Objective Studies of Psychoanalytic Concepts*, Social Science Research Council, New York, 1943.

R. R. Sears, 'Experimental analysis of psycho-analytic phenomena', in J. McV. Hunt (ed.), *Personality and the Behavior Disorders*, Ronald Press, 1944, pp. 306–32.

J. R. Smythies (with A. Coppen and N. Kreitman), 'The theoretical basis of psychoanalysis', in *Biological Psychiatry: A Review of Recent Advances*, Heinemann, 1968.

P. M. Turquet, 'Criteria for a psycho-analytic explanation', *Aristotelian Society Supplement*, vol. 36, 1962.

J. M. Whiting and O. H. Mowrer, 'Habit progression and regression – a laboratory study of some factors relevant to human socialization', *Journal of Comparative Psychology*, vol. 36, 1943, pp. 229–53.

Acknowledgements

Permission to reproduce the Readings in this volume is acknowledged from the following sources:

Reading 1   *New Society* and B. A. Farrell
Reading 2   Stanford University Press
Reading 3   *New Society* and B. A. Farrell
Reading 4   The British Psychological Society and R. C. Albino
Reading 5   The Journal Press and Arnold Bernstein
Reading 6   The Journal Press and Halla Beloff
Reading 7   Duke University Press, Gerald S. Blum and Daniel R. Miller
Reading 9   Oxford University Press and Saul Rosenzweig
Reading 10   *Psychological Reports* and Vincent J. Tempone
Reading 11   The Journal Press, William D. Wells and Rachel L. Goldstein
Reading 12   American Psychological Association and O. H. Mowrer
Reading 13   Holt, Rinehart & Winston, Inc.
Reading 14   American Psychological Association and Neal E. Miller
Reading 15   American Psychological Association and Paul Mussen
Reading 16   Coward-McCann, Inc.
Reading 17   *Psychoanalytic Quarterly* and Milton H. Erickson
Reading 18   *Archives of General Psychiatry* and K. Z. Altshuler
Reading 19   *Science* and David Foulkes
Reading 20   The British Psychological Society and B. A. Farrell

Author Index

Author Index

Subject Index

Subject Index